A GRADED SPANISH REVIEW GRAMMAR

3rd Edition

A GRADED SPANISH REVIEW GRAMMAR

F. Courtney Tarr

Augusto Centeno

Revised by
Paul M. Lloyd

University of Pennsylvania

PRENTICE HALL, Englewood Cliffs, New Jersey 07632

Library of Congress Cataloging-in-Publication Data

TARR, F. COURTNEY (FREDERICK COURTNEY), 1896–1939.
  A graded Spanish review grammar / F. Courtney Tarr, Augusto
Centeno.—3d ed. / revised by Paul M. Lloyd.
      p. cm.
  Rev. ed. of: A graded Spanish review grammar with composition. 2nd
ed. 1973.
  Includes index.
  ISBN 0-13-362146-4
  1. Spanish language—Grammar—1950– I. Tarr, F. Courtney
(Frederick Courtney), 1896–1939. A graded Spanish review grammar
with composition. II. Centeno, Augusto, 1901–1965. III. Lloyd,
Paul M. IV. Title.
PC4112.T35 1991
468.2'421—dc20   90-7582
                                                            CIP

Editorial/production supervision
  and interior design: *Mary Kathryn Leclercq*
Cover design: *Joe DiDomenico*
Prepress buyer: *Herb Klein*
Manufacturing buyer: *Dave Dickey*
Acquisitions editor: *Steve Debow*
Editorial assistant: *María F. García*

 © 1991, 1973, 1933 by Prentice-Hall, Inc.
A Division of Simon & Schuster
Englewood Cliffs, New Jersey 07632

Printed in the United States of America
10 9 8 7 6 5 4 3 2 1

ISBN   0-13-362146-4

Prentice-Hall International (UK) Limited, *London*
Prentice-Hall of Australia Pty. Limited, *Sydney*
Prentice-Hall Canada Inc., *Toronto*
Prentice-Hall Hispanoamericana, S.A., *Mexico*
Prentice-Hall of India Private Limited, *New Delhi*
Prentice-Hall of Japan, Inc., *Tokyo*
Simon & Schuster Asia Pte. Ltd., *Singapore*
Editora Prentice-Hall do Brasil, Ltda., *Rio de Janeiro*

To Joan

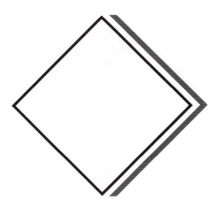

CONTENTS

PREFACE

When I was asked by Prentice Hall to prepare a third revised edition of Tarr and Centeno, I had to consider to what extent any further changes might be advisable (aside from correcting the obvious errors of the second edition). At first I had thought that a simple correction of those errors might be sufficient, but a number of suggestions from teachers experienced in the use of the text plus my own experiences in classes in advanced grammar finally convinced me that it would be best to make a somewhat more extensive revision than I had originally anticipated.

I have therefore made a number of changes in detail, although those who have known the book in its previous forms will not perceive any alteration in its basic structure. Tarr and Centeno has been a success in its basic form for over fifty years, something which can be said of practically no other Spanish textbook published in the United States. One should be extremely cautious about tampering with success. Still, the end of the twentieth century is fast approaching, and it can hardly be expected that no changes would be appropriate. In particular, my own experiences have shown me that a number of the grammatical explanations needed to be reworded to some extent so that modern American college students may find them somewhat easier to read and understand. For example, those familiar with previous editions will find that Sec. 120 (Chap. 10) dealing with conditional sentences is mostly new. I have also reorganized in some places the translation sections.

Since Tarr and Centeno has been used by most teachers as an advanced grammar review, it also appeared to the editor that there is relatively little need these days for lengthy paragraphs to be translated from English to Spanish, especially in view of the numbers of texts now available which concentrate on composition alone. Therefore, the sections labelled "composition" (actually just more translation sentences) have been omitted, although the various "temas" which ask the student to make up his or her own paragraphs, using material from the text, have been retained as final sections of some chapters for optional use by teachers.

I hope that this third edition of Tarr and Centeno will continue to find the same acceptance that the previous editions did, and will serve teachers and students of Spanish as it has in the past. Those who use the text are cordially invited to send me any suggestions for further changes in the future that might seem appropriate.

Thanks are due to a number of persons who have made suggestions for corrections and revisions: Lee Fontanella, Raúl Ianes, Félix Larrea, José Regueiro, Ernest Rehder, and Jim Tatum. Very special thanks are due to John H. R. Polt, Edward Neugaard, and Pierre Ullman, who very generously provided me with detailed analyses of numerous points in the second edition. If in some cases, I have, perhaps perversely, neglected to follow their advice they can put the full blame on me for any remaining errors and infelicities in the text.

Paul M. Lloyd

A GRADED
SPANISH
REVIEW
GRAMMAR

PRELIMINARY LESSON ONE

NOTE. Neither the rules nor the exceptions in the two preliminary lessons are complete. Reference is made in parentheses after each paragraph heading to the more extended treatment of the same topic.

1. FORMS OF THE DEFINITE ARTICLE *THE* (SEC. 155)

	SINGULAR	PLURAL
MASC.	**el**	**los**
FEM.	**la**	**las**

2. GENDER OF NOUNS (SEC. 165)

1. Nouns in Spanish are either masculine or feminine.
2. Nouns ending in **-o** are usually masculine; nouns ending in **-a** are usually feminine.

el edificio	*building*	**la casa**	*house*
el retrato	*portrait*	**la alcoba**	*bedroom*
el aeropuerto	*airport*	**la pierna**	*leg*

EXCEPTIONS: **la mano** *hand,* **el día** *day*; many masculine nouns ending in **-a** (Sec. 165); and short forms of words such as **la foto (fotografía)** and **la moto (motocicleta).**

3. Normally the grammatical gender of a noun is arbitrary and has no relationship with the meaning of the noun. However, nouns denoting male beings are masculine (except for such general terms as **persona** *person,* **víctima** *victim,* etc., which are always feminine), and those denoting female beings are feminine— regardless of ending.

el guía	*guide*	**la actriz**	*actress*
el marinero	*sailor*	**la prima**	*cousin*
el conferenciante	*lecturer*	**la madre**	*mother*
el actor	*actor*	**la modelo**	*the (artist's) model*

4. The names of the days and months are masculine.

3. CONTRACTION OF THE DEFINITE ARTICLE (SEC. 156)

The article **el** contracts with the prepositions **a** *to* and **de** *of* to form **al** and **del** respectively.

los árboles del jardín	*the trees of the garden*
Vamos al teatro.	*We are going to the theater.*

4. PLURAL OF NOUNS AND ADJECTIVES (SEC. 166)

The plural of Spanish nouns and adjectives is formed (*a*) by adding **-s** to words ending in an unaccented vowel or diphthong, (*b*) by adding **-es** to those ending in a consonant (including **y**). (*c*) Nouns with final unaccented syllable ending in **-s** do not change their form in the plural.

Plural of Nouns and Adjectives		
SINGULAR		*PLURAL*
a. **el caballo**	*the horse*	**los caballos**
la torre	*the tower*	**las torres**
blanco	*white*	**blancos**
b. **la virtud**	*virtue*	**las virtudes**
el papel	*the paper*	**los papeles**
la ley	*the law*	**las leyes**
fácil	*easy*	**fáciles**
c. **el lunes**	*Monday*	**los lunes**
la tesis	*the thesis*	**las tesis**

5. ORTHOGRAPHIC CHANGES

In spelling the plural of nouns and adjectives, (*a*) final **-z** changes to **c**, (*b*) words having a final stressed syllable ending in **-n** or **-s** lose the written accent in the plural, (*c*) words having a final unstressed syllable ending in **-n** must have a written accent over the vowel in the stressed syllable.

Plurals with Orthographic Changes

SINGULAR		PLURAL
a. **el lapiz**	*the pencil*	**los lápices**
la luz	*the light*	**las luces**
b. **la reunión**	*the gathering*	**las reuniones**
cortés	*courteous*	**corteses**
c. **el joven**	*the youth*	**los jóvenes**
el margen	*the margin*	**los márgenes**

EJERCICIO

Escríbase el plural de las palabras siguientes:
1. juez   2. origen   3. tradición   4. fugaz   5. ramplón   6. vez   7. fácil
8. aleman   9. crisis   10. holgazán   11. tenaz   12. burlón.

6. PERSONAL A ("PERSONAL ACCUSATIVE")
(SECS. 99, 118, 168, 173)

When the noun object of a verb is a definite person or personified thing (including animals), it is preceded by the preposition **a**.

He visto a mi amigo.	*I have seen my friend.*
Amo a España.	*I love Spain.*
Tuvieron que matar al perro.	*They had to kill the dog.*

EJERCICIO

Añada las preposiciones necesarias con cada una de las palabras entre paréntesis en las frases siguientes:
1. Vamos a visitar _____ . (mis abuelos, la catedral, don Luis, el profesor, el barrio viejo)
2. Echaron a la calle _____ . (el muchacho, la basura, el gato, el viejo, la amiga de María)
3. Mañana van a recoger _____ . (Diego, los papeles, el aparato, nuestros compañeros, mi tío)
4. Recuerdo mucho _____ . (Margarita, Sevilla, la tertulia, el curso anterior, el tío de Alicia)

Preguntas

1. ¿Qué ciudades vamos a visitar? ¿A quién (quiénes) vamos a visitar?
2. ¿Qué echaron a la calle? ¿A quién echaron a la calle?
3. ¿Qué van a recoger mañana? ¿A quién van a recoger mañana?
4. ¿Qué quiere Ud. mucho? ¿A quién quiere Ud. mucho?

7. USES OF THE DEFINITE ARTICLE (SECS. 157, 159)

1. The Spanish definite article is used in a number of situations where English does not need it. It is used (*a*) with abstract nouns, (*b*) with nouns used in a generic or general sense, both singular and plural, (*c*) with days of the week and other expressions of time, (*d*) with parts of the body and articles of personal wear (instead of the possessive adjectives, as in English. See Sec. **73**).

a. **La religión, la ciencia y el arte son las grandes creaciones de la humanidad.**	*Religion, science, and art are the great creations of humanity.*
b. **El petróleo y la electricidad son muy necesarios en la vida moderna.**	*Oil and electricity are very necessary in modern life.*
Las abejas poseen una organización social.	*Bees possess a social organization.*
c. **Saldremos el lunes.**	*We will leave Monday.*
Llegaremos a las cinco y media.	*We will arrive at half past five.*
El verano pasado estuvimos en la Argentina.	*Last summer we were in Argentina.*
Eran las tres menos cuarto.	*It was quarter to three.*

EXCEPTION: After **ser** the article is usually omitted: **Ayer fue jueves, hoy es viernes, mañana será sábado.** *Yesterday was Thursday, today is Friday, tomorrow will be Saturday.*

d. **Puso el reloj en el bolsillo.**	He put his watch in his pocket.
Tiene los ojos negros.	He has dark eyes.
Me quité la blusa.	I took off my blouse.

EJERCICIO

Reemplácense las palabras subrayadas con las palabras entre paréntesis:
1. La civilización es un producto de los esfuerzos de hombres extraordinarios.
   (arte, ciencia, literatura, gobierno, técnica, transportes modernos)
2. Los jóvenes[a] suelen preocuparse más por los asuntos personales[b].
   a. (las mujeres, los hombres, los estudiantes, los americanos)
   b. (las enfermedades, la sociedad, la contaminación, la economiá)
Reemplácense las palabras subrayadas con otros nombres de días de la semana:

3. Estarán aquí para el <u>viernes</u>.

4. Mañana es <u>jueves</u>, ¿no?

5. Me gusta ir al parque todos los <u>días</u>.

Reemplácense las palabras subrayadas con las palabras entre paréntesis:

6. El viejo se puso <u>los zapatos</u>. (el abrigo, la camisa, la corbata, los pantalones)

7. Elena tiene <u>los ojos azules</u>. (el pelo rubio, las pestañas largas, la boca chica, las piernas delgadas, las manos grandes)

8. Felipe se quitó <u>el sombrero</u>. (la corbata, el jersey, la chaqueta, los anteojos).

Preguntas

1. ¿Qué es la civilización?
2. ¿Quiénes se preocupan más por los asuntos personales?
3. ¿Cuándo estarán ellas aquí?
4. ¿Qué día es mañana?
5. ¿Le gusta a Ud. ir al parque todos los días?
6. ¿Qué se puso el viejo?
7. ¿Cómo es Elena?
8. ¿Qué se quitó Felipe?

---

2. The definite article is also used—but with specific exceptions—(*a*) before **señor** (but not **don**) and other titles, except in direct address, (*b*) with adjectives of nationality denoting language, except after the preposition **en** and the verbs **hablar** *to speak,* **escribir** *to write,* **estudiar** *to study,* and **aprender** *to learn.*

a. **El señor Martínez ha llegado hoy.**	*Mr. Martínez has arrived today.*
El general Marina y el cardenal Casares paraban en el mismo hotel.	*General Marina and Cardinal Casares were staying at the same hotel.*
But: **—Por aquí, señora Rodríguez.**	*(Come) this way, Mrs. Rodríguez.*
Don Miguel Gómez es amigo mío.	*Mr. Miguel Gómez is a friend of mine.*
b. **El español no es difícil.**	*Spanish is not difficult.*
But: **Me gusta hablar español.**	*I like to speak Spanish.*
La señorita Sierra estudia alemán.	*Miss Sierra is studying German.*

NOTE. The definite article is also omitted after **de** or before adjectives of nationality denoting language, in cases such as **la clase (lección) de español** *the Spanish class (lesson),* **el profesor (libro) de inglés** *the English teacher (book).*

8. INTERROGATION AND NEGATION

In an interrogative sentence (*a*) the subject usually follows the verb; (*b*) in a negative sentence the adverb **no** *not* precedes the verb.

a. **¿Está Juan en Madrid?**   *Is John in Madrid?*
   ¿Está cerrada la puerta?   *Is the door locked?*
b. **Juan no está en Madrid.**   *John is not in Madrid.*

NOTE. The English negative adjective *no = not any* is usually rendered by the adverb **no** in Spanish: **No tengo libros** *I have no books* (*= I don't have any books*).

EJERCICIO

Póngase la forma correcta de los nombres y títulos siguientes en los espacios en blanco: (el general Marina, el señor Alvar, doña Antonia, la señorita Alonso, el capitán Moreno, el profesor Carvajal, don Miguel)
1. Hoy llega _____ .
2. —Pase Ud., _____ .
3. En el nuevo parador se encontraban _____ y _____ .
4. ¿Quiere Ud. algo, _____ ?

Preguntas

1. ¿Quién llega hoy?
2. ¿Quién va a pasar?
3. ¿Quiénes se encontraban en el nuevo parador?
4. ¿Quién quiere algo?

Traducción

1. I have five pencils, but those young people don't have any.
2. The gardens are very large.
3. The nations of the world must seek peace.
4. Many of the cities of South America are very modern.
5. Mr. Iglesias and Mr. Domingo are singers.
6. We visited the President and his wife.
7. People often fear death without need.
8. Dogs are domestic animals and man's best friends.
9. Miss Vela is very pretty.
10. Senator Montoya will arrive tonight.
11. Modern science has conquered time and space.
12. Today is Sunday. We do not work (on) Sundays.
13. Write this exercise in Spanish.
14. Yesterday I saw Mrs. López.
15. He picked up his gloves and his hat.
16. I will go to Montevideo next week.
17. Italian, French, and Spanish come from Latin.
18. Has Mr. Domínguez sent the package?
19. The house has four bedrooms.

20. Classes begin at eight thirty.
21. I cannot mail this letter; I haven't any stamps.
22. Petroleum has many uses.
23. Your parents are very young.
24. We go every morning to the Spanish class.
25. Mr. Alvarez is our Spanish teacher.
26. I am going to speak to (greet) a friend.
27. We are sailing next Monday.
28. I like coffee, but I don't like wine.

Verbos y Modismos

Review the conjugation of regular verbs (Sec. **222**).

Echar *to pour, throw, cast;* **echarse a** *to start to, burst out, etc.;* **echarse a perder** *to spoil.*

Etc. is not used vaguely here and in all subsequent sections on verbs and idioms, but to indicate that there are other meanings used in the translations which are related to or derived from those given in the definitions at the head. These meanings and idioms are either given in parentheses or recorded in the vocabulary. One of the purposes of these translations is to impart a feeling for some of the most widely used verbs in Spanish by showing not only the variety of their uses but also the underlying connections between them. It must be constantly kept in mind that frequently the "idiom" is in English rather than in the Spanish expression, which may be more literal, direct, and concrete. In order to facilitate the acquisition of a real feeling for the literal meaning of the Spanish expression, this is given in parentheses whenever necessary or possible.

1. Don't put (throw) the blame on him.
2. They threw him out of the theater.
3. Will you (please) mail (drop in the mailbox) this letter?
4. I am going to lie down (refl.) a while.
5. Do you want more coffee?—Yes, pour me a little more.
6. She gave me an angry look.
7. You are very fond of paying compliments.
8. Let's take (**por**) the short cut.
9. We started to run down the street (**calle abajo**).
10. They all burst out (**echarse a**) laughing.
11. This has spoiled all my plans.
12. He thinks he is a (**se las echa de, se las da de**) Don Juan.

Tirar(se) *to draw, pull, throw (violently), pitch, hurl; throw away,* etc.; *to fire (a shot);* **tirarse de** *to pull.*

1. A cart drawn by oxen passed slowly.
2. Military life attracts him.

3. It's about (**habrá**) five kilometers at most.
4. She has blonde hair approximating reddish.
5. He threw a book at my head.
6. The poor woman threw herself off the bridge.
7. Throw away that cigar; it smells bad.
8. Let's take (**por**) the short cut.
9. The soldiers were firing at the presidential palace.
10. Don't go back on it! (**no te eches atrás**).

Saltarse *to jump (over), come out* or *off (suddenly)*.

1. He jumps over all obstacles.
2. I skipped all the descriptions in the book.
3. Tears came to his eyes (**se le saltaron las lágrimas**).
4. A button has come off my (**del**) coat.
5. It is obvious (**salta a la vista**).

PRELIMINARY LESSON TWO

9. THE INDEFINITE ARTICLE, FORMS AND USES
(SECS. 158, 161–163)

1.

	SINGULAR		PLURAL	
MASC.	un	} a, an (one)	unos	} some
FEM.	una		unas	

2. English frequently uses the indefinite article where in Spanish no article is needed. The most frequent omission of this article in Spanish is before an unmodified predicate noun or adjective denoting social class, nationality or an occupational, political, or religious group.

Mi cuñado es arquitecto.	*My brother-in-law is an architect.*
El primer ministro es socialista.	*The prime minister is a socialist.*
La mujer de Miguel es católica.	*Miguel's wife is a Catholic.*
Pepe es panameño.	*Pepe is a Panamanian.*

3. Spanish often expresses the concept of *some* or *any* by omitting the article. Spanish possesses no unstressed adjective corresponding to the English unstressed *any, no.*

En esta tienda se venden plantas y flores.	*In this shop plants and flowers are sold.*
¿Tiene Ud. fósforos?	*Have you any matches?*
No tengo fósforos.	*I have no matches.*
No tenemos automóvil.	*We don't have a car.*

EJERCICIO

Reemplácense las palabras subrayadas con las palabras entre paréntesis:
1. Mi padre[a] es abogado[b].
   a. (tu hermano, el presidente, el comandante, nuestro tío)
   b. (aristócrata, médico, estudiante, republicano, izquierdista, protestante)
2. En España se cultivan naranjas. (aceitunas, manzanas, uvas, toronjas)
3. Lucila tiene libros[a] interesantes[b].
   a. (parientes, profesores, hermanas, obras de arte)
   b. (importantes, excelentes, tradicionales, extraordinarios).

Preguntas

1. ¿Qué es su padre? 2. ¿Qué se cultiva en España? 3. ¿Qué tiene Lucila? 4. ¿Qué es Ud.? 5. ¿Qué no tiene Ud.?

10. THE NEUTER ARTICLE *LO* (SECS. 78, 126, 164)

The neuter article **lo** *the* is not used with nouns. It is used with adjectives (and participles) to form concepts equivalent to abstract nouns. (This construction is often equivalent to the English *thing, part,* or the suffix *-ness*.)

lo mejor del libro	*the best part of the book*
lo raro de la situación	*the strangeness of the situation*
lo nuevo del caso	*the newness of the matter*

EJERCICIO

Pónganse las palabras entre paréntesis en lugar de las palabras subrayadas:
Me gusta[a] lo bueno[b] del libro[c].
a. (extraña, molesta, intriga, encanta)
b. (raro, extraordinario, interesante, nuevo, original)
c. (caso, situación, cosa, asunto)

Preguntas

1. ¿Qué le gusta a Ud.? 2. ¿Qué le extraña a Ud.? 3. ¿Qué le molesta a Ud.? 4. ¿Qué le intriga a Ud.? 5. ¿Qué le encanta a Ud.?

11. FEMININE FORMS OF ADJECTIVES (SEC. 176)

The masculine and feminine forms of adjectives are (*a*) identical, except: (*b*) when the masculine ends in **o**, the feminine ends in **a**, (*c*) adjectives of nationality ending in a consonant add **a** to form the feminine, and lose the written accent if the final syllable of the masculine form is stressed and ends in **n** or **s**.

    a. **difícil** *difficult,* **gris** *gray,* **audaz** *audacious, daring* **fuerte** *strong.*
    b. **blanco, -a** *white,* **bonito, -a** *pretty,* **maravilloso, -a** *marvelous.*
    c. **español, -a** *Spanish,* **francés, francesa** *French,* **alemán, alemana** *German.*

NOTE. Adjectives of nationality are not capitalized in Spanish, even when used as nouns.

12. AGREEMENT OF ADJECTIVES (SECS. 179, 184)

An adjective agrees in gender and number with the noun it modifies.

La casa amarilla estaba rodeada de árboles frutales.	*The yellow house was surrounded by fruit trees.*

EJERCICIO

Combínense los sustantivos y adjetivos siguientes:
1. nación, juventud, cuñado, paisaje, fenómeno, sombrero, lápiz
2. triste, alemán, hermoso, andaluz, pintoresco, malo.

13. SHORTENED FORMS OF ADJECTIVES (SECS. 185, 205)

Certain adjectives have shortened (apocopated) forms when used in unstressed position before the noun. They fall into the following groups: (*a*) those which lose the final **o** before a masculine singular noun, (*b*) those which lose the final syllable.

a. **uno**	*one*	**un**	**ninguno**	*none, no*	**ningún**
bueno	*good*	**buen**	**alguno**	*some, any*	**algún**
malo	*bad*	**mal**	**primero**	*first*	**primer**
			tercero	*third*	**tercer**

    b. **ciento** *(a, one) hundred* becomes **cien** before all nouns, and often when used alone in colloquial usage;

grande becomes **gran** before any noun in the singular;
Santo *Saint* which becomes **San** before any masculine singular name unless it begins with **To-** or **Do-**.

c. **Cualquiera** *any* is in a class by itself since it drops the final **-a** before all nouns.

a. **Estas naranjas tienen muy buen sabor.**	*These oranges have a very good flavor.*
Algún día se lo contaré a Ud.	*I will tell you someday.*
Ningún ser humano puede ser perfecto.	*No human being can be perfect.*

NOTE. The shortened forms **algún** and **ningún** have written accents.

b. **Hemos recorrido hoy cien kilómetros.**	*We have covered one hundred kilometers today.*
Aquí hay casi cien.	*Here there are almost a hundred.*
San Jerónimo y Santo Tomás fueron doctores de la iglesia.	*Saint Jerome and Saint Thomas were doctors of the church.*
c. **Podemos hacerlo cualquier día.**	*We can do it any day.*

EJERCICIO

Combínense los adjetivos de Sec. **13** con los sustantivos siguientes: médico, princesa, estudio, manzana, libro, esfuerzo.

---

14. POSITION OF ADJECTIVES (SECS. 180, 187)

1. Limiting (determinative) adjectives (that is, articles, demonstratives, possessives, numerals, and indefinites) precede the noun they modify.

mis libros	*my books*	**unos sellos**	*some stamps*
esta falda	*this skirt*	**doce habitaciones**	*twelve rooms*

2. Descriptive adjectives normally follow the noun when they differentiate the noun modified from others of the same class. A few common adjectives (**bueno, malo, grande**) generally precede because in most cases they have lost most of their differentiating force.

la torre blanca	*the white tower*	**un viaje marítimo**	*a sea trip*
un gato persa	*a Persian cat*	**un buen rato**	*a good time*

3. In interrogative sentences, the predicate adjective precedes the subject, if the latter is a noun.

¿Es muy caro el libro?	*Is the book very expensive?*

EJERCICIO

Combínense los adjetivos y sustantivos siguientes:
1. este, cinco, nuestro, malo, grande, bueno
2. adjetivo, fotografías, traje, perro, novelas, sillas.

15. *QUE*

Que may be (*a*) a conjunction (English *that*), (*b*) a relative pronoun (*that, who*), and (*c*) the comparative adverb *than*.

a.	**Dice que llega esta tarde.**	*He says that he will arrive this afternoon.*
b.	**El niño que abrió la puerta es su sobrino.**	*The boy who opened the door is his nephew.*
c.	**Dolores estudia más que su hermano.**	*Dolores studies harder (more) than her brother.*

NOTE. *Than* is **de** before numerals: **Tengo más de mil fotografías en mi álbum** *I have more than a thousand photographs in my album.*

EJERCICIO

Combínense las frases siguientes en una sola frase con el relativo **que**, por ejemplo, **Pedro dice algo. Le gusta nadar.** → **Pedro dice que le gusta nadar; Leemos el libro. El libro es importante.** → **El libro que leemos es importante.**
1. Juan dice algo. Su madre viene.
2. El hombre indica algo. Hay que dar una vuelta.
3. La niña abrió la puerta. La niña es su sobrina.
4. Mi hermano vive en Madrid. Mi hermano es un abogado famoso.
5. El viaje fue interesante. Hicimos un viaje.
6. La computadora es cara. Compramos la computadora.

Preguntas

1. ¿Qué dice Juan?
2. ¿Qué indica el hombre?
3. ¿Qué es la niña? ¿Quién abrió la puerta?
4. ¿Qué es su hermano? ¿Dónde vive su hermano?
5. ¿Qué hicieron Uds.?
6. ¿Qué compraron Uds.?

Si Enrique trabaja mucho, su hermano Pedro trabaja poco, y su primo Jacinto no trabaja nunca.

7. ¿Quién trabaja menos que Pedro?
8. ¿Quién trabaja más que Jacinto?
9. ¿Quién trabaja más que Enrique?
10. ¿Quién trabaja menos que Enrique?

16. ADVERBS IN -*MENTE* (SEC. 191)

Adverbs of manner are freely formed by adding **-mente** to the feminine singular of adjectives. If the adjective has a written accent, the latter is retained when forming the adverb.

lento	*slow*	**lentamente**	*slowly*
frío	*cold*	**fríamente**	*coldly*
rígido	*rigid*	**rígidamente**	*rigidly*

Traducción

1. That gentleman is an Englishman; his wife is a very tall blonde.
2. Mr. Rivas is an employee of the company.
3. Charles is not a doctor; he is a good accountant.
4. I am going to buy some bread rolls.
5. This map costs more than two dollars.
6. We haven't any money.
7. The most interesting (part) of the trip was the visit to the Roman ruins.
8. These armchairs are very uncomfortable.
9. We had very bad weather.
10. We could see the English coast.
11. Those mountains are not very high.
12. I like this gray overcoat.
13. My study is very small.
14. He wrote an essay on the Spanish novel.
15. He won the third prize.
16. He played several Portuguese fados.
17. We are taking (following) a course in (of) contemporary art.
18. The first lessons are not very difficult.
19. Are these girls Irish?
20. This author writes very confusedly.
21. He also talks very rapidly.
22. It is evident that you haven't read the book.
23. This is the absurd (side) of the project.
24. The gardens (which) we are going to visit belong to the Governor.
25. He earns more than the maid.

Verbos y Modismos

NOTE. References to other sections are made to call attention to irregularities in the conjugation.

Review radical (stem) changing verbs of Class I (Sec. **226**).

Sentar *to seat, lay down, agree with, be becoming to;* **sentarse** *to sit down, be seated.*

1. This climate does not agree with me.
2. The new suit was very (**muy bien**) becoming to her.
3. Let's sit down here.
4. In the picture (photograph) some persons were seated and others (were) standing.
5. Before discussing the matter we should (**conviene**) lay down a few principles.
6. Mix (**mézclense**) the ingredients and let (**déjese**) set for (during) an hour.

Contar *to count, recount, tell;* **contar con** *to count on or with, have.*

1. He couldn't get to sleep, so (**y**) he began to count (up) to a thousand.
2. The president (**rector**) of the University was (counted) at that time some fifty years (old).
3. The shoemaker's wife would tell us stories every night.
4. Don't tell it to me, tell it to him.
5. He manages (directs) everything; the director is of no importance (does not count for anything).
6. You (may) count on my help.
7. This province has great (natural) resources.

Perder *to lose, miss;* **perderse** *get lost.*

1. We missed the train by a few minutes.
2. Don't miss (for yourself) the trip to the mountains.
3. I got lost in the big city.

Volver (Sec. **266**) *to go back, return (intrans.), turn (trans.);* **volver a** *to (do) again;* **volverse** *to turn (over, back), become (turn, go).*

1. Let's go back (to) home.
2. Don't do it again.
3. Please recopy this letter.
4. Turn the page.
5. That noise is driving me crazy.
6. I don't know why he turns his back (on) me.
7. I have a pain in this shoulder which will (does) not let me turn over on (**de**) that (this) side.
8. The deal is closed; don't go back on it (**atrás**).
9. That fellow must have gone crazy.

10. These people have become (turned) very suspicious.
11. There are nothing but (everything becomes) difficulties.

Soler *to be accustomed (used) to, to (do) usually.*

1. I usually stay at home at night.
2. We used to go together to the café.
3. What do you (does one) usually give as a (**de**) tip?

SER AND ESTAR: EXPRESSIONS SIGNIFYING "TO BECOME"

1

17. *SER* (SEC. 259) AND *ESTAR* (SEC. 245)

1. **Ser** and **estar** both mean *to be.* **Ser** means *to be* in essence, while **estar** means *to be* in location, state, or condition.

2. **Ser** is used when the predicate is (*a*) a noun or an adjective used as a noun, (*b*) an adjective denoting an essential quality or characteristic, (*c*) a prepositional phrase denoting origin, material, or ownership, (*d*) an expression of time, (*e*) part of an impersonal expression. The distinction between **ser** and **estar** is also reflected in the nouns **ser** *being* and **estado** *state, condition.*

a.	**Pedro es arquitecto.**	*Peter is an architect.*
	Carmen es madrileña.	*Carmen is a Madrilian.*
	El sol es una estrella.	*The sun is a star.*
	Soy casado.	*I'm married (i.e., a married man).*
b.	**La torre es muy alta.**	*The tower is very high.*
	El señor Martínez es viejo.	*Mr. Martinez is old.*
c.	**La mesa es de madera.**	*The table is (made) of wood.*
	Este abrigo es de mi hermano.	*This overcoat is my brother's.*
	Soy de Caracas.	*I am from Caracas.*
d.	**Son las tres y media.**	*It is half past three.*
	Es de día.	*It is daytime.*
	Hoy es el quince de marzo.	*Today is the 15th of March.*

e. **Es probable.**	*It is probable.*
Es evidente.	*It is evident.*
Es tarde.	*It is late.*

3. The difference between **ser** and **estar** appears clearly when the verbs are used with adjectives (see Sec. **20**). (*f*) When adjectives such as **interesante, claro,** and **cómodo** denote essential characteristics, they are used with **ser.** (*g*) The same adjectives used with **estar** indicate a condition that the subject has come into, rather than an inherent or essential characteristic.

f. **El libro era muy interesante.**	*The book was very interesting.*
La silla es cómoda.	*The chair is comfortable.*
g. **Yo estoy cómodo.**	*I am comfortable* (condition).
Está muy claro.	*It is very clear.*

EJERCICIO

Combínense los nombres en la sección (*a*) con los adjetivos y sustantivos en la sección (*b*) usando el verbo **ser**:
   a. Carolina, Miguel, Antonio, el médico, mi tío, María
   b. profesor, famoso, estudiante, escritor, muy popular, soltero, rico, guapo, alto

Preguntas

   ¿Qué es *Carolina* (Miguel, etc.)? ¿Cómo es el *médico*?

EJERCICIO

Combínense los sustantivos de la sección (*a*) con los de (*b*) para indicar que los de (*b*) son el material de que están hechos, por ejemplo, **cuaderno, papel** → **el cuaderno es de papel.**
   a. cuaderno, casa, máquina de escribir, vestido, reloj
   b. papel, piedra, aluminio, seda, plata

Preguntas

   ¿De qué es el *cuaderno*? (la casa, etc.)?

EJERCICIO

Combínense los sustantivos de la sección (*a*) con los nombres de (*b*) para indicar pertenencia, por ejemplo, **libro, tío** → **el libro es de mi tío.**
   a. artículo, automóvil, edificio, barco, pistola
   b. hermano, Jorge, gobierno, Jacinto, guardia

Preguntas

¿De quién es el *artículo* (el automóvil, etc.)?

---

4. The more frequent uses of **estar** are: (*h*) to express location, (*i*) with present participles, to form the so-called progressive tenses, (*j*) with past participles, to denote the condition resulting from the action of a verb, and (*k*) with adjectives signifying state or condition.

h. **Estamos en los Estados Unidos.**	*We are in the United States.*
La Giralda está en Sevilla.	*The Giralda is in Seville.*
El sol está lejos de la tierra.	*The sun is distant from the earth.*
i. **Estamos estudiando.**	*We are (in the act of) studying.*

NOTE. The progressive tenses in English are used with much more frequency than in Spanish where the ordinary present tense is normally used. English often uses a progressive tense as the equivalent of the ordinary present: *he is working a lot these days* would usually be translated as **trabaja mucho estos días. Está trabajando** would be interpreted as meaning that he is in the act of working at this moment. Speakers of English must beware of always translating the English present progressive by a Spanish progressive. It must be especially noted that the Spanish progressive construction can never be used to indicate a future, e.g., **Mañana voy a Lisboa** *Tomorrow I'm going to Lisbon.*

j. **La ventana está cerrada.**	*The window is closed.*
El artículo está bien escrito.	*The article is well written.*
El cielo está nublado.	*The sky is cloudy.*
Mi abuela está muerta.	*My grandmother is dead.*
k. **Juan está contento.**	*Juan is happy.*
Mi primo está enfermo.	*My cousin is ill.*
Marta está triste.	*Martha is sad.*

EJERCICIO

Contéstense las preguntas siguientes, usando los siguientes sujetos entre paréntesis: **¿Dónde está** _____ ? (su padre, la Giralda, el Prado, los astronautas, nosotros, yo)

---

5. From the preceding summary, it should be evident that the distinction between **ser** and **estar** will generally offer no difficulty except when the predicate contains an adjective (*b* and *k*). When this occurs, a choice is made between the two verbs according to whether the predicate adjective denotes (*b*) an essential quality or characteristic, or (*k*) a state or condition.

Isabel es muy morena.	*Isabel is very dark (of complexion—essential characteristic).*
Isabel está muy morena.	*Isabel is very dark (tanned, a condition).*

6. If the subject of **ser** is a person, the predicate adjective usually is equivalent to a noun denoting a general class or type and may be the equivalent of a noun in English.

Mi sobrina es rubia.	*My niece is (a) blonde.*
Mi cuñada es joven.	*My sister-in-law is (a) young (woman).*
Mi amigo Daniel es costarricense.	*My friend Daniel is a Costa Rican.*
El señor de la Renta es rico.	*Mr. de la Renta is a rich man.*

NOTE. **Ciego** *blind,* **sordo** *deaf,* and the like, usually belong to this category, as does **feliz: soy feliz** *I am happy* (but **estoy contento**).

7. **Estar** may be regarded as the graphic verb *to be* and, in contrast to the more abstract **ser**, often has the force of *look, feel, taste,* or *act.* **Estar** emphasizes the effect that a quality has on the person perceiving it. (See Sec. **270** for a list of adjectives whose English translation is different after **ser** and **estar**.)

Antonio es malo.	*Antonio is bad (wicked).*
Antonio está malo.	*Antonio is ill (feels bad).*
Rosario es pálida.	*Rosario is pale (by nature).*
Rosario está pálida.	*Rosario is (looks, has become) pale.*
Luis es muy raro.	*Luis is very peculiar.*
Luis está muy raro hoy.	*Luis acts very peculiar today.*
El caldo es muy bueno para los enfermos.	*Broth is very good for sick people.*
Este caldo está muy bueno.	*This broth tastes very good.*

EJERCICIO

Combínense las palabras en la sección (*a*) con las de (*b*), primero con el verbo **ser** y después con el verbo **estar**:

a. Luis, el jefe, yo, Jacinto y su amiga, las muchachas, nuestros padres, el agua
b. malo, aburrido, cansado, extraño, listo, divertido, frío

Preguntas

¿Cómo está *Luis* (el jefe, etc.)? ¿Cómo es *Luis*?

---

8. The graphic quality of **estar** is well illustrated in the progressive tenses, which in Spanish always refer to action in progress. (See Sec. **17.5**.)

	Estoy leyendo una novela.	*I am (in the act of) reading a novel.*
But:	**Leo muchas novelas.**	*I read many novels (general statement).*
	Ahora vivo en Nueva York.	*I am living (live) in New York.*

Cámbiense los verbos en las frases siguientes del presente al progresivo con **estar,** añadiendo la frase **en este momento,** p.ej., **estudio mis apuntes** → **en este momento estoy estudiando mis apuntes.**
1. Mi profesora nos *ayuda.*
2. Los obreros *construyen* un edificio nuevo.
3. Los estudiantes *protestan* las injusticias.
4. La autora de esa novela *escribe* otra.
5. El tren *llega* a la estación.

18. EXPRESSIONS SIGNIFYING *TO BECOME*

Spanish has no verb with a general meaning like English *to become.* Instead, it has a variety of equivalents. If the predicate (*a*) is a noun or an adjective used as a noun, **hacerse** is used to denote the result of conscious effort; if the predicate is (*b*) an adjective or participle, **ponerse** is used to indicate changes in physical, mental, or emotional states.

a. **Miguel se hizo periodista.**	*Miguel became a journalist.*
Un pobre puede hacerse rico.	*A poor man can become rich.*
b. **Fernando se puso pálido.**	*Fernando became pale (furious, fat).*
(furioso, gordo).	
El cielo se puso muy oscuro.	*The sky became very dark.*

EXCEPTIONS: **se hace tarde** *it is getting (becoming) late;* **se hace (de) noche** *it is getting dark (night time).*

Combínense las palabras en la sección (*a*) con las de (*b*) y los verbos **hacerse** o **ponerse**:
a. yo, mi compañera de cuarto, el profesor, los ciudadanos, la actriz
b. rico, enojado, abogado, ingeniero, enfermo

Traducción 1A

1. Who is that gentleman?—He is a friend of my father.
2. What are those papers?—They are letters.
3. How is your brother?—He is sick.
4. My nephew wants to be an engineer.
5. We would like to be in Seville during (the) Holy Week.
6. That building is high. It is (made) of steel and concrete.

7. These apples are not ripe.
8. I am from Montevideo; my parents are still there. They are old.
9. This house belongs to my sister-in-law.
10. The door is closed and the lights are out.
11. My office is not far from your hotel.
12. These shoes are comfortable, but too expensive.
13. I don't like the soup. It is cold.
14. Today is the first of June. Next month we will be in Europe.
15. Be generous.
16. Be ready at five o'clock.
17. The book I am reading now is interesting and is very well written.
18. You are very busy this morning.—I have been busy the whole week.
19. I am not (a) nervous (person), but I feel restless today.
20. You have become pale. Are you ill?
21. The proprietor of the store was lame.
22. Do you like this ice cream?—Yes, it is (tastes) good.
23. How beautiful the sea is (looks) this evening!
24. It became late and we had to return.
25. My roommate has become (a) lawyer.
26. We were eating when he came in.

II

19. ADDITIONAL REMARKS ON *SER*

1. **Ser,** not **estar,** is used in the following cases, where occurrence and definition, not actual location, are expressed.

La escena es en Madrid.	*The scene is (takes place) in Madrid.*
La guerra fue en el Paraguay.	*The war was (occurred) in Paraguay.*
La conferencia es en el museo.	*The lecture is at the museum.*

NOTE. In a sentence like **Aquí es donde vive** *This* (here) *is* (the place) *where he lives,* **ser** is simply used as a linking verb, as in **este es el lugar** *this is the place.*

EJERCICIO

Reemplácense los verbos en las frases siguientes con la forma debida del verbo **ser:**
1. La ceremonia tuvo lugar en el ministerio.
2. La batalla occurrió en el campo.
3. La conferencia empieza a las ocho.
4. El martes se celebra el concierto.
5. Darán la fiesta en casa de mi tío.

---

2. In Spanish the subject frequently follows the verb. Consequently, **ser** sometimes agrees in number with the predicate, not the subject, especially if the predicate is felt to be the logical subject.

Lo más interesante de la obra son las escenas cómicas.	*The most interesting part of the work is the comic scenes.*

3. **Ser de** gives to a following infinitive an impersonal, passive meaning.

Es de esperar . . .	*It is to be hoped . . .*
Era de lamentar . . .	*It was regrettable . . .*

20. ADDITIONAL REMARKS ON *ESTAR*

1. **Estar** also indicates location in time in the following idiomatic expressions:

¿A cuántos (del mes) estamos hoy?	*What date is today?*
Estamos a quince de marzo.	*It is the fifteenth of March.*

NOTE. These sentences may also be translated **¿Qué fecha es hoy?** and **Hoy es el quince de marzo.**

2. As a result of the difference between **ser** and **estar,** certain adjectives and participles vary distinctly in meaning (and in their English equivalents) according to whether they are used with one or the other. (For a longer list of these adjectives and participles see Appendix, Sec. **270.**)

Este producto es muy rico en vitaminas.	*This product is very rich in vitamins.*
Este plato está muy rico.	*This dish is (tastes) delicious.*
Joaquin está muy cansado.	*Joaquin is very tired.*
Joaquin es muy cansado.	*Joaquin is very tiresome (a bore).*
La nieve es fría.	*Snow is cold.*
Este café está frío.	*This coffee is cold.*
Hermenegildo es muy distraído.	*Hermenegildo is a very absent-minded man.*
Estaba distraído.	*He was distracted (i.e., wasn't paying attention).*

3. The graphic character of the progressive tenses and especially of resultant conditions may be increased by replacing **estar** with auxiliaries of more concrete meaning, such as verbs of motion:

Voy cansándome de esto.	*I am getting tired of this.*
Anda distraído.	*He is (going around) absent-minded.*

Vengo indignado.	*I am* (coming from somewhere) *indignant.*
Vengo coleccionando relojes desde hace tiempo.	*I have been collecting watches for a long time.*

EJERCICIO

Cámbiense los verbos en las frases siguientes a las construcciones con **-ndo** y los verbos **estar, ir, andar,** y **venir**: p. ej., **escucho los chismes → estoy (vengo, etc.) escuchando los chismes.**
1. Cantamos las canciones populares.
2. Mi mejor amigo escucha todo lo que dicen.
3. Ese tonto molesta a todos.
4. Aquella muchacha hermosa atrae a todos los jóvenes.
5. Nuestros compañeros se cansan de los estudios.
6. Te lo digo desde hace años.

---

4. The use of **estar** to stress the impact that something makes on the speaker is revealed with special force when it appears with adjectives which usually are found with **ser** or even, in a few rare cases, with nouns. In such sentences the emphasis is not on the identification of the subject with the predicate as with **ser** but on how the subject appears to the speaker, independent of what or how it is in reality. The best English equivalent of this use is *seem* or *look.*

El pobre de don Alejandro está tan viejo estos días.	*Poor Mr. Alexander looks so old these days.*
¡Estaba tan niña, tan muñeca!	*She seemed so child-like, so doll-like!*
¡Qué idiota estás!	*How idiotic you're acting!*

NOTE. After **ser** and **estar** the distinction between nouns and adjectives is largely neutralized. (See Sec. **17.5**.) Compare also **él es muy caballero** *he is very gentlemanly;* **es muy verdad** *it is very true;* **esos chicos son muy amigos** *those boys are great friends.*

21. EXPRESSIONS SIGNIFYING *TO BECOME* (SEC. 139.1 NOTE)

Spanish possesses no general equivalent to the abstract English verb *to become.* The Spanish equivalent will vary according to the specific meaning in each case. In addition to **hacerse** and **ponerse,** the following are also used:

(*a*) **llegar a ser** (with nouns) to indicate the final result or culmination of a process,
(*b*) **volverse** (with adjectives) to denote a violent or radical change,
(*c*) **convertirse en** (with nouns) to denote any change, natural or unexpected,

(*d*) **meterse a** (with nouns) to denote an unexpected change of occupation,

(*e*) certain reflexive verbs like **calentarse** *grow warm, warm up,* **enfriarse** *grow cold,* and a number of verbs ending in **-ecer**:

endurecer	harden	**empobrecer**	*become poor*
enriquecer	grow rich	**entristecer**	*become sad*
esclarecer	grow light	**oscurecer**	*grow dark*
atardecer	grow dark	**anochecer**	*become night*

a. **Napoleón llegó a ser emperador.**   *Napoleon became emperor.*
Llegaron a ser amigas inseparables.   *They became (came to be) inseparable friends.*

b. **Se volvió loca.**   *She became (went) crazy.*
Se volvió republicana.   *She became (turned) republican.*

c. **El agua se convierte en vapor.**   *Water becomes (turns into) steam.*
El mitin se convirtió en un motín.   *The (political) meeting became (turned into) a riot.*

d. **Se metió a novelista.**   *She became (turned into) a novelist.*

NOTE. With **monja** *nun* and **fraile** *monk, friar,* **meterse** is used: **se metió a monja** *she became a nun.* *To become* (go) *blind* is **quedarse ciego.**

e. **La comida se ha enfriado.**   *The meal has become cold.*
Anochece.   *It is getting dark.*
Se ha enriquecido.   *He has become rich.*

NOTE. The English idiom *What has become of?* is translated **¿Qué ha sido de?** or **¿Qué se ha hecho de? ¿Qué se hizo de?**

EJERCICIO

Contéstense, utilizando en las respuestas las palabras entre paréntesis y las expresiones de la Sección **21**:

1. ¿Qué ha sido de su primo? (ingeniero, rico, programador, loco, maestra, dibujante)
2. ¿Qué le pasó al amigo de usted? (socialista, reaccionario, amigo del presidente)

Cámbiense las frases siguientes, utilizando los verbos inceptivos, según el modelo: **La comida está fría → la comida se ha enfriado.**

3. Mi madre está triste.
4. El cielo está claro (oscuro).
5. El agua está caliente.
6. La tierra está dura.
7. La muchacha tiene la cara roja.

Traducción 1B

1. What date is today?—It is the 18th of February. (two ways)
2. I was talking with Miss Pardo. She is a very intelligent girl.
3. Her parents are spending the winter in Majorca. They are both painters.
4. The plays of Zorrilla were very popular.
5. The hill is very steep.
6. This coffee is very hot.
7. I have been awake the whole night and now I am tired.
8. Your mother-in-law is always in a (of) good humor.
9. The resemblance of the portrait was astonishing.
10. Charles is a writer. He is never satisfied with (**de**) his work.
11. What (how) is your fiancée (like)?—She is tall and blonde.
12. I want to buy this hat. How much is it?—It is very cheap.
13. Mr. Sánchez is (a) very silent (individual), but tonight he has been talking all the time.
14. I have never been so happy.
15. You act very strange.—Yes, I am worried.
16. You are (a) very absent-minded (person).—Oh, no, you are mistaken.
17. We were very bored because the film was boring.
18. The waiter became so furious that I thought he had gone crazy.
19. She is getting fat. It is very disagreeable.
20. What has become of your cousin George?—He is married now.
21. He has become president of the firm.
22. You are becoming very intolerant.
23. Is it here that you bought the suit?
24. The word "speed" has become the symbol of our age.
25. It is to be expected.
26. The (**lo**) best (part) of the program are the works of Albéniz.

III

Verbos y Modismos

Review radical-changing verbs of Classes II and III (Secs. **227, 228**).

1. I regret I did not do (not having done) it before.
2. He heard (felt) a tremendous noise.
3. I don't think we will sleep at all (**nada**) tonight.
4. Where is John?—Upstairs, sleeping soundly.
5. His father died (**morírsele**) yesterday.

Pedir *to beg, ask for, request.*

1. He asked her to go with him.
2. Ask him for it.
3. You (one) can't ask for anything better (more).
4. Ask for (it) in all good drug stores.
5. I have borrowed his tuxedo.
6. I am going to ask you a favor.
7. We saw some beggars asking for money.

Servir (de) *to serve (as);* **servir para** *to be of use* or *good for;* **servirse de** *make use of;* **sírvase** *please.*

1. His daughter was employed (serving) in the house of a doctor.
2. In this hotel they serve very good meals (**muy bien de comer**).
3. Help (serve) yourself (to) bread.
4. At night the patio served as a dining room.
5. The boy acted as a chauffeur, a waiter, and even a secretary for him.
6. This key is no good.
7. What is this used for?—It is no good at all (for nothing).
8. He is no good as a (for) pilot.
9. What is the use of denying it?
10. Please, close the door.

Entender *to make out (hear, understand) in contrast to* **oír** *(Sec. **151**) to hear (physically) and* **comprender** *to comprehend (rationally);* **entenderse** *to come to an understanding or agreement, to get along together;* **entender de** *to know about (through practice).*

1. Speak louder; I can't (do not) hear (understand) you well.
2. I can't read (do not make out) his handwriting.
3. (It is by) talking (that) people come to understand each other.
4. Those two do not get along well together.
5. Is it clear?—Yes, sir.
6. He knows a lot about machinery.
7. Apparently you know (something) about everything.

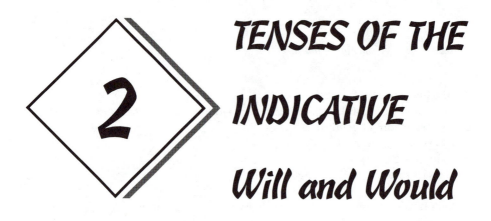

2 TENSES OF THE INDICATIVE

Will and Would

(For tense forms of the indicative, see Sec. **222**.)

22. THE PRESENT TENSE

The simple present tense is employed more frequently in Spanish than in English, being used (*a*) as the equivalent of the ordinary English present progressive tense and (*b*) to render the English present perfect when the act or state lasts down to the present. This latter construction is particularly identified with impersonal **hace** (Sec. **137**), with temporal **desde (que),** and with the verb **llevar** used with temporal meaning.

> *a.* **¿Adónde va Ud.?**   *Where are you going?*
> **Ahora vivo en el campo.**   *I am living in the country now.*

NOTE. The progressive tenses in Spanish have much more graphic force than their English equivalents and are used only when the action is actually taking place (see Sec. **17.7; 20.3**).

> *b.* **Hace una semana que estamos**   *We have been here a week.*
> **aquí.**

28

Estamos aquí desde el lunes.	*We have been here since Monday.*
No la veo desde que estoy aquí.	*I haven't seen her since I have been here.*
Llevamos aquí una semana.	*We have been here a week.*

NOTE. Similar to (*b*) is the idiomatic use of **acabar de** to represent action just previously completed: **acaba de llegar el tren** *the train has just arrived.*

EJERCICIO

Contéstense:
1. ¿Desde cuándo estudia usted español?
2. ¿Cuánto tiempo hace que usted vive aquí?
3. ¿Lleva usted mucho tiempo estudiando en esta universidad?
4. ¿Cuántos días hace que usted no ve a sus padres?

23. THE PRETERIT

1. English has but one simple past tense. Spanish possesses two, the *preterit* and the *imperfect*. Of these, the preterit is the one that more closely corresponds to the English simple past. It is essentially a narrative tense, presenting facts viewed as a completed and undivided whole, regardless of duration. Consequently it is used (*a*) to record a single completed fact or phenomenon, and (*b*) to sum up a series of acts or states which, viewed as a whole, constitute a single completed fact or phenomenon. In other words, the preterit puts the emphasis on either the beginning or the end of an action or a state.

a. **Cerró la puerta con violencia.** *He slammed the door.*
Ayer llovió. *Yesterday it rained.*
Estuvimos en España en el verano de 1992. *We were in Spain in the summer of 1992.*
El viaje duró seis días. *The trip lasted six days.*

b. **La semana pasada escribí dos cartas a mi hermana.** *Last week I wrote two letters to my sister.*
Mataron ocho toros en la corrida. *Eight bulls were killed in the fight.*
En el siglo XVI los españoles hicieron muchos viajes de exploración. *In the sixteenth century the Spaniards made many voyages of exploration.*

2. The English *ago* is rendered by **hace . . . que** with the preterit. **Hace** may follow the verb, in which case **que** is omitted.

Hace una semana que llegué. Llegué hace una semana. *I arrived a week ago (lit., it makes a week since I arrived).*

EJERCICIO

Cámbiense las frases siguientes al pretérito:
1. Me levanto y me lavo la cara.
2. Luego me visto y me pongo el mejor traje que tengo.
3. Suena el teléfono.
4. Descuelgo el receptor y digo: —Diga.
5. Después me desayuno y voy a ver a mi amiga.

24. THE IMPERFECT

1. The imperfect tense corresponds roughly to the English past progressive. Consequently, the imperfect indicates that an act or state is viewed (*a*) as being in progress. Therefore it is used in past descriptions of states or actions that continue throughout a past period. It is also used (*b*) to indicate habitual, recurrent, or continuous action in the past, corresponding to the English *used to, would* (when it means the same thing as *used to*); (*c*) to represent indirect discourse, and (*d*) to give the time of day.

a. **Estaba en Sevilla cuando la vi por primera vez.**	*I was in Seville when I first saw her.*
Llovía sin parar.	*It was raining continuously.*
La comitiva fúnebre pasaba lentamente.	*The funeral procession was passing slowly.*
Las olas se estrellaban contra las rocas.	*The waves were breaking on the rocks.*
b. **Iba al café todas las tardes.**	*He would (used to) go to the cafe every afternoon.*
c. **Dijo que lo sabía.**	*He said he knew it.*
d. **Eran las seis en punto cuando terminé.**	*It was six o'clock on the dot when I finished.*

2. The imperfect is used in the **hace . . . que, desde, llevar,** and **acabar de** constructions (Sec. **22**) as equivalent of the English pluperfect.

Hacía una semana que estábamos allí.	*We had been there (for) a week.*
Llevábamos una semana allí.	
Estábamos allí desde principios de mes.	*We had been there since the first of the month.*
El tren acababa de llegar.	*The train had just pulled in.*

EJERCICIO

Cámbiense las preguntas en el ejercicio de la sección **22** al imperfecto. Cámbiense las frases siguientes al imperfecto:
1. Hace un día espléndido.
2. Los pájaros cantan en los árboles.
3. El cielo está azul.
4. Oigo los ruidos de la calle.
5. Son las siete y cuarto.
6. Voy a levantarme. Soy feliz.

25. THE FUTURE

The Spanish future tense corresponds in general to the English future. The following differences are to be noted: (*a*) the future is used in Spanish to indicate probability or a conjecture which the speaker is reasonably certain will prove to be true ("future of probability"); (*b*) the future is not used in Spanish to render the English *will* when the latter means *be willing, want to.*

a. **¿Quién llama?—Será el cartero.**	*Who's knocking?—It must be the postman.*

NOTE. This use of *must* in English has to be differentiated from the *must* meaning *obliged to* or *required to.*

b. **No quiere venir con nosotros.**	*He will not ("won't," i.e., does not want to) come with us.*

NOTE. The future is used after **si** *whether,* but not after **si** *if:* **no sé si vendrá o no** *I don't know whether he will come or not,* but **si le veo, se lo daré** *if I see her, I'll give it to her.*

26. THE CONDITIONAL

The conditional tense represents the future in the past. The Spanish tense corresponds in general to the English construction using *would,* but with the same differences as noted in Sec. **25** for the future. Thus, the conditional can be used to mean conjecture in the past, in English *must have, might have.*

English speakers must be especially aware that the English word *would* has a variety of different meanings and is not automatically to be interpreted as the equivalent of the Spanish conditional tense. (See Sec. **28**.)

a.	**Marta dijo que vendría mañana.**	*Marta said that she would come tomorrow.*
	No sabíamos si estarían aquí o no.	*We didn't know if they would be here or not.*
	¿Quién llamaba?—Sería el cartero.	*Who was knocking?—It must have been the postman.*
b.	**No querías venir con nosotros.**	*You would not (did not want to) come with us.*

EJERCICIO

Cámbiense los verbos de las frases siguientes al futuro:
1. Mañana voy a Nueva York.
2. Dentro de poco estamos allí.
3. Muy pronto lo sabes todo.
4. Jorge puede hacerlo.
5. No quieren hacer el trabajo necesario.

En las frases siguientes cámbiense las expresiones con **deber (de)** + infinitivo al futuro y luego al condicional, p. ej., **debe de verlo → lo verá → lo vería.**
1. Deben de ser las cuatro.
2. Debe de ser mi hermana.
3. Mi libro debe de estar perdido.
4. Aquella vieja debe de tener más de ochenta años.
5. Deben de haber ido al teatro.

27. THE PERFECT (COMPOUND) TENSES

The perfect (compound) tenses are formed with **haber** and the invariable past participle. The present perfect and pluperfect are (*a*) normally used more or less as in English—except in constructions denoting lapse of time (Secs. **22** and **24**). The future perfect and conditional perfect express (*b*) in past time the same functions as the future and the conditional.

a.	**Le he dado mi opinión sobre el asunto.**	*I have given you my opinion on the subject.*
	Le había dado mi opinión sobre el asunto.	*I had given you my opinion on the subject.*
b.	**¿Quién ha mandado el paquete?—Habrá sido mi primo.**	*Who has sent the package?—It must have been my cousin.*

NOTE. The conditional perfect of probability is rare.

¿Quién lo habría hecho?	*Who could have done it?*

EJERCICIO

Cámbiense los verbos en las frases siguientes del presente al presente perfecto:
1. Vamos muchas veces al teatro.
2. Allí se presentan muchas obras dramáticas.
3. Hasta ahora no vuelvo a mi patria.
4. ¿Ves una cosa semejante?
5. No lo hace nunca.

28. *WILL* AND *WOULD*

The student should bear in mind that the English auxiliaries *will* and *would* represent not only the future and conditional tenses but also the present and past tenses of **querer** *to be willing, to want,* and that *would* often is the equivalent of the imperfect tense in the meaning *used to.*

Dijo que vendría.	*He said he would come.*
No quiere (quería) venir con nosotros.	*He won't (wouldn't) come with us.*
Iba al café todos los días.	*He would go to the cafe every day.*

Traducción 2A

1. I have been studying for two hours and now I'm tired.
2. Somebody is calling you on the (by) telephone.
3. I didn't hear what he was saying.
4. She says we are going to the theater. Are you coming too?
5. She told me she would see me tomorrow.
6. I have been here for three months. Tomorrow I am leaving for Spain.
7. I haven't been to (in) the movies since I have been here.
8. I saw your grandfather in Philadelphia, but I didn't talk to him.
9. The Secretary of (the) Treasury arrived this morning.
10. The conductor asked us for the tickets.
11. The sea was very rough.
12. Last year I used to take my meals in a restaurant.
13. The steamer was entering the bay when the collision occurred.
14. It was half past one when the game started.
15. When we lived in the country we would (i.e., used to) get up at six o'clock every morning.
16. Charles V was King of Spain and Emperor of Germany.
17. In the Middle Ages Medina del Campo was famous for its fairs.
18. He had been sick for a long time.
19. I had been in Mexico for two years when we became friends.
20. (I wonder) where my dictionary is?—It must be on the shelf.

21. The child must have been four years old.
22. Vargas Llosa's latest novel has just come out.
23. I wouldn't like to live in this town.
24. The owner of the dog said that she would not sell him.
25. I must have lost the key of my trunk.
26. We had forgotten that it was Sunday and the stores were closed.

II

29. SOME USES OF THE PRESENT

The present tense is used, especially in the spoken language, as a graphic substitute for other tenses in the following constructions: (*a*) as an emphatic future, when certainty is implied, (*b*) in interrogations, when immediate future time is involved, (*c*) for the conditional perfect, in contrary-to-fact conditions (see Secs. **120, 123**); (*d*) for the simple past, in historical narrative, in rapid sequences, or with **por poco**, (*e*) for the imperative, by stating the command not as a wish but as a fact.

a.	**Mañana le despido.**	*I (surely) will fire him tomorrow.*
	Nos reunimos esta tarde.	*We will get together (for sure) this afternoon.*
	Eso lo hago yo cualquier día.	*I'll do that any day.*
b.	**¿Vamos ahora?**	*Shall we go now?*
	¿Pongo el desayuno en la mesa?	*Shall (should) I put the breakfast on the table?*
	¿Me ayudas?	*Will you help me?*

NOTE. In negative sentences the Spanish present often is the equivalent of *can* or *will* in English: **no entiendo su letra** *I can't make out his handwriting;* **el ruido no me deja dormir** *the noise will not let me sleep.*

c.	**Si hubiera entrado,** (or **entra**) **en aquel momento, le tiro algo a la cabeza.**	*If he had entered at that moment, I would have thrown something at his head. (See Secs. 120, 123.)*
d.	**Salgo de casa, me encuentro con Enrique, me convida a café y luego nos fuimos al teatro.**	*I left the house, I met Henry, he "treated" me to coffee, and then we went to the theater.*
	Por poco me caigo.	*I almost fell down.*
e.	**Deja Ud. el paquete en el correo y vuelve aquí.**	*Leave the package at the post office and return here.*

30. PRETERIT AND IMPERFECT (CONTINUED)

1. The difference between the preterit and the imperfect is a modal rather than a temporal one. Both are past tenses, but each tense stresses not time but rather the way in which the state or action of the verb is presented.

The preterit stresses final result; the imperfect stresses process. It follows, therefore, that the same statement may have a different meaning according to which past tense is used. When the imperfect is used, the speaker regards the meaning of the verb as being in progress and forming the background of other acts that may be taking place.

The difficulty encountered by speakers of English lies in the fact that while in English one may often use a past progressive in the same sense as a Spanish imperfect, the English simple past may also be used in sentences which in Spanish would require an imperfect. In other words, the distinction, which in English is optional, is required in Spanish. Also, there are some verbs in English which rarely appear in the progressive construction, e.g., *to be, to have, to seem,* etc.

A las once de la mañana el barco entró en el puerto.	*At eleven o'clock in the morning the ship entered the port.*
A las once de la mañana el barco entraba en el puerto.	*At eleven o'clock the morning the ship was entering the port.*

In the preceding examples, we can see that the first sentence simply reports a past fact as completed, while the second sentence implies that while the action was in process, i.e., while the ship was entering the port, some other events were taking place and the entering of the ship was simply a background for them. For example, while the ship was entering the port, it struck a sand bar, or the captain had a heart attack, etc. In isolated sentences where there is no visible context, it is the speaker's mental attitude, i.e., the unexpressed context, that determines the tense of the verb used.

En el siglo XVI España fue una gran potencia europea.	*In the sixteenth century Spain was a great European power* (viewed in résumé and implying contrast with some subsequent situation, e.g., **hacia 1800 España había perdido mucha de su importancia anterior**).
En el siglo XVI España era una gran potencia europea.	*In the sixteenth century Spain was a great European power* (viewed as the background for further statements about what was happening during the time that Spain was a great power, e.g., **en esa época se llevó a cabo la conquista de mucho del Nuevo Mundo**).
En el verano de 1992 estuvimos en España.	*In the summer of 1992 we were in Spain* (summed up as a single experience, possibly implying just a short visit).
En el verano de 1992 estábamos en España.	*In the summer of 1992 we were in Spain* (implying that the speaker spent

the whole summer in Spain). He may go on to relate what happened during that period. In English, it would be impossible to say, *we were being in Spain*).

EJERCICIO

Cámbiense las frases siguientes al pasado:
1. Mi amigo Peña me acompaña todos los días al parque.
2. Cada mañana llega a mi casa a las diez.
3. Por lo general tomamos una taza de café y luego salimos.
4. Un día Peña toca el timbre mientras todavía duermo.
5. De repente me despierto y veo que son las siete.
6. —¿Qué diablos será eso?—me pregunto.
7. Abro la puerta y Peña me saluda cordialmente.
8. Entra y me explica que unos compañeros suyos que viajan por el país quieren hacer una excursión a El Escorial.
9. Por eso nos invitan a ir con ellos.
10. Acepto la invitación, nos desayunamos, y vamos. Nos divertimos mucho.

---

2. As a result of the difference between the preterit and imperfect, certain verbs such as **conocer, saber, poder, tener,** and **querer** have different English equivalents in these two tenses, since English normally does not have any imperfect distinction for these verbs. That is, it is usually impossible to say something like: *I was knowing it; *he was being able to swim; *we were having five dollars.*

No lo sabía.	*I did not know it.*
Lo supe ayer.	*I found it out (learned it) yesterday.*
No conocía a ese señor.	*I did not know that gentleman.*
Le conocí ayer.	*I met him (made his acquaintance) yesterday.*
No quería salir.	*He would not (did not want to) go out.*
No quiso salir.	*He refused to go out.*
No podía olvidarlo.	*He could not (was not able to) forget it.*
No pudo olvidarlo.	*He could not (tried but failed) forget it.*
Ayer tuve carta de su madre.	*I received a letter from his mother yesterday.*

NOTE. With **poder** and **querer** the difference in meaning between the preterit and imperfect is much more evident when the sentence is negative.

3. The imperfect is sometimes used as a vivid substitute for the conditional or conditional perfect, especially in colloquial speech.

Si no hablaba, se moría.	*If he couldn't have talked, he would have died.*
Si hubiera entrado en aquel momento, le tiraba (tiro) algo a la cabeza.	*If he had entered at that moment, I would have thrown something at his head.*
Yo que tú no lo hacía (haría).	*If I were you, I wouldn't do it.*

4. The preterit (usually with **ya**) stresses the completion of action in immediate past time.

Ya terminamos.	*We have finished.*
Ya se acabó.	*It's all over.*

5. The imperfect is frequently used instead of the present tense (*a*) in polite questions with **desear** *to desire* or its equivalent, and (*b*) with **merecer** *to deserve.*

a. **¿Qué deseaba el señor?**	*What would you like? (lit., What did the gentleman wish? (Often used by waiters and shopkeepers.)*
b. **Merecía que le ahorcaran.**	*He deserves to be hanged.*

EJERCICIO

Cámbiense los infinitivos entre paréntesis a la forma debida del pasado:
1. Ayer yo (conocer) al nuevo decano cuando fui a la reunión.
2. Enrique tenía el brazo roto y no (poder) levantar el peso.
3. Manuel esperaba un regalo de Alberto pero sólo (tener) una carta.
4. Las dos camareras (conocer) a muchos de los parroquianos de la cafetería.
5. Un día nosotros (saber) una noticia importante.
6. Pedro me dijo que no (querer) salir porque estaba muy ocupado.
7. Las tropas insurgentes fracasaron porque no (poder) apoderarse de la capital.

---

31. THE FUTURE AS IMPERATIVE

The future is occasionally used as a categorical imperative.

Hará Ud. lo que le digo.	*You will do what I say.*

32. SPECIAL USES OF THE PRESENT PERFECT

The present perfect may be used (*a*) in clauses introduced by **hace . . . que,** especially if negative, (*b*) in colloquial speech in Spain as equivalent to the simple past when referring to recent events, where in American Spanish the preterit would be used, or even (*c*) with the force of an imperative, stating the command as an already accomplished fact.

a. **Hace mucho que no la he visto.**	*I haven't seen her for a long time.*
b. **Han llegado esta mañana.**	*They arrived this morning.*
¿Lo han entendido?	*Did they understand it?*
c. **¡Ya se ha callado Ud.!**	*You shut up!*

EJERCICIO

Póngase el presente del perfecto o el presente de los verbos entre paréntesis:
1. Hace muchos días que Pepe no (trabajar).
2. Hace mucho que nosotros (estar) en esta ciudad.
3. Hace sólo una semana que yo te (conocer).
4. Hace un rato que él no (venir) por aquí.
5. Hace tiempo que ellos no (salir) de casa.

33. THE ARCHAIC PLUPERFECT

In literary Spanish one may still find a sporadic case of the archaic pluperfect, identical in form with the imperfect subjective in **-ra.**

La niña se guardó el dinero que le diera su abuela.	*The little girl kept the money her grandmother gave (had given) her.*

34. FURTHER CONSTRUCTIONS WITH *DESDE* (TEMPORAL)

1. In expressing an act or state that lasts down to a point in the present (or the past), **desde hace** (or **desde hacía**) may be used to indicate the time elapsed.

Estoy aquí desde hace una semana.	*I have been here a week.*
Estaba allí desde hacía una semana.	*I had been there a week.*

2. In past time the preterit (not the imperfect) is used with **desde que,** which expresses the moment from which (not the time during which).

No la he visto desde que llegué.	*I have not seen her since I arrived.*
No la había visto desde que salí del Perú.	*I had not seen her since I left Peru.*

Traducción 2B

1. I (will) stay (at) home tomorrow.
2. The vendor of lottery tickets was crying: "It comes out tomorrow."
3. What (do you say), shall we dance?
4. You go to the store, pay the bill, and come back at once.
5. We went to get our passports, but the office was closed.
6. That very day the troops entered the city.
7. Eight o'clock had just struck; when we arrived at the station the train was pulling out.
8. It was a cool and pleasant morning; the walk didn't tire us at all.
9. There were many people there whom I did not know, but later on I made friends with some of them.
10. The taxi driver refused (did not want) to accept the tip the lady gave (had given) him.
11. I tried to call her on the telephone, but I couldn't.
12. We went to see you last night, but you were not (in).
13. I had not been to (at) a horserace for several years.
14. I have not gone out to the street since I fell sick.
15. He said that if he did not arrive on (**a**) time he would lose the position.
16. It is useless. He won't listen.
17. We will come back right away.
18. I would not take it seriously.
19. She and I were then very good friends, but later on we quarreled.
20. I took out my wallet and noticed that I did not have any money.
21. In 1840 my great-grandfather made a trip from Bogotá to Caracas; it lasted twenty days. Journeys were very long in those times.
22. I thought you were away. When did you return?
23. I learned the news this afternoon.
24. If I don't (get an opportunity to) talk, I (shall) die.
25. Shall we leave now?
26. The danger is over (passed) now.

III

Verbos y Modismos

Review verbs with orthographic changes (Sec. **229**).

1. Don't begin yet.
2. I began the work.
3. Nobody can (**no hay quién**) convince him (Sec. **118**).
4. Don't I convince you?
5. Send (address) the mail to this address (**señas**).

6. Go (direct yourself) to the manager.
7. Find out what is going on.

Tocar *to touch, play (an instrument or music), knock (ring a bell);* (impers.) *to be one's turn, get (as one's share or lot).*

1. Do not (it is prohibited) touch the objects.
2. You (one) must not mention (touch on) this topic to him, because he gets angry.
3. His oldest daughter plays the piano very well.
4. The orchestra played several modern Spanish works.
5. Don't ring the doorbell, it is out of order. Knock (with your hand).
6. I have just had my examination in (**examinarme de**) chemistry; it's your turn tomorrow.
7. How much does each one (of) us get?

Pegar(se) *to stick, beat, strike, give (blow, shot, kick, shout, jump,* etc.).

1. I am putting (sticking) these pictures in my album.
2. Don't beat the child!
3. I shot one of the robbers.
4. You can't fool me (**pegármela**).

Jugar (Sec. **250**) *to play, gamble.*

1. Did you play (at) tennis yesterday?—Yes, I played three sets (**partidos**).
2. If you don't want to play, don't play.
3. I don't like to gamble because I always lose my money.

Coger *to gather, catch, take (pick, select).* **Tomar** can often be used in the sense of *to pick, select* and is the preferred word for this meaning in American Spanish.

1. Anna was gathering flowers in the garden.
2. Don't catch your finger!
3. His coming took (caught) me unawares.
4. I must catch the seven o'clock train.
5. He has caught a cold.
6. He took me by (**de**) the hand and led me to his study.
7. Here is (you have) the box of cigars; take a few.

Tema

Escriba Ud. varios párrafos, utilizando para cada frase las palabras y modismos indicados. Por ejemplo, de **oyo/salir/antes/ver/amigo** se podría formar una frase sencilla como: **yo salí antes de ver a mi amigo.** O, si se quiere, se puede formar una frase un poco más complicada: **yo saldré de la estación antes de ver a mis amigos,** o **yo salía mucho antes, pero no veía a tu amigo,** o **yo había salido antes que me viera mi amigo.**

A. El viaje

1. aeropuerto/animado/yo/tomar/avión
2. avión/no salir/la gente/echar la culpa/línea aérea
3. azafata/echar una mirada/compañero de viaje/cuando/oírnos/hablar español
4. compañeros/echarse a reír/cuando/avión/temblar
5. yo/no querer/perder/vista/Lisboa
6. yo/contar con/ayuda/amigos/para ver/cosas/interés

B. La llegada

7. avión/aterrizar/8:30/mañana
8. oficiales de inmigración/pedirnos/pasaporte
9. oficiales de aduana/pedirme/abrir/maletas
10. después/revisarme la ropa/permitirme/salir
11. yo/salir/aeropuerto/tomar/autobús/ciudad
12. yo/no tener dinero/tener que/cambiar

C. En el hotel

13. yo/bajar del autobús/el centro/ir al hotel
14. dejar caer/maleta/al entrar
15. botones/tomarme/maleta/sonrisa
16. yo/firmar/tarjeta/presentar/pasaporte
17. yo/subir/habitación/dar propina/botones

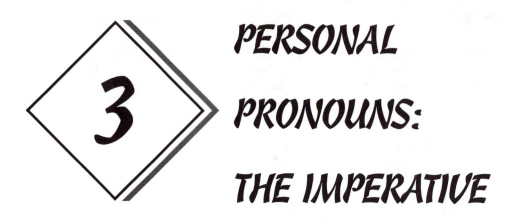

PERSONAL PRONOUNS: THE IMPERATIVE

35. TABLE OF PERSONAL PRONOUNS
(FOR NEUTERS AND REFLEXIVES, CF. SECS. 52, 55).

| PERSON | Subject | SINGULAR | | |
		Indirect Object	Direct Object	Prepositional Form
1.	yo	me	me	mí
2.	tú	te	te	ti
	usted	le	lo (m.)	usted
			la (f.)	
3.	él	le	le (Spain)	él
			lo (America)	
	ella	le	la	ella
	(objects)		lo (m.)	ello
			la (f.)	
		PLURAL		
1.	nosotros	nos	nos	nosotros
	nosotras	nos	nos	nosotras
2.	vosotros	os	os	vosotros
	vosotras	os	os	vosotras
	ustedes (Am.)	les	los (m.)	ustedes
			las (f.)	ustedes
3.	ellos	les	los, les	ellos
	ellas	les	las	ellas

36. PRONOUNS OF ADDRESS

1. **Usted** (often abbreviated **Ud., Vd., V.**) and **ustedes** (abbreviated **Uds., Vds.,** or **VV.**) are the pronouns that ordinarily correspond to the English *you.* Being contractions of the older forms **vuestra merced** and **vuestras mercedes**, they are third person pronouns, as are the object forms **le, la, les, las.**

2. The second person forms **tú** and **vosotros** (**-as**) are used only in intimate or familiar address. (The same holds true for **te** and **os**.) Traditionally these second person forms are chiefly used between relatives, young people (including university students even when they do not know each other), and close friends of any age. In recent years the casual use of **tú** has been spreading in Spain, even among people who are not close acquaintances. In Andalusia and in Spanish America **vosotros** and the corresponding verb forms have been replaced by **ustedes** plus the third person plural forms of verbs.

37. TITLES OF ADDRESS

1. **Señor** *Mr.,* **Señora** *Mrs.,* and **Señorita** *Miss* (abbreviated **Sr., Sra., Srta.**), **don** and **doña** (abbreviated **D.** and **Da.**) are used, especially in addressing letters, according to the following scheme: **Sr. Gómez, Sr. D. Miguel Gómez, D. Miguel, D. Miguel Gómez.**

NOTE. **Don** was formerly used in Spain chiefly by nobles.

2. For the use and omission of the definite article with **Señor,** see Sec. **7.2a**. **Señor, señora,** and **señorita** may be used as nouns meaning *gentleman, lady,* and *young lady.*

38. CONVENTIONAL AND INTIMATE IMPERATIVE
(SEE SEC. 29.e; 31; 32.c; 58; 108.3; 115; 132.4, NOTE)

1. The third person forms of the present subjunctive are used with **usted** to form (*a*) the formal imperative. The forms of (*b*) the imperative mood are second person forms and are used only when **tú** and **vosotros** would apply.

IMPERATIVE MOOD (COMMANDS)		
a. **compre Ud.**	**coma Ud.**	**viva Ud.**
compren Uds.	**coman Uds.**	**vivan Uds.**
b. **compra**	**come**	**vive**
comprad	**comed**	**vivid**

NOTE. In colloquial speech the second person plural imperatives have become identical with the infinitive: **¡hijos, venir aquí!** *Children, come here!* Instructions for exercises and examinations also use this form: **escribir una composición sobre los mayas.**

EJERCICIO

Cámbiense los verbos en las frases siguientes al imperativo según el modelo: **La señora Alas habla → hable Ud., señora Alas; Tomás me habla → háblame, Tomás.**
1. El señor Gómez viene mañana.
2. Elena tiene cuidado en la autopista.
3. Los señores traen los papeles al juez.
4. Isabel me dice la verdad.
5. El capitán obedece las órdenes del general.
6. La señorita Ramírez pedirá ayuda a su padre.
7. Tomás se pone el jersey.
8. Antonia nos compra unos recuerdos en España.

    2. The first person plural of the present subjunctive is used for the first person plural imperative, equivalent to English *let's*. . . . The only exception is **vamos** *let's go.* The object pronouns must be attached to the end of the verb in the positive imperative. If the object pronoun is the reflexive **nos** the final **-s** of the first person plural ending is dropped (see Secs. **41.2** and **58**).

> **Estemos contentos por ahora.**   *Let us be satisfied for the present.*
> **Defendamos nuestros derechos.**   *Let us defend our rights.*

NOTE. **Vamos a** + the infinitive of a verb may be used instead of the imperative form whenever the action is to be performed immediately: **vamos a comer** *Let's eat (now),* in contrast to the more general **no comamos demasiado** *let us not eat too much (at any time).*

EJERCICIO

Contéstense las preguntas utilizando primero la construcción con **vamos a** y luego el subjuntivo según el modelo: **¿Entramos? → Sí, vamos a entrar; entremos.**
1. ¿Salimos?
2. ¿Comemos?
3. ¿Trabajamos?
4. ¿Escribimos?
5. ¿Bailamos?
6. ¿Bebemos?

39. SUBJECT PRONOUNS

    Usted is the only subject pronoun normally expressed with the verb, the others being adequately indicated by the inflectional ending. Any subject pronoun may be used, however, when needed for clearness, contrast, or emphasis. The subject pronouns **él, ella, ellas, ellos,** when so used always refer to persons, never to things. Subject pronouns referring to things are not expressed.

Speakers of English must be aware that the subject pronoun *it* has no equivalent in Spanish, which uses only the third person singular form of verbs as indication.

Él pintaba y ella escribía.	*He was painting and she was writing.*
Él lo dijo, yo no.	*He said it, not I.*
Son grandes y cómodos (los autobuses).	*They are large and comfortable* (the buses).
Ella es muy buena.	*She is very kind.*

NOTE. To render the English impersonal *it is I, it was I*, etc., Spanish uses the inflected forms of **ser: soy yo (somos nosotros), eran ellos,** etc.

EJERCICIO

Quítense los sujetos de los verbos en las frases siguientes, reemplazándolos con el pronombre donde sea necesario:
1. Carlos iba mucho al teatro pero María prefería ir al cine.
2. Mis padres suelen viajar mucho.
3. Las chicas juegan después que terminan las clases.
4. Ese señor lleva mucho tiempo aquí y su mujer también.
5. La cocinera no quiso preparar lo que le mandó su patrona.

---

40. OBJECT PRONOUNS OF THE THIRD PERSON

The following peculiarities of object pronouns of the third person must be noted:

(*a*) **lo** as direct object ordinarily refers to things, **le, la** to persons in the Castilian dialect in Spain.

(*b*) **los** and **las** as direct objects refer to both persons and things;

(*c*) **le** and **les** as indirect objects are both masculine and feminine;

(*d*) **usted (ustedes)** has the direct object masculine form **le (les)** and the feminine form **la (las).** In American Spanish **lo** is usually used for all masculine direct objects, both persons and things.

41. POSITION OF VERB OBJECT PRONOUNS

1. Verb object pronouns ("conjunctive pronouns"), both direct and indirect, are normally placed immediately before the verb. They are unstressed and in contrast with the pronoun objects of prepositions ("disjunctive pronouns"), which are stressed.

Le hablé ayer.	*I spoke to him (her) yesterday.*
Hablé con él ayer.	*I talked with him yesterday.*

2. When, however, the object pronoun is object of (*a*) an infinitive, (*b*) a present participle, or (*c*) an affirmative (not negative) imperative, the pronoun follows the verb and is attached to it.

a. **Tenemos que copiarlas. (cartas)**	*We have to copy them. (letters)*
b. **Estaba leyéndola. (novela)**	*He was reading it. (novel)*
c. **Démelo Ud. (lápiz)**	*Give it to me. (pencil)*
But: **No me lo dé Ud.**	*Do not give it to me.*

NOTE. When the pronoun is attached to a verb form, the stressed syllable of the verb remains the same, and thus requires a written accent in all cases, except when only one pronoun is appended to an infinitive.

EJERCICIO

Reemplácense primero los sustantivos objetos de los verbos con los nombres en paréntesis y después éstos con los pronombres correspondientes.
1. Los estudiantes van a ver al <u>señor rector</u>. (decano, secretaria, muchachas)
2. Mi primo verá <u>la exposición</u> pronto. (las pinturas, los monumentos, el museo)
3. Señalamos <u>el peligro</u> a nuestros compañeros. (los colores, el palacio, la casa)
4. El obrero invitó a <u>los forasteros</u> a tomar una copa. (la gente, los hombres, las chicas)
5. Tienen que comunicar <u>la noticia</u> a los demás. (los informes, las ideas, la decisión)
6. ¿Por qué no nos muestran <u>los ejemplos</u>? (las pinturas, los periódicos, el programa)

En las frases del Ejercicio **E3.1** pónganse los pronombres en lugar de los sustantivos objetos de los verbos en las frases 3-8. Luego háganse todas las frases negativas, p.ej., **La señora Alas toma café → Señora Alas, tómelo Ud.; no lo tome Ud.**

---

42. THE REDUNDANT CONSTRUCTION

1. When the context does not clearly indicate the antecedent of **le, la, los, las,** or **les,** ambiguity can be avoided by adding after the verb the proper prepositional phrase.

Le di el libro ⎰ **a él.** ⎱ **a ella.** **a Ud.**		*I gave the book to him (her, you).*

2. This construction is also used (*a*) for purposes of emphasis, contrast, or clearness; (*b*) when the indirect object is a noun denoting a person (or personified thing) the indirect object pronoun **le** is often used with the verb.

a. **No me lo diga Ud. a mí.**   *Don't tell it to me.*

NOTE. For further emphasis, the prepositional form may precede: **a mí no me importa** *I don't care.*

b. **Le expliqué el caso a mi hermana.**	*I explained the matter to my sister.*

NOTE. When **todo(s)** is the direct object, **lo(s)** must also be used: **lo tengo todo aquí** *I have everything here;* **los he visto todos** *I have seen them all.*

EJERCICIO

Reemplácense los objetos de los verbos con los pronombres en las frases siguientes, utilizando siempre la construcción enfática **a él, a ella,** etc.
1. Le ofrecí el dinero al <u>conserje</u>, no al <u>portero</u>. (mujer—hombre, empleados—jefe)
2. Les escribimos la tarjeta postal a <u>nuestros padres</u>, y también a <u>nuestras hermanas</u>. (los amigos—el profesor, mi madre—mi sobrino)
3. ¿Podemos enseñar la lección a <u>los alumnos</u>? (el profesor, nuestros compañeros)
4. Le entregaron los paquetes <u>al cartero</u>. (la bibliotecaria, el artista)
5. José le pidió diez mil pesetas a <u>su padre</u>. (su madre, sus compañeros)

---

43. VERBS THAT FOLLOW THE PATTERN OF *GUSTAR*

With certain verbs and verb phrases the English direct object becomes the subject (and follows the verb). The English subject becomes the indirect object.

Me gustan los perros.	*I like dogs.* (Lit. *Dogs are pleasing to me.*)
Me hace falta un sombrero.	*I need a hat.*
Me falta dinero.	*I lack money.*
Le encanta la literatura.	*Literature delights her.*
Me agradan mis compañeros.	*I like my companions.*
¿Te sienta bien ese traje?	*Does that suit suit you?*
Nos parece aburrido.	*We think it's boring.* (It seems boring to us.)

EJERCICIO

Pónganse las palabras en las secciones *a.* y *b.* en lugar de las palabras subrayadas:
1. Me <u>gusta</u>[a] la <u>pintura moderna</u>.[b]
   a. atraer, agradar, aburrir
   b. los viajes, el Quijote, el vino francés, los periódicos extranjeros

2. ¿Le <u>falta</u>^{a} a Ud. <u>dinero</u>?^{b}
   a. hacer falta, parecer interesante, contentar, espantar
   b. el perro, el gato, sellos nuevos, joyas raras, la información

---

Traducción 3A

1. Please show me that hat.
2. Buy me that typewriter, Dad. I need one.
3. Let's go to my study. We'll talk there.
4. Son, open the window.
5. Let's forget the incident.
6. Let's go for a walk.
7. She was reading and he was sewing.
8. You suggested it, he didn't.
9. They have a country house. It is small, but very pretty.
10. Who is downstairs?—It's them. (masc.)
11. We sent you (sing.) a present. Did you (sing.) receive it?
12. We used to visit him every evening.
13. I met Miss García in the post office and accompanied her home.
14. We saw them (masc.) and greeted them.
15. Where are your glasses?—I have left them home.
16. How many sentences are there in this section?—I don't know; I haven't counted them.
17. I intend to give them a copy.
18. Here are the suitcases. I am going to check them.
19. All right, do it now, don't leave it for tomorrow.
20. Did you write down the address of the boardinghouse?—I am doing it at this moment.
21. It would be better to talk to him, not to them.
22. Well, don't accuse *me*!
23. Tell them (masc.) what happened.
24. Last night I sent (**poner**) a telegram to the cashier of the bank.
25. Address the letter to Mr. Pedro Fernández Carvajal, calle San Bernardo, (number) 32.

II

44. PRONOUNS OF ADDRESS (*CONTINUED*)

Following are some special uses of pronouns of address: (*a*) **tú** (and **te**) are used in invocations and apostrophes, (*b*) **vosotros** and corresponding forms are frequently used in addressing an audience, in advertisements, and in general notices. As pointed out in Sec. **36**, **vosotros** does not appear in American Spanish, being replaced by **ustedes.**

a. **Padre nuestro que estás en los cielos . . .**   *Our Father who art in Heaven . . .*

b. **Quisiera presentaros esta noche . . .**	*I should like to present to you tonight . . .*
Comprad la hoja de afeitar "Toledo."	*Buy Toledo razor blades.*

NOTE 1. **Vos** (second person plural, with singular or plural meaning) is used in archaic or poetic style. **Nos,** the paternal *we,* is still used by high ecclesiastical authorities and by the king of Spain.

NOTE 2. In many parts of Spanish America **vos** is colloquially used instead of **tú,** with special verb endings which may vary from region to region, e.g., Argentine **amás, comés, escribís** *you love, eat, write.*

NOTE 3. Certain offices and ranks have a special form of address (**tratamiento**), such as **Usía** (contraction of **Vuestra Señoría**) and **Vuecencia** (contraction of **Vuestra Excelencia**).

45. TITLES OF ADDRESS AND FAMILY NAMES (*APELLIDOS*)

1. **Señor** is used in addressing or referring to titled persons and officials.

¿Está el señor rector?

　　　Is the President (of a university) in?

2. *Officially in Hispanic countries, each person has two family names (***apellidos***), the father's and the mother's:* D. Manuel Carrillo (**y**) Gayangos. (In modern usage the **y** is usually omitted.)

3. A married woman retains her own family name as her legal name, adding to it her husband's, preceded by **de**. thus Mercedes Linares Castellanos becomes, on marrying the above-mentioned gentleman, Doña Mercedes Linares de Carrillo, and their son Rafael is called Rafael Carrillo Linares.

EJERCICIO

La señorita Nieves Muñoz Castro se casa con Francisco Salinas e Ibáñez.
1. ¿Cómo la llaman después del casamiento?
2. ¿Cuál es el nombre completo de su hija Pilar?
3. Si Pilar se casa con Diego Aguilar Pastor, ¿cómo la llamarán?

---

46. COMPOUND SUBJECT

In the case of compound subjects of different persons, the verb is first person plural if one of the subjects is first person, and second person plural if they are second and third person.

Usted y yo vamos.	*You and I go.*
Tú y él vais.	*You and he go.*

47. FORMS OF THE VERB OBJECT ("CONJUNCTIVE") PRONOUNS (*CONTINUED*)

The following uses of object pronouns are frequently found:

1. **lo** instead of **le** as direct object referring to masculine persons (standard in American Spanish);
2. **les** instead of **los** as direct object referring to masculine persons;
3. **la** as the indirect object pronoun referring to feminine persons (**laísmo**) is a regionalism.

NOTE. The use of **le** as masculine direct object referring to things (**leísmo**) is provincial and archaic.

48. SPECIAL USES OF VERB OBJECT ("CONJUNCTIVE") PRONOUNS

Following are some important idiomatic uses of the conjunctive pronouns: (*a*) when the direct or indirect noun object precedes the verb, the corresponding conjunctive pronoun is usually used also; (*b*) the feminine pronoun **la** (also **las,** and rarely **ella**) is used elliptically in many idiomatic and colloquial expressions, as equivalent to an indefinite *it* (see Sec. **77.2** for **la(s)** used in set expressions); (*c*) in literary style (and in archaic and provincial speech) the conjunctive pronouns are occasionally annexed to finite forms of the verb, especially at the beginning of a sentence or clause.

a. **El apartamento lo tiene alquilado.**	*He has the apartment rented.*
b. **¡Buena la has hecho!**	*You've made a fine mess of it!*
Las caza al vuelo.	*He (she) catches on quick.*
Se las echa de Don Juan.	*He puts on airs of being a Don Juan.*
Se las da de intelectual.	*He pretends to be an intellectual.*
Voy a habérmelas con él.	*I'm going to have it out with him.*
¡Me las pagará!	*He'll pay for that!*
Quiero arreglármelas.	*I want to settle things.*
No las tenía todas conmigo.	*I didn't have all my wits about me.*
c. **Hallóse sin protección de nadie.**	*He found himself without any backing.*

49. SPECIAL USES OF THE PREPOSITIONAL FORMS

(*a*) The prepositional forms of the pronouns are employed to replace the verb object forms when the verbs are omitted. (*b*) After **entre** *between,* the subject pronouns are used:

a. **¿Le gusta a usted? A mí no.**	*Do you like it? I don't.*
Vi a su madre, a ella no.	*I saw her mother, not her.*

b. **Entre tú y yo, me parece muy raro.**	*Between you and me, it seems very strange.*

Traducción 3B

1. Buy national products.
2. Advertise in this magazine.
3. Ladies and gentlemen: I would like to indicate to you. . . .
4. He and I were classmates.
5. (As for) the house, he has it mortgaged.
6. (As for) his son, he has him in a military academy.
7. We approached them to hear what they were saying.
8. The man was running towards us.
9. We moved away from them.
10. The Ambassador will see you later.
11. Consult the secretary.
12. Those girls are talking about us.
13. They have invited **you,** not **me.**
14. Does the project interest you?—Not me.
15. I haven't answered them (masc.) yet. I am going to dictate the letter to you.
16. Don't type it. Write it in (with) pencil.
17. I can't go to see them (fem.). Give them (fem.) (my best) regards.
18. I gave you the stamps. Where have you put them?
19. We would like to hear her sing. Have you heard her?
20. Men do not like to shop. Women do.
21. This soil needs water.
22. Is it you, Frank?—Yes, it's me.
23. He wouldn't tell them, but I did (**yo sí**).
24. Are you going to the theater with them?—No, I am not (in the mood) for it.
25. He'll pay me (for) this (fem. pl.).

III

Verbos y Modismos

Verbs ending in **-aer, -eer, -eír, -oír, -uir, -üir,** and those whose stem ends in **-ll** or **-ñ** (see Sec. **222, 230, 231**).

1. I found (saw) myself in a very difficult situation.
2. The night was so dark that nothing could be (was) seen.
3. I can't stand (see) that fellow.
4. Thinking that you were not coming, we (have) started to eat.
5. They believed that we had heard the conversation.
6. I have always thought so (the same).

7. She is always laughing.
8. He laughed (refl.) loudly (much) when I told him (it).
9. I do not hear well.
10. He said it in (a) loud voice so that we (could) hear it.
11. Look here! Porter!
12. Let's wait until he finishes talking.
13. They finished the job and left (went away).
14. He dyed his hair and moustache.

Caer (Sec. **236**) *to fall, get (fall to one's lot), fit (become);* **caer en (la cuenta de)** *to remember (see the point);* **caerse** *to fall (of persons).*

1. A tree has fallen (invert).
2. Look out! (¡**Cuidado!**) Don't fall!
3. I almost (**por poco**) fell (fall).
4. (To) my friend Mercedes has won (fallen) a prize in the lottery.
5. Don't drop it (let fall).
6. You know to whom I refer.—Yes, now I remember! (**ya caigo**).
7. The children have taken a liking to their father's friend (**les ha caído en gracia**).

PERSONAL, REFLEXIVE, AND NEUTER PRONOUNS

50. TWO-VERB OBJECT PRONOUNS

When both the direct and the indirect verb object pronouns appear together, in most cases the indirect object precedes the direct. The two pronouns either precede or follow the verb according to the rules for the position of a single pronoun object.

Me lo dio esta mañana.	*He gave it to me this morning.*
Démelo Ud.	*Give it to me.*
No quiso dármelo.	*He refused to give it to me.*

NOTE. The pronoun **se** always precedes other objects. In cases in which first and second person pronouns appear together or in combination with **se** and **le(s), lo(s),** or **la(s),** the following order is required:

se + te (os) + me (nos) + le(s), lo(s), or **la(s).**

51. THE VERB OBJECT PRONOUN *SE*

If both object pronouns are of the third person, the indirect object invariably has the form **se** (instead of **le** or **les**). The redundant construction with **se** is used in accord with the principles of Sec. **42.**

Juan se lo vendió	a él. a ella. a usted. a ellos. a ellas. a ustedes.	*John sold it to him (her, you, them).*

Se lo dio a mi hermana.	*He gave it to my sister.*
Yo se lo expliqué a Pedro.	*I explained it to Peter.*

NOTE. The pronoun **se** is the equivalent of **le** and **les** and should not be confused with the reflexive pronoun **se.**

EJERCICIO

Primero pónganse las palabras entre paréntesis en lugar de las palabras subrayadas, y luego reemplácense los objetos de los verbos con los pronombres:
1. Le mostraron <u>las casas</u> nuevas[a] <u>al señor ministro</u>[b].
2. Le dio <u>el aparato</u>[a] a <u>tu hermano</u>[b].
3. Le da <u>los fondos</u>[a] <u>al banquero</u>[b].
4. Les ofreció <u>la oportunidad</u>[a] a <u>los extranjeros</u>[b].
   a. (los libros, la flor, las armas, el barco)
   b. (el rector, los oficiales, la señora, el profesor)

---

52. REFLEXIVE PRONOUNS

Reflexive pronouns are object pronouns referring to the grammatical subject of the verb. The reflexive pronouns of the first and second persons have the same forms as the corresponding personal object pronouns: **me, nos, te,** and **os.**

(*a*) The third person object pronoun, both singular and plural, direct and indirect, is **se.**

(*b*) The corresponding prepositional object is **sí.**

(*c*) With the preposition **con** the special forms are **conmigo, contigo,** and **consigo.**

(*d*) **Se,** whether reflexive or indirect object, always precedes any other verb object pronoun.

a.	**Ellas se están vistiendo.**	*They are getting dressed (i.e., dressing themselves).*
b.	**Hablaba para sí.**	*He was talking to himself.*
c.	**Lo trajo consigo.**	*He brought it with him(self).*
d.	**Se me acercó.**	*He came up to me.*

EJERCICIO

Pónganse los pronombres reflexivos en los espacios, cambiando los sujetos a
yo, tú, nosotros, y **ellos**:
1. Pedro _____ quitó los zapatos.
2. María _____ compró unos bombones.
3. Fidel _____ rascó la cabeza.
4. Miguel nunca _____ niega nada.
5. Ricardo lo trajo con _____.

53. "DATIVE OF INTEREST" (INDIRECT OBJECT)

The Spanish indirect object (person to whom one gives or says something) expresses more varied relations than its English counterpart. It denotes, in general, the person to whose benefit or disadvantage the notion of the verb occurs. (Cf. colloquial English *I bought me a new car.*) This relation is traditionally called the "dative of interest." (Contrast **me dio el libro** *he gave me the book* with **me cambió el libro** *he (ex)changed the book for me.*) The more usual types of relation expressed by this use of the indirect object are (*a*) possession and (*b*) separation which is frequently expressed in English with the preposition *from.* Since in Spanish parts of the body and objects of clothing and other possessions are normally preceded by the definite article (see Secs. **7** and **73**), the possessor is indicated by the indirect object pronoun. When the reflexive object is used with verbs which in English normally are not reflexive (*c*) it often serves to give an intensifying force to the verb by doubling the reference to the subject.

a. **Me duele la cabeza.** *My head aches.*
    Les rompí la ventana. *I broke their window.*
    Me hizo una fotografía. *He (She) took my picture (for me).*
    Se puso el sombrero. *She put on her hat.*

b. **Le compramos el automóvil.** *We bought the car from him.*
    El ruido me quitó el sueño. *The noise prevented me from sleeping (i.e., took sleep away from me).*

c. **Se fue (se marchó).** *She went away (left).*
    Se estaba días enteros sin hablar. *She would remain whole days without speaking.*

    Se bebió una botella de vino. *She drank (up) a bottle of wine.*
    Se comió un bistec. *She ate (gobbled up) a steak.*

NOTE. The more usual verbs in this category are: **irse, marcharse** *go away,* **quedarse, estarse** *remain, stay,* **llevarse** *carry off, away,* **caerse** *fall down,* **pararse** *stop* (intransitive). In American Spanish, **pararse** also means *stand up.*

EJERCICIO

Pónganse los pronombres correctos en los espacios según los objetos entre paréntesis:

1. _____ robaron el reloj.
2. _____ perdió una gran oportunidad.
3. _____ pueden hacer la ropa para mañana.
4. _____ dejó el recado.
5. _____ han explicado el caso.
6. ¿_____ puede planchar la camisa?

(a él, a ella, a nosotros, a Miguel y Jacinto, a mí, a ti, a ustedes)

54. VERBS HAVING MATERIAL AND PERSONAL OBJECTS

When a Spanish verb has two objects, one personal and the other material, the person affected usually becomes the indirect object and the thing affected the direct object. In English the reverse is often the case; note the English equivalents of the Spanish construction with the verbs **pagar, pedir, agradecer, avisar, impedir,** and the like.

Se lo agradezco mucho. (el regalo)	*I am grateful to you for it. (the gift)*
Me la pagó en seguida. (la cuenta)	*He paid me right away. (the bill)*
Se lo impedimos. (el acto)	*We prevented him (from doing it).*
Me lo pidió. (el libro)	*He asked me for it. (the book)*

NOTE. **Pagar** *to pay* can also take a personal object as in English: **me pagó en seguida** *he paid me at once.*

EJERCICIO

Úsense los pronombres en lugar de los sustantivos objetos de los verbos en las frases siguientes:

1. Le agradezco mucho a Ud. la carta de recomendación.
2. Te pidió el regalo.
3. Nos avisó que había peligro.
4. Les pagaron la cuenta.
5. Nos impidieron la salida.

55. NEUTER PRONOUNS

Neuter personal pronouns, like neuter demonstratives (Sec. **69**), have as their antecedents a phrase, a clause, a general idea, or a specific object without definite gender, either expressed or understood. They have the following forms:

(*a*) the subject pronoun **ello,** which in modern usage is rarely employed,

(*b*) the verb object pronoun **lo,** (see Sec. **56**), and

(*c*) the prepositional form **ello.**

a. **Ello es que nunca volvió.**	*The fact is he never came back.*
b. **Tiene Ud. que contármelo.**	*You must tell me* (it).
Pregúnteselo.	*Ask him* (it).
¡No me lo digas!	*Don't tell me* (it)!
c. **Cuente Ud. con ello.**	*Count on it* (what I said).

56. PREDICATE *LO*

Spanish, in contrast to English, requires objects in a number of places in which English is satisfied with a simple verb form:

(*a*) Thus with the verbs **ser** and **estar,** the neuter pronoun **lo** is used when a previously mentioned adjective or noun is omitted, regardless of whether the omitted words are masculine or feminine.

(*b*) After the verbs **creer, decir, preguntar,** and similar verbs of asking or telling, where in English the object is either unexpressed or implied by the adverb *so* (see Sec. **55**)

a. **¿Es Ud. chileno (chilena)?—Lo soy.**	*Are you Chilean?—I am.*
¿Está Ud. enfermo?—Lo estoy.	*Are you ill?—I am.*
Note: **¿Quién es? ¿Paco?—No, soy yo.**	*Who is it? Frank?—No, it's me.*
b. **Dígaselo Ud.**	*Tell it to her (him).*
¿Cree Ud. que perderemos el tren?—No, no lo creo.	*Do you think we will miss the train?— No, I don't think so.*
Voy a preguntárselo.	*I am going to ask her (him) (it).*

EJERCICIO

Contéstense con el pronombre correcto, poniendo las palabras entre paréntesis en lugar de las palabras subrayadas, p.ej., **Sí, lo soy:**

1. ¿Es Ud. americano (-a)? (español, francés, chino)
2. ¿Es abogado su padre? (arquitecto, médico, periodista)
3. ¿Están Uds. contentos? (tristes, alegres)

4. ¿Son <u>interesantes</u> los cursos? (aburridos, técnicos)
5. ¿Cree Ud. que <u>todo va bien</u>? (la vida es mala, el mundo se acaba)
6. ¿Dijeron Uds. a sus padres <u>qué van a hacer durante las vacaciones</u>? (por qué no van a casa, cómo están)

---

57. *MISMO (-A, -OS, -AS)*

Mismo *self* is used to intensify both subject pronouns and pronoun objects of prepositions. Students should note especially that in English the pronouns such as *myself, ourselves, yourself,* etc. are also used as reflexive pronouns. In Spanish reflexive verb object pronouns are different in form (see Sec. **52**) and are never stressed. Native speakers of English must be careful not to confuse the two.

Él mismo tuvo que reconocerlo.	*He himself had to admit it.*
Me lo repetía muchas veces a mí mismo (-a).	*I used to repeat it to myself many times.*

Traducción 4A

1. They want to sell it (fem. sing.) to her.
2. I am going return it (masc. sing.) to you.
3. Don't send them (fem. pl.) to Charles. He has them already.
4. Where is the umbrella?—George took it away (with him).
5. He got up from the chair and came toward us.
6. Put your coat on. Don't take it off.
7. I am going away tomorrow. Why don't you come with me?
8. When I went to your house, you had gone.
9. Stay here while I shave (refl.).
10. Who was talking with him?—Nobody, he was talking to himself.
11. The injured (man) came to.
12. Did you fall down?—No, but I thought I was going to (fall down).
13. Don't be grateful to *me*; be grateful to *her*.
14. Are you ready?—Yes, I am.
15. Did you pay the shoemaker for the shoes?—I think so, but ask him (it).
16. The thieves disarranged my papers and broke my ash tray.
17. Well, the fact is that we never saw them again.
18. They've ruined my suit!
19. It was very unpleasant; I don't want to think of it.
20. Don't lose heart. Cheer up!
21. I don't want to get involved (**meterme**) in it.
22. That man is an Englishman, isn't he?—Yes, he is.
23. He doesn't look old.—No, he doesn't, but he is.
24. I'm going to borrow these books from him.

25. If you want his permission, ask him for it.
26. Let him know about it.
27. The janitor told me all (about) it.
28. Please copy this page for me.
29. He ate it all up.
30. She told me herself.

II

58. IMPERATIVE OF REFLEXIVE VERBS

In the first person plural imperative, reflexive verbs lose the final *s* of the ending when the pronoun **nos** is added (Sec. **38.2**); in the second person plural (intimate) imperative the final *d* is similarly dropped when **os** is attached.

Sentémonos aquí.	*Let's sit down here.*
Pongámonos de acuerdo.	*Let's come to an agreement.*
Sentaos, muchachos.	*Sit down, boys.*

The only exception is **idos** *go away.*

EJERCICIO

Cámbiense las expresiones siguientes al subjuntivo, primero en sentido afirmativo, y luego en forma negativa, poniendo las palabras entre paréntesis en lugar de las palabras subrayadas, p.ej., **Vamos a ponernos los guantes** → **pongámonos los guantes** → **no nos pongamos los guantes.**

Vamos a ponernos el sombrero (quitarnos los zapatos, acordarnos del asunto, divertirnos, atrevernos, casarnos, apresurarnos, despedirnos, quedarnos).

59. FURTHER USES OF THE PREPOSITIONAL FORMS

As a result of the rules for position of pronoun objects, when the direct object of a verb is a pronoun of the first or second person and the indirect object is a pronoun of the third person, the latter takes the prepositional form.

Me presentó a ella.	*He introduced me to her.*
Nos acercamos a él.	*We approached him.* (See Sec. **49**.)
Te recomendamos a ella.	*We recommended you to her.*

NOTE. **Me la presentó** can only mean *he introduced her to me.* But **se le acercó** may mean *he approached her* because **se,** whether direct or indirect object, always precedes other pronouns.

EJERCICIO

Constrúyanse frases completas con las palabras dadas según el modelo:
Manuel/presentar/a mí/a ella → Manuel me presentó a ella.
1. Eduardo/presentar/a nosotros/a él.
2. Mi amigo/recomendar/a ellos/a ella.
3. Nuestros padres/presentar/a él/a ellos.

60. POSITION OF PRONOUN OBJECTS (*CONTINUED*)

There is a growing tendency in modern Spanish to place the pronoun
objects of the infinitive or the present participle immediately before the auxiliary
instead of attaching them to the dependent verb.

No me lo quiso dar or **No quiso dármelo.**	*He wouldn't give it to me.*
Se lo voy a dar or **Voy a dárselo.**	*I am going to give it to him.*
Le estoy escribiendo or **Estoy escribiéndole.**	*I am writing to him.*

EJERCICIO

Pónganse los pronombres en lugar de los objetos de los verbos en las frases
siguientes: p.ej. **El jefe quiere darle el puesto → El jefe se lo quiere dar o El
jefe quiere dárselo.**
1. El gerente va a ofrecerme el dinero.
2. Silvia quería escribir la solicitud al director.
3. Ana puede encontrar los periódicos.
4. Vamos a decir el cuento de hadas a las niñas.

61. "DATIVE OF INTEREST" (*CONTINUED*)

The indirect object is often used to express many subtle shades of
advantage or disadvantage, which in English are often translated as (*a*) often
by *on, at* or (*b*) occasionally are impossible to translate directly.

a. **Me hizo una jugada.**	*He played a dirty trick on me.*
La niña le ponía una carita muy graciosa.	*The little girl would make a cute little face at him.*
b. **Me temo que no resulte.**	*I am afraid that it will not work out.*
Sé lo que me hago.	*I know what I am doing.*

NOTE. Sometimes two dative values may be combined: **se le murió el caballo** *his horse died ("on him")*. **Morir** states a bald fact (**murió el rey** *the king died*, **murieron muchos en el combate** *many died in the battle*) while **morirse** indicates a personal concern on the part of the speaker or a natural or uneventful death.

62. REFLEXIVE VERBS WITH A PREPOSITION

In contrast to the situation in Sec. **54**, a number of reflexive verbs require a preposition to introduce the object, e.g., **alegrarse de, enterarse de, oponerse a, contentarse con.** See Sec. **269** for a list of frequently used verbs that require a preposition.

Me alegro de su éxito.	*I am glad of your success.*
Se enteraron del asunto.	*They learned about the matter.*
Me opuse al arreglo.	*I opposed the arrangement.*

63. RECIPROCAL PRONOUNS

The plural reflexive pronouns may be used with reciprocal meaning (= *each other*.) The redundant constructions **uno a otro, el uno al otro, una a otra,** etc., are employed when needed for clearness or emphasis.

Se ayudaban en sus estudios.	*They helped each other in their studies.*
No podían soportarse el uno al otro.	*They couldn't stand each other.*
Nos llevábamos muy bien, él y yo.	*We got along very well (together), he and I.*

64. PREDICATE *LO* (*CONTINUED*)

Predicate **lo** is used to recapitulate, not only adjectives, but also nouns regardless of gender.

Parece mentira, pero no lo es.	*It seems incredible but it is not.*
Creen que para mí es una satisfacción, y lo es, lo es.	*They think it is a pleasure for me. And it is, it is.*

65. PERSONAL PRONOUNS WITH "PARTITIVE" VALUE

If the antecedent of a verb object (conjunctive) pronoun is partitive, i.e., indicates only a part of the thing or quality mentioned, the pronoun likewise has the same meaning. In such cases the English either omits the pronoun or uses the indefinites *any, some, none,* etc.

¿No tiene vergüenza? Sí, la tiene.	*Hasn't he any shame?—Yes, he has.*
¿No hay árboles en este país?—No, no los hay.	*Are there no trees in this country?—No, there aren't any.*
¿Hay leche?	*Sí, la hay.*

NOTE 1. The object pronoun used with **haber** in the sense of *there is, there are* (*was, were,* etc.) must agree in gender and number with the thing mentioned. Thus, in the examples above, **los** refers to **los árboles** and **la** to **la leche.**

NOTE 2. The omission of the pronoun is gaining ground in modern colloquial Spanish: **¿Tiene Ud. fósforos?—Sí, tengo.** *Have you any matches?—Yes, I have.*

Traducción 4B

1. Let's get up very early.
2. Let's get together later on.
3. Be happy, friends!
4. He recommended me to you.
5. He recommended you to me.
6. We are going to organize it (masc.).
7. Be careful with the radio; you are going to get it out of order.
8. "Buy a dozen from me," the flower vendor said to us.
9. Translate this poem for me. I don't understand it very well.
10. He ate up all the grapes.
11. He would come late to the office (on me), he would carry off my writing paper and even sell my books.
12. His mother died a year ago.
13. She died from grief.
14. His illness grew worse.
15. Love took away my appetite.
16. The dog got away from him.
17. We shall oppose it.
18. Let's be contented with this solution.
19. They used to see each other in the café.
20. When I entered the room, they were kissing each other.
21. I myself opened the door for them.
22. We ourselves had warned (it to) him.
23. We were afraid of finding some difficulties, but there were none.
24. Is there running water in this room?—Yes, there is.
25. Were there any visitors this afternoon?—Yes, there were.
26. She seized the letter and prevented me from reading it (Sec. **114a**).
27. Are you the landlady?—Yes, sir, I am.

III

Verbos y Modismos

Review verbs ending in **-ecer** and **-ocer** (Sec. **239**).

Saber (Sec. **257**) *to know (have information concerning:* **sabe mucho español** *he knows a great deal of Spanish); know how to, find out;* **saber a** *taste of;* **conocer** *to know (be acquainted with persons or things:* **conoce muy bien el español** *he knows Spanish very well), recognize, be evident.* **Conocer** cannot be used with an infinitive.

1. He does not know how to read or (**ni**) write.
2. I did not know that you were here.
3. I know that the road is in very bad condition (pl).
4. He knows a great deal of medicine.
5. Do you know (any) French?
6. Do you know (the way) to the post office?
7. I know (**me sé**) that book by heart.
8. She never knows her (**la**) lesson.
9. What is she going to say when she finds it out? (Sec. **119.2**)
10. It isn't known where he is.
11. This water tastes of iron.
12. Do you know General Domínguez?
13. She is well acquainted with Spanish customs.
14. She also knows Spanish music.
15. He met (got acquainted with) her at the seashore.
16. I had changed so much that he did not know me.
17. At the station I spoke (**saludar**) to several acquaintances.
18. It is evident that you do not live here.
19. I did not know that this gentleman was a foreigner; he does not show it at all.
20. We know a great deal about this fellow.
21. We know this fellow very well.
22. You will find out tomorrow.
23. (I want you to) know that that is not true.

Tema

Escriba Ud. un diálogo entre Ud. y el conserje de un hotel. Ud. le pregunta si hay una habitación libre y el precio por día. El conserje le explica que hay varias habitaciones disponibles a precios diferentes; por ejemplo, una habitación exterior costará 400 pesos diarios pero que hay otras habitaciones más razonables para una persona que son mas pequeñas o dan a un patio interior, o que no tienen baño privado. Ud. tratará de obtener la mejor habitación posible al precio más bajo posible. El conserje pide que Ud. firme la tarjeta y entregue su pasaporte. Ud. quiere saber por qué quiere el pasaporte y el conserje le explica que la ley dicta que los hoteles den a la policía todos los días una lista de los nombres de todos los que se alojan en el hotel, y que tienen que poner también el número del pasaporte de todos los extranjeros en el hotel. Ud. trata de hacer que el conserje le explique las razones de tal práctica y compara esto con lo acostumbrado en los Estados Unidos. Al fin le da el pasaporte. El conserje dice que le devolverá el pasaporte en unos minutos, y entonces llama al botones y le dice que suba el equipaje. Ud. quiere saber también qué clase de comida sirven en el hotel, y si hay buenos restaurantes cerca, y si el desayuno está incluido en el precio de la habitación.

Escriba Ud. este diálogo en sus propias palabras y utilice por lo menos cinco de los verbos de la sección Verbos y Modismos.

5 > DEMONSTRATIVES AND POSSESSIVES

I

66. DEMONSTRATIVE ADJECTIVES

Spanish possesses three demonstrative adjectives corresponding to the demonstrative adverbs **aquí** *here* (near to the speaker), **ahí** *there* (near the person addressed), and **allí** *there* (removed from both, over there).

SINGULAR			PLURAL		
Masc.	Fem.		Masc.	Fem.	
este	**esta**	*this (here)*	**estos**	**estas**	*these (here)*
ese	**esa**	*that (there)*	**esos**	**esas**	*those (there)*
aquel	**aquella**	*that (yonder)*	**aquellos**	**aquellas**	*those (yonder)*

(a) The demonstrative adjective agrees in gender and number with the accompanying noun and is repeated before nouns of different gender.

(b) **Este** indicates an object near to, associated with, or possessed by the speaker.

(c) **Ese** indicates an object near to, associated with, or possessed by the person spoken to.

(d) **Aquel** indicates an object distant from both or unrelated to either.

    a. **Este hombre y esta mujer.**   *This man and woman.*

    b. **Esta silla es muy cómoda.**   *This chair* (I am sitting in) *is very comfortable.*

65

No veo bien con estos lentes.	*I don't see well with these glasses* (I have on).
c. **Deme Ud. esa pluma.**	*Give me that pen* (you have).
Me gusta ese sombrero.	*I like that hat* (you are wearing).
d. **Mire Ud. aquella casa.**	*Look at that house* (yonder).
Aquellos árboles son robles.	*Those trees* (over there) *are oaks.*

EJERCICIO

Úsense los adjetivos demostrativos en lugar de los artículos definidos en las frases siguientes, y luego pónganse las palabras entre paréntesis en lugar de las palabras subrayadas:
1. El <u>libro</u> que tengo aquí es más interesante que el libro que Ud. tiene. (la revista, las fotos)
2. Vemos <u>los árboles</u> en las montañas distantes. (la nieve, las rocas, los esquiadores)
3. <u>El monumento</u> que tú has visto es muy famoso. (la iglesia, el museo, las casas antiguas)
4. <u>La pluma</u> aquí es más cara que la pluma allí en la mesa. (el aparato, los platos, la radio)

---

67. PRONOUNS RESULTING FROM DELETION OF A NOUN

One of the most common processes of Spanish grammar is the formation of a pronoun by deleting the noun found in a noun phrase. (See Secs. **68, 72, 84, 181, 186** for examples.) Thus one may form the demonstrative pronoun by removing the noun modified by a demonstrative adjective. (In writing, the demonstrative pronoun may have an accent written over the stressed vowel, if there might be some ambiguity.) For example, from **aquellas corbatas** one may get **aquéllas, este coche → éste,** etc.

No me gustan estas corbatas, pero aquéllas, sí.	*I don't like these neckties, but I do (like) those.*
Esta silla es más cómoda que esa.	*This chair is more comfortable than that one.*

EJERCICIO

Quítense los sustantivos modificados por los demostrativos, reemplazando las palabras subrayadas con las palabras entre paréntesis:
1. Quiero ver estas <u>cosas</u>, no aquellas <u>cosas</u>. (libros, camisas, caja, guantes)
2. Se me acercaron esos <u>muchachos</u>, pero aquellos <u>muchachos</u> se marcharon. (hombres, guardias, señoritas)

3. Deme Ud. esa <u>pluma</u> porque esta <u>pluma</u> está rota. (plato, lápiz)
4. ¿Prefiere Ud. esta <u>manzana</u> o esa <u>manzana</u>? (melón, galletas, vasos)
5. Este <u>sombrero</u> me sienta mejor que ese <u>sombrero</u>. (traje, camisa, vestido)

68. THE PRONOUNS *EL, LA, LOS, LAS*

Another example of the formation of a pronoun by deleting a noun is seen in the use of the definite article plus the relative pronoun **que** or the preposition **de** by removing the noun between them. Thus from **el hombre que vino → el que vino, la mujer que trabaja → la que trabaja, la plata del Perú,** etc. (See Sec. **84** for further examples.)

Los recursos de Chile y los del Perú.	*The resources of Chile and those of Peru.*
Esta tienda y la de la esquina.	*This store and the one on the corner.*
Este diccionario y el que Ud. tiene.	*This dictionary and the one (which) you have.*
La del vestido azul marino.	*The (woman) in the navy blue dress.*

EJERCICIO

Reemplácense los sustantivos subrayados, sólo donde sea necesario, con los sustantivos entre paréntesis según el modelo, p.ej., **este helado es el helado que más me gusta → este helado es el que más me gusta.** Háganse los cambios necesarios.

1. Estas <u>flores</u> son las flores que prefiero. (calcetines, corbatas, zapatos)
2. Mi prima es la muchacha del <u>vestido verde</u>. (pelo largo, ojos azules, sonrisa alegre)
3. Estos libros son <u>los libros</u> que Ud. quería ver. (cuadros, objetos, fotos, vasos)

69. NEUTER PRONOUNS

The neuter pronouns **esto, eso, aquello,** and **lo** are used to refer to a general idea, a phrase, a clause, or an object of indeterminate gender. **Lo** is chiefly used in the combination **lo que** *what (that which)*.

Esto me preocupa.	*This (situation) worries me.*
Eso no es verdad.	*That (what you have said) is not true.*
Lo que ocurrió ayer	*What (that which) happened yesterday*

70. POSSESSIVE ADJECTIVES

1. There are two forms of possessive adjectives in Spanish, the stressed and the unstressed. The former follow the noun and are used only under special circumstances. The latter precede the noun and are the ones normally used.

POSSESSIVE ADJ. UNSTRESSED			POSSESSIVE ADJ. STRESSED FORM	
Singular	Plural		Singular	Plural
1. mi	mis	my	mío, mía	míos, mías
2. tu	tus	your	tuyo, tuya	tuyos, tuyas
3. su	sus	his, her its, your	suyo, suya	suyos, suyas
1. nuestro, -a	nuestros, -as	our	nuestro, -a	nuestros, -as
2. vuestro, -a	vuestros, -as	your	vuestro, -a	vuestros, -as
3. su	sus	their your	suyo, -a	suyos, -as

2. The possessive adjective agrees in gender and number not with the possessor (as in English) but with the thing possessed. **Mi, tu,** and **su,** however, have the same form for masculine and feminine. They are repeated before nouns of different gender or number.

Éstas son mis habitaciones.	*These are my rooms.*
Han traído Uds. su baúl?	*Have you (pl.) brought your trunk?*
Este escritor me regala todos sus libros.	*This author gives me all his books.*
mi tío y mis primos	*my uncle and cousins*

3. The stressed forms are chiefly used only (*a*) in direct address, (*b*) exclamations, (*c*) as equivalents of the English *of mine, of yours,* etc., and (*d*) after forms of **ser** (see Sec. **72c**).

a. **No tardes, hijo mío.**	*Don't be late, my son.*
b. **¡Dios mío!**	*My goodness!*
c. **Consuelo es muy amiga suya, ¿verdad?**	*Consuelo is a good friend of yours, isn't she?*
d. **Este coche es mío.**	*This car is mine.*

4. The English possessive case ending (*'s*) is rendered by **de** with the possessor noun or pronoun.

la casa de mi amigo	*my friend's home*
Esto no es de nadie.	*This is nobody's (i.e., does not belong to anybody).*

EJERCICIO

Colóquense los sustantivos entre paréntesis en lugar de las palabras subrayadas, y entonces úsense otros adjetivos posesivos en lugar de los adjetivos posesivos dados:
1. ¿Dónde está su madre? (sobrino, tío, abuela, padres)
2. Mi coche es nuevo. (barco, sandalias calcetines, tocadiscos)
3. El violinista es un amigo mío. (compañero, primo, pariente)

71. SUBSTITUTES FOR *SU*

Since **su** (and **suyo**) may mean either *yours* (singular and plural), *his, hers, theirs,* or *its,* it is very frequently replaced to avoid ambiguity by the phrases **de él, de ella, de usted,** etc., following the noun.

Es una idea de ella.	*It's (one of) her idea(s).*
He leído el artículo de Ud.	*I have read your article.*

NOTE. In conversation **su** (and **suyo**) normally mean *yours* (referring to the person addressed). In more formal style the **su** may be retained in addition to the explanatory **de usted: he leído su artículo de Ud.** *I have read your article.*

EJERCICIO

Pónganse los pronombres con **de** que correspondan a los nombres entre paréntesis por el adjetivo **su(s)** en las frases siguientes: e.g., **la clase de ella** (María), **la clase de ellos** (Ana y Jorge), etc.
1. Vamos a ver su casa.
2. Sus ideas son siempre interesantes.
3. Sus cuadernos están en la mesa.
4. Josefa es una amiga suya.
   (María, Ana y Jorge, Jacinto, los hermanos de Pablo, las señoras, usted, ustedes)

72. POSSESSIVE PRONOUNS

(*a*) Possessive pronouns, being stressed words, are formed by deleting the noun in noun phrases composed of the article, the noun, and the stressed possessive adjective or the possessive expressed by **de** plus a noun or pronoun, **la casa tuya → la tuya, el libro mío → el mío, los perros de él → los de él, las flores de usted → las de usted,** etc. (*b*) **El suyo** normally means *yours*; in other meanings it is replaced, to avoid ambiguity, by **el de él, el de ella,** etc. (*c*) The article **el** may be omitted only after the verb **ser** (Secs. **17.2c, 70.3c**).

a.	**Este comedor es más grande que el nuestro.**	*This dining room is larger than ours.*
	Sus maletas están aquí, las mías no.	*Your suitcases are here, mine are not.*
b.	**Aquí está mi abrigo. ¿Dónde están el suyo y el de Pilar?**	*Here is my overcoat. Where are yours and Pilar's?*
	Aquí está el de élla, pero no veo el mío.	*Here is hers, but I don't see mine.*
c.	**Esta corbata es mía.**	*This necktie is mine.*
	Esta cochera es del vecino; la de la esquina es la nuestra.	*This garage is our neighbor's; the one on the corner is ours.*

NOTE. The demonstrative **el** may be retained after **ser** to indicate contrast or emphasis.

EJERCICIO

Reemplácense los sustantivos subrayados con los pronombres posesivos, cambiando las palabras subrayadas por las palabras entre paréntesis:
1. Ud. tiene <u>mi paraguas</u>. (guantes, billete, libro)
2. <u>Nuestro coche</u> está en la calle. (bicicletas, amigo)
3. <u>Sus maletas</u> están en el pasillo. (compañero, gato, amiga)
4. ¿No tienes <u>tus billetes</u>? (pasaporte, corbata, pantalones)
5. Éste es <u>mi número</u>. (libro, permiso, cartas)
6. ¿Ése es su <u>libro</u>? (guante, coche, impermeable)

---

73. SUBSTITUTES FOR THE POSSESSIVE ADJECTIVE

The possessive adjective is used less frequently in Spanish than in English. Its place can be taken by the definite article (Sec. **7.1d**) or by the dative of interest or possession (Sec. **53**).

Saqué el reloj.	*I took out my watch.*
Me duele la cabeza.	*My head aches.*
Nunca se sabe la lección.	*He (she) never knows his (her) lesson.*
Estoy perdiendo el tiempo.	*I am wasting my time.*

NOTE. This construction is not confined to parts of the body or objects of personal wear, but may be extended to any object directly associated with the subject of the sentence.

Traducción 5A

1. Mr. Barrientos is talking to his son, a university student.
2. My son, don't neglect your studies.
3. That impatience of yours will be your ruin.
4. Why do you say that?
5. I have told you many times that that is your room and that this one is mine.
6. This writing desk is too (very) low. I like better (more) the one you have in your study.
7. What you ask for is impossible.
8. Have you seen this?—No, what is it?
9. What are you doing with that knife?
10. Who is that girl seated at the window?
11. These shoes are (too) big for me.
12. Which of those gentlemen is your friend, Dad?—The one with the moustache.
13. I'm very glad to meet you.—The pleasure is mine.
14. Is this her briefcase?—No, hers is on the table.
15. Please show me that overcoat. No, not that one, the one with the belt.
16. I have met Mrs. Torrijos; her daughter Teresa is studying at (**en**) the university.
17. Are all these prints yours?—No, these are my brother's.
18. Our house is near theirs.
19. The editor of that newspaper is a classmate of mine.
20. I don't share your opinion.
21. That was a remark of hers.
22. Are those dresses yours?—No, mine are in the trunk.
23. This car is his; ours is in the garage.
24. Those mountains are higher than the ones we saw on our trip.
25. I don't remember what she said.
26. These handkerchiefs are not ours; they must be somebody else's.
27. I have lost my hat.
28. Don't put your head out (through) the window.

II

74. *ACÁ* AND *ALLÁ*

The adverbs **aquí** and **allí** have the more indefinite forms **acá** *(over) here* and **allá** *(over) there*. They are also used with verbs of movement.

Allá en las montañas hace frío.	*Over there in the mountains it is cold.*
Venga Ud. acá.	*Come over here.*

NOTE. These adverbs when used with **por** have many special meanings: **por aquí** *around here, this way;* **por ahí** *somewhere around, around town;* **por allí** *around there, that way;* **por acá** *in this region, neighborhood:* **Venga Ud. por acá** *Call on us some time.*

75. AGREEMENT

A demonstrative adjective modifying two nouns of different gender need not be repeated if the nouns are plural and form a single concept.

estas ideas y proyectos   *these ideas and plans*

76. SPECIAL USES OF THE DEMONSTRATIVES

Following are some special uses of **este, ese,** and **aquel:**

(*a*) with temporal, as well as locative, meaning: this use is particularly characteristic of **aquel;**

(*b*) in a series of two, **éste** (the last mentioned) means *the latter* and **aquél** (the first mentioned) *the former;*

(*c*) in correspondence **en (a, por) esta** and **en (a, por) esa** mean *here* and *there,* respectively, a noun such as **ciudad** being understood;

(*d*) the pronoun **ese (esa,** etc.) when applied to persons conveys an idea of contempt;

(*e*) the adjective imparts a graphic flavor, especially in certain set phrases with **por.**

NOTE. When the referent is clear, demonstrative pronouns do not need accent marks, but they are sometimes used.

a. **en estos días**	*in these days*
en esa época	*at that time*
en aquel entonces	*at that time* (definitely past)
Aquel asunto me salió mal.	*That (past) affair turned out badly for me.*
b. **Bolívar y Wáshington son los dos grandes libertadores americanos; éste murió en 1830, aquél en 1799.**	*Bolivar and Washington are the two great American liberators: the former died in 1830, the latter in 1799.*
c. **Llegan a esa el lunes próximo.**	*I shall arrive there next Monday.*
d. **¿Quién es ese?**	*Who is that fellow?*

NOTE. **Éste (ésta,** etc.) is used familiarly with the meaning *he* (*she,* etc.) when pointing to a person present: **eso es lo que éste dice** *that's what he says.* In literary style, **este** (etc.), when beginning a sentence, is equivalent to the English *emphatic he* (*she, it,* etc.) or *the latter.*

e. **por esas calles**	*through the streets (graphic)*
por esos mundos de Dios	*throughout the wide world*

77. SPECIAL USES OF *EL* AND *AL*

1. **De los (las) que** and **de lo que** may be used as equivalent to the English *of the kind (sort) which.*

Ese es de los que tiran la piedra y **esconden la mano.**	*That fellow is the kind who throws stones without showing his hand.*
Es de lo que no hay.	*There's nothing better than this (i.e., its like does not exist).*

2. The feminine **la** and **las** are used with **de** (*a*) to refer familiarly to the female members of a family, (*b*) in a number of set idiomatic phrases, exactly parallel to the use of **la(s)** as an object pronoun (Sec. **48.b**), (*c*) with adjectives in certain idiomatic expressions.

a. **la de Bringas**	*Mrs. Bringas (or the Bringas woman)*
las de Fernández	*the Fernández girls*
b. **Pasó las de Caín.**	*He went through great suffering.*
Hubo la de San Quintín.	*There was a big fight.*
Se armó la de Dios es Cristo.	*A big fight started.*
Tomó las de Villadiego.	*He took to his heels.*
¡La de gente que había!	*What a big crowd there was!*
¡La de preocupaciones que tenemos!	*What a lot of worries we have!*
c. **Esta es la nuestra.**	*This is our opportunity.*
Se armó la gorda.	*They started a good one (fight).*
Pasamos las negras.	*We had a tough time.*
Me llevas la contraria.	*You oppose me.*
Miguel ha hecho una de las suyas.	*Michael has pulled one of his tricks.*
Se salió con la suya.	*He got his own way.*

NOTE. A similar construction is found in the idioms **fue ella, será ella: Cuando llegamos a casa, fue ella** *When we got home, she started the trouble.*

78. SPECIAL USES OF THE NEUTER DEMONSTRATIVES

The neuter demonstratives **lo, esto, eso, aquello** are used frequently (*a*) to form adverbial phrases, (*b*) with **de** to form appositional phrases and clauses. **Lo** in these phrases is the same as the neuter article. (See Secs. **10, 164**.)

a. **por eso**	*for that reason, therefore, that's why*
en esto	*at this juncture, in this matter*
con esto	*thereupon*

b. **lo de ayer**	*the (incident) of yesterday*
Eso es lo de menos.	*That is the least important (part).*
Esto de escribir a ordenadora me molesta.	*This (business) of writing on a computer annoys me.*
Eso de que lo niegue Ud. ahora . . .	*(The idea) that you should deny this now . . .*
aquello del "Titanic"	*the Titanic disaster*

NOTE. **¡Eso es!** or simply **¡Eso!** means *That's it!, Exactly!*

EJERCICIO

Reemplácense las palabras subrayadas con **eso, esto, aquello o lo (de).**

1. La idea de que no hay que trabajar es absurda.
2. El incidente de don Juan y su vecino debe olvidarse.
3. ¡Qué rara la manía de Enrique, no querer volver a casa!
4. El accidente que tanto daño hizo a Susana nos pesó a todos.
5. La cosa de tu abuelo y el mono sí que fue interesante.

---

79. ADDITIONAL REMARKS ON POSSESSIVES

1. The stressed form of the possessive adjective is used in a number of prepositional phrases.

de parte mía	*on my behalf, from me*
a pesar suyo	*to his (her, etc.) regret*
por cuenta mía	*on my account*
a costa nuestra	*at our expense*
en busca suya	*in search of him*
en contra tuya	*in opposition to you*

NOTE. The unstressed form may also be used in the above phrases: **de mi parte,** etc.

2. The neuter possessives **lo mío, lo tuyo,** etc., are used with various shades of meaning: indefinite, abstract, or collective.

Siempre has confundido lo mío y lo tuyo.	*You have always confused my property and yours.*
Ellos van a lo suyo.	*They are going after what they want.*
Se llevó lo suyo.	*He got what was coming to him.*

NOTE. But **los míos,** etc., may mean *my people,* etc. *(family, partisans, etc.).*

Traducción 5B

1. García Márquez and Vargas Llosa are two Spanish American novelists; the latter was born in Perú, the former in Colombia.
2. He (*pointing*) says he has nothing to do with that.
3. When shall we see you in this (city)?
4. That (fellow) is the one who wanted to sell me those shares.
5. He is the kind that never says anything.
6. The (countess) of Cantarranas and her friends were still there.
7. Come this way. The children must be over there in the garden.
8. Do you remember those wonderful mornings in Bogotá?
9. She has gone looking for you (in search of you).
10. I will do it on (for) my own account.
11. I haven't been able to attend to that (affair) of your son.
12. Do you mean to tell me that those documents were false?—Yes, that's it.
13. I don't like this (idea) of eating so late.
14. We were all talking there and at this moment we heard a great noise.
15. All I have is at your disposal.
16. Where is the servant?—She must be somewhere around.
17. That (affair) of the strike was a very serious thing.
18. The revolutionary leader and his (followers) were arrested.
19. She was always wasting time in the (those) cafés.
20. They took to their heels.
21. They gave him his (deserts).
22. They laughed at his expense.
23. In those moments of affliction the workers showed their great courage and heroism.
24. That was a blessing from God.

III

Verbos y Modismos

Review verbs in **-ucir** and **-ducir** (Sec. **238**)

1. Please, translate five pages.
2. I should like you to translate this page for me.
3. I want you to conduct the negotiations.
4. He took (conducted) us to his study.

Parecer *to have the appearance of (seem, look like);* **aparecer** *to put in an appearance (turn up, show up);* **parecerse a** *to resemble.* (**Parecer** is very frequently used impersonally: **me parece** *it seems to (strikes, impresses) me, I believe:* **¿qué le parece?** *how do you like?* (= *what do you think of?*); **¿le parece que . . . ?** *what do you say to . . . ? shall we . . . ?*)

NOTE. **Aparecer** means *to put in an appearance*. Hence it may also be used in 5 and 6.

1. They are so sunburned that they look like Indians.
2. He seems to be happy (**contento**).
3. She doesn't look like the same person.
4. Those jokes are unseemly (do not look well) in a person like you.
5. The child was not to be seen anywhere.
6. The papers I lost (**que se me . . .**) have (**ya**) turned up.
7. Emilia looks a great deal like (resembles) her grandmother.
8. It is a very original work; it is not like (resembles) anything which I am acquainted with.
9. The picture is (**tiene**) a good likeness (**parecido**).
10. Apparently (it seems to be that) he has given up the plan.
11. His conduct is to all appearances (**al parecer**) quite innocent.
12. It seems unbelievable (**mentira**) that you should say that (Sec. **113.2**).
13. I believe it is going to rain.
14. That does not strike me favorably (**bien**).
15. How did you like the bullfight?
16. Shall we leave now?
17. He does all that for appearances' sake (**por el buen parecer**).

Quitar(se) *to remove, take away (off, from)*, etc.

1. Take the books off the table.
2. She took off her coat.
3. I took the collar off the dog.
4. Don't take away his illusions.
5. Get (yourself) out of here.
6. He must be gotten out of the way (**de en medio**).
7. Love keeps me from sleeping (takes sleep away from me).
8. The one (thing) does not exclude the other.
9. Cut it out! (**¡Quita!**)

6 RELATIVE PRONOUNS

80. SIMPLE AND COMPOUND RELATIVE PRONOUNS

There are two fundamental distinctions which must be clearly understood before the use of relative pronouns in Spanish can be mastered. These distinctions concern the use, not the form of relative pronouns. The first is between simple and compound relatives: (*a*) a simple relative pronoun has an antecedent in the main clause; (*b*) a compound relative pronoun contains its own antecedent.

a.	**La carretera que Ud. ve es la de Madrid.**	*The road that you see is the one to Madrid.*
b.	**Quien calla otorga.**	*He who keeps silent gives consent.*

81. COMPLEMENTARY AND SUPPLEMENTARY RELATIVE CLAUSES

The second fundamental distinction concerns complementary and supplementary (limiting) relative clauses: (*a*) a complementary (or restrictive) relative clause is one which is necessary to complete the meaning of the antecedent, the two forming a single concept; (*b*) a supplementary (or non-restrictive or non-limiting) relative clause is one which adds an accessory or parenthetical fact, not an essential part of the antecedent. This latter type of relative clause is usually indicated by a comma in writing or by a pause in speaking.

a. **El señor que acaba de llegar ha subido a su habitación.**

The gentleman who has just arrived (i.e., the newcomer) has gone up to his room.

b. **El señor Herrera, que acaba de llegar, ha subido a su habitación.**

Mr. Herrera, who has just arrived, has gone up to his room.

82. *QUE*

Que (uninflected) *which, that, who, whom* is by far the most frequent relative pronoun. It is the ordinary simple relative and is used (*a*) in complementary relative clauses both as subject and object and referring to both persons and things; (*b*) similarly in supplementary relative clauses; (*c*) after the common simple prepositions **de, a, en, con,** especially when referring to things. (When **de** is a part of a compound preposition like **debajo de, antes de,** etc., relative pronouns are treated differently; see Sec. **85b**.)

a. **La chica que vino a verme es una prima mía.**

The girl who came to see me is a cousin of mine.

Este es el libro que me dieron.

This is the book (that) they gave me.

NOTE 1. Speakers of English should note especially that **que** can refer to persons as well as things. English normally requires that *who(m)* must be used as a relative pronoun, if the relative is not omitted.

NOTE 2. The object relative pronoun is never omitted in Spanish as in English:

el asunto a que Ud. se refiere   *the matter you refer to*

NOTE 3. The personal **a** is normally not used in complementary relative clauses: **el hombre que acabo de saludar**   *the man I have just spoken to*

b. **Mi tío, que es un hombre de buen humor, nos divirtió mucho.**

My uncle, who is a humorous man, amused us very much.

c. **el avión en que fuimos a Cuba**

the plane on which we went to Cuba

la reunión a que asistimos

the meeting which we attended

EJERCICIO

Combínense los pares de frases siguientes en frases completas, p.ej., **Este es el libro. Me dieron el libro. → Este es el libro que me dieron.**

1. Los amigos nos saludaron. Los amigos llegaron ayer.
2. Mi plan es de viajar por México. Mi plan no está completo.

3. El estilo de arquitectura de los edificios es muy moderno. Vimos los edificios.
4. La residencia es vieja. Vivo en la residencia.
5. Esa muchacha es amiga mía. Usted vio a la muchacha ayer.
6. La conferencia fue interesante. Fuimos a la conferencia.
7. El auto es de mis padres. Viajamos en el auto.
8. El profesor es de España. Te hablé del profesor.

83. *QUIEN* (PL. *QUIENES*) WHO, WHOM

Quien refers only to persons, never to things. It may be used (*a*) after prepositions, (*b*) as a compound relative, especially in set phrases. It is not normally used as a subject relative pronoun in restrictive clauses.

a. **la persona de quien Ud. me habló**	*the person of whom you spoke to me*
el amigo por quien me enteré	*the friend through whom I found out*
Quien calla, otorga.	*He who keeps silent gives consent.*

NOTE. **Quien** (and **el cual**) may be found in supplementary relative clauses: **lo consulté con mi padre, quien (el cual) me dio buenos consejos** *I talked it over with my father, who gave me good advice.* This use of **quien** and **el cual,** which purists insist on, is more characteristic of the written than the spoken language.

EJERCICIO

Combínense los pares de frases siguientes en frases completas, p.ej., **El chico es guatemalteco. Hablo con el chico.** → **El chico con quien hablo es guatemalteco.**
1. Los muchachos son de Chile. Viajamos con los muchachos.
2. Esta mujer es mi prometida. Compré el regalo para la mujer.
3. Los pasajeros eran ciudadanos americanos. Dejaron desembarcar a los pasajeros.
4. No conozco al hombre. Usted habló con el hombre.
5. El perro ladra. El perro no muerde.
Úsese **quien** por **el que** en las frases siguientes:
6. El que no se atreve no pasa la mar.
7. El que da luego, da dos veces.
8. El que lo dijo, lo afirma.

84. *EL QUE (LA QUE, LOS QUE, LAS QUE, LO QUE)*

El que, composed of the articles **el, la, los, las** and the relative **que** (see Sec. **68**) refers to both persons and things. It is used (*a*) as the compound relative pronoun equivalent to the English *he who, etc., the one which, etc.,* and (*b*) as a simple relative in competition with **el cual** and **quien,** especially after prepositions. (*c*) The neuter form **lo que** is the equivalent of the English *what* (= *that which*).

a.	**El que tiene dinero lo gasta.**	*He who has money spends it.*
	Las que vinieron ayer son unas estudiantes argentinas.	*Those (girls) who came yesterday are (a group of) Argentine students.*
	Este helado es el que más me gusta.	*This ice cream is the (kind) I like best.*
	mi prima, la que está casada con el ingeniero	*my cousin, (the one) who is married to the engineer*
b.	**Los pueblos por los que pasamos eran muy pintorescos.**	*The towns through which we passed were very picturesque.*
	El amigo por el que me enteré.	*The friend through whom I found out.*
c.	**Lo que me cuenta Ud. me asombra.**	*What you tell me astonishes me.*
	Lo que llevaba en la cabeza era un cántaro.	*What she was carrying on her head was a water jar.*

EJERCICIO

Quítense las palabras subrayadas en las frases siguientes, reemplázandolas con las palabras entre paréntesis; luego quítense los sustantivos, haciendo los ajustes necesarios, p. ej.: **Los muchachos que vienen a trabajar son los programadores → Los que vienen a trabajar son los programadores.**

1. El hombre que lo dice, miente. (la mujer, los muchachos, las personas)
2. Las muchachas que nos saludaron son mis compañeras de clase. (los chicos, el estudiante, la señorita)
3. La persona que trabaja más, debe recibir más. (el estudiante, los hombres, las mujeres)

Combínense los pares de frases siguientes en frases completas.

4. Las montañas estaban cubiertas de nieve. Pasamos por las montañas.
5. El pueblo está lejos de aquí. Partí desde el pueblo.
6. La iglesia grande es la catedral. Hay una cruz encima de la iglesia.

Combínense los pares de frases siguientes en frases completas, cambiando **algo** por **lo que,** p.ej., **Ud. me cuenta algo. Me asombra. → Lo que Ud. me cuenta me asombra.**

7. Algo ocurrió. Fue increíble.
8. Vimos algo. No es nada raro.
9. Ese individuo decía algo. No me llamó la atención.
10. Le regalaron algo. Era un libro recién publicado.

85. *EL CUAL (LA CUAL, LOS CUALES, LAS CUALES, LO CUAL)* WHICH, WHO, WHOM

El cual also refers to both persons and things. It is never used as a compound relative. **El cual** is used (*a*) to indicate the more distant of two possible antecedents, thus preventing ambiguity, and alternates with **el que** (*b*) after prepositions other than **de, a, en, con.** (*c*) The neuter **lo cual** is used in supplementary clauses when the antecedent is a clause or a phrase.

a. **Comí con el hijo de la casera, el cual fue compañero mío.**	*I dined with my landlady's son, who was a classmate of mine.*
b. **Había una torre muy alta desde la cual (la que) se veía toda la ciudad.**	*There was a very high tower from which the entire city could be seen.*
c. **Se negó a verme, lo cual (lo que) me extrañó mucho.**	*He refused to see me, which (fact) astonished me greatly.*

NOTE. **Lo cual** can never be used as equivalent to the compound relative **lo que** *what, that which.*

EJERCICIO

Combínense los pares de frases siguientes en frases completas, utilizando **el cual, la cual, lo cual,** etc.

1. La hija del presidente hizo una visita a los Estados Unidos. Ella había estudiado inglés.
2. Los pastores eran enemigos del gobierno. El fugitivo vivía entre los pastores.
3. El edificio es el ayuntamiento. Hay un museo detrás del edificio.
4. Recibió un gran premio por sus esfuerzos. Le agradó mucho.

---

86. SUMMARY

The chief uses of the relative pronouns are summarized in the following table, the forms in parentheses being alternative but less frequent.

ANTECEDENT	COMPLEMENTARY	SUPPLEMENTARY	COMPOUND	AFTER PREPOSITIONS
Person	**que**	**que** (**el cual, quien**)	**el que**	**quien** (**el que, que**)
Thing	**que** (**el cual**)	**que**		**que** (after **de, a, en, con**) **el que, el cual** (after other prepositions)

NOTE. **Donde** *where* (*= in which*) is frequently used in relative clauses: **el pueblo donde viven mis padres** *the town where my parents live.*

87. *CUYO* AND *CUANTO*

1. **Cuyo(-a, -os, -as)** *whose, of which* is the possessive relative adjective referring to both persons and things and agreeing in gender and number with the thing possessed.

el terremoto cuyos efectos fueron tan desastrosos — *the earthquake, the effects of which were so disastrous*

2. **Cuanto(-a, -os, -as)** is a compound relative (both pronoun and adjective) equivalent to **todo el que,** etc. The neuter **cuanto** is the form most frequently used.

Le debo a Ud. cuanto soy y cuanto tengo. — *To you I owe all I am and all I have.*

NOTE. **Todo** and **cuanto** may be used in combination: **estoy conforme con todo cuanto Ud. dice** *I agree with everything you say.*

EJERCICIO

Combínense los pares de frases siguientes en frases completas, p.ej., **Ese hombre es guapo. Vemos su casa. → Ese hombre cuya casa vemos es guapo.**
1. Aquella casa es bonita. La puerta está abierta.
2. Aquel estudiante no se preocupa. Sus padres pagan todos los gastos.
3. Los alumnos tienen que gastar mucho. Sus libros son caros.
4. Los chicos van a México. Sus padres van de vacaciones.

Traducción 6A

1. Who are the gentlemen who were here this morning?
2. Mr. La Barrera, who is on his way to France, will stop here tomorrow.
3. I like immensely the photograph you sent me.
4. We couldn't find the man to whom we had given our check.
5. The man through whom I got the job has just telephoned me.
6. He who perseveres goes very far.
7. My partner's secretary (f.), who left last week, is a Puerto Rican.
8. The maid said they weren't at home, which surprised me a good deal.
9. We read many essays, among which was yours.
10. What he said was untrue, but very amusing.
11. Of all the museums we have visited this is the one we like best (most).
12. Now we are studying Goya, whose influence on contemporary art has been so great.
13. Don't pay any attention to what they say.
14. I will give you all the envelopes I have.
15. There are three trains every day; the one which has just left is the express.
16. Why don't you publish that story you read us?

17. The girl you were talking to is the same one I was telling you about.
18. I will have to borrow some money from my cousin Albert, (the one) who is in Belgium.
19. The driver, who was not what we would call an expert, did not turn on time.
20. The gardener, who was a Mexican, spoke no English.
21. The writer, whose works you admire so much, died yesterday.
22. My friends, who were Americans, landed before I (did).
23. The passengers who were American citizens could land before those who were not.
24. All I have is at your disposal, he said.
25. What she told us was incredible.
26. We lived in a large house on top of which there was a roof-garden.
27. The square has high arcades under which the people walk.
28. The town we stopped in was very small.
29. We saw for the first time the Spanish flag, the colors of which are red and yellow.
30. I have finished the job your friend gave (**encargar**) me.
31. This is the café where we get together.

II

88. AGREEMENT

The verb in the relative clause usually agrees with the antecedent in person and number.

Tú, que la conoces bien, habla primero.	*You, who know her well, speak first.*
Yo soy el que (quien) lo digo.	*It is I who says it.*

NOTE. In sentences such as the latter, the third person is more frequent: **el que (quien) lo dice soy yo** *I am the one who says it.*

89. SPECIAL CONSTRUCTIONS WITH *QUE*

Que may be used (*a*) referring to persons after the prepositions **de** and **con**, (*b*) as a relative adverb equivalent to **en que** *on which, when,* (*c*) a compound relative when followed by an infinitive.

a. **el empleado de que le hablé a Ud**	*the employee about whom I spoke to you*
la gente con que suele reunirse	*the people with whom he usually associates (in gatherings)*

NOTE. The use of **que** instead of **en que** gives a more indefinite or general meaning to the antecedent.

b. **el dia que nací**	*the day (when) I was born*
c. **Esto me da que pensar.**	*This gives me something to think about (cause for reflection).*

NOTE. **Donde** may be used similarly: **no había donde sentarme** *there wasn't any place to sit down.*

EJERCICIO

Combínense los pares de frases siguientes en frases completas:
1. El oficial nos ayudó. Te hablé del oficial.
2. Los muchachos son simpáticos. Vivo con los muchachos.
3. El día fue mi cumpleaños. Fui a ver a mi madre ese dia.

---

90. INDEFINITE *QUIEN*

Quien is used with indefinite value, in certain set constructions.

hay quien asegura . . .	*some people assert . . .*
como quien dice	*as one might say*

91. SPECIAL CONSTRUCTIONS WITH *EL QUE*

1. **El que** is sometimes found as a stressed alternative for simple **que** after prepositions:

Con un desdén al que no fue insensible.	*With a scorn to which he was not insensible.*

2. When the compound relative is object of a preposition the following features are to be noted: (*a*) **el que** and **lo que** cannot be split so that any preposition always comes before them unless (*b*) the **el** may be replaced by the more emphatic **aquel** or **ese.**

a. **¿Sabe Ud. al que me refiero?**	*Do you know the one I am referring to?*
Sé de lo que eres capaz.	*I know what you are capable of.*

NOTE. By attraction, a similar construction is occasionally used with nouns: **al único que hace caso es a Ud.** *the only person he pays attention to is you.* Furthermore, the preposition may be repeated: **es por él por quien me preocupo** *he is the one I am worried about;* **¡a ése es al que (a quien) se lo di!** *that's the fellow I gave it to!*

b. **Aquello a que me referí . . .**	*What I referred to . . .*
Fueron pocos aquellos a quienes no invitaron.	*There were (very) few who were not invited.*

3. **Lo que es** in initial position has the special meaning *as for*.

Lo que es simpatía, sí que la tiene.	*As for charm, she certainly has it.*
Lo que es yo, no voy.	*As for me, I'm not going.*

92. SPECIAL CONSTRUCTION WITH *CUYO*

Cuyo (*a*) is replaced by **a quien** in constructions corresponding to the dative of interest (Sec. **53**) or possession, and (*b*) is occasionally used as a relative adjective replacing adjectival **el cual,** which is still more infrequent.

a. **el señor a quien robaron la cartera**	*the gentleman whose wallet was stolen (they stole)*
b. **por cuya razón (or por la cual razón** or **por lo cual)**	*for which reason*
Salieron para Cuernavaca, a cuyo pueblo llegaron al mediodía.	*They left for Cuernavaca, at which town they arrived at noon.*

NOTE. **Pueblo a que** is more usual in such constructions.

93. CORRELATIVES

Both **quien** and **cual** are used (*a*) in literary style as correlatives—with the written accent to distinguish them as such—either in the singular or plural. (*b*) **Tal** and **cual** (sometimes **como**) also form a correlative pair, as do **el que más y el que menos** *the best and the worst (of them)*.

a. **Quiénes (cuáles) a pie, quiénes (cuáles) a caballo, los campesinos acudían al mercado.**	*Some on foot, others on horseback, the peasants were hastening to market.*
b. **Tal para cual.**	*Two of a kind.*
Pinta el carácter del pueblo tal cual (como) es.	*It depicts the character of the people just as it really is.*

94. THE RELATIVE CONJUNCTION *QUE*

In colloquial speech especially, a verb object pronoun may be used to recapitulate the antecedent, with the relative acting as a connective.

Tiene una letra que no la entiende nadie.	*He has (so bad) a handwriting that nobody understands it.*
Tendrá sus defectos, que no los veo yo.	*He may have his faults, but I don't see them.*

EJERCICIO

Combínense los pares de frases en frases completas con **que**:
1. ¡Tiene un geniazo! Nadie lo aguanta.
2. Es un tipo. No sé por qué no lo meten en el manicomio.
3. La pobre lloraba. Daba lástima.

Traducción 6B

1. The afternoon I saw you I had an accident.
2. It was the bad condition of the road that made us give up our trip.
3. We will go to the beach where we used to swim last summer.
4. As for courage, he certainly has it.
5. You, who are a good friend of his, ought to tell him.
6. I am the one who proposes it.
7. We visited Quito, which (city) pleased us greatly.
8. Most of the tourists who come here are Americans.
9. The villagers, who are very shrewd people, wanted to cheat us.
10. As for her, she said nothing.
11. From (by) what I have just seen, we cannot come to an agreement.
12. The prisoner, whose hands and feet they tied, could not escape.
13. He is one of those for whom idleness doesn't exist.
14. That's the one I want to talk to.
15. He maintains that he speaks seven languages, which I know isn't true.
16. You are the one who has to decide.
17. Tell (talk to) us about what you did.
18. It's the translation that is difficult.
19. We had an interview with those against whom the accusation had been made.
20. It's a critical situation (the one) we are in.
21. We who love him well will try to dissuade him.
22. The actors he can rely on are all amateurs.
23. There wasn't any place to put the car.
24. Children give a great deal of trouble (to do).
25. It is a difficulty which I had not realized.
26. He has (such) a temper that nobody can stand him.

III

Verbos y Modismos

Dar (Sec. **241**) *to give*, etc.; *to strike, hit*, etc.; **darse** *to occur;* **darse por** *to consider oneself,* **dar la lata** *to be boring.* (**Dar** is frequently used to form verb phrases out of nouns, e.g., **dar la vuelta** *to go back,* **dar vueltas** *to turn round and round.*)

1. What is on (are they giving) at the theater tonight?
2. This soil produces splendid melons.
3. Various cases of typhus have occurred (invert).
4. It makes no difference to me.
5. The windows faced on the garden.
6. He thanked me for the favor.
7. You have to hurry.
8. I did not realize it.
9. He caused a scandal.
10. They gave us very good meals.
11. Let's take a stroll through the streets.
12. You can't get around it (**no hay que darle vueltas**).
13. I have forgotten to wind the clock.
14. He gave me to understand that the article was his.
15. He did not consider himself beaten.
16. I will not let on.
17. It struck twelve.
18. You have hit (**en**) the mark.
19. I have just got (**me ha dado**) a pain in my arm.
20. It makes me feel sorry (**da pena**) to see him like that (**así**).
21. It made him feel ashamed to have to borrow money.
22. I feel afraid to go in.
23. I (suddenly) felt like (**ganas de**) hitting him with my umbrella.
24. The clerk answered insolently: I won't (**no me da la gana**).
25. He came upon his friend.
26. I have taken to (**se me ha dado por**) collecting stamps.
27. They slapped each other.
28. At it again (**¡dale!**).
29. That fellow is always boring.
30. He put the bite on me for some money (**Me dio un sablazo**).
31. My girlfriend jilted me (**dar calabazas**).
32. He misrepresented the matter to me (**me dio gato por liebre**).
33. He never does things right (**dar pie con bola**).

Tema

Escriba Ud. un diálogo entre Ud. y un amigo con que se encuentra en una terraza en un país hispánico. Ud. le dice cuánto le gusta verle después de tanto tiempo y el amigo dice que a él también le agrada muchísimo verle a Ud. Ud. le cuenta algo de lo que ha visto, qué tal fue el viaje, que es lo que espera ver durante su visita, etc. El amigo se ofrece como guía a algunos puntos de interés. Luego le invita a Ud. a una tertulia que se reúne esa noche en un café muy cerca del hotel. Le explica cómo se ha de portarse en una tertulia y cómo serán los que van a esta tertulia que se compone de un grupo de jóvenes con aspiraciones literarias.

Escriba Ud. este diálogo en sus propias palabras y utilice por lo menos cinco de los verbos o modismos de la sección Verbos y Modismos.

7 INTERROGATIVES AND NEGATIVES

I

95. INTERROGATIVES

1. All interrogative adjectives and pronouns have a written accent to differentiate them from relatives and conjunctions of identical form. This accent is retained in indirect questions.

¿Quién ha dicho eso?	*Who has said that?*
¿Adónde va Ud.?	*Where are you going?*
No sé cuándo llegará.	*I do not know when he will arrive.*

2. **¿Quién?** (*pl.* **quiénes?**) *who?* refers only to persons. *Whom?* is **¿a quién?** and *whose?* is **¿de quién?** (always followed immediately by **ser**).

¿Quiénes eran esos señores?	*Who were those gentlemen?*
¿A quién saluda Ud.?	*Whom are you greeting?*
¿De quién es este libro?	*Whose book is this?*

NOTE. **Cuyo** is not used as an interrogative.

3. **¿Qué?** *what? which?* is both (*a*) pronoun and (*b*) adjective.

a.	**¿Qué dijo él?**	*What did he say?*
b.	**¿Qué montañas son éstas?**	*What mountains are these?*
	¿En qué barco viajó Ud.?	*In what (which) boat did you travel?*

4. **¿Cuál?** (*pl.* **¿cuáles?**) *which (one)?* is used only as a pronoun.

¿Cuál es su habitación?	*Which (one) is your room?*
¿Cuál es su tío?	*Which one is your uncle?*

NOTE. In American Spanish **cuál** is also used as an adjective. **¿Cuál libro quiere Ud.?** *Which book do you want?*

5. The English *what* is rendered in Spanish (*a*) by **¿qué?** (= **¿qué cosa?**) when definition or identification rather than selection is called for, or (*b*) by **¿cuál?** when selection out of a group, rather than definition, is stressed (also = English *which*).

a. **¿Qué es esto?**	*What is this?*
¿Qué es la justicia?	*What is justice?*
¿Qué es ese señor?—Es médico.	*What is that gentleman? (i.e., What does he do?)—He is a doctor.*

NOTE. Contrast **¿Quién es ese señor?—Es el señor Ruiz.**

b. **¿Cuál es la capital de Chile?**	*What (i.e., which city) is the capital of Chile?*
¿Cuál es el número de su teléfono?	*What (which one) is your telephone number?*

6. **¿Cómo** *how* always implies *manner (in what way?)*.

¿Cómo está Ud.?	*How are you?*
¿Cómo le gusta el café?—Lo prefiero con azúcar.	*How do you like your coffee (prepared)?—I prefer it with sugar.*

NOTE. The English *how do you like?* in the sense of *What do you think of?* is rendered by **¿Qué le parece (parecen) a Ud.?: ¿Qué le parece a Ud. Montevideo?—Me gusta muchísimo.** *How do you like Montevideo?—I like it very much.*

7. **¿Cuánto(s)?** *how much? how many?* is fully inflected and is used as both (*a*) adjective and (*b*) pronoun.

¿Cuánto es?	*How much is it?*
¿Cuántas semanas dura el viaje?	*How many weeks does the trip last?*

8. *What kind of?* is normally **¿qué clase de?**

¿Qué clase de madera es ésta?	*What kind of wood is this?*

EJERCICIO

Háganse preguntas que tendrán como respuestas las frases siguientes, p.ej., **Esa mujer es mi madre** → **¿Quién es esa mujer?; Vine aquí en avión.** → **¿Cómo vino Ud. aquí?**

1. Ese señor será el nuevo juez.
2. Aquellos edificios son del Ministerio de Gobernación.
3. Los árboles en este jardín fueron plantados hace muchos años.
4. Los turistas pueden ir en avión de Nueva York a Madrid en seis horas.
5. El Cuzco es una de las ciudades más pintorescas de la América del Sur.
6. Le encantan a Ud. los cuadros de Diego Rivera.
7. Hablé con mi consejero.
8. Prefieres el café con leche.
9. Ese libro me costó un ojo de la cara.
10. El número de mi cuarto es 212.

96. INTERROGATIVES USED AS EXCLAMATIONS

1. **¡Qué!** corresponds (*a*) to English *how!* before adjectives and adverbs and (*b*) to English *what!* or *what a!* before nouns; if the noun (*c*) is modified by a following adjective, **tan** or **más** is placed before the adjective.

a.	**¡Qué bonito!**	*How pretty!*
	¡Qué lejos vive Ud.!	*How far (away) you live!*
b.	**¡Qué paciencia tiene Ud.!**	*What patience you have!*
c.	**¡Qué edificio tan (más) alto!**	*What a tall building!*

2. **¡Cuánto(s)!** *how much! how many!* always agrees in number and gender with the noun it modifies (or replaces) and is used as both pronoun and as adjective.

¡Cuántos árboles hay en esta finca!	*How many trees there are on this estate!*
¡Cuánto me alegro!	*How happy I am!*

NOTE. The shortened adverb **¡cuán!** *how!* (used only before adjectives and adverbs as an equivalent of **qué**) is exclusively literary.

EJERCICIO

Háganse frases exclamativas de las frases siguientes, p.ej., **Estamos tristes** → **¡Qué tristes estamos!**

1. Estoy muy contento.
2. Tenemos que leer muchos libros en este curso.
3. Aquel parque es muy pintoresco.
4. Me fastidia la conducta de algunos estudiantes.
5. La conferencia fue muy interesante.

97. SIMPLE NEGATION

1. Simple negation is expressed in Spanish by the adverb **no,** which precedes the verb and its unstressed pronoun objects. Spanish **no** translates both (*a*) the English *do not, is not,* plus *any* etc., (*b*) the English adjective *no.*

a. **No lo hice.**	*I did not do it.*
¿No viene esta tarde?	*Isn't he coming this afternoon?*
Viene esta tarde, ¿no es verdad?	*He is coming this afternoon, isn't he?*
No tengo dinero.	*I don't have any money.*

NOTE. **¿No es verdad?** is frequently shortened to **¿no?** or **¿verdad?**

b. **No tengo suerte.**	*I have no luck (I haven't any luck).*

2. If no verb is present, **no** usually follows nouns, pronouns, and adverbs, as does **sí** when similarly used.

Todavía no.	*Not yet.*
Ahora no.	*Not now.*
Me gusta a mí, pero a él no.	*I like it but he doesn't.*

98. STRONG NEGATION

NEGATIVE EXPRESSIONS	
no	*no*
ningún, ninguna	*no*
sin	*without*
ninguno, -a	*none, no one*
sin ninguno, -a	*without any*
nada	*nothing*
nadie	*nobody*
ni . . . ni . . .	*neither . . . nor . . .*
sin . . . ni . . .	*without . . . or . . .*
nunca	*never*
nunca jamás	*never ever*
tampoco	*not either (at the beginning of a sentence)*
no . . . tampoco	*not either*
ni tampoco	*and neither*
Other somewhat negative expressions	
apenas	*barely, scarcely*

1. Negative (*a*) adverbs, (*b*) pronouns, and (*c*) adjectives may be used to reinforce the negation or define it more specifically. Of these the more usual are (*a*) **nunca, jamás** *never,* (*b*) **nada** *nothing,* (*c*) **ninguno** *no.* If these negatives

follow the verb, **no** must also be used before the verb; if they precede the verb, **no** is not required. Consequently, Spanish, unlike English, may have more than one negative in the same sentence. In fact, in the Spanish negative sentence all forms are negative.

a. **No lo he visto jamás.**	*I have never seen it.*
Ni yo tampoco.	*Nor I either (me neither).*
Nunca dice nada a nadie.	*He never says anything to anybody.*

NOTE. **Tampoco** is the negative corresponding to **también** and is used after a preceding negative statement.

b. **Aquí nadie sabe nada.**	*Here nobody knows anything.*
No he visto a ninguno de esos hombres.	*I have seen none of those men.*
c. **No voy a ninguna parte.**	*I am going nowhere (I'm not going anywhere).*

NOTE. **Ninguno** is used much less before direct objects in negative sentences than is *any* in English. When there is no particular stress on the object, it is normally sufficient to use the object without any modifiers.

No tengo dinero.	*I don't have any money.*
No hemos comprado libros.	*We haven't bought any books.*

2. The negative forms are also used in the following circumstances: (*a*) after comparatives and in relative clauses following superlatives:

Comió más que nunca.	*He ate more than ever.*
Baila mejor que nadie.	*She dances better than anyone.*
Yolanda es la mujer más hermosa que he visto jamás.	*Yolanda is the most beautiful woman I have ever seen.*

(*b*) After expressions implying negative meanings:

Era imposible comprender nada.	*It was impossible to understand anything.*
Es inútil tratar de hacer nada.	*It is useless to try to do anything.*

(*c*) In questions that imply negative answers:

¿Ha estado Ud. jamás en Venezuela?	*Have you ever been in Venezuela?*

(*d*) After **sin, antes de,** and **apenas:**

Una llanura sin agua ni árboles.	*A plain without water or trees.*
Antes de hacer nada, vamos a pensarlo bien.	*Before doing anything, let's think about it.*
Apenas se ve nada desde aquí.	*One can scarcely see anything from here.*

Háganse negativas las frases siguientes:
1. Tengo mucho.
2. Fuimos algunas veces a la capital.
3. Algunos de esos papeles pertenecen al profesor.
4. Él va y yo también.
5. Un día recibimos una carta.
6. Alguien puede ayudarme.
7. Visité muchos lugares.

99. *ALGUIEN, ALGO, ALGUNO*

1. Corresponding to the negatives **nadie, nada, ninguno** are the affirmative indefinites **alguien** *somebody, anybody,* **algo** *something, anything,* **alguno** *some, any.*

Alguien llama a la puerta.	*Somebody is knocking at the door.*
Que conteste alguien.	*(Let) anybody answer.*
¿Hay algo de particular?	*Is there anything special?*
Sí, algo que me extraña.	*Yes, something which surprises me.*
Algún día lo sabrá Ud.	*Some day you will find (it) out.*
Conozco a algunos pero no a todos.	*I know some but not all.*

NOTE. The personal **a** is used with **alguien, nadie, alguno,** and **ninguno.**

Háganse positivas las frases siguientes:
1. Nadie vendrá con nosotros.
2. Nunca dirá nada de lo que le pasó.
3. Aquí no hay nada de interés.
4. Ninguno de esos chicos me saludó.
5. Ella no estudió ni él tampoco.

2. **Algo** and **nada** may be used as adverbs.

El libro es algo pesado.	*The book is somewhat (rather) dull.*
No son nada orgullosos.	*They aren't a bit (at all) proud.*

EJERCICIO

Pónganse **algo** o **nada** en lugar de **muy** en las frases siguientes:
1. Aquel señor es muy pesado.
2. Esos estudios no son muy estimulantes.
3. Mi viaje a Puerto Rico no fue muy caro.
4. Los que no aprecian el arte son muy ignorantes.

Traducción 7A

1. Frank (**Paco**) and Mike (**Miguel**) are roommates who have just met (each other).
2. Frank is very curious and wants to know something about his new friend.
3. F: Has anyone been here this afternoon?
4. M: No, no one.
5. F: What a cool morning! Which is your desk?
6. M: I don't care (**me da igual**). I like this (one).
7. F: Hey (**oye**), whose glasses are these?
8. M: Which ones?
9. F: The ones (which are) on the dresser.
10. M: They're not mine.
11. F: What is your second family name?
12. M: Martín. What's yours?
13. F: Ibáñez. Do you want something?
14. M: No, I don't want anything.
15. F: What kind of book is that?
16. M: A book for my English class.
17. F: That class is rather (somewhat) difficult, isn't it?
18. M: No, not at all.
19. F: Have you ever been to (in) the United States? What's this?
20. M: It's a photo of my family.
21. F: Which is your mother?
22. M: The one (who is) dressed in (**de**) white.
23. F: What is your brother?
24. M: He is a bullfighter.
25. F: Really? What is this (made) of?
26. M: (*Doesn't say anything, and tries to read.*)
27. F: The bank is closed. What is today?
28. M: (*Mike turns a page.*) What did you say? I can't hear anything.
29. F: What date is today?
30. M: I don't know. What is the date of the discovery of America?
31. F (*showing Mike two shirts*): Which color do you like best?
32. M: What is your opinion?
33. F: I don't have any opinion. What was the result (*pl.*) of your test?
34. M: I flunked (**¡Me suspendieron!**) Now I have to study!

II

100. INTERROGATIVES (*CONTINUED*)

1. It must be noted (*a*) that the adjective **¿qué?** often has the same value as the pronoun **¿cuál?**, (*b*) that the pronoun **¿qué?** may be replaced in colloquial and emphatic style by **¿qué cosa?**

a.	**¿En qué barco vino Ud.?**	*What (which) boat did you come in?*
	¿Cuál es el barco en que vino?	*Which is the boat you came in?*
b.	**¿Qué cosa es la propiedad?**	*What is property?*

2. **¿Cómo?** is also used as the polite equivalent of the English *what (did you say)?* and is equivalent to the English emphatic question *what (do you mean)?*

Esa señorita es su herman.	*That young lady is his sister.*
¿Cómo su hermana?	*What do you mean his sister?*
No lo sé.—¿Cómo que no lo sabe?	*I don't know.—What (do you mean) you don't know?*

3. **¿A cómo?** and **¿a cuánto?** are used in asking the price of articles sold by the kilo, the dozen, etc.

¿A cómo (cuánto) se vende la docena de naranjas?	*What is the price of oranges by dozen?*
¿A cuánto (cómo) está la merluza?	*What is the price of hake (today)?*

4. **¿Qué tal?** *how (what kind of)?* is used when *function* (**ser**), *condition*, or *result* (**estar**) is involved.

¿Qué tal es el coche?	*What is the car like?*
¿Qué tal abogado es Vallejo?	*What kind of a lawyer is Vallejo?*
¿Qué tal está el camino?	*In what shape is the road?*
¿Qué tal estuvo el concierto?	*How was the concert?*

EJERCICIO

Háganse preguntas cuyas respuestas serán las frases siguientes:
1. La tecnología es un peligro para la humanidad.
2. La mantequilla se vende a cien pesos el kilo.
3. Los camarones están a ciento cincuenta pesos el kilo hoy.
4. El señor Gómez es un músico muy dotado.
5. El estreno del drama estuvo magnífico.

101. EXCLAMATIONS (*CONTINUED*)

1. The following special constructions should be noted: (*a*) **¿a qué?** in the sense of *why, for what purpose?*; (*b*) **¡qué de!** meaning *what a (lot of)! how many!* (*c*) **¡lo que!** for **¡cómo!** and **¡cuánto!** in exclamations, and (*d*) indirect exclamations. In this latter type, an inflected adjective may intervene between **lo** and **que**.

<table>
<tr><td>a.</td><td>¿A qué viene todo esto?</td><td>Why all this?</td></tr>
<tr><td>b.</td><td>¡Qué de gente!</td><td>What a (big) crowd!</td></tr>
<tr><td>c.</td><td>¡Cómo
¡Cuánto } nos divertimos
¡Lo que } con eso!</td><td>How we enjoyed that!</td></tr>
</table>

NOTE. The construction **¡La de gente que había!** (Sec. **77.2b**) is an outgrowth of the exclamatory and quantitative **lo que**.

<table>
<tr><td>d.</td><td>No sabe Ud. lo que le aprecia.</td><td>You don't know how much he esteems you.</td></tr>
<tr><td></td><td>No tiene Ud. idea de lo bonitas que son.</td><td>You haven't an idea how pretty they are.</td></tr>
</table>

EJERCICIO

Cámbiense las frases siguientes según el modelo: **Las playas de la Costa Brava son muy hermosas.** → **¡Ud. no sabe lo hermosas que son!** **Jorge sabe mucho.** → **¡Ud. no se imagina lo que sabe!**

1. El paisaje de México nos encantó.
2. Sentimos mucho no haber podido ir.
3. La vida hoy es muy cara.
4. Los precios han subido mucho.
5. Estas cartas son muy importantes.

---

102. INTERJECTIONS

Interjections are used much more frequently in Spanish than in English. (For a list of the more common interjections, see Appendix, Sec. **278**.) Some of the most frequent are:

¡Pero mujer! *Wow!*	**¡Oye, chico (viejo, hijo)!** *Hey! (not related to age)*
¡Hombre! *Man! Wow!*	**¡Oiga!** *Hey! Listen!*
¡Cuidado! *Look out!*	**¡Ay!** *Ow! Ouch!*

NOTE. Note the following uses of **¡ay!** and **¡cuidado!: ¡Ay de mí!** *¡Woe is me!* **¡Cuidado con los rateros!** *Look out for pickpockets!*

103. NEGATIVES (*CONTINUED*)

1. Except for the cases cited in Sec. **97,** the position of **no** when the verb is not expressed is usually the same as in English.

He escrito la mayor parte, pero no todo.	*I have written most, but not all.*

2. Some expressions, affirmative in origin, have acquired negative force:

(*a*) **alguno** following the noun at the end of a negative sentence is equivalent to an emphatic negative;

(*b*) **en mi vida, en absoluto,** and similar expressions, by analogy to **nunca** and the like, have acquired a strong negative value even when used before the verb or as independent expressions;

(*c*) **dejar de** means to *leave off, stop* and, by extension, *to fail to, refrain from.*

a. **No tengo inconveniente alguno.**	*I have no objection (at all).*
b. **En mi vida he oído tal cosa.**	*I have never heard such a thing in all my life.*
En absoluto.	*Not at all.*
Me importa un bledo.	*I don't care a bit.*
c. **No deje Ud. de escribirme.**	*Don't fail to write me.*

3. The adverb **nada** is frequently used (*a*) as an exclamation and (*b*) in the form **nada de.**

a. **¡Nada, mujer, nada!**	*Of course, of course!*
Descuide Ud.	*Don't worry.*
b. **Hacía un tiempo magnífico; nada de calor, nada de humedad.**	*The weather was splendid; no heat, no humidity.*

4. **Ni** is used (*a*) in the correlative **ni . . . ni** *neither . . . nor* (usually with plural verb, except when logic requires a singular verb) and (*b*) in the combinations **ni siquiera, ni aun** *not even,* **ni un(o)** *not a (single).*

a. **Ni Juan ni Jorge dijeron nada.**	*Neither John nor George said anything.*
Ni Andrés ni Carlos es el padre de aquel niño.	*Neither Andrew nor Charles is the father of that child.*
Ni bueno ni malo.	*Fair.*

NOTE. When **no** is used, the first **ni** is often omitted: **no** tiene padre **ni** madre *he has neither father nor mother.*

b. **Ni siquiera me escribe.**	*He doesn't even write to me.*
No tengo ni un céntimo.	*I haven't even a cent.*

NOTE 1. **Ni** often has the value of *not even:* **ni su mismo padre le hubiera reconocido** *not even his own father would have recognized him;* **quedó que ni pintado** *it was just right (i.e., not even if specially painted could it have been better).*
NOTE 2. **Ni** is used in certain colloquial expressions as an emphatic negative: **¡ni hablar!** *by no means!* e.g., **¿Vienes con nosotros?—¡Ni hablar! Tengo demasiado que hacer.** It is also used to emphasize a statement: **Ellos son tan tontos, de estudios ¡ni hablar!** *They're so dumb, there's no question of studying!* Other emphatic negative expressions are: **ni pensarlo, ni en sueños, ni soñarlo, ni de milagro,** etc.

EJERCICIO

Cámbiense las frases siguientes según el modelo: **No tengo libros → No tengo ni un libro; no tengo libro alguno. Pedro no escribe a sus padres. → Pedro ni (siquiera) escribe a sus padres.**
1. Aquí no tenemos las comodidades de la vida moderna.
2. Desde aquí el humo es tan espeso que no se ve el fin de la calle.
3. No hay esperanzas para la paz mundial.
4. Los de esa familia no trabajan un solo día de la semana.
5. Esos revolucionarios no han aprendido las lecciones de la historia.
Cámbiense las frases según el modelo: **Escríbame → No deje de escribirme.**
6. Llámame por teléfono el lunes.
7. Tráigame Ud. unos churros.
8. Saluden Uds. de mi parte a su padre.

---

5. A redundant **no** is occasionally used in Spanish, when the sense of the subordinate element is negative.

Prefiero morir a no vivir así.	*I prefer to die to living this way.*

Traducción 7B

1. In which house do you live?
2. To which club does he belong?
3. What's all this noise for?
4. How they shouted!
5. How many tourists on the streets!
6. I couldn't tell you how angry they were!
7. How was the game?—Fair.
8. How does she drive?—Pretty well.
9. What kind of a student is she?—One of the best.
10. I am in no hurry (at all).
11. Don't fail to give him the message.
12. Neither you nor he has any reason to complain.
13. When are you going to stop typing? I can't sleep.
14. Thank you very much.—Don't mention it (man).

15. (Be) careful! The sidewalk is very slippery.
16. He had neither work nor money.
17. I haven't had a single moment's rest.
18. I (never) laughed more in my life.
19. Don't (answer back), don't (answer back)! Do what I tell you.
20. Not even you will be able to convince him.
21. I didn't pay the bill.—What (do you mean) you didn't pay?
22. You can't imagine how lively the dance was.
23. How (much) we danced last night!
24. Would you like an ice cream?—No, no ice cream (pl.) for me.

III

Verbos y Modismos

Poner (Sec. **254**) *to place, put, etc.;* **ponerse** *to put on, start to, become, set (the sun);* **poner casa** *to have one's own house*

1. He put the bread on the table.
2. What are they putting (on) tonight at the Opera?
3. You have got (put) me in a predicament.
4. Let's send him a telegram.
5. This always puts him in a (**de**) bad humor.
6. Such things make me nervous.
7. They have made him (**de**) overseer of the estate.
8. They are to start housekeeping in Madrid.
9. What name have they given the child?
10. Keep me informed (**al corriente**) of what goes on.
11. This hen does not lay.
12. Put on your overcoat.
13. We all stood up (**de pie**).
14. I am (**estoy**) getting old.
15. The sky became very dark.
16. It was impossible to come to an agreement.
17. The girl started to sing.
18. The train started off (**en marcha**).
19. In summer the sun sets very late.

Meter *to put into,* etc.; **meterse en** *to get (put) oneself (into), intervene, get mixed up in;* **meterse con** *to provoke, quarrel with,* etc.; **meter la pata** *to make a mistake*

1. I have to put all this into the trunk.
2. He put his hand in his pocket.

3. We went into the woods.
4. Now he has gone in for painting (**a pintar**).
5. I don't like to get (involved) in other people's affairs.
6. I don't want to get (mixed up) in that.
7. They've gotten into a mess.
8. Don't get (into a conflict) with him.
9. We put our foot (**la pata**) (in it).
10. He is always butting in (**meter la cuchara**).

Tema

Escriba Ud. un párrafo de unas cien a ciento veinticinco palabras sobre su deporte favorito. Las preguntas siguientes pueden servir de guía en la composición del párrafo:

1. ¿Cómo se organiza este deporte?
2. ¿Es un deporte al que juegan sólo los profesionales o hay también aficionados?
3. ¿Le gusta a Ud. (o le gustaría) participar en el deporte?
4. ¿Es un deporte muy popular y suele haber muchos espectadores en los partidos?
5. ¿Es un deporte que requiere mucha preparación y entrenamiento?
6. ¿Se puede comparar el deporte con la corrida de toros?
7. ¿Cree Ud. que los deportes reflejan el carácter nacional? ¿Cómo y por qué?

8 THE INFINITIVE

Por and Para

I

104. THE INFINITIVE: NOUN CLAUSES

1. The infinitive is the verbal noun. Therefore it always functions like a noun; that is, it is either (*a*) subject or (*b*) object of a verb or (*c*) introduced by preposition. Since it is also a verb in meaning, the infinitive may have its own subject, object, or other verbal modifiers (see example *a*).

a.	**Me gusta acostarme tarde.**	*I like to go to bed late.*
	¿Ir yo? ¡No, señor!	*Me go? No, sir!*
b.	**Quería ir al teatro.**	*I wanted to go to the theater.*
c.	**No tengo ganas de comer.**	*I don't feel like eating.*

2. The Spanish infinitive corresponds not only to the English infinitive with *to* but also to the verbal noun ending in *-ing*. Hence, after prepositions it is the infinitive and not the participle ending in **-ndo** which is used in Spanish.

Ver es creer.	*Seeing is believing.*
No tardará en llegar.	*He will not be long in arriving.*
Hable Ud. con él antes de marcharse.	*Speak with him before leaving.*

3. The dependent infinitive is used regularly in Spanish when there is no change in subject, where in English a dependent clause introduced by *that* is more likely. When there is a change in subject the dependent clause is usually introduced by the relative **que** followed by a finite verb form (i.e., a noun or an adverb clause—see Secs. **111, 112**).

Siento no poder ir.	*I am sorry I can't go. (I regret not being able to go.)*
Afirma haberlo visto.	*He claims that he saw it. (He claims to have seen it.)*
Sigamos hasta concluir.	*Let's keep on until we finish. (. . . until finishing.)*
But: **Afirma que ella se lo dijo.**	*He asserts that she told him (so).*
Sigamos hasta que él llegue.	*Let's keep on until he arrives.*

EJERCICIO

Cámbiense las frases según el modelo, usando el infinitivo: **No lo ha visto (afirma)** → **Afirma no haberlo visto.**
1. Volamos por avión. (pienso, quiero, espero)
2. Han jugado a los naipes. (confiesan, sienten, olvidan)
3. Tomás toca el piano. (propone, prefiere, necesita)
4. Hiciste todas tus tareas. (lograste, olvidaste, intentaste)
5. Vuelvo a casa. (espero, me gusta, temo)

---

4. In Spanish certain verbs, verb phrases, adjectives, and nouns require a preposition as a link to their noun complements. This preposition is retained when the noun is replaced (*a*) by an infinitive or (*b*) by a noun clause. See Sec. **269** for a list of verbs requiring a prepositional complement.

a. **Me alegro de saberlo.**	*I am glad to know it.*
Insiste en hacerlo.	*He insists on doing it.*
Estoy seguro de convencerle.	
Tengo la seguridad de convencerle.	*I am sure of convincing him.*
b. **Me enteré de que no había venido.**	*I found out that he had not come.*
Insistí en que no lo había dicho.	*I insisted that he had not said it.*
Tengo la seguridad de que no lo dijo.	*I am certain that he did not say it.*

NOTE. The preposition **a** is regularly used with verbs signifying motion like **ir, venir,** etc., and a few other verbs: **voy a hablarle** *I am going to speak to him,* **vinieron a recogernos** *they came to pick us up,* **me obligan a hacerlo** *they oblige me to do it.*

Cámbiense las frases siguientes según el modelo: **No puedo hablarte. (me avergüenzo de)** → **Me avergüenzo de no poder hablarte.**
1. Oí la noticia. (me contenté con, me asusté de, me pareció)
2. No vamos al teatro. (nos disculpamos de, nos resignamos a, nos extrañamos de)
3. Pilar hace un viaje a Europa. (insiste en, se compromete a, no se atreve a)
4. Mis padres me ayudarán. (se alegran de, se desviven por, se cansan de)
5. Sacaste buenas notas. (te alegras de, te niegas a, te preocupas por)

5. Conversely, when the noun complement is not introduced by a preposition, there is no preposition corresponding to the English *to* used with the infinitive.

Me gusta el teatro—ir al teatro.	*I like the theater—to go to the theater.*
Le prometí el dinero—dárselo.	*I promised him the money—to give it to him.*

105. INFINITIVE AFTER VERBS OF CAUSATION AND PERCEPTION

1. The dependent infinitive with its immediate modifiers usually comes directly after the main verb. This is especially to be noted—in contrast to the English usage—after verbs of perception (i.e., seeing, hearing) and causation (i.e., making someone do something).

Oyeron cantar a Plácido Domingo.	*They heard Plácido Domingo sing.*
Hizo venir al medico.	*He had the doctor come.*
Vimos caer al suelo al oficial herido.	*We saw the wounded officer fall to the ground.*

2. When a verb of causation or perception and its dependent infinitive both have noun objects, (*a*) the object of the main verb is the indirect object of the main verb and the subject of the infinitive and usually comes last. (*b*) If the object of the main verb is a pronoun, it naturally precedes the verb. (*c*) If both objects are third person pronouns, the indirect object becomes **se** and both precede the main verb.

a.	**Mandó traer el desayuno al criado.**	*He ordered the servant to bring breakfast.*
	Oyeron hablar español al camarero.	*They heard the waiter speaking Spanish.*
	Oímos cantar "La Paloma" a una chica guapa.	*We heard a pretty girl sing "La Paloma."*

b. **Le vi dejar caer el periódico.**   *I saw him drop the newspaper.*
    Nos miraron firmar nuestros   *They watched us sign our names.*
      nombres.
c. **Se lo vi esconder.**   *I saw him hiding it.*
    Ya se la oí cantar.   *I already heard her sing it (i.e., the song).*
    Se lo mando hacer.   *I order him (or her) to do it.*

3. If the dependent infinitive has no object, the object of the main verb is the direct object.

    La vimos entrar.   *We saw her enter.*
    Oigo sonar las campanas.   *I hear the bells ring.*
    Las oigo sonar.   *I hear them ring.*

EJERCICIO

Cámbiense las frases siguientes según el modelo: **El médico vino. (vieron)** →
Vieron venir al médico.
1. El pianista tocó una pieza de Falla. (escuchamos)
2. Los muchachos corrieron por la calle. (vi)
3. Las azafatas ayudaron al pasajero enfermo. (hicieron)
4. La mujer gritaba desesperadamente. (oyó)
5. Los bomberos se acercaron al incendio. (miramos)

Pónganse las formas debidas de los pronombres en lugar de los nombres subrayados:
6. Vi acercarse a nosotros a <u>un viejo extraño</u>.
7. Escuchamos gritar al <u>marido furioso</u>.
8. Yo oía cantar a <u>los pájaros</u>.
9. El chófer mira reparar el auto <u>al mecánico</u>.
10. Vieron al hombre pegar a <u>su compañero</u>.

106. SPECIAL CONSTRUCTIONS

(*a*) **al** + infinitive is equivalent to the English *on, when,* + *-ing.* (*b*) **Que** introduces the infinitive depending on an indefinite pronoun or on a noun modified by an indefinite or numerical adjective. (*c*) Certain verbs (e.g., **dejar, consentir, pensar**) vary in constructions with the dependent infinitive, according to their variations in meaning. (*d*) **aprender, empezar,** and **enseñar** take **a** before a complementary infinitive.

a. **al entrar en la casa**   *on entering (when he entered) the house*
b. **Tengo algunas cartas que**   *I have some letters to answer.*
      contestar.
    Deja mucho que desear.   *It leaves much to be desired.*
    No hay nada que decir.   *There is nothing to say.*

     c. **Déjeme Ud. hacerlo.**   *Let me do it.*
        Deje Ud. de hacerlo.   *Stop doing it.*
        Él piensa en su deber.   *He thinks of his duty.*
        Piensa salir mañana.   *He intends to leave tomorrow.*
     d. **Estamos aprendiendo a conducir.**   *We are learning to drive.*
        Empezó a llover.   *It started to rain.*

NOTE. **Seguir** and **continuar** *to keep on, continue* are followed by the present participle in **-ndo,** not the infinitive: **siga Ud. leyendo** *keep on reading* (see Sec. **132.3**).

EJERCICIO

Cámbiense las frases siguientes según el modelo: **Cuando entré en la casa, me fijé en el espejo roto. → Al entrar en la casa, me fijé en el espejo roto.**
1. Cuando nos enteramos de la verdad, fuimos a verlo.
2. Cuando hizo el trabajo, olvidó sus problemas.
3. Cuando terminé la carta, dejé de llorar.
4. Cuando la vi por primera vez, me enamoré en seguida.

Pónganse las formas de **tener, dejar** y **haber (hay, había, habrá, hubo)** en el espacio y pónganse las palabras entre paréntesis en lugar de las palabras subrayadas:
5. _____ poco*ᵃ* que decir*ᵇ*.
    a. (mucho, algo, nada, varias cosas, algunos asuntos)
    b. (hacer, sugerir, proponer, acabar)

---

107. *POR* AND *PARA*

    The preposition **por** must be clearly differentiated from **para,** especially in translating the English *for.* **Para** is more restricted in meaning and consequently it is more helpful to learn its uses first.
    1. **Para** corresponds to the English *for* in the sense of (*a*) aim, destination and purpose, (*b*) comparison, and (*c*) limit of time (usually = *by* in English). It is frequently used (*d*) to introduce infinitives indicating purpose (*to, in order to*). In other words, **para** generally looks ahead (broadly speaking).

     a. **Estas cartas son para Ud.**   *These letters are for you.*
        Mi sobrino estudia para   *My nephew is studying (to be) an*
         arquitecto.   *architect.*
        Salimos para La Habana.   *We left for Havana.*
     b. **Tiene muy buena pronunciación**   *He has very good pronunciation for a*
         para un extranjero.   *foreigner.*
     c. **Dejémoslo para mañana.**   *Let's leave it for tomorrow.*
        Se concluirá para el sábado.   *It will be over by Saturday.*

  d. **Estoy esperándole para hablarle.**   *I'm waiting for him (in order) to talk to him.*

   Estás aquí para estudiar, no para jugar.   *You're here to study, not to play.*

EJERCICIO

Pónganse las palabras entre paréntesis en lugar de las palabras subrayadas:
1. El <u>libro</u>^a es para <u>usted</u>^b.
 a. (este papel, los billetes, las cartas)
 b. (mí, ti, mi amigo, Carlos)
2. Ud. es muy <u>discreto</u>^a para ser <u>joven</u>^b.
 a. (listo, cínico, inteligente)
 b. (secretaria, estudiante, portero)
3. Lo <u>tendremos</u>^a para <u>mañana</u>^b.
 a. (sabrá, comprarán, venderás, obtendrán)
 b. (jueves, la semana que viene, pasado mañana, esta noche)
4. <u>Trabajo</u>^a mucho para <u>ganar</u>^b mucho.
 a. (estudiamos, gastan, Ud. habla)
 b. (aprender, gozar de la vida, estar a gusto, no aburrirse)

---

  2. **Por** has a greater variety of uses than **para** and corresponds to the English *for* in the sense of (*a*) *because of, on account of, in behalf of, in exchange for, during, as,* (*b*) It may also be translated as *through* (*along, around*). (*c*) It also expresses agency (as in the passive voice, Sec. **148.2**), means, manner, unit of measure = *per.* (*d*) It is also used as equivalent of *by* in oaths and exclamations. (*e*) The expression **por mí** can be interpreted as *as far as I'm concerned....*

  a. **Le suspendieron en los exámenes no por su mala suerte sino por falta de preparación.**   *He failed (they flunked him) in the examinations not because of his bad luck but for lack of preparation.*

   Hágalo Ud. por mí.   *Do it for me (for my sake).*

   Recibió muy poco por su trabajo.   *He received very little for his work.*

   Pagué mucho dinero por mi casa.   *I paid a lot of money for my house.*

   ¿Por cuánto tiempo va Ud. a España?   *For how long are you going to Spain?*

   por ejemplo   *for example*

  b. **Vamos a dar una vuelta por las calles.**   *Let's take a walk through the streets.*

   Pase Ud. por aquí.   *Come this way.*

  c. **Estaba muy tostado por el sol.**   *He was very sunburned.*

   Consiguió el cargo por su propio mérito.   *He obtained the position by his own merit.*

   Íbamos a cien kilómetros por hora.   *We were going at 100 kilometers an (per) hour.*

  d. **Juro por mi honor.**   *I swear by (on) my honor.*

   ¡Por Dios!   *For Heaven's sake!*

  e. **Por mí, puedes hacer lo que quieras.**   *As far as I'm concerned, you can do as you want.*

NOTE. *Because* (conjunction) is **porque,** but *because of, on account of* is **por** or **a causa de.**

EJERCICIO

Pónganse las palabras entre paréntesis en lugar de las palabras subrayadas:
1. Dimos un paseo*ᵃ* por el parque*ᵇ*.
    a. (caminé, andaban, paseamos)
    b. (el barrio viejo, la plaza, las calles)
2. Pedro me gusta*ᵃ* por su buen humor*ᵇ*.
    a. (nos ayudó, te encanta, estudia mucho)
    b. (generosidad innata, buenas cualidades, deseo de ser ingeniero)
3. Pagamos*ᵃ* poco (mucho) por esos libros*ᵇ*.
    a. (hacemos, trabajan, gané)
    b. (nuestra patria, sus ideales, mis esfuerzos)
4. Culparon*ᵃ* Pepe por su inatención*ᵇ*.
    a. (multaron, condenaron, pagaron)
    b. (infracción de la ley, traición a la causa, trabajo)
5. Estuvo*ᵃ* allí por varias semanas*ᵇ*.
    a. (va, se quedó, estará)
    b. (tres días, el resto de la vida, un mes)

Traducción 8A

1. We were very tired from playing (**al**) tennis.
2. We were going to stop playing.
3. Let's go for a walk along the bank of the river.
4. It's very warm for April.
5. I don't feel like going out. I prefer to stay here reading.
6. Let's keep on walking until we get (arrive at) to the bridge.
7. There is nothing to see there.
8. They refused to sign the petition.
9. They insisted that they had signed it.
10. Don't bother to copy it.
11. We heard the night watchman move away (**irse**)
12. He is teaching us to ride horseback.
13. I don't think I've seen him before.
14. He makes many gestures when he talks.
15. He broke a leg jumping through the window.
16. Will you let him talk? (See Sec. **25.b.**)
17. He hastened to close the deal.
18. I intend to answer his letter this morning.
19. He was thinking of resigning.
20. I couldn't put up with that.
21. At last he consented to lower the price.

22. He has much to learn.
23. I'm convinced that you are right.
24. I hold (consider) your project (for) impossible.
25. He had the road repaired.
26. Be careful not to burn your fingers.
27. The pier was destroyed by the storm.
28. What's this?—It's a machine for cutting papers.
29. How much do you want for the painting?
30. There was room at the table for six people.
31. This company pays a dividend of seven percent.
32. He remained silent out of (because of) prudence.
33. We're leaving for London tonight and we'll be back by September.
34. I'll see you tomorrow morning.
35. Answer by telegram, not by letter.
36. Leave the door open when you go out.

II

108. THE INFINITIVE (*CONTINUED*)

1. The definite article **el** may be used with an infinitive or a noun clause to heighten its noun force, especially if the infinitive or noun clause precedes the main verb or is separated from it.

El callar a tiempo es una virtud.	*To be silent at the right time is a virtue.*
El que diga Ud. eso tiene mucha gracia.	*Your saying that is very amusing.*

NOTE. The subjunctive is used in this type of clause. See Sec. **116.3.**

2. The use of the infinitive as a noun is (*a*) especially characteristic of poetic style, and (*b*) in some cases such infinitives have come to be felt as pure nouns.

a.	**el susurrar de las hojas**	*the rustling of the leaves*
b.	**sus gestos y andares**	*her gestures and manner of walking*
	mis pesares	*my troubles*

3. Infinitives, like nouns, are sometimes used in exclamations equivalent to commands or entreaties, either (*a*) with **a** or (*b*) absolutely. A similar use occurs (*c*) in interrogations. (*d*) The infinitive can also be used in exclamatory and emotional sentences.

a.	**¡A la cama y a descansar!**	*Go to bed and rest!*
	¡A trabajar, compañeros!	*(Let's get) to work, fellows!*
	A ver.	*(Let's or let me) see (it).*

b. **¡Serenidad, muchachos, y apuntar bien!**

(Let's have) calm, men, and take good aim!

Callarse. No hacer ruido.

Be quiet. Let's have no noise.

No fijar carteles.

Post no bills.

NOTE. Compare the frequent use of the general **hay que** with much the same meaning: **hay que tener cuidado** *one (we) must be careful.* Compare also a similar use of the perfect infinitive: **¡Pues no haberlo hecho!** *Well then, I (you, he, etc.) shouldn't have done it!* In these cases the infinitive refers to a specific person or persons made clear by the context. The negative infinitive is not used as frequently for general prohibitions as in English. The Spanish formula **Se prohibe fumar (aparcar, la entrada,** etc.**)** is usually the equivalent of English *No smoking (parking, admittance, etc.)* However, the absolute infinitive is gaining ground in general directions and in advertisements as an alternative for the imperative ending in **-d** (Sec. **44.c**).

c. **¿Qué hacer?**

What (is there) to be done? (What to do?)

¿Cómo volver a casa?

How (are we) to get home?

d. **Y decían, "¡Nosotras a coser, nosotras en la cocina, nosotras a planchar!"**

And they said, "We women always sewing, always in the kitchen, always ironing!"

NOTE. The infinitive is used absolutely in the following construction: **entender, lo han entendido** *as far as understanding goes, they have understood it.*

EJERCICIO

Cámbiense las frases siguientes según el modelo: **Descansen Uds.** → **A descansar.**

1. Cállese.
2. Vuelvan Uds.
3. Estudien Uds.
4. Llamen Uds.

Contéstense según el modelo: **Ud. se ríe.** → **¿Yo? ¿Reírme yo?**

5. Uds. se burlan.
6. Ud. canta bien.
7. Uds. no estudian.
8. Ud. se olvida.
9. Uds. faltan a clase.

---

4. Even when there is no change in subject, the more concrete and graphic **que** clause is frequently used in the spoken language, instead of the infinitive, especially after verbs of saying and thinking.

Dice que no lo ha visto.

He says he didn't see it.

Cree que lo sabe todo.

He thinks he knows everything.

Fingí que dormía.

I pretended I was asleep.

5. **De, a,** and **con** are occasionally used in conditional sentences (Secs. **120, 123**) before the infinitive in place of the *if*-clause: (*a*) **de** can be used in any conditional clause, and (*b*) **a** may appear in contrary-to-fact conditions. (*c*) **Con** may be used in concessive clauses.

<table>
<tr><td>a.</td><td>**De no poder hacerlo, avíseme Ud.**</td><td>*If you aren't able to do it, let me know.*</td></tr>
<tr><td>b.</td><td>**A no tener a mano el diccionario, no podría trabajar.**</td><td>*If I didn't have the dictionary at hand, I couldn't work.*</td></tr>
<tr><td>c.</td><td>**Con tener tantos amigos, ninguno le socorrió.**</td><td>*Although he had so many friends, none helped him.*</td></tr>
</table>

6. For Spanish equivalents of the English passive infinitive, see Sec. **154.**

EJERCICIO

Cámbiense las frases según el modelo: **De no querer ir, llámeme.** → **Si Ud. no quiere ir, llámeme.**

1. De estar de acuerdo, no tendremos inconveniente.
2. De decir la verdad, no podrán errar.
3. De haber bastante para todos, nadie se quejará.

Cámbiense las frases según el modelo: **A no ser que nos ayudes, no terminamos.** → **Si no nos ayudas, no terminamos.**

4. A decir la verdad, la culpa es nuestra.
5. A juzgar por las apariencias, puedo creer que sí.

Cámbiense las frases según el modelo: **Con tener tanto dinero, no es popular.** → **Aunque tiene mucho dinero, no es popular.**

6. Con trabajar tanto, nunca gano bastante.
7. Con cumplir con sus deberes, no están satisfechos.
8. Con tratar de parecer muy intelectual, todos saben que es tonto.

---

109. POR AND PARA (*CONTINUED*)

1. After **ir, venir,** and other verbs of motion, and also after **mandar, preguntar,** and similar verbs, the English *for* is translated by **por,** possibly because the relationship seems to be rather of motive and not so much destination or purpose.

<table>
<tr><td>**Tengo que ir a la ventanilla por los billetes.**</td><td>*I have to go to the window for the tickets.*</td></tr>
<tr><td>**Vino aquí por sus libros.**</td><td>*He came here for his books.*</td></tr>
<tr><td>**Envió por su baúl.**</td><td>*He sent for his trunk.*</td></tr>
</table>

NOTE. In conversational usage in Spain one may hear **voy a por agua.**

2. After **estar, para** denotes (*a*) disposition (physical and mental), *to be about to, to be ready for,* while **por** denotes (*b*) *desire, inclination, in favor of.* Consequently, **estar por** in this sense is used only with personal subjects.

a. **Está para nevar.**	*It's about to snow.*
No estoy para bromas.	*I'm in no mood (disposition) for jokes.*
b. **Está por las cosas prácticas.**	*He is in favor of practical things.*
Estoy por quedarme en casa.	*I am in favor of staying at home.*

In American Spanish, on the other hand, *to be about to* is expressed with **estar por.** *To be in favor of* is **estar a favor de.** Thus, in America, the first sentence in *a.* would be: **Está por nevar.** The sentences in *b.* would be: **Está a favor de las cosas prácticas,** etc.

3. In general, the infinitive with **para** indicates (*a*) purpose or intention; with **por** it indicates (*b*) cause, desire, or motive, and (*c*) unfinished or future action. In the last use, English normally uses the passive infinitive, e.g., *to be* + the past participle.

a. **Es un día muy hermoso para ir a la playa.**	*It is a very beautiful day to go to the beach.*

NOTE. After verbs of motion **para** may be used instead of **a** if the idea of purpose is to be stressed: **fue a Filadelfia a (para) ver a un amigo** *he went to Philadelphia to (in order to) see a friend.*

b. **No le dije a Ud. nada por no disgustarle.**	*I didn't say anything to you (because I didn't want) to upset you.*
c. **El puente está por construir.**	*The bridge is (yet) to be constructed.*
Eso está por ver.	*That is to be seen.*

NOTE. The infinitive with **por** often corresponds to a whole clause in English: **no asistió a la reunión por estar enferma su madre** *he didn't attend the meeting because his mother was ill.*

4. In a number of cases English *in order to* may be translated by either **por** or **para,** depending on the shade of meaning desired, with **para** indicating intention or purpose, and **por** meaning cause or motive.

Estudio derecho por complacer a mi padre.	*I am studying law in order to please (because of, for the sake of) my father.*
Estudio derecho para complacer mis padres.	*I am studying law in order to (with the purpose of, with the intention) please my parents.*

Summary of the use of **por** and **para**

Para

- destination
  El tren va para Toledo. *The train is going to Toledo.*
  ¿Es este regalo para mí? *Is this gift for me?*
- purpose
  Ahorro para viajar. *I save in order to travel.*
- time limit
  He de terminar para mañana. *I have to finish by tomorrow.*
- comparison
  Juega muy bien para no ser *For a non-professional, he plays very well.*
  profesional.

Por

- relationship to space or place *I was walking along the street.*
  Iba por la calle.
- movement (*through*)
  Mira por la ventana. *Look through the window.*
- time at which
  Me voy por la tarde. *I am leaving in the afternoon.*
- duration
  Me quedé por un año. *I stayed (for) a year.*
- manner or means
  Lo oí por radio. *I heard it on the radio.*
  Envíalo por avión. *Send it by air.*
- proportion, rate, or exchange
  Lo vendió por $100. *He sold it for $100.*
  No vayas a 85 kilómetros por hora. *Don't go 85 km. an hour.*
- cause or motivation
  Lo hice por ti. *I did it because of you.*
  Fue por culpa tuya. *It was your fault.*

EJERCICIO

Pónganse las palabras entre paréntesis en lugar de las palabras subrayadas:
1. Estamos para terminar. (salir, rendirnos, dormir)
2. Es buen día[a] para estudiar[b].
   a. (lugar, oportunidad)
   b. (divertirse, cantar, trabajar)
3. Ernesto está por quedarse. (dejarlo todo, probarlo, irse)
4. El puente[a] está por construir[b].
   a. (la tarea, las palabras, el problema)
   b. (concluir, aprender, resolver)

Traducción 8B

1. Your coughing woke me.
2. Smoking like that is not good for your health.
3. That you don't want to admit it is one thing, and that it isn't true is another.
4. We stopped at a country house called "Quitapesares."
5. I count on being back tomorrow.
6. If you can't take the seven o'clock train, wait until tomorrow.
7. Children, (go) to sleep!
8. Come, (you must) cheer up.
9. But, how (are we going to) tell him?
10. (As for) writing I haven't written.—Well, (you should) have told me before.
11. I did not find it out until I arrived at Gibraltar.
12. He is going for the mail.
13. I have come from New York to have the pleasure of meeting you.
14. I don't know what I would do if I didn't have you here.
15. (My) not having written does not mean that I have forgotten you (Sec. **116.1**).
16. She said that to tease him.
17. I am (in favor of) telling him no.
18. The party is (yet) to be organized.
19. We aren't here to waste time.
20. That's arguing for the sake of arguing.
21. Go on playing the piano. Don't stop on my account.
22. I will do my best to find work for you.
23. Although he is such a good lawyer, he couldn't win the case.
24. This happens to you for being so stubborn.
25. They didn't have any friends because they couldn't speak the language.
26. She is living here now in order to be near her son.
27. We will accept the invitation in order not to slight them.
28. The show is about to start.

III

Verbos y Modismos

Sacar (Sec. **229.1**) *to take out, pull out, bring out, get out, get, obtain, infer,* etc.

1. He took a letter from his pocket.
2. Get me out of this predicament!
3. The dentist will have to pull this tooth (for me).
4. Don't stick your arm out.
5. It's impossible to get her away from her books.
6. Sugar is obtained from beets (sing.).

7. She has won the first prize.
8. He has gotten a great deal (**gran partido**) out of his travels.
9. You don't gain anything by (**con**) getting angry.
10. Have you bought (got) seats for the bullfight?
11. I have gotten a headache from this argument.
12. Make out two copies of this letter.
13. What is (to be) inferred from that?
14. He has not gotten anything clear (**en limpio**) out of his reading.
15. He has taken care of (**sacar adelante**) the entire family.
16. I asked her to (**sacar a**) dance.

Tomar *to take, have* (usually in the sense of *choose* or *receive*, used chiefly with food, drink, etc., and in various special meanings).

1. What are you going to have (take), tea or coffee?
2. Have you had breakfast?
3. Finish drinking your coffee.
4. I am going to have an ice cream.
5. The doctor took his pulse.
6. We have taken an apartment in Madrid.
7. He used to take many sun baths.
8. Let's take a taxi.
9. Do you have any cigarettes?—Yes, have (one).
10. Everywhere they took him for a Spaniard.
11. We shall have to take a hand (**cartas**) in the matter.
12. He got ahead (**la delantera**) of us.
13. You are teasing me.
14. Why, of course! (**Toma!**) That's true.

Tema

Escriba Ud. unas cien palabras sobre la época histórica que más le interesa a Ud. o algún acontecimiento histórico que le atrae, p. ej., la guerra de la independencia de los Estados Unidos o de España o de las repúblicas hispanoamericanas; la conquista de Granada o de América; el descubrimiento de América, etc. Conteste Ud. las preguntas siguientes:

1. ¿Cuál es la época (o el acontecimiento) de la historia humana que más le atrae a Ud.?
2. ¿Qué hay en esta época o acontecimiento que le suscita más interés?
3. ¿Quiénes son los personajes históricos que tuvieron más influencia en este período?
4. ¿Qué hicieron estas personas que fue importante?
5. ¿Qué impresión hicieron en sus contemporáneos?
6. ¿Cuál ha sido el juicio de la historia sobre estos personajes y la importancia de este acontecimiento?

7. ¿Qué efecto tuvo esta época en el desarrollo del mundo moderno?
8. ¿Qué sería diferente hoy si este acontecimiento hubiera sido diferente?
9. ¿Sería mejor el mundo entonces?

Escriba Ud. este párrafo en sus propias palabras y utilice por lo menos cinco de los verbos de la sección Verbos y Modismos.

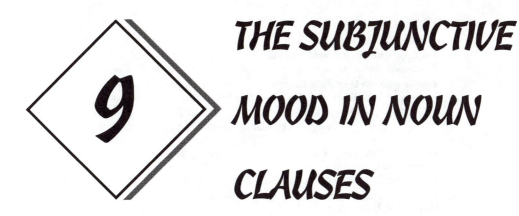

THE SUBJUNCTIVE MOOD IN NOUN CLAUSES

110. TENSES OF THE SUBJUNCTIVE (SEC. 222)

1. In English the subjunctive mood has almost died out, its place being taken by the modal auxiliaries *may, might, should, would, could,* but in Spanish the subjunctive is still very much alive.

2. The present subjunctive is formed on the stem of the first person singular present indicative (the only exceptions are **sea, sepa, vaya,** and **haya**). The two forms of the past subjunctive are formed on the preterit stem. Of these two forms the one ending in **-ra** is the more common, especially in spoken usage.

(a) The present subjunctive is used for the future as well as the present.

(b) In the past, the two past subjunctives are used, as well as the subjunctive forms of the compound perfect tenses.

(c) The use and sequence of tenses is normally as in English dependent clauses. That is, if the main verb is in the present or future tense, the present subjunctive or the present perfect subjunctive with the auxiliary **haber** is used. If the main verb is in a past tense, the past subjunctive or the past perfect subjunctive with **haber** is used.

(d) If, however, the clause containing the subjunctive refers to the past, the past subjunctive may be used, as well as the present perfect subjunctive.

(e) The conditional is normally used with the past subjunctive.

a. **No creo que llegue esta noche.** *I do not think he will arrive tonight.*
   Dudamos que esté aquí. *We doubt that he will be here.*

b. **Temía que no llegara a tiempo.** *I feared he would not arrive on time.*
   Sentí que lo hubiera hecho. *I regretted that he had done it.*

c. **Es posible que haya llegado.** *It is possible that he has arrived.*
   ¿Será posible que vengan pronto? *Could it be possible that they will arrive soon?*

   El rey quería que todos le prestaran ayuda. *The king wanted everyone to give him help.*
   Sentí que lo hubiera hecho. *I was sorry that she had done it.*

d. **Dudo que fuera ella.** *I doubt it was she.*
   Dudo que haya sido ella.

e. **Le gustaría que sus amigos le invitaran a la fiesta.** *He would like his friends to invite him to the party.*

111. THEORY OF THE SUBJUNCTIVE

The *subjunctive* ("subjoined") *mood* possesses two essential characteristics: (*1*) it is used primarily in subordinate clauses, and (*2*) the assertion contained in the subordinate clause is dependent upon the meaning of the main verb, and is not related as an independent fact. Thus a statement of fact will appear in the indicative in an independent sentence.

Juan está aquí.
Los seres humanos no viven en paz.

If these statements are not related as facts, but are somehow dependent upon other statements, especially those denoting emotion (doubt, uncertainty, joy, etc.), volition (ordering, advising, requesting, asking, etc.), or causation, they will appear in a dependent clause in the subjunctive.

The Subjunctive

Me alegro de		
Siento		
Le molesta		
Temen		
Queremos	QUE	{ **Juan esté aquí.**
Es dudoso		{ **los seres humanas vivan en paz.**
Es imposible		
Es difícil		
Confío		

A convenient method for learning the uses of the Spanish subjunctive is to classify them according to the type of clause in which they occur.

112. TYPES OF CLAUSES

Clauses are either principal or subordinate. A subordinate clause is dependent for its full meaning on the nature of its relation to the principal clause. This relation may be that of (*a*) a noun, (*b*) an adjective, (*c*) an adverb. Noun clauses are introduced (*a*) by the conjunction **que** *that*, (*b*) adjective (or relative) clauses by relative pronouns (chiefly by **que** *that, which*), and (*c*) adverb clauses by adverbial conjunctions of time, cause, purpose, result, manner, concession, etc. The majority of these clauses is formed by adding **que** to adverbs and prepositions. Noun clauses (*a*), like nouns and infinitives, function either as subject, object, or object of a preposition.

a. **Creo que se ha ido.**	*I think he has gone.*
Es verdad que se ha ido.	*It is true he has gone.*
Estoy seguro de que se ha ido.	*I am sure he has gone.*

NOTE. **Que,** unlike English *that,* is rarely omitted in Spanish.

b. **Me gusta la casa que ha comprado Ud.**	*I like the house you have bought.*
c. **Se lo digo a Ud. para que se lo repita a él.**	*I am telling it to you so that you (may) repeat it to him.*
Estoy comiendo aunque no tengo ganas.	*I eat although I don't feel like it.*
Ella salía cuando yo llegué.	*She was leaving when I arrived.*

113. THE SUBJUNCTIVE IN NOUN CLAUSES

1. Noun clauses are more frequent in Spanish than in English, which often uses the infinitive, especially in cases where the subjunctive is required in Spanish.

Quiero que Ud. vaya.	*I want you to go.*
Me opongo a que Ud. vaya.	*I am opposed to your going.*

2. The subjunctive is used in noun clauses when the governing verb or expression denotes or even implies any subjective attitude of (*a*) volition, causation, necessity, or advisability, (*b*) emotion, (*c*) doubt, uncertainty, or denial.

a. **Conviene que Ud. le hable.**	*It is advisable that you talk to him.*
Les dije que esperaran.	*I told them to wait.*

Some of the more frequent verbs and expressions of this type are:

aconsejar *to advise*	**es necesario** *it is necessary*
aprobar *to approve (of)*	**hacer** *to cause to, (have somebody do*
basta *it is sufficient*	*something)*
conseguir, lograr *to attain, succeed*	**impedir** *to prevent*
in	**importa** *it matters*
conviene *it is advisable*	**permitir** *to permit*
mandar *to order, command*	**preferir** *to prefer*
decir *to tell (and other verbs of*	**oponerse a** *to oppose*
saying used in the sense of	**pedir** *to ask for, request*
command)	**querer** *to will, wish, want*
dejar *to let, allow*	**rogar** *to beg*
desear *to desire*	

b. **Siento que no se quede Ud. aquí unos días.**	*I'm sorry you're not staying here a few days.*
Se alegró de que fuéramos a visitarle.	*He was glad that we went (came) to visit him.*
Es lástima que no podamos vernos a menudo.	*It's a pity that we can't see each other often.*

Some of the more frequent verbs and expressions of this type are:

alegrarse *to be glad*	**es lástima** *it is a pity*
asombrarse *to be astonished*	**extrañar(se)** *to be surprised*
celebrar *to be glad*	**sentir** *to be sorry, regret*
esperar *to hope*	**temer** *to fear*

c. **No creo que vayamos al baile.**	*I don't believe we'll go to the dance.*
Es probable que le veamos a Ud. pronto.	*It's probable that we will see you soon.*
Es difícil que me encuentre en casa.	*It's unlikely that you will find me at home.*

The most frequent verbs and expressions in the negative (when doubt or mental reservation is implied) are:

creer	*to believe*
decir	*to say*
pensar	*to think* (and the like)

Others are:

dudar	*to doubt*
es fácil (difícil)	*it is likely (unlikely)*
es posible (imposible)	*it is possible (impossible)*
es probable	*it is probable*
negar	*to deny*

EJERCICIO

Pónganse los verbos de Sec. **2.** (*a*) (*b*) y (*c*) en lugar de los verbos principales de las frases siguientes, y cámbiense los verbos subrayados, utilizando los que están entre paréntesis: p.ej., **Desean que Ud. estudie.** → **(pagar) Desean que Ud. pague.**

1. Quieren que Ud. trabaje.
2. Prefería que nos quedáramos.
3. Se alegraban de que llegara Pedro.
4. Siento que hayas ido.
5. No creemos que Jacinto haya venido.
6. Es probable que María venga.

(estudiar, pagar, escuchar, entrar, ponerse el sombrero, comer, tener paciencia, aprender, fijarse, decidir, huir, despedir)

114. THE INFINITIVE USED INSTEAD OF THE NOUN CLAUSE

(*a*) If the subject of the dependent verb is the same as that of the main verb, the infinitive of the dependent verb is normally used instead of the subjunctive. In certain cases the infinitive may be used instead of the noun clause even when the subject of the subordinate clause is different from that of the main verb. This usually occurs when the subordinate subject is a pronoun which may be regarded as the indirect object of the principal verb, e.g., after (*b*) **mandar, hacer, dejar, permitir,** and (*c*) after certain expressions such as **me conviene, me importa, me es preciso (necesario, imposible).**

a. **Siento no poder hacerlo.**	*I'm sorry I can't do it.*
Se alegraba de estar contigo.	*He was happy to be with you.*
b. **No le dejaron entrar en el local.**	*They didn't let him enter the place.*
Me mandaron volver.	*They ordered me to return.*
Me impidió trabajar.	*He prevented me from working (see Sec. 105.2).*
c. **Me conviene hacerlo.**	*It is advisable for me to do it.*
Le fue imposible acudir a la cita.	*It was impossible for him to keep the appointment.*

NOTE. The construction with the infinitive is not used after **querer, pedir, rogar,** or **decir** in the sense of order, command.

EJERCICIO

Cámbiense las frases siguientes según el modelo, reemplazando los verbos subrayados con los verbos en paréntesis del Ejercicio **E9.1**: p.ej., **No dejan que**

<u>entremos</u> → **No nos dejan entrar; Es difícil que Juan <u>vaya</u>.** → **A Juan le es difícil ir.**

1. Dejó que yo <u>pagara</u>.
2. Es preciso que <u>ayudemos</u>.
3. Mandan que <u>vuelvas</u>.
4. Es imposible que Tomas <u>se quede</u>.
5. Pedro permitió que <u>fuéramos</u>.

115. THE SUBJUNCTIVE IN PSEUDO-PRINCIPAL CLAUSES

Even when used in what seems to be a principal clause, the subjunctive must be considered as depending upon some subjective attitude (one of wishing, commanding, surprise, incredulity, etc.) on the part of the speaker. The English equivalent of these expressions is the construction with *let, may, have, I wish (understood), to think (imagine) that!*, etc. Such constructions are similar to the use of the first person plural of the present subjunctive as the equivalent of English *let's* (see Sec. **38**).

Que entre.	*Let (have) him enter.*
¡Que lo hagan en seguida!	*Have them (I wish them) to do it at once.*
¡Que se diviertan Uds.!	*(I hope you) have a good time.*
¡Que diga una cosa así!	*(To think) that he should say such a thing!*

NOTE. The use of **que** clearly shows the subordinate character of the above type of clause. It is omitted only in set phrases or formulae:

En paz descanse.	*May he rest in peace.*
¡Viva el rey!	*Long live (hurrah for) the king!*

EJERCICIO

Utilícense los verbos del ejercicio de **E9.2** en frases con el subjuntivo: p.ej., **¡Que se queden Uds! ¡Que llegue Pedro! ¡Que trabaje Ud.!**

Traducción 9A

1. I'm sorry you weren't here last night.
2. I'm very glad that you are feeling better.
3. Tell him not to wait for us.
4. I don't think I'll be able to go with you (pl.).
5. It's a pity she can't accompany us.
6. It's useless for you to insist.

7. She begged me to keep the secret.
8. I fear they won't be able to finish it on time.
9. It's enough that you promise it.
10. It surprises me that she hasn't said anything to me.
11. We hope she isn't offended.
12. I'm not sure this package is for him.
13. He denied that the signature was his.
14. I asked him to bring me an envelope.
15. We would like you to stay for dinner (to dine).
16. I don't mean to say you are wrong.
17. We would regret very much your misinterpreting the situation.
18. He had us carry the armchair upstairs.
19. It is necessary that we change our clothes.
20. She had the doctor come.
21. I forbade them to bring books to the examination room.
22. I advised all the students to take notes.
23. Long live the President!
24. Have the janitor come up.
25. Good night! (I hope) you sleep well!
26. (To think) that they have deceived us so!

II

116. THE SUBJUNCTIVE IN NOUN CLAUSES

1. As a corollary of the principle discussed in Sec. **113.2,** many verbs of the **decir** and **creer** types take the indicative when straight assertion or belief is involved, and the subjunctive whenever volition, emotion, uncertainty, supposition, etc. is implied. Verbs like **sospechar(se)** *to suspect,* **recelar** *to distrust,* and **quejarse** *to complain* are likewise usually followed by the indicative but may be followed by the subjunctive when some emotion like doubt or uncertainty is implied.

Telefoneó que vendría por la noche.	*She telephoned she would come in the evening.*
Le telefoneé que viniera por la noche.	*I telephoned her to come in the evening.*

In the first example the main verb simply conveys information and is therefore followed by the indicative. In the second example the same verb is used as an equivalent of verbs like **mandar, pedir, querer, aconsejar,** etc., and is followed by the subjunctive.

Se empeñaron en que no tenía razón.	*They insisted I was wrong.*

Se empeñaron en que tomáramos un taxi.	*They insisted that we take a taxi.*
Sospecho que está aquí ya.	*I suspect (i.e., believe) he is already here.*
Sospecho que haya hecho un disparate.	*I suspect (i.e., fear) he has done something foolish.*
¿Está Ud. segura de que ha sido él?	*Are you sure it was he?*
¿Está Ud. segura de que haya sido él?	*Are you really sure it was he? (implying doubt)*
Esto significa que tiene esas intenciones.	*This means (proves) that he has those intentions.*
Esto no significa que tenga esas intenciones.	*This does not mean (prove beyond doubt) that those are his intentions.*
Niego que sea verdad.	*I deny that it is true.*
No niego que es verdad.	*I do not deny (I believe) it is true.*
No niego que sea verdad.	*I do not deny that it may (possibly) be true.*

Some of the more common verbs and expressions in this category are:

confesar	**quejarse**
no hay duda	**recordar**
escribir	**suponer**
insistir	**es verdad**

The subjunctive is less frequent than the indicative after negative **saber:**

No sabía que estaba (estuviera) Ud. aquí.	*I didn't know you were here.*

Esperar and occasionally **temer(se)** may be followed by the indicative when no emotional reaction is implied: **espero que tendrá Ud. éxito** *I hope (expect) you will be successful.*

Suponer may be followed by the future of probability: **supongo que será él** *I suppose it must be he.* For *si* (= *whether*) clauses with the future of probability, see Sec. **123.7.**

2. In Spanish, the tendency is to interpret the noun clause as a reflection of the emotional attitude of the speaker rather than as a material fact. This type is especially common in subject clauses, e.g., after impersonal expressions that imply that what is being affirmed is dependent on the speaker's mental attitude.

Basta que Ud. lo afirme.	*It is sufficient that you affirm it.*
Es natural que sea así.	*It is natural that it should be so.*
Comprendo (me explico) que no se lleven bien.	*I understand (it is explicable to me) that they do not get along.*
But **Es innegable que el triunfo ha sido completo.**	*It is undeniable that the victory was complete (a material fact).*

Similarly, **consta** *it is a fact,* **resulta** *it turns out,* **se ve, es evidente, se conoce** *it is evident* are followed by the indicative.

3. In subordinate clauses which precede the main verb there is an even stronger tendency to use the subjunctive, since the speaker is often undecided as to what is to follow, and after expressing some doubt, then changes to a statement of certainty.

Que lo haya hecho es innegable.	*That he did it is undeniable.*

4. When the subjunctive is used instead of the infinitive after verbs and expressions of the **mandar, me conviene** type (Sec. **114**), a less general and more emphatic turn is given to the statement.

Le mandé salir del cuarto.	*I ordered him to leave the room.*
Le mandé que saliera del cuarto.	*I told him to get out of the room.*
Le conviene hacerlo.	*It would be a good thing for you to do it.*
Conviene que Ud. lo haga.	*You ought to do it.*

EJERCICIO

Cámbiense las frases siguientes según el modelo, reemplazando las palabras subrayadas con los verbos entre paréntesis: p.ej., **Le mandé hacerlo.**[a] → **Le mandé que lo hiciera; Permiten**[b] **que lo hagamos.** → **Nos permiten hacerlo.**
1. Conviene quedarnos[a] aquí.
2. Le mandaron[b] que saliera.
   - *a.* (ir al teatro, estar tranquilo, dar un paseo)
   - *b.* (nos importa, nos es preciso, dejan)

---

5. In Spanish the noun clause is retained in cases where the English varies the construction.

Les agradecería que me enviaran . . .	*I should appreciate (it) if they would send me . . .*

117. THE SUBJUNCTIVE PSEUDO-PRINCIPAL CLAUSES (*CONTINUED*)

1. The subjunctive is used (*a*) in elliptical contrary-to-fact conditions when the conclusion is omitted (see Sec. **120**), (*b*) after the adverbs **ojalá** and **así** *I wish that, may,* and (*c*) usually with adverbs signifying uncertainty such as **tal vez, quizá** (or **quizás**), and **acaso,** *perhaps.*

a. **¡Si me vieras ahora!**	*If you could see me now!*
¡Nunca lo hubiera hecho!	*I wish I had never done it!*
b. **¡Ojalá estuviera aquí ahora!**	*I wish he were here now!*
¡Así me cayera muerto!	*May God strike me dead!*

NOTE. The exclamatory **¡quién!** used with a past subjunctive always refers to the speaker: **¡Quién fuera actor de cine!** *I wish I were a movie actor!*

    c. **Quizá sea verdad.**   *Perhaps it's true.*

2. Similar to the hortatory use treated in Sec. **115** is the concessive use of the subjunctive in alternative clauses with or without the correlatives **ora . . . ora, (ya) que . . . (ya) que . . .** *whether . . . whether. . . .*

Pase lo que pase no pienso desistir.	*Come what may (come), I do not intend to stop.*
Que lo crea Ud. o que no lo crea, es la verdad.	*Whether you believe it or not it is the truth.*

EJERCICIO

Añádanse **ojalá** y **quién** a las frases siguientes, según el modelo: **No puedo ir.**
→ **¡Ojalá pudiera ir! ¡Quién pudiera ir!**
1. No soy un gran amante.
2. No entiendo esas cosas.
3. No te veo ahora.
4. No sé la verdad.

Añádase **quizá** a las frases siguientes, cambiando los verbos al subjuntivo:
5. Vienen a vernos mañana.
6. Volvemos a casa después del concierto.
7. Me olvidarás.

Reemplácense los verbos subrayados con los verbos entre paréntesis.
8. <u>Pase</u> lo que <u>pase</u>, no volveremos atrás. (hacerse, venir)
9. Que lo <u>haga</u> o que no la <u>haga</u>, me es igual. (querer, ver, traer)

Traducción 9B

1. It's unquestionable that they did their duty.
2. It's understandable that he should be so bored.
3. Is it natural that he should take that point of view?
4. It's sufficient that you recommend him to me.
5. He wrote me that he would arrive at three o'clock and to wait for him in the office.
6. I suppose you are going away this summer.
7. Let us suppose he said that.
8. Don't you think he is a man of ability?
9. Do you suspect he is deceiving you?
10. I admit that he is impatient, but not that he is indiscreet.
11. I (can) well understand that you should oppose it.
12. Can't you understand what you ask (for) is impossible?

13. I can't conceive your taking that job.
14. We can't explain to ourselves that he should be so careless.
15. She can't understand that we should live modestly.
16. He complains that you don't write to him.
17. We don't doubt that you are sincere.
18. It is evident that he is not to blame for what has happened.
19. That they were here last night is evident.
20. Would that you were here!
21. Let him do what he will, don't pay any attention to him.
22. Let him come and tell me himself.
23. Perhaps I am mistaken.
24. It would be a good thing for them to rent that house.
25. They ought to rent that house.
26. She had the boy bring up the suitcases.
27. We heard them discuss the matter.
28. Don't let yourself be carried away by your enthusiasm.

III

Verbos y Modismos

Hacer (Sec. 247) *to do, make, become, try, be (of weather conditions and duration of time);* **hacer por** *to strive to;* **hacer (el papel) de** *to take the part of, act as;* **hacerse el . . .** *pretend to be;* **estar hecho(s) a** *to be accustomed to.* (**Hacer** *is frequently used to make phrases out of nouns.*)

1. Don't make me miss the train.
2. They had the doctor summoned.
3. It's a splendid day.
4. This room is very cold (it's very cold in this room).
5. Have you been waiting for me long?
6. He had arrived two weeks previously.
7. What has become of your friend?
8. He became a lawyer in three years.
9. The two became friends immediately.
10. Let's go before it gets dark (**de noche**).
11. He has become a real (**está hecho un**) character (**personaje**).
12. We are accustomed (**hechos**) to all kinds of inconveniences.
13. We were soaked to the skin (**hechos una sopa**).
14. I shall try to see him.
15. He took a very important part in the uprising.
16. I have been acting as a carpenter all day.
17. I pretended not to hear (to be deaf).
18. They make up (**las paces**).

19. Do you need the pencil?
20. Have you hurt yourself?
21. Nobody paid any attention to him.
22. It doesn't please me a bit (**no me hace maldita la gracia**).
23. They've played him a dirty trick.
24. He was afraid he would make himself ridiculous (**hacer el ridículo**).
25. We have made a fine mess of it (**¡Buena la . . .**)
26. I thought (**hacía**) you (were) in Quito.
27. He makes (out) he does not hear.
28. It seems to me (**a mí se me hace**) that that is not the way it is said.
29. He pretends not to see what is going on (**hace la vista gorda**).
30. They took advantage of their opportunities (**hacer su agosto**).

THE SUBJUNCTIVE IN ADJECTIVE AND ADVERB CLAUSES

10

118. THE SUBJUNCTIVE IN ADJECTIVE (I.E., RELATIVE) CLAUSES

The subjunctive is used only in complementary relative clauses. It is used to indicate that the antecedent is (*a*) indefinite, (*b*) hypothetical, or (*c*) non-existent. It imparts to the antecedent a value corresponding in general to the English *any, whatever, whoever.* The idea of futurity is frequently involved, especially in types (*a*) and (*b*).

a.	**Haré lo que Ud. me dice.**	*I shall do what (the specific thing) you tell me.*
	Haré lo que Ud. me diga.	*I shall do whatever you tell me.*
b.	**Se lo pregunté a un hombre que pasaba.**	*I asked a (definite) man who was passing.*
	Se lo preguntaré al primero que pase.	*I shall ask the first person (whoever he may be) who passes.*
c.	**¿Hay alguien aquí que lo sepa?**	*Is there anybody here who knows it?*
	No conozco aquí a nadie que juegue al golf.	*I don't know anybody here who plays golf.*
	No hay quien le aguante.	*There is no one who can stand him.*

NOTE. The personal **a** is always retained with the indefinite pronouns and adjectives (Sec. **99**), but not necessarily with nouns used indefinitely: **envíenos (a) un hombre en quien tenga confianza** *send us a man in whom you have confidence.*

EJERCICIO

Pónganse los verbos entre paréntesis en lugar de los verbos subrayados.
1. Busco un muchacho que me <u>ayude</u>.
2. Necesito al mozo que me <u>ayudaba</u> ayer.
   (servir, acompañar, hacer el trabajo)
3. Vamos a coger las frutas que <u>estén</u> maduras.
4. Compramos sólo las frutas que <u>están</u> maduras.
   (saber bien, costar poco, contener vitaminas)
Háganse negativas las frases siguientes:
5. Hay un alumno que sabe hacerlo.
6. Conocemos a alguien que habla ruso.
7. Aquí hay un avión que va a Madrid.

---

119. THE SUBJUNCTIVE IN ADVERB CLAUSES

1. The subjunctive is always used in the following types of adverb clauses: (*a*) purpose, (*b*) with **sin que** (unaccomplished result) (*c*) proviso, supposition, and exception. This latter category does not include conditional sentences (with **si** *if*) (see Sec. **120**) or concessive clauses (with **aunque,** etc. *although, even if*) (see Sec. **122**).

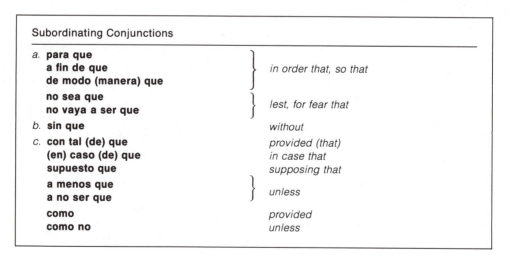

Subordinating Conjunctions	
a. **para que** **a fin de que** **de modo (manera) que**	*in order that, so that*
no sea que **no vaya a ser que**	*lest, for fear that*
b. **sin que**	*without*
c. **con tal (de) que**	*provided (that)*
(en) caso (de) que	*in case that*
supuesto que	*supposing that*
a menos que **a no ser que**	*unless*
como	*provided*
como no	*unless*

    a. **Lo dijo en voz alta para que nosotros lo oyéramos.**   *He said it in a loud voice so that (in order that) we could hear it.*

    b. **Salimos sin que nadie nos viera.**   *We left without anyone seeing us.*

c. **Haré mi parte con tal que Ud. haga la suya.**	*I shall do my part provided you do yours.*
Como no esté en su cuarto, no sé dónde encontrarle.	*Unless he is in his room, I don't know where to find him.*

EJERCICIO

Reemplácense las palabras subrayadas con los verbos entre paréntesis:
1. Me dio ayuda <u>para que</u> (de modo que, a fin de que) <u>fuera su amigo</u>. (no dejarle, prestarle dinero, presentarle a mi hermana)
2. Lo hice <u>sin que</u> los otros <u>lo supieran</u>. (darse cuenta, no hacer nada, ayudarme)
3. No comprenderán nada <u>a menos que</u> (a no ser que) alguien <u>se lo explique</u>. (decir la verdad, darles la solución)
4. Con tal que todo <u>vaya</u> bien, tendremos buenos resultados. (salir, andar)

---

2. The subjunctive is used under certain conditions in the following types of adverb clauses:

(*a*) in temporal clauses when the time is future to that of the principal clause, and
(*b*) in concessive clauses, unless the statement is clearly conceded as a material fact.

More subordinating conjunctions

a. **antes (de) que** *before*
así que *as soon as*
cuando *when*
después (de) que *after*

en cuanto *as soon as*
hasta que *until*
mientras que *during*
tan pronto como *as soon as*

b. **a pesar de que** *in spite of the fact that*
aun cuando *even though*
aunque *although, even if*

---

a. **Se lo daré cuando le vea.**	*I shall give it to him when I see him.*
Esperaré aquí hasta que vuelva.	*I shall wait here until you return.*
Tan pronto como Ud. llegue, póngame un telegrama.	*As soon as you arrive, send me a telegram.*
b. **No es buen estudiante aunque su padre sea muy rico.**	*He's not a good student, even though his father is (may be) very rich.*
Salió sin paraguas, aunque estaba lloviendo.	*He left without an umbrella although it was raining (a material fact).*
Si yo tuviera bastante dinero me compraría un coche nuevo.	*If I had enough money, I would buy myself a new car (i.e., I don't have enough money).*

EJERCICIO

Cámbiense las frases siguientes del pasado al futuro:
1. Entramos en la casa cuando empezó a llover.
2. Se lo dio a su amigo tan pronto como llegó.

3. Te lo repetí en cuanto me lo pediste.
4. Jugaron hasta que se cansaron.
5. Pudimos discutirlo mientras que estuvimos juntos.

Contéstense según el modelo: **¿Cuándo nos veremos? (ser posible) Nos veremos cuando sea posible.**
6. ¿Cuándo llegará su hermano? (terminar su trabajo)
7. ¿Cuándo podemos hacerlo? (estar listo)
8. ¿Cuándo me pagará Ud.? (tener el dinero)
9. ¿Cuándo se marchan Uds.? (venir nuestro padre)
10. ¿Cuándo me escribe Ud.? (llegar a Bogotá)

Pónganse **después que** y **tan pronto como (en cuanto)** en lugar de **cuando** en las frases **6–10.**

---

120. CONDITIONAL SENTENCES

1. Conditional sentences have certain characteristics which require a separate treatment. A conditional sentence is basically one in which there are two clauses: one beginning with **si** *if* which states a condition (the "protasis"), and one which declares what the result of that condition will be (or might be) (the "apodosis").

(*a*) In conditional sentences which speak of real conditions or actual possibilities, the indicative mood is used in both clauses.

Si llueve no iré.	*If it rains (does rain) I shall not go.*
Si estaba en casa entonces no lo sabíamos.	*If he was at home then, we didn't know it.*

(*b*) Other conditional sentences present less likely conditions and results. In English, those conditional sentences in which we find the auxiliary verb forms *would (should)* in the result clause use the past tense in the *if*-clause. In these cases, the past tense no longer refers to a true past time, but is simply the form used to indicate the unreality (or supposed unreality) of the condition. Equivalents of these sentences in Spanish use the past subjunctive in the *if*-clause. In the result clause the conditional form of the verb appears.

Si lloviera ahora, no iría.	*If it were raining now, I wouldn't go.*
Si estuviera en casa hoy, le veríamos.	*If he were at home today, we would see him (i.e., he is not at home).*

(*c*) If the reference is to the past, in English we find the pluperfect tense in the **if**-clause. In equivalent Spanish sentences the pluperfect subjunctive is used in the **if**-clause. Occasionally, especially in colloquial usage, the present indicative is used in the result clause (see Sec. **29c**). This type of conditional sentence is usually said to contain a condition which is "contrary to fact" or completely unreal.

Si hubiera estado en casa ayer, le habríamos visto.	*If he had been at home yesterday, we would have seen him* (i.e., he wasn't home).
Si hubiera llovido, no habría ido.	*If it had rained, I wouldn't have gone* (i.e., it didn't rain).

(*d*) Some sentences have the same form as those in (*b*) even though they may well appear to refer to real possibilities. However, in order to stress great doubt or uncertainty, the speaker wishes to present the condition as though it were really almost impossible and "contrary to fact."

Si yo ganara el premio gordo en la loteria, iría a Europa.	*If I won the first prize in the lottery, I would go to Europe* (i.e., it is very unlikely that I will win).
Si lloviera, no iría.	*It it should rain, I wouldn't go.*

NOTE. The present subjunctive is never used after **si** meaning *if*. Contrast with **en caso de que** (and other conjunctions of Sec. **119.1.c**) where the subjunctive is required:

En caso de que llueva no iré.	*In case it rains (should rain) I will not go.*
Si llueve, no iré.	*If it rains, I won't go.*

2. **Hubiera** etc. is frequently used instead of **habría** etc. in the conclusion of contrary to fact sentences.

Si hubiera llovido no hubiera ido.	*If it had rained I would not have gone.*

NOTE. **Como si** *as if* is especially identified with contrary to fact clauses and is always followed by the past subjunctive:

Lo dijo como si no le importara nada.	*He said it as if it were of no importance to him.*

3. **Si** meaning *whether* introduces an indirect question and is followed either by the infinitive or the future (or conditional) of probability.

No sabía si ir o no.	*I did not know whether to go or not.*
Me pregunto si será cierto.	*I wonder if it is (can be) true.*
¿Si será cierto?	

EJERCICIO

Cámbiense los verbos en las frases siguientes según el modelo: **Si Luis viene, le veremos.** → **Si Luis viniera, le veríamos.**
1. Si estamos de acuerdo, podemos irnos.
2. Si te lo dicen, lo crees.
3. Si es necesario, lo pagaré.
4. Si tienen bastante dinero, harán un viaje a Chile.
5. Si me lo pides, te lo daré.

Cámbiense las frases siguientes según el modelo: **Ramón no vino y no le vimos.** → **Si Ramón hubiera venido, le habría (hubiera) visto.**
6. Mis amigos no estudiaron y no aprendieron la lección.
7. Fernando no se cuidaba, y se enfermó.
8. Llovió ayer y no fuimos al campo.
9. No trabajé mucho y no gané mucho.
10. No me mandaron la carta y no supe la verdad.

Traducción 10A

1. Let them do whatever they wish.
2. Let us stop at (in) a hotel where they have (an) orchestra.
3. This apartment has only four rooms. I want one that has seven.
4. Isn't there anyone here who knows you?
5. I can't find the bellboy who has my baggage.
6. I couldn't find a porter to carry my baggage.
7. The tailor has brought some samples for us to choose.
8. What are you going to do when you finish your work?
9. You can start your lecture when (ever) you want.
10. Don't do anything until we see each other tomorrow.
11. When the professor arrives, let's tell him (it).
12. Unless you hurry, we will never get there (arrive).
13. In case he is not in his office call him at his house.
14. I will take charge of the matter provided you give me liberty of action.
15. Before the student could answer, the bell rang.
16. The child crossed the street without anyone seeing him.
17. I couldn't finish the translation although I worked all night.
18. I will not be able to finish the translation even though I study all night.
19. The ambassador spoke so slowly that we could understand him very well.
20. I will speak very slowly so that everybody can understand me.
21. The dentist pulled my tooth out without my realizing it.
22. You shout at me as if I were deaf.
23. If we had walked faster we wouldn't have missed the trolley.
24. If you wait a moment we will go out together.
25. If you don't like it, don't buy it.

26. If you should need me tomorrow, call me on the telephone.
27. He did not say whether he would accept or not.
28. Write it down now, so that you won't forget it.
29. I will give it to him as soon as I see him.
30. (There is) nobody (who) can convince him of the contrary.

II

121. THE SUBJUNCTIVE IN RELATIVE CLAUSES (*CONTINUED*)

1. The subjunctive is used whenever the antecedent carries merely an implication of uncertainty or negation. **Apenas** *scarcely* can be considered a negative word, and therefore it requires the subjunctive.

Hay pocos que lo sepan.	*There are few (persons) who know it.*
Apenas había quien hablara de otra cosa.	*There was scarcely a person who would talk of anything else.*

2. The subjunctive is also used (*a*) in relative clauses of concession introduced by **por (más) . . . que** *however (much) that* and (*b*) occasionally after a superlative, in order to emphasize the statement by including all possibilities.

a. **Por más esfuerzos que haga, no lo conseguirá.**	*No matter what efforts he may make, he will not obtain it.*
Por mucho (más) que corra Ud., no le alcanzará.	*No matter how hard you run, you will not overtake him.*

NOTE. The indicative may be used when an actual fact is stressed, rather than with future possibilities: **Por mucho que trabajo . . .** *No matter how hard I (actually) work . . .*

b. **Darío es el poeta más grande que Nicaragua haya producido.**	*Darío is the greatest poet that Nicaragua has ever produced.*

3. The following types of relative clauses, corresponding to (*a*) parenthetical and (*b*) hypothetical or concessive clauses in English, are extensions of the hortatory subjunctive (i.e., "*Let's . . .*") treated in Sec. **115**. This construction is especially characteristic of colloquial speech and set phrases. In some instances, these clauses may be interpreted as those having an indefinite antecedent.

a. **Su padre, que en paz descanse (q.e.p.d.) . . .**	*Your father, may he rest in peace . . .*
El finado, que santa gloria haya . . .	*The deceased, may he be in heaven . . .*
Mi abuelo, que de Dios goce (q.d.D.g.) . . .	*My grandfather, may he be with God . . .*

Tu mujer, que en gloria esté (q.e.g.e.) . . .	*Your wife, may she rest in heaven . . .*
b. **La vida que le pidieran, la daría.**	*He would give his life if they asked him.*
Con dos letras que le pongas, se arregla el asunto.	*If you will only drop him a few lines, the matter will be settled.*

NOTE 1. The set phrases **que yo sepa (recuerde, vea)** *that (as far as) I know (can remember, see)* have lost in most cases their original relative value: **no es hombre rico, que yo sepa** *he is not a rich man, that I know of.*

NOTE 2. The parenthetical **que digamos** *to say the least* is used to intensify a preceding negative: **no es muy justo que digamos** *it is not very fair, to say the least.*

EJERCICIO

Reemplácense las palabras subrayadas con las palabras entre paréntesis:
1. Por mucho que <u>haga</u>, no tendrá éxito. (gritar, trabajar, saber)
2. Por más <u>cartas</u>^a que <u>escriba</u>^b nadie le hará caso.
   a. (esfuerzos, oficiales)
   b. (hacer, ver)
3. Por muy listo que <u>sea</u>, no puede engañar a todos. (parecer, creer ser, aparentar)

---

122. THE SUBJUNCTIVE IN ADVERB CLAUSES (*CONTINUED*)

1. The subjunctive is used (*a*) in causal clauses of doubtful or rejected reason and, in antiquated style, after **como** indicating cause, (*b*) in result clauses, when a desired, not an accomplished, result is stated, or when a result is denied, (*c*) after **aunque,** when an acknowledged fact is emotionally stressed.

a. **No lo hago porque sea conveniente, sino porque es justo.**	*I do not do it because it is convenient but because it is right.*
No es que sea fea; es que es antipática.	*It isn't that she is homely; it's that she is disagreeable.*
Como no pudiera ir contra la opinión pública, tuvo que dimitir.	*As he could not go against public opinion, he had to resign.*
b. **Arregle Ud. el programa en tal forma que todos queden satisfechos.**	*Arrange the program so that everybody will be pleased.*
No soy tan tonto que me lo crea.	*I am not so foolish as to believe that.*
c. **Aunque sea Ud. mi jefe, no le puedo obedecer en esto.**	*Even though you are my boss, I cannot obey you in this.*

NOTE. Compare **por muy alcalde que sea, a mí no me da órdenes** *no matter how much of a mayor he may be, he can't give me orders.* **Y eso que,** *on the other hand,* carries no emotional value and always takes the indicative: **me pasé el día trabajando, y eso que era domingo** *I spent the day working, although it was Sunday.*

EJERCICIO

Reemplácense las palabras subrayadas con las palabras entre paréntesis:
1. No trabajo porque <u>sea agradable</u>, sino porque es necesario. (gustarme, obligarme tú)
2. No es que <u>no me guste</u>; es que no tengo tiempo. (ser desagradable, irritarme, no poder hacerlo)
3. Aunque <u>vengan</u> muchos, no lo voy a tolerar. (no creerlo, esforzarse)

---

2. The following are developments of clauses originally temporal in value: (*a*) **ya que** *now that, since, granted that* and (*b*) **siempre que** *whenever, provided that* take the subjunctive when futurity, possibility, or an emotional attitude is stressed; (*c*) **mientras que** *as long as, until* and **hasta que** *until* when referring to future time (and hence to action not yet accomplished) often have a redundant *no*.

   a. **Ya que a Ud. no le hace falta . . .**   *Since (now that) you do not need it . . .*
      Ya que no trabaja éste, que nos   *Since (granted that) this fellow won't*
      deje en paz.   *work himself, let him not disturb us.*

NOTE. **Ya que** with the subjunctive is found especially in negative clauses.

   b. **Siempre que viene nos trae un**   *Whenever he comes he brings us a*
      regalo.   *present.*
      Siempre que a Ud. no le haga   *Provided, of course, you will not need*
      falta . . .   *it . . .*
   c. **Mientras que no lleguen las**   *As long as the orders don't come (i.e.,*
      órdenes no podemos hacer   *until they do come) we can do nothing.*
      nada.
      No haga Ud. nada hasta que no   *Don't do anything until I call you.*
      le llame.

EJERCICIO

Reemplácense las palabras subrayadas con las palabras entre paréntesis:
1. Ya que <u>todo va bien</u> ahora, podemos terminar a tiempo. (todos trabajar, no haber dificultades)
2. Ya que <u>no hay remedio</u>, me encomendaré a Dios. (nadie ayudarme, haberlo perdido todo, no tener éxito)
3. Siempre que <u>van allí</u>, se divierten mucho. (ver a sus padres, aprender algo, beber vino)

4. Siempre que <u>no haya dificultades</u>, todo irá a las mil maravillas. (hacer buen tiempo, alguien ayudarnos, conservar mi salud)
5. Mientras <u>no hagamos nada</u>, no le veremos. (quedarnos aquí, estar viajando, no llamarle)

---

3. **Como** (causal) when used with the subjunctive and referring to future time, takes on a concessive or conditional value equivalent to *in case, provided,* or *if.* **Como no** in this use is equivalent to *unless.* These constructions are frequent in colloquial speech.

Como tenga suerte con este negocio, doblo mi fortuna.	*If (provided) I am lucky in this business, I'll double my fortune.*
Como no llegue en este tren ya no llega hoy.	*Unless he arrives on this train he won't be here today.*

123. CONDITIONAL SENTENCES (*CONTINUED*)

1. Distinction must be made between (*a*) neutral conditions in past time (indicative) and (*b*) conditions stressing uncertainty or that are contrary to fact (subjunctive).

a. **Si Arturo no estaba enfermo, lo parecía.**	*If Arthur wasn't sick, he looked it.*
b. **Si Arturo no estuviera enfermo, vendría a verte.**	*If Arthur weren't sick, he would come to see you.*

2. **Por si** *in case* is construed like **si,** either with the present indicative or the past subjunctive.

Deje Ud. el almuerzo en la mesa por si viene (viniera).	*Leave the lunch on the table in case he comes (should come).*

NOTE. **Por si** always follows the main clause. **Por si acaso** (colloquially **por si las moscas**) means *just in case.*

3. **Si** is frequently used in colloquial speech to introduce an emphatic assertion equivalent to the English *why.* This construction is in origin an elliptical conditional sentence (**Si me lo dijo él, ¿por qué no lo he de creer?**), but the ellipsis is no longer felt.

¡Si me lo dijo él mismo!	*Why, he told me himself!*

4. **Ni que** is occasionally used colloquially in elliptical clauses with either concessive or contrary to fact value.

¡Ni que estuviera loco!	*Not even if I were mad (would I do such a thing)!*

5. The forms in **-ra** are occasionally found in principal clauses as equivalents of the conditional. Especially common are **quisiera** *I (he, she) would like,* and **pudiera** *I (he, she) would be able (to)* (see Sec. **129**).

Más te valiera callar.	*It would be better for you to keep silent.*
Dijérase que nunca había hablado con mujer.	*One would have said that he had never talked with a woman.*
Debieras dedicarte al trabajo.	*You ought to dedicate yourself to work.*
Quisiera saber qué pasa aquí.	*I'd like to know what is going on here.*

6. The condition is occasionally stated as an alternative clause (Sec. **117.2**). In this case **si** is omitted and the conclusion is introduced by **y.**

7. The condition is occasionally given in the form of the prepositions **de, a,** or **con** plus the infinitive (see Sec. **108**).

Fuera el discurso menos violento de forma y nos satisfacería por completo.	*Were the speech less violent in form, it would satisfy us completely.*

EJERCICIO

Pónganse las palabras entre paréntesis en lugar de las palabras subrayadas:
1. Quedémonos aquí, por si <u>llega Victor</u>. (llamarnos Patricio, pasar algo, haber un motín)
2. ¡Ni que <u>me hicieran rey!</u> (ser presidente, tener un dineral)
3. ¡Si lo <u>trajeran</u> ellos! (hacer, decir, comprar)
4. ¿Si <u>vendrá</u> Jacinto mañana? (llegar, salir, estar aquí)

---

8. **Si** *whether,* followed by the future or conditional of probability, may be used (*a*) after **dudar, suponer, sospechar, pensar,** etc. (Sec. **116**, note **3**) and (*b*) in elliptical indirect questions.

a. **Dudaba si aceptaría.**	*He was in doubt whether to accept or not.*
b. **¿Si será ella?**	*I wonder if it can be her?*

9. For the use of the graphic present and imperfect in conditional sentences, see Sec. **29c, 30.3**.

124. THE FUTURE SUBJUNCTIVE

The future subjunctive has disappeared from living Spanish speech and is used only **(a)** in legal phraseology and **(b)** in a few antiquated set phrases, especially proverbs. Its form is almost the same as that of the past subjunctive in **-ra,** except that the final vowel is **-e.**

a. **Si la Asamblea determinare** . . .	*If the Assembly should determine* . . .
b. **Adonde fueres, haz lo que vieres.**	*When in Rome, do as the Romans do.*
Sea lo que fuere.	*Be that as it may (be).*

NOTE. Even in these cases the present subjunctive is the usual form: **sea lo que sea, pase lo que pase** *come what may.*

Traducción 10B

1. Is there anything he does not know?
2. No matter how much you shout, he will not hear you.
3. However difficult the situation may appear, we will not lose hope.
4. Lope de Vega is the most fertile author the world has ever (**jamás**) known.
5. Is the drug store very far?—No, in two strides (that you take) you (will) be there.
6. If you would only study one hour longer (more) you could finish the work.
7. Has anyone been here to see me?—Not that I know.
8. Even if the book is very amusing, I don't think it has any literary value.
9. It isn't that I don't approve (of) your plans, (it is that) the moment to put them in practice hasn't yet come.
10. In case they aren't at home leave them a note (message).
11. We will be very glad to do it provided that we can count on the necessary authorization.
12. Since I will not be able to (go to) meet you personally, I will send a friend of mine.
13. Even though you say it, I prefer not to believe it.
14. Why, he told me he didn't know (any) German!
15. Who sent you this gift?—Unless it is my wife I don't know who it can be.
16. If I catch him in a (**de**) good humor, I('ll) convince him.
17. Let's walk slowly, so that we do not tire ourselves too much.
18. Not even if I had seen it with my own eyes (could I be more certain)!
19. Don't forget to take an umbrella with you, in case it rains.
20. What a way of spending money! Not even if he were a millionaire (could he spend more)!
21. Should the party refuse . . .
22. If they invited him to dinner (dine), he would always accept.
23. If they did not invite him to dinner, he would not eat.
24. The longer I live in this town, the less I like it.
25. Since I can't tell him, I'll tell you.
26. No matter how often I read it, I do not understand it.
27. He is afraid of firearms, although he is a soldier.
28. He is not so far away that he cannot hear us.
29. I wondered whether I could be wrong.
30. It would be better for you not to tell them unless they ask you.

III

Verbos y Modismos

Decir (Sec. **242**) *to say, tell, speak, mean;* **Ud. dirá** *speak up*

1. They say you are leaving.
2. It apparently (one would say that) is of no consequence to you at all.
3. Who would have thought (would say) it!
4. All right, I am listening (**¡Bien. Ud. dirá!**).
5. Time (God) will tell.
6. I have finished (spoken).
7. The fear of gossip (**el qué dirán**) does not hold him back.
8. This music means (says) nothing to me.
9. What do you mean (wish to say)?
10. His brother, I mean (say) his cousin, keeps a grocery store.
11. This law, or rather (**mejor dicho**) this bill, will be discussed tomorrow.
12. He didn't say a word (**no decir esta boca es mía**).
13. As we said before (**lo dicho**), we'll meet at ten o'clock.
14. There is no need to say (**excuso decir**) what happened next.
15. Your grandfather is not a boy, to say the least (**que digamos**).

Dejar *to leave (behind, unmolested, untouched, etc.) let, allow, keep from;* **dejar de** *(with inf.) to stop, fail to;* **dejarse de** *(with noun) to quit, stop (to leave [= go out] is* **salir**)*,* **dejar por imposible** *to give up*

1. I have left the money at home.
2. You get out (**bajarse**) here; I'll look for a place to park (leave the car).
3. I don't want you to leave it for tomorrow.
4. Let him (alone).
5. Let me (have) the book when you finish it.
6. The illness has left him very weak.
7. We will have to (impers.) give him up as (**por**) impossible.
8. You astonish me (express as resultant condition, i.e., **me dejas . . .**).
9. He has (left) forgotten his overcoat.
10. With all this (**tanta**) conversation you keep me from (do not let me) working.
11. Don't let yourself be convinced.
12. I am going to stop smoking.
13. Don't fail to write me.
14. Quit your joking (**bromas**).
15. Quit (it)!
16. She stood me up (**dejar plantado**).

Tema

Escriba Ud. un párrafo de cien palabras sobre un paseo por un lugar favorito de Ud. Al escribir, conteste Ud. las preguntas siguientes:

1. ¿Dónde y cuándo empezó el paseo?
2. ¿Por qué medio de transporte fue Ud.?
3. ¿Qué le atrae a Ud. más en aquel lugar?
4. ¿Qué hay de interés allí?
5. ¿Es un lugar muy recorrido o es Ud. uno de pocos que lo visitan?
6. ¿Qué cosas suele Ud. hacer allí?
7. ¿Tiene Ud. amigos que también van allí o prefiere ir solo?
8. ¿A qué clase de personas le gusta ese lugar?

Escriba Ud. este párrafo en sus propias palabras y utilice por lo menos cinco de los verbos y expresiones de la sección Verbos y Modismos.

PARTICIPLES AND AUXILIARIES

11

I

125. THE PRESENT PARTICIPLE

1. The present participle in Spanish (Sp. **gerundio**) is used as an adverb—without prepositions—for various adverbial relations: (*a*) instrument (or means) and its derivatives: manner, cause, etc.; and (*b*) to indicate the time during which an action takes place. This type of clause occurs more frequently in Spanish than in English, which in many cases employs a preposition with the participle or a complete adverbial clause.

a. **Arrojándose al agua, salvó la vida de su amigo.** — *(By) throwing himself into the water, he saved his friend's life.*

Vino corriendo. — *He came running.*

Estando Juan enfermo, no pudo ir. — *Since John was ill, he could not go.*

Andando despacio no se cansará Ud. — *Going slowly you won't be tired.*

b. **Viviendo en Buenos Aires solía asistir a los conciertos.** — *When I lived in Buenos Aires I used to go to the concerts.*

NOTE 1. The subject, if expressed, follows the participle.

NOTE 2. English speakers must be especially aware that the English verbal form ending in *-ing* has many more uses than the Spanish participle ending in

-ndo which is never used as an adjective or a noun. The Spanish verbal form used as a noun is the infinitive (see Sec. **104**).

2. The present participle is used with **estar** to form the graphic or progressive tenses (see Secs. **17.7; 20.3.**).

EJERCICIO

Pónganse las palabras (en la forma en **-ndo**) entre paréntesis en lugar de las palabras subrayadas:
1. <u>Va</u> cantando una melodía popular. (andar, venir, seguir)
2. Nadie gana nada <u>quejándose</u>. (hablar, dormir, estudiar)
3. Siendo estudiante, <u>iba mucho a Nueva York</u>. (vivir en Filadelfia, estar cerca, tener la oportunidad)

---

126. USES OF THE PAST PARTICIPLE

(For a list of the irregular past participles, see Sec. **266**.)
1. The past participle functions as an adjective and as a verb. Its chief function as a verb is to form the compound past tenses. (See Sec. **27**.)
2. Participles are frequently used as adjectives with the neuter article **lo** to form an abstract concept (Sec. **10**.) The English equivalent of this construction is usually either an abstract or a relative clause.

lo arriesgado de la situación	*the riskiness of the situation*
Entre lo dicho y lo hecho, hay un gran trecho.	*Actions speak louder than words. (There is a great difference between what is said and what is done.)*
Pues, lo dicho. Hasta mañana.	*As we agreed, then. Until tomorrow.*

3. The English present participle ("action in progress") is often rendered by the Spanish past participle when what is referred to is actually the final result of an action. Thus in English, *sitting* often refers to the result of having sat down, so that in Spanish the past participle must be used.

Había dos sombreros colgados en la percha.	*There were two hats hanging on the rack.*
Dos hombres estaban sentados en el sofá.	*Two men were sitting on the sofa.*
La recién llegada era una señora muy divertida.	*The newcomer was a very amusing lady.*

4. The past participle denoting resultant condition is frequently used with **tener.** This construction must be differentiated from the perfect tenses, for which it may serve as a graphic substitute.

Tengo escrita la carta.	*I have the letter written.*
el dinero que tenía guardado	*the money I had put aside*
como te tengo dicho	*as I have (repeatedly) told you*

EJERCICIO

Reemplácense las palabras subrayadas con las palabras entre paréntesis:
1. Estaba <u>dormido</u> cuando llegamos. (acostado, ocupado, preocupado, entretenido)
2. Lo <u>conocido</u> siempre sirve para algo. (amado, aprendido, ahorrado)
3. Tenían <u>compradas</u> algunas cosas útiles. (vendidas, preparadas, encerradas, hechas)

---

127. MODAL AUXILIARIES

Modal auxiliaries are verbs that modify other verbs. They may be classified accordingly as they express (*a*) desire and willingness: **querer,** (*b*) ability and possibility: **poder, saber,** (*c*) obligation and necessity: **haber de, deber, tener que,** and the impersonal **hay que,** (*d*) inference and assumption: **deber de, haber de.** Note carefully the different meanings of **poder, deber (de),** and **haber de.**

a.	**Quiero hacerlo.**	*I want to do it.*
	¿Quiere Ud. venir mañana?	*Would you like to come tomorrow?*
b.	**No puedo hacerlo.**	*I can't do it.*
	Puede ser.	*It may be.*
	¿Se puede (entrar)?	*May I come in?*
	Puede Ud. pasar ahora.	*You may go in now.*
	No sé decirle.	*I can't tell you.*

NOTE. **Poder** is equivalent to the English *may* (permission, possibility) as well as *can, be able;* **saber** denotes mental, in contrast to physical, ability.

c.	**Ha de venir mañana.**	*He is to come tomorrow (certainty with a shade of obligation).*
	Debió venir ayer.	*He should have come yesterday (moral obligation).*
	Tiene que venir mañana.	*He must come tomorrow (necessity).*
	Hay que hacerlo ahora.	*It has to be done now (necessity).*

NOTE. The English *we must (have to)* is often rendered **hay que: hay que trasborder ahora** *we have to change trains (planes) now.*

d.	**Debe de ser así.**	*It must be so.*
	La enfermedad debió de ser grave.	*The illness must have been serious.*

Las consecuencias han de ser estas.	*The consequences are sure to be these.*
¿Qué ha de hacer uno?	*What can one do?*

NOTE 1. **Haber de** and **deber de** may be regarded as strong forms of the future and conditional of probability. **Será, sería,** and **serán** could be used in the first three of the above examples.

NOTE 2. **Haber de,** being a graphic form of the future, is used only of reasonably certain inferences and assumptions. From this use is derived the faint shade of obligation recorded in (*c*).

NOTE 3. The distinction between (*c*) **deber** and (*d*) **deber de** is not strictly observed in actual usage.

EJERCICIO

Añádanse verbos modales a las frases siguientes según el modelo: **Hago el trabajo.** → **Puedo hacer el trabajo; debo hacer el trabajo, tengo que hacer el trabajo,** etc.

1. Ricardo vendió su coche.
2. Mi madre preparará la comida.
3. Los estudiantes estudian más de lo común.
4. Nos vemos pronto.
5. Regresaron antes de lo pensado.

---

128. CORRESPONDENCE OF TENSES

Many of the English modal auxiliaries are defective verbs, but their Spanish equivalents are used with full tense distinctions.

Podrá venir mañana.	*He will be able to come tomorrow.*
Querrá hacerlo ahora.	*He will want to do it now.*
Debí hacerlo.	*I ought to have done it.*

129. POLITE OR SOFTENED STATEMENT

The imperfect subjunctive forms (*a*) **quisiera** and (*b*) **debiera** are used in polite or softened statements as equivalents of the English (*a*) *should like* and (*b*) *should, ought* (see Sec. **123.5**).

a. **Quisiera que me recomendara Ud.**	*I should like you to recommend me.*
b. **Debiera Ud. tener un poco de paciencia.**	*You ought to (should) have a little patience.*
Debiera haberlo hecho.	*I should have done it.*

NOTE. **Pudiera** is sometimes used as a substitute for **podría**.

EJERCICIO

Cámbiense las formas de **deber, poder,** y **querer** al subjunctivo en **-ra:**
1. Debes llamar a tu padre.
2. Podemos arreglarlo ahora.
3. Quieren mantener la paz.
4. Deben esforzarse, si van a salir adelante.
5. Josefa no debe preocuparse tanto.

---

130. SPANISH EQUIVALENTS OF *MAY* AND *MIGHT*

1. The English *may* and *might* denoting possibility are often rendered in Spanish by **puede que** or **es posible que.**

Puede que sea verdad.	*It may be true.*

2. The English-speaking student of Spanish should keep in mind that the chief difficulties in the use of modal auxiliaries arise from the peculiarities of the English rather than the Spanish usage. In English, modal auxiliaries like *can, may, ought,* etc. do not have full tenses as they do in Spanish.

Traducción 11A

1. Taking off his cap, he showed us the wound.
2. Suddenly getting up, she rushed towards the door.
3. That happened a long time ago when I was a student.
4. The driver, putting the brakes on quickly, avoided an accident.
5. There were many people looking out of the window.
6. He is a very daring man.
7. I might see her this afternoon.
8. He fulfilled his promise (what had been promised).
9. Give me everything concerning (referring to) this fellow.
10. What a boring speech!
11. Will you (please) be quiet?
12. I have to finish my work before going out.
13. I don't know (how) to translate this passage. Can you help me?
14. I had to rewrite the lesson.
15. The doctor said that you ought to stay in bed, and you should follow his advice.
16. All students should learn (how) to use (handle) the dictionary.
17. I should like to see you as soon as possible.
18. Could you come to my office right away?
19. We must hurry if we want to arrive on time.

20. We are to sign the contract tomorrow morning.
21. The (sum) collected so far amounts to several million(s of) pesos.
22. The actors have the play very well rehearsed.
23. I received your letter when I was in the hospital.
24. You should have sent it sooner.
25. If (since) you read so fast, I can't understand you.
26. You may come when(ever) you wish.
27. It must be very late. We have to go.
28. I want to play tennis today because it may rain tomorrow.
29. That is not what (we) agreed (to do).
30. We must go out now.

II

131. PRESENT PARTICIPLE

1. The Spanish verbal adjective in **-ante** and **-iente** (or **-ente**) often corresponds to English words ending in *-ing.* Some of these forms are used as adjectives, nouns, or even as prepositions. **Corriente** *running, current, ordinary;* **(el) amante** *loving, lover;* **el estudiante** *student;* **presente** *present;* **durante** *during.*

NOTE. *The participles* **hirviendo** *boiling and* **ardiendo** *burning, unlike the other* participles in **-ndo,** are used as adjectives: **agua hirviendo** *boiling water.*

2. The adjectival present participle in English in *-ing* is often rendered in various ways in Spanish: (*a*) by the verbal adjective or by adjectives in *-oso, -or,* etc., (*b*) by a relative clause, (*c*) after verbs of perception, by the present participle or the infinitive, (*d*) by the past participle signifying resultant condition (Sec. **126.3**).

a. **un palacio flotante**	*a floating palace*
el caballo ganador	*the winning horse*
el equipo victorioso	*the winning team*
la sociedad bancaria	*the banking firm*
b. **Encontré los papeles que faltaban.**	*I found the missing papers.*
c. **Oímos ladrar a un perro.**	*We heard a dog barking.*
Veíamos a los niños jugando en la plaza.	*We could see the children playing in the square.*
d. **No lo dejes tirado en el suelo.**	*Don't leave it lying (thrown) on the floor.*

EJERCICIO

Fórmense palabras en **-nte** de los verbos siguientes. Los verbos en **-ar** toman el sufijo **-ante,** y los verbos en **-er** e **-ir** casi siempre toman el sufijo **-iente:**
1. andar, bastar, brillar, cambiar, cantar, emocionar, hablar, impresionar,

insultar, participar, penetrar, representar, terminar, tirar, viajar.

2. sorprender, existir (**-ente**), maldecir (**-diciente**), salir, sonreír, contender.

132. THE PRESENT PARTICIPLE (*CONTINUED*)

1. Even when used adjectivally (*a*) in the so-called "pictorial" gerund or (*b*) when modifying the object of a verb, the Spanish gerund or present participle retains its verb force. This latter construction (*b*) is equivalent to a supplementary relative clause.

a.	**Wáshington cruzando el Delaware**	*Washington crossing the Delaware*
b.	**Acabo de recibir un prospecto anunciando una nueva edición del "Quijote."**	*I have just received a prospectus announcing a new edition of the "Quixote."*

NOTE. Thus, *we saw them move away* may be **los vimos alejarse (alejándose, que se alejaban).** But when the English present participle is equivalent to a complementary relative clause, e.g., *the missing papers,* the gerund ending in **-ndo** cannot be used (**los papeles que faltaban**).

2. The only preposition used with the **gerundio** is **en.** This infrequently used construction has a temporal or conditional meaning, *as soon as, (immediately) after, when, if.*

En terminando de comer, venga Ud. a mi casa.	*As soon as you finish dinner, come to my house.*
En teniendo salud, no hay que apurarse.	*As long as (if) one has his health, there is no need to worry.*

3. (Sec. **20.3**) In the progressive or graphic tenses **estar** is often replaced by verbs of motion (**ir, andar, venir, llevar**) which give an added graphic force to the expression in keeping with their literal meaning (often rendered in English by an adverbial modifier). **Seguir** and **continuar** *to continue* are always followed by the present participle.

Venía andando por la carretera.	*He came walking along the highway.*
Me voy cansando de esto.	*I am getting (gradually, beginning to get) tired of this.*
Andaba escribiendo para los periódicos.	*He was writing for the newspapers (sporadically).*
Seguí viéndola todos los días.	*I kept (on) seeing her every day.*
Llevo dos horas estudiando.	*I have been (spending) two hours studying.*
Vengo diciéndoselo hace tiempo.	*I have been telling him so for some time.*

EJERCICIO

Reemplácese **estar** con verbos de moción en las frases siguientes:
1. Estoy aburriéndome de esto.
2. Todos estaban diciendo lo mismo.
3. Los radicales están molestando a mucha gente.
4. Estamos aguantando lo malo de este mundo.

Cámbiense las construcciones siguientes según el modelo: **Hace unos días que estudio la materia.** → **Llevo unos días estudiando la materia.**
5. Hace poco tiempo que el médico visita a los enfermos.
6. Hace un año que mi cuñado trabaja aquí.
7. Hace varias semanas que nos vemos diariamente.

4. The present participle is frequently used in familiar epistolary and journalistic style to represent an attendant circumstance or result which, in English, would take the form of a coordinate clause or even a separate sentence.

Se ha declarado la huelga general cerrándose todas las tiendas.	*General strike declared. All stores closed.*
El automóvil chocó contra un árbol, resultando heridos de gravedad todos sus ocupantes.	*The car crashed into a tree, and all the passengers were seriously injured.*

NOTE. The adverbial present participle is sometimes used colloquially as an exclamatory imperative: **¡Andando!** *Come along!* **¡Callandito!** *Hush!*

133. PAST PARTICIPLES (*CONTINUED*)

1. Past participles (and adjectives with verbal meaning) may be used in the absolute construction to express time. In this construction the participle always agrees in gender and number with the noun it modifies and always precedes it.

Firmado el pagaré, me entregaron el dinero.	*After the note was signed, they delivered the money to me.*

NOTE. Compound prepositions such as **antes de** *before,* **después de** *after,* and **luego de** *immediately after* may be used to specify the exact temporal relation: **luego de firmado el pagaré,** etc. The participial construction with the preterit of the auxiliary in apposition (**firmado que hube el pagaré**) is a survival found only (and rarely) in literary style.

EJERCICIO

Reemplácense las palabras subrayadas con las formas debidas de las palabras entre paréntesis:

1. Después de (luego de) <u>pagadas las deudas</u>, pudimos respirar un poco. (terminar la guerra, cumplir los ejercicios, hacer los trabajos)
2. (Antes de) <u>contado el dinero</u>, tuvieron que llegar a un acuerdo. (escribir el contrato, empezar la tarea)

---

2. With the past participle (as well as with the gerund) **estar** may be replaced by related verbs of more specific meaning: **quedarse, hallarse, encontrarse, verse.** Verbs of motion (**ir, andar, venir, seguir,** etc.) may also be used to impart a graphic quality in keeping with the literal meaning of the auxiliary.

Spanish uses many more graphic and objective auxiliaries with the present and past participles than does English, which, on the other hand, uses many subjective (or modal) auxiliaries. Compare in this connection the Spanish use of the past participle stressing final result where English uses the present participle stressing "being in progress."

Se hallaba muy desanimado.	*He was very discouraged.*
Andaba preocupado.	*He was (went about) worried.*
Se vieron obligados a retirarse.	*They were forced to retire.*
Me encuentro desganado.	*I'm not hungry.*

NOTE. Past participles may lose most or all of their verb force, becoming pure adjectives (or even nouns) in value, and being construed as a consequence with **ser** (Sec. **17.5**). A true participle always takes **estar,** etc., except to form the passive voice.

EJERCICIO

Cámbiense las frases siguientes según el modelo: **La nieve cubrió el techo.** →
El techo está (se halla, se encuentra, queda) cubierto de nieve.
1. Destruyeron la casa.
2. Ocuparon la ciudad.
3. Excluyeron a los radicales.
4. Suprimieron los periódicos liberales.
5. Cerraron los teatros.

---

134. SUBSTITUTE VERBS

1. The English auxiliary verbs *do, have, be* are used in English in elliptical expressions which omit the principle verb, e.g., *Has he left yet? No, he hasn't; Who knows the answer? I don't.* The verb forms omitted in these examples are *left, know.* Since Spanish lacks, for the most part, this kind of verb auxiliaries, it makes use of other constructions for elliptical expressions: (*a*) by repeating the original verb, (*b*) by omitting the verb and using the personal pronoun followed by an adverb (**sí, no,** etc.) or (*c*) by the propeer form of **ser** with personal pronoun subject.

a. **¿Ha visto Ud. a D. Benito? Sí, le he visto.**	*Have you seen D. Benito?—Yes, I have.*
b. **¿Va Ud. a esperar a Jorge? Yo no.**	*Are you going to wait for George? I'm not (not me).*
c. **¿Quién se ha llevado mi cuaderno?—Yo no he sido.**	*Who has taken away my notebook?—I haven't.*

NOTE. The English query *Do you?* or *Really?* indicating surprise or interest is rendered in Spanish by **¿De veras?** or **¿Ah, sí?**

Contéstense las preguntas según el modelo: **¿Quién ha recibido una carta?— Yo no. (Yo sí)**
1. ¿Quién ha traído un periódico?
2. ¿Quién ha ido a ver el museo?
3. ¿Quién ha gritado?
4. ¿Quién ha estado aquí antes?

---

135. MODAL AUXILIARIES (*CONTINUED*)

1. With **poder** and **deber** either the present or the perfect infinitive may be used, the latter as in English.

He debido hacerlo.	*I should have done it.*
Debe de haberlo hecho.	*He must have done it.*
Hubiera podido hacerlo. ⎫	⎰ *I could have done it.*
Podría (pudiera) haberlo hecho. ⎭	⎱

NOTE. In sentences such as the preceding, **podía** and **debía** may be used instead of the conditional.

2. **Convenir** is frequently used to render the English *should* or *ought* in the sense of *to be to one's advantage.*

Conviene hacerlo ahora.	*It ought to be done now.*
Convendría que Ud. le hablara.	*You ought to talk to him.*

Cámbiense las frases siguientes según el modelo: **Han podido ganarlo.** → **Pueden haberlo ganado. Podría haberlo hecho.** → **Habría podido hacerlo.**
1. Debemos haber estudiado más.
2. Puede haberlo visto.

3. Debieron de pagar la cuenta.
4. Has podido encontrarlo.

Traducción 11B

1. I am reading a very interesting book.
2. The author is very impertinent.
3. Rice is very nourishing.
4. She has a good singing voice.
5. There is running water in all the rooms.
6. We saw the boat sinking and disappearing under the waves.
7. A man riding on horseback came down the street.
8. The box containing fifty pills costs seven dollars and ninety-eight cents.
9. This is a passing fashion.
10. (A) barking dog never bites.
11. We met many women carrying baskets on their heads.
12. The print represents Hernán Cortés burning his ships.
13. As soon as the game is over we will go home.
14. I see you are still very busy.
15. I will go on writing until you are ready.
16. The patient is still confined to bed.
17. We had been waiting for two hours.
18. He has been engaged in politics for ten years.
19. After the necessary preparations had been made, they started the work.
20. I don't feel well.
21. You ought to take (do) some exercise.
22. I should have moved to another house.
23. I could have gone abroad, but I didn't want to.
24. Who (has) said that?
25. Didn't you like the concert? I did.
26. He ought to know what he is doing, but I don't think he does.
27. We must do (fulfill) our duty.
28. When will you find (it) out?
29. Yesterday I wanted to talk to you, but I couldn't find you.

III

Verbos y Modismos

Querer (Sec. **255**) *to will, wish, want, love.*

1. Will you come in?
2. He would not (did not want to) admit it.
3. I tried to save him, but it was too (**ya era**) late.

4. He will surely (**sin duda**) want the performance to continue.
5. Do you really love her?
6. The torments of love are the subject of many poems.
7. This means that I shall not see him again (**más**).
8. He did it without meaning to (unwillingly).
9. (Just) as you wish; it makes no difference to me.

Poder (Sec. **253**) *to be able, can, may; power, might;* **¿Se puede?** *May I come in?;* **no puedo más** *I can't stand it any longer*

1. The power of illusion can blind a man.
2. I cannot (fut.) do it until tomorrow.
3. How can such a thing have occurred?
4. The sick man could not (was unable to) speak.
5. I was looking (*present participle*) for you yesterday, but I could not find you.
6. The situation may change from one moment to another.
7. It may be true as far as (**por lo que**) I know.
8. May I come in? (**¿Se puede?**)
9. This is my opinion, but (it) might very well turn out (**ocurrir**) quite the contrary.
10. His ambition was stronger (**pudo más**) than his love.
11. Let's rest a while, I am all in (I can do no more).
12. I must (**no puedo menos de**) accept his decision.
13. I like it immensely (**a más no poder**).
14. I can't stand (**poder con**) that fellow; he is very boring.

Convenir (Sec. **163**) *to agree to* (**en**), *etc.; (impers.) to suit, befit, be a good thing for one, ought, etc.*

1. I admit (agree) that he meant well (his intention was good).
2. It's a deal! (**¡Convenido!**)
3. If the time does not suit you, set (**señalar**) another.
4. I don't think it would be (is) a good thing for me to accept the position.
5. You had better (**conviene**) go slowly.
6. It would be better if (**convendría más que**) I went with him.

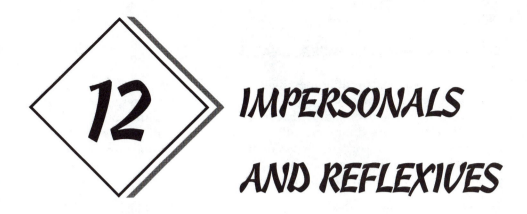

12 IMPERSONALS AND REFLEXIVES

136. THE IMPERSONAL CONSTRUCTION

The term "impersonal" applied to a verb or verb phrase signifies that it is used without a personal subject and, consequently, only in the third person. In English the impersonal construction is formed by using the neuter pronoun *it* to represent a subject which is (*a*) nonexistent, (*b*) unexpressed, or (*c*) postponed. In Spanish no such pronoun is required, since any verb may be used with the subject either unexpressed or postponed. As a result the impersonal construction is much more widely used in Spanish.

a.	**Llueve.**	*It is raining.*
	Amanece.	*It is dawn(ing).*
	Truena.	*It is thundering.*
	Escampa.	*It is clearing up.*
	Hiela.	*It is freezing.*
b.	**No me importa (eso que Ud. dice).**	*It is immaterial to me (what you say).*
	Es lástima.	*It's a pity.*
c.	**Me conviene hacerlo.**	*It's to my advantage to do it.*
	Es preciso que vaya Ud.	*It's necessary that you go.*

137. *HACER* AND *HABER* USED IMPERSONALLY

1. Impersonals with non-existent subjects are used only in the singular. In Spanish the chief members of this group are (*1*) verbs describing natural phenomena (see *a*. above) and (*2*) **hacer** and **haber** used impersonally.

2. **Hacer** is used impersonally (*a*) in expressions of weather and (*b*) in temporal clauses to record the lapse of time during or since an act or state (e.g., **hace tres meses que estudio aquí** *I have been studying here for three months*) (see Secs. **22b; 23.2; 24.2; 32a; 34**).

a. **Hace calor (frío, fresco).**	*It is warm (cold, cool).*
Hace buen (mal) tiempo.	*It is nice (bad) weather.*

EJERCICIO

Pónganse las formas debidas de los verbos siguientes en el presente, el presente progresivo, imperfecto, y pretérito:

nevar, tronar, helar, lloviznar, granizar, amanecer, anochecer, atardecer, oscurecer, esclarecer.

---

3. **Haber,** when not used as an auxiliary to form the compound tenses, is an impersonal verb equivalent to the English *there is, are; there was, were*, etc. It has the special form **hay** only in the present tense.

¿Hay algo de particular?	*Is there anything new?*
Hubo una gritería formidable.	*There was a huge hubbub.*
Ha habido dificultades.	*There have been difficulties.*
Había seis libros en la mesa.	*There were six books on the table.*
¿Hay sandías? Las hay.	*Are there any watermelons? There are.*

4. The demonstrative *there is* (**allí está**) must be differentiated from the impersonal *there is, are* (**hay**). **Hay** etc. stresses mere existence and is always used when the predicate is indefinite. **Estar** stresses actual presence and is always used when the English *there is* is equivalent to *there stands*.

Hay barcos en la bahía.	*There are (some) ships in the bay.*
But: **Allí (en la bahía) están los barcos.**	*There (in the bay) are the ships.*
Abajo hay (or **está**) **un señor que pregunta por Ud.**	*Downstairs there is a gentleman asking for you.*
Estaban dos hombres en el muelle.	*There were two men (standing) on the dock.*

NOTE 1. **He aquí (ahí)** corresponds to the English *here (there) is, here (there) you have, behold:* **he aquí el resultado** *here you have the result.* The personal pronouns, when used, are annexed to **he,** e.g., **helos aquí** *here they are, here you have them.*

NOTE 2. The preterit **hubo** is used when *there was (were)* is the equivalent of **tuvo lugar, ocurrió,** etc.

EJERCICIO

Cámbiense las frases siguientes al pasado:
1. Hay un mitin estrepitoso en la plaza.
2. Hay muchos espectadores.
3. Hay varias razones para su conducta.
4. No hay clase hoy.
5. Hay una gran explosión en el barco.

Háganse preguntas de las frases precedentes y contéstense con los pronombres según el modelo: **¿Hay muchos estudiantes?—Sí, los hay. (¿Había muchos estudiantes?—Sí, los había.)**

---

138. VERBS WITH NON-PERSONAL SUBJECT

Some verbs are used (*a*) exclusively as impersonals, but (*b*) many transitive verbs, especially those denoting thought, feeling, or obligation, are used in a construction with the indirect object referring to the person affected (dative of interest) in cases where the English would use a personal subject. (Compare the archaic English *methinks, melikes*.)

a. **Sucedió que el presidente no pudo asistir.**	*It happened that the president couldn't attend.*
Basta que seas amigo mío.	*It suffices that you're a friend of mine.*

NOTE. The more usual verbs of this type are:

bastar *to suffice, be enough*
convenir *to suit, be to one's advantage*
doler *to grieve, pain*
estar visto *to be obvious, clear*
importar *to matter*
ocurrir *to occur, happen*
pesar *to grieve, to be sorry for*
resultar *to turn out*
suceder *to happen*

Some of these verbs may be used in a personal sense: **María me conviene como esposa** *Mary suits me as a wife*; **el dolor no importa** *pain doesn't matter.*

b. **Me parece que tiene Ud. razón.**	*I think you are right.*
Me gusta leer en la cama.	*I like to read in bed.*
Le extrañó mi comportamiento.	*He was surprised at my conduct. (My conduct surprised him.)*

NOTE. **Ser** is always used to form impersonal phrases (**es lastima, es tarde,** etc.) except in the case of **está bien** (*it's*) *all right.*

EJERCICIO

Pónganse los verbos **gustar, parecer, importar, convenir, extrañar, pesar** en lugar de los verbos subrayados, haciendo los cambios necesarios en el verbo subordinado: p.ej., **Nos gusta que todos presten atención.** → **Importa que todos presten atención,** etc.

1. <u>Parece</u> que todos prestan atención.
2. <u>Me gustaba</u> que tuvieran encerrados a los insurgentes.
3. <u>Le extraña</u> que nadie lo reconozca.
4. ¿<u>Te pesa</u> que nos quedemos aquí?
5. <u>Les importaba</u> que el decano les escuchara.

---

139. SPANISH REFLEXIVE VERBS AS EQUIVALENT TO ENGLISH INTRANSITIVES

1. Reflexive verbs are much more frequent in Spanish than in English. Where English tends to create intransitives out of transitives, Spanish creates reflexives. Hence the Spanish equivalents of many English intransitives are reflexive.

TRANSITIVE		REFLEXIVE	INTRANSITIVE
acercar	*to bring near or nearer*	**acercarse**	*to approach, draw near*
acostar	*to put to bed*	**acostarse**	*to go to bed*
adelantar	*to advance, put ahead*	**adelantarse**	*to advance, go ahead*
alegrar	*to cheer, make glad*	**alegrarse**	*to rejoice, be glad*
casar	*to marry (off)*	**casarse**	*to marry, get married*
despertar	*to wake, rouse*	**despertarse**	*to awaken*
detener	*to stop, arrest*	**detenerse**	*to stop (oneself)*
levantar	*to raise*	**levantarse**	*to rise, get up*

NOTE. The English *become (get, grow)* is often rendered in Spanish by the reflexive: **cansarse** *to become tired,* **enfriarse** *to grow (get) cold* (see Sec. **21**).

2. A few verbs are always used reflexively in Spanish, e.g., **atreverse (a)** *to dare,* **arrepentirse (de)** *to repent,* **desvivirse (por)** *to do one's utmost for,* **dignarse** *to deign,* **jactarse (de)** *to boast,* **quejarse (de)** *to complain,* **preciarse (de)** *to pride oneself.*

140. THE "QUASI-PASSIVE" (SEE SECS. 150, 152)

The English intransitive often approaches a passive in meaning, particularly in general statements. In such cases the Spanish again uses the reflexive.

La nieve se derrite.	*The snow melts (is melting).*
Las puertas se cierran a las once.	*The doors close (are closed) at eleven.*
Se rompió la cuerda.	*The rope broke (is broken).*

EJERCICIO

Cámbiense los verbos siguientes a la forma impersonal con **se:**
1. Rompieron las cuerdas.
2. Abren las tiendas a las nueve y media.
3. Tocan las campanas los días de fiesta.

141. THE IMPERSONAL REFLEXIVE

1. The reflexive construction is further extended in Spanish (*a*) to transitive and intransitive verbs used impersonally, corresponding to the English use of *one, they, we, you (indefinite), people* (*b*) to form impersonal constructions similar to those treated in Sec. **138,** but which indicate a fortuitous occurrence that affects someone. The person affected is the indirect object. (*c*) In general directions or announcements.

a. **¿Se fuma aquí?**	*Can one smoke here?*
Se come bien en este hotel.	*They serve good meals in this hotel.*
Se entra por aquí.	*You go in this way.*
Se hablaba agitadamente.	*They talked in great excitement.*
Se dice que habrá cambios en el gobierno.	*It is said there will be changes in the government.*
Esto no se hace.	*This isn't done.*
b. **Se me figura.**	*I imagine.*
Se me olvidó.	*I forgot.*
Se le ocurrió una idea.	*An idea occurred to him.*
Se le rompió la pluma.	*His pen got broken (on him).*
Se nos acabó el dinero.	*Our money ran out.*
Se nos murió el padre.	*Our father died.*

NOTE. This construction is used to render the English construction of the type (i.e., *to me*) *I was told that* **se me dijo que. . . .**

c. **Escríbase en español.**	*Write in Spanish.*
Se alquila.	*For rent.*
Se compran libros de texto.	*Textbooks bought.*

EJERCICIO

Cámbiense las frases siguientes según el modelo: **Ganan mucho en esa fábrica.**
→ **Se gana mucho en esa fábrica.**
1. Venden autos de ocasión aquí.
2. Entran por la derecha.
3. Pagan bien por la mano de obra.
4. Cantan canciones populares.
5. Trabajan poco durante el verano.

Cámbiense las frases siguientes según el modelo: **El espejo se rompió.** → **Se me (nos, te, le, les) rompió el espejo.**
6. La gasolina se acabó.
7. Un incidente cómico ocurrió.
8. La botella se cayó.
9. El número se olvidó.
10. Los libros quedaron en casa.

Traducción 12A

1. It rains a great deal in this part of the country.
2. Do you think it is going to snow?—I don't think (**parecer**) so.
3. It doesn't make any difference to me what they say.
4. I should like to meet your son-in-law.
5. It seems unbelievable that you should say that.
6. It is so cold in this room that it is impossible to study.
7. Is there (any) news?—No, I think it is too soon.
8. There were many people on the streets.
9. Where is my raincoat?—There it is, on the armchair.
10. There is no need to worry.
11. There were three men in the store.
12. Who is in the dining room?—There isn't anybody.
13. A very queer thing has happened to me.
14. It is strange that he hasn't telephoned me.
15. It would interest me very much to read your essay.
16. It surprised us that he hadn't accepted the offer.
17. Are you getting tired?—Yes, I'll take a bath now and go to bed.
18. I looked out of the window to see the parade.
19. Be careful, don't make a mistake.
20. It's my turn to talk.
21. I didn't dare to give him the news.
22. Don't complain of your luck. It seems to me that you have been very fortunate.
23. This fabric tears (is torn) easily.
24. Water turns (is turned) to steam.
25. This can't be permitted.

26. How (**por dónde**) do you get out of this building?
27. A good idea occurs to me.
28. One travels comfortably in Spain.
29. May I (one) (come in)?
30. Don't forget to send her flowers.
31. Five years ago he did not have a cent.
32. How long have you been living here?
33. Umbrellas repaired.
34. Translate into English.
35. That is not said in Spanish.
36. In one room people were smoking and chatting; in another they were dancing.

II

142. IMPERSONAL VERBS USED WITH PERSONAL SUBJECT

Impersonal verbs describing natural phenomena are sometimes used with the personal subject.

Anochecimos en La Mancha.	*It was nightfall when we entered La Mancha.*
Tronó la artillería.	*The artillery thundered.*

143. IMPERSONAL VERBS (*CONTINUED*)

1. **Haber** is occasionally used impersonally in (*a*) expressions of weather when the phenomenon is observed rather than felt (**hacer**) and (*b*) to express distance.

a. **Hay viento** (observed).
 Hace viento (felt).   } *It is windy.*

 Hay sol (observed).
 Hace sol (felt).   } *It is sunny.*

b. **¿Cuánto hay de aquí a Londres?**   *How far is it from here to London?*

But: **Lisboa está a 10 horas de Madrid por tren.**   *Lisbon is 10 hours from Madrid by train.*

NOTE. **Ha** meaning *ago* as in **mucho tiempo ha** *a long time ago* is an archaism.

2. Personal **haber** is found as an archaic survival in certain set phrases. In the preterit, **haber de** may merely reinforce the preterit meaning.

Su padre, que santa gloria haya . . .	*His father, may his soul rest in peace . . .*
Tendrá que habérselas conmigo.	*He'll have to fight it out with me.*
Hubieron de quedar sorprendidos.	*They were surprised.*

144. CAUSATIVE REFLEXIVES

A few reflexive verbs may have causative meaning. (In the example given, for example, we interpret the meaning of the sentence causatively because people do not normally cut their own hair.)

Voy a cortarme el pelo.	*I am going to have my hair cut.*

145. IMPERSONAL PRONOUNS

Impersonal **uno (una)** has a more colloquial flavor than the English *one.*

No para uno de trabajar.	*One never stops working.*
Una no puede estar en todas partes.	*One can't be everywhere.*

NOTE. The second person (including **usted**) may be used colloquially in the sense of the English impersonal *you* when the speaker wishes to dramatize his story: **Vas por la calle y de pronto se te acerca un individuo y te dice . . .**   *You are (one is) going along the street and suddenly a fellow comes up to you and says to you . . .*

146. IMPERSONAL CONSTRUCTION WITH *THERE*

The English impersonal construction with the anticipatory *there* is rendered in Spanish (*a*) by merely postponing the subject, (*b*) by using **haber** with a noun object, or (*c*) by using the impersonal reflexive construction.

a. **Llegó un momento . . .**	*There came a moment . . .*
b. **Hubo gritos y tiros.**	*There was shouting and firing.*
c. **Por Navidad se come mucho.**	*There is a great deal of eating at Christmas time.*

147. WORD ORDER

Spanish word order is much less fixed than is English word order. Consequently, while in English the vast majority of sentences follow the order Subject–Predicate (Verb–Object), in Spanish the order Predicate–Subject is as frequently found as the reverse order. The choice of order seems to depend upon which element presents new information and is therefore stressed. Thus, **Juan trabajó** puts the emphasis on the verb, while **trabajó Juan** emphasizes the subject. For a simple rule to aid the student in deciding which order to use, one may ask which implied question is being answered by a simple declarative sentence. **Juan trabajó** is the answer to the implied question **¿Qué hizo Juan? Trabajó Juan** corresponds to the question **¿Quién trabajó?** This rule applies best to simple sentences and, of course, is only a rule of thumb, and not a complete analysis of Spanish sentence structure. Factors of sentence stress, formalized order, etc. may complicate matters. The basic idea that new information comes last, however, seems to be a valid one.

In complex sentences, the predominant order is Predicate–Subject in the dependent clause, probably because the subject is usually the new information.

Ayer estábamos en casa, cuando llegó un telegrama urgente.	*Yesterday we were at home, when an urgent telegram arrived.*
Me di cuenta de que había ocurrido algo muy raro.	*I realized that something very strange had happened.*

Traducción 12B

1. I woke up with a headache.
2. It was sunny but very windy.
3. There is moonlight.
4. How far is Montevideo from Buenos Aires?
5. I didn't think it was so near.
6. The door opened and there entered the colonel.
7. I was surprised to see him here.
8. There was complete silence.
9. Is there much snow around here?
10. There will be (a) banquet and (a) dance.
11. There is much talking and little deciding.
12. It is a question of his future.
13. We would like to accept your invitation, but I don't think it will be possible.
14. (It) worried her what you told him.
15. It would be a good thing for you to learn to swim.
16. There is your friend. Shall I tell him to come in?
17. It seems unbelievable that there is no good hotel in this town.
18. The plan doesn't suit me.
19. It seems to me that we are never going to get there.
20. Don't forget to turn the lights out.
21. A great deal of time is lost discussing.
22. And now it turns out that they don't agree.
23. I don't like to have my picture taken.

24. It is hard for me to believe it.
25. One has too many worries.

III

Verbos y Modismos

Haber (Sec. 246) *to be (impersonal), have (in a few set phrases as auxiliary to form compound tenses);* **haber de** *should* (**hube de** *I had to*)

1. There are no stars (out); the sky is very cloudy.
2. Were there many people at (**en**) the dance?
3. When (**al**) the speech was over, there were protests and hisses.
4. There will not be (enough) time for everything.
5. He must have come before.
6. Many thanks!—Don't mention it (**no hay de qué**).
7. What's the news? (**¿Qué hay de nuevo?**)
8. Hi! (**¿Qué hay?**) (informal)
9. We are to sail next week.
10. I don't know why it has to be this way (**así**).
11. We (impersonal) must get up earlier.
12. You should (**habrá que**) hear him!
13. There was no reason (**para qué**) to hide it from (i.e., to) him.
14. How far is it from Havana to Santiago?
15. My grandfather—may he rest in peace (**que santa gloria haya**)—always stopped at (**en**) this inn.
16. He will have to have it out (**habérselas**) with me.

Tener (Sec. 260) *to have, hold, be (when followed by nouns, especially those referring to physical and emotional states, i.e.,* hambre, miedo*);* **tener gracia** *to be funny*

1. He is (you have) the book you were looking for.
2. He was thirsty (hungry, sleepy, cold, warm, afraid).
3. I don't think you are right.
4. I don't know what is the matter withs41me (what I have).
5. How old (**¿Cuántos años**) were you then?
6. I don't feel like (**ganas de**) going out.
7. My feet were (I had) swollen.
8. We must (*impersonal*) have pity on him.
9. We have to return tonight.
10. I had to dismiss the servant for (being) insolent.
11. We have no need (**por qué**) to hide it.
12. I have the letter written.
13. He has told me so many times.

14. The sickness had us quite worried.
15. The joke was not funny (**gracia**).
16. The scene takes place in the Sierra Nevada.
17. Hold the wheel while I light a cigaret. Be careful!

Tema

Escriba Ud. un párrafo de unas ciento cincuenta palabras sobre el artista favorito de Ud. Puede ser artista en cualquier arte, la pintura, la escultura, la arquitectura, la literatura, o la cinematografía. Al escribir, conteste Ud. las preguntas siguientes:

1. ¿Dónde y cuándo vivió este artista?
2. ¿Cuáles son sus obras más importantes y conocidas?
3. ¿Cuáles son las obras que más le agradan a Ud.? ¿Por qué?
4. ¿Cuáles son los rasgos más notables del arte de este artista?
5. ¿Cuáles han sido los rasgos más apreciados por los conocedores del arte?
6. ¿Qué importancia tuvo este artista en la historia de su arte?
7. ¿Qué influencia ha tenido en otros artistas?
8. ¿Quisiera Ud. ser artista?

Escriba Ud. este párrafo en sus propias palabras y utilice por lo menos cinco de los verbos y expresiones de la sección Verbos y Modismos.

THE PASSIVE VOICE AND RELATED CONSTRUCTIONS

13

I

148. THE PASSIVE VOICE ("*SER* PASSIVE")

1. The passive voice always involves action; it is used when the action is viewed from the standpoint, not of the subject acting, but of the object acted upon. In the sentence *the bridge was built by the Romans*, the object of the action (the bridge) becomes the grammatical subject of the verb, while the active subject (the Romans) becomes the agent.

2. The passive voice is formed in Spanish by **ser** with the inflected past participle, which agrees in gender and number with the passive subject. The agent (or instrument) is introduced by **por.**

El puente fue construido por los romanos.	*The bridge was built by the Romans.*
Guernica fue destruida por un bombardeo.	*Guernica was destroyed by a bombing raid.*

NOTE. The "**ser** passive" is almost never found in the present tense, usually being replaced by other constructions (Sec. **150**).

EJERCICIO

Cámbiense las frases siguientes a la voz pasiva con **ser:**
1. Las tropas rebeldes atacaron el cuartel.
2. El presidente alzó la bandera blanca.
3. Los tanques ganaron los objetivos.
4. El ministro nombrará un nuevo embajador.
5. El gobierno censuró la prensa.
6. Los empleados limpiaron la sala.

149. EXPRESSIONS OF RESULTANT CONDITION

1. English, in most cases, fails to distinguish (except by the context) between the passive voice and expressions of resultant condition (Sec. **17.3h**). In Spanish the construction with **estar** (or its substitutes) is to be used to refer to the condition resulting from an action, unless action is clearly performed, in which case the passive voice (or its equivalent) is called for.

El libro está bien escrito.	*The book is well written (resultant condition).*
La ventana estaba cerrada.	*The window was shut (resultant condition).*
La ventana fue cerrada por el viento.	*The window was (blown) shut by the wind (action = The wind shut the window).*

NOTE. The imperfect (**era**) is more frequent in resultant conditions (description), while the preterit (**fue**) is more frequent in the passive and its equivalents (action).

2. In expressions of resultant condition the instrument or agent (with, by) is usually expressed by **de.** The participle may be understood as stressing that the condition described is a natural, expected one, rather than being the result of some fortuitous action.

Las montañas cubiertas de nieve.	*The snow-covered mountains.*
La casa estaba rodeada de árboles.	*The house was surrounded by trees.*

EJERCICIO

Cámbiense las frases siguientes según el modelo: **El libro fue escrito por el autor. → El libro está escrito.**
1. La calle fue iluminada.
2. Las tiendas fueron abiertas a las ocho.

3. La casa fue inundada por el agua del río.
4. El castillo fue rodeado por las tropas.
5. Los documentos fueron firmados.

Cámbiense las frases del ejercicio de Sec. **148** al pasivo con **se,** quitando el agente: p.ej., **La puerta fue cerrada** → **La puerta se cerró.**
Cámbiense las frases siguientes según el modelo: **El vaso se rompió** → **El vaso está roto.**

6. La novela se escribió en inglés.
7. Se cerraron las tiendas.
8. Se murió mi tío.
9. Se suprimió el periódico.
10. Se prohibió toda manifestación pública.

---

150. SPANISH EQUIVALENTS OF THE ENGLISH PASSIVE

1. The passive voice is used much less in Spanish than in English. Even in cases where the agent is expressed, the active voice is often retained, especially when the passive subject is a pronoun. In such cases, the grammatical subject follows the verb.

Le detuvo un guardia.	*He was arrested by a policeman.*

2. In English the passive voice is widely used, not only to express resultant condition but also action performed by an unnamed agent. This latter construction—the "impersonal construction" (see Sec. **141**)—is rendered in Spanish (*a*) by the reflexive (with the passive subject usually following the verb), especially if the subject is a thing, or (*b*) by the impersonal use of the third person plural of the active voice, especially if the passive subject is a living being. This latter construction (*c*) lays more stress on the action than does the more indefinite construction with the reflexive.

a.	**Se prohibe fumar.**	*No smoking (smoking is forbidden).*
	Se sospechaba algo pero no se decía nada.	*Something was suspected but nothing was said.*
	Se suspendió la función.	*The performance was called off.*
	Se construyó la casa el año pasado.	*The house was built last year.*
	Las oficinas se abren a las nueve.	*The offices are opened at nine. (The offices open at nine.)*

NOTE. The reflexive construction is especially frequent with the present tense, and in announcements and general statements. (See Secs. **140, 141.**)

b.	**Detuvieron al criminal.**	*The criminal was arrested.*
	Nombraron alcalde al señor Montes.	*Mr. Montes was appointed mayor.*

NOTE. This construction is used more frequently in Spanish than the indefinite *they* in English: **me han dicho que se marcha usted** *I've been told you are leaving.*

c. **Cerraron la ventana.**	*The window was shut. (Somebody shut the window.)*
Se cerró la ventana.	*The window was shut. (Mere statement of a fact).*

NOTE. When the passive subject is a living being, the straight reflexive construction is not used to render the English passive because it might be confused with the literal reflexive meaning. *The horses were killed* would not be **se mataron los caballos** since this would mean *the horses killed themselves.* In order to give an equivalent of the English passive, the third person plural must be used: **mataron los caballos.**

EJERCICIO

Cámbiense de la voz pasiva con **ser** a la voz pasiva con **se,** p.ej., **El libro fue escrito → El libro se escribió.**
1. El palacio fue destruido.
2. Las comidas fueron preparadas.
3. El grupo fue organizado.
4. Los manuscritos fueron vendidos.
5. Las cartas fueron mandadas.
6. Las lecciones fueron entregadas.

Cámbiense las frases precedentes a la tercera persona del plural según el modelo: **El espejo fue roto. → Se rompió el espejo. → Rompieron el espejo.**

---

151. SUMMARY

The following summary may be helpful in determining the more usual Spanish equivalents of the English passive:

A. Resultant Condition: result of action = **estar** + past participle.
B. True Passive: action performed with agent expressed or clearly implied = **ser** + past participle (passive voice).
C. "Impersonal construction": action performed but agent unnamed =
    1) reflexive with **se,** especially in general statements of fact and if the subject is a thing.
    2) third person plural active voice, especially if action is stressed, and passive subject is a living being.

Traducción 13A

1. We were arrested, but when we showed our passports, we were set free.
2. The town was destroyed by an earthquake.
3. These books are not well bound.
4. When he was a student, he was appointed president of the committee.
5. Spanish is spoken here.
6. The newspaper was suppressed by the government.
7. The streets were crowded and traffic (was) stopped.
8. All the furniture has been sold.
9. The ceremony has been postponed until tomorrow.
10. The damages are estimated at (in) a million (of) pesetas.
11. The house was very well built.
12. The travelers were robbed last night.
13. My friend the major was promoted yesterday.
14. At what time does the bank close?—It closes at three.
15. The decision was made public.
16. In England tea is served every afternoon at five o'clock.
17. Eight bulls were killed at the bullfight.
18. An agreement was arrived at after a short discussion.
19. We are told that (the) tickets can be exchanged here.
20. The road was full of mud.
21. Energetic measures will be taken.
22. Foreign money is not accepted.
23. He was convinced by his friends.
24. Classes will be resumed after New Year's.
25. The mystery has been cleared up.
26. The mystery is cleared up.
27. The famous scientist was surrounded by his friends (condition).
28. The famous scientist was surrounded by his friends (action).

II

152. THE REFLEXIVE PASSIVE ("*SE* PASSIVE")

The Spanish use of the reflexive as equivalent to the English passive is fundamentally the same construction as the use of the reflexive as equivalent to the English intransitive (see Secs. **139–141**). In both cases the English omits entirely the unnamed element (the object, or the agent) whereas in Spanish the reflexive construction achieves grammatical completeness without adding the unnamed element. The pronoun object **se** makes up, in a purely grammatical sense, for the absence of an active subject (i.e., passive agent). This fact accounts (*a*) for the post-position of the grammatical subject which is the logical object of the action, and (*b*) for the cases in which **se** has become the equivalent of an indefinite subject pronoun similar to the English *one, you, we, they, people* (see Sec. **141**).

a. **Aquí se venden flores.**	*Flowers are sold here.*
Se levantó la sesión a las nueve de la noche.	*The meeting (was) adjourned at nine p.m.*

NOTE. In the true reflexive and the "quasi-passive" (Sec. **140**) the grammatical subject normally precedes: **Concha se está peinando** *Concha is combing her hair;* **esta tinta no se borra fácilmente** *this ink is not easily erased.* But in the impersonal passive, where the action is more prominent than the unnamed actor, the verb normally precedes.

b. **Se estaba muy bien junto al fuego.**	*It (one) was very comfortable by the fire.*
Cuando se es buena persona, no se es mal ciudadano.	*When one is a good person, one is not a bad citizen.*

NOTE. A similar use of **se** is seen in the type **se fusiló al espía** *the spy was shot* (Sec. **153.4**).

153. SPECIAL VARIATIONS IN THE USE OF THE PASSIVE VOICE AND RELATED CONSTRUCTIONS

1. **De** occasionally introduces the agent when an emotional attitude (of love, hate, respect, etc.) rather than specific action is stressed.

Es respetado (de parte) de amigos y enemigos.	*He is respected by friends and enemies.*
Fueron bien recibidos de todos.	*They were well (courteously) received by everybody.*

EJERCICIO

Cámbiense las frases siguientes a la voz pasiva con **ser:**
1. Todos estiman mucho a los que buscan la paz.
2. Sus amigos le aman.
3. Los soldados respetaban a la mujer del coronel.
4. Las mujeres admiran al actor famoso.
5. Los jornaleros odian a los terratenientes.

---

2. The passive voice is sometimes avoided in Spanish even when the agent is expressed, since the effect of the passive (that of stressing the object acted upon) can be obtained with the active voice by placing the object before

the verb (Sec. **150.1**). When a noun object precedes, the proper object pronoun must also be used (Sec. **48a**).

La finca la compró mi padre.	*The estate (farm) was bought by my father.*

NOTE. The Spanish change in word order obtains the same result (and the same order of ideas) as the English change in construction.

3. The passive voice is frequently used in past tenses (especially in the present perfect) when the agent is not expressed, but clearly implied.

El baile ha sido suspendido.	*The dance has been called off (i.e., by the persons in charge).*
El conferenciante fue muy aplaudido.	*The lecturer was much applauded (i.e., by the audience).*

4. When the passive subject is a living being, the impersonal reflexive—always with the singular verb—may be used with the personal **a**. But in these cases the third person plural is a more graphic and colloquial alternative.

Se fusiló al espía.	*The spy was shot (summary statement of fact).*
Fusilaron al espía.	*The spy was shot (graphic presentation of an act).*
Se nombró alcalde al señor Montes.	*Mr. Montes was appointed mayor (more formal).*
Nombraron alcalde al señor Montes.	*Mr. Montes was appointed mayor (more colloquial).*

EJERCICIO

Cámbiense las frases siguientes según el modelo: **Fusilaron al espía.** → **Se fusiló al espía.** → **Se le fusiló.**
1. Detuvieron a muchos estudiantes.
2. Libertaron al prisionero.
3. Esperaban a la señora.
4. Eligieron presidente al señor González.
5. Recibieron con entusiasmo a los astronautas.

---

5. The third person plural has a greater indefinite value in Spanish than in English. It is sometimes used when only one person is involved.

Llaman a la puerta. Abren y entra un desconocido.	*There is a knock at the door. It is opened and a stranger enters.*

EJERCICIO

Cámbiense las frases siguientes según el modelo: **Alguien llamaba a la puerta.**
→ **Llamaban a la puerta.**
1. Alguien ha preguntado por Ud.
2. Alguien empezó a tirar piedras al ministro.
3. Alguien abrió las puertas.
4. Alguien rompió el paraguas.
5. Alguien iba cantando por la calle.

6. Spanish uses the resultant condition (with **resultar, salir, quedar,** etc.) to render the English passive in the sense of *turn out.*

> **El caballo resultó muerto, pero el jinete salió ileso.**
> *The horse was killed but the rider was unhurt.*

7. The agent is occasionally added to the reflexive passive, thus resulting in a combined **se** and **ser** passive construction.

> **Los rumores se desmintieron ayer por el gobernador.**
> *The rumors were denied yesterday by the governor.*

8. In addition to the guiding principles stated in Sec. **151**, the attitude of the speaker is an important factor in determining the choice between the various possibilities of rendering the English passive. Thus, in the example *the tourists were entertained* the statement may be presented in relation to (*a*) the tourists, (*b*) the entertainers, or (*c*) objectively and impersonally.

> *a.* **Los turistas fueron agasajados.**
> *b.* **Agasajaron a los turistas.**
> *c.* **Se agasajó a los turistas.**

154. THE PASSIVE INFINITIVE

The same distinctions apply to the passive infinitive as to the passive voice in general. It is used only (*a*) when the active or reflexive form cannot be employed. The English passive infinitive is usually rendered (*b*) by a noun clause with the indefinite third person plural, (*c*) by the active infinitive, (*d*) by **de** + the active infinitive after **ser** used impersonally (Sec. **19.3**), and (*e*) by **hay que** (Sec. **127c**).

> *a.* **Más vale ser temido que ser querido.**
> *It is better to be feared than to be loved.*

b. **No quiero que me molesten.**	*I don't want to be bothered.*
c. **Hizo derribar la tapia.**	*He had the wall torn down.*
No es para leerlo en un día.	*It cannot be read in a day.*
d. **Es de creer que el pueblo prefiere un gobierno democrático.**	*It is to be believed that the people prefer a democratic government.*
Una nueva crisis gubernamental es de temer.	*A new government crisis is to be feared.*
Sus acciones son de condenar.	*His actions are to be condemned.*
e. **Hay que enfrentarse con la verdad.**	*The truth must be faced.*

NOTE 1. In certain set phrases with **para** the past participle alone is occasionally used: **no es para dicho en público** *it is not* (a thing to be) *said in public.*

NOTE 2. The English passive infinitive indicating action to be performed in the future is occasionally rendered in Spanish by the active infinitive: **las deudas a extinguir** *the debts to be liquidated.* **Por** in this construction (Sec. **109.3c**) would have the value of *still to be, yet to be.*

EJERCICIO

Cámbiense las frases siguientes según el modelo: **Se construyó una casa nueva.** → **Mandaron construir una casa nueva; Juan construyó una casa.** → **Juan hizo (mandó) construir una casa.**

1. Se terminó el trabajo.
2. Se vendió la colección de arte moderno.
3. Se despidió a los trabajadores.
4. Se suspendió el vuelo a la Habana.
5. Se anunció el nuevo consejo de ministros.

Cámbiense las frases siguientes según el modelo: **Se teme que la paz no pueda durar mucho.** → **Es de temer que la paz no pueda durar mucho.**

6. Se cree que todavía hay esperanza.
7. Se esperaba que los enemigos llegaran a un acuerdo.
8. Se oía la melodía que hacían los pajarillos.
9. No se olvidaba que la guerra era una tragedia.
10. Se nota que no permiten conducta escandalosa en España.

Traducción 13B

1. The watch was given to me by my uncle.
2. He will be given a banquet by his friends.
3. Samples will be sent on request.
4. The tennis court was rarely used.
5. Houses are being built along the road.
6. Free delivery.
7. The firemen were decorated before a numerous public.

8. We were overtaken by a motorcycle.
9. The enterprise is being financed by several bankers.
10. Constitutional guarantees have been suspended and martial law declared.
11. One cannot believe everything that is said.
12. People dine very late in Spain.
13. The governor is expected tonight.
14. He is accused of embezzlement.
15. I was received with (the) open arms.
16. We were not allowed to smoke.
17. You never hear him around the house.
18. His conduct is to be respected and admired.
19. His conduct is respected and admired by everybody.
20. What I am telling you is not to be repeated.
21. His orders are to be obeyed by all persons surrounding him.
22. Several appointments will be announced tomorrow.
23. We weren't at all bothered by the customs officials.
24. The astronauts were enthusiastically received.
25. They had the collection sold.
26. He is to be feared when he gets angry.
27. This play is rather to be read than to be performed.
28. Somebody was playing the piano in the next house.
29. It is preferable to suffer injustice rather than to be unjust.

III

Verbos y Modismos

Ser (Sec. **259**) *to be* (essentially) and **estar** (Sec. **245**) *to be (located, look, act, feel)*. Review of Chapter 2.

1. The scene is (takes place) in Madrid.
2. What has become (been) of your brother? (Sec. **21f** Note)
3. It would be desirable (**de desear**) that they (should) come to an agreement.
4. The joke was your brother-in-law's idea (**cosa**).
5. It was not (anything) to be taken (**tomarlo**) seriously.
6. It is not impossible, but it is rather difficult to do it.
7. The furniture in (of) the living room was (of) mahogany.
8. The house was painted (**de**) yellow.
9. They are very good friends; they are always together.
10. He is very cultured; he is well informed about literary matters.

Estar and **andar** (Sec. **133**) *to walk, go around, go* (especially of mechanisms), *be* (moving about doing something). (Note that in sentences 1–8 **andar** may be used as a more graphic substitute for **estar**.)

1. How's everything (are we)?
2. I am not in very good health (**bien de salud**).
3. He is very much worried about (**por**) business.
4. He is (engaged in) writing a book.
5. I don't like to be always traveling (**de viaje**).
6. These days we are having (**de**) examinations.
7. What is your friend doing now?—He has a job (**está de**) as steward on a boat.
8. I am wild; I have no (am without) money and I don't know what to do.
9. People are (going around) saying you are going to resign.
10. Why are you going around with such a serious look (face)?
11. He liked to walk about the streets at night.
12. How is the affair going?
13. Is your watch going? Mine has stopped.
14. This clock is slow (fast).
15. We must (*impers.*) go very carefully.
16. Go (on)! I can't believe it.
17. Come (on), tell me now.
18. Let's get down to business (**vamos al asunto, al grano**), don't beat about the bush (**andarse por las ramas, con rodeos**).

THE ARTICLE

155. FORMS OF THE ARTICLE

1. See Secs. **1, 9, 10.**
2. The feminine singular has the special forms **el** and **un** before feminine nouns (not adjectives) beginning with a stressed **a** or **ha.** The plural forms are regular.

el agua	*(the) water*	**las aguas**	*(the) waters*
el hacha	*(the) axe*	**las hachas**	*(the) axes*
un águila	*an eagle*	**unas águilas**	*(some) eagles*

But: **la alta cima** *the high peak*

EXCEPTIONS: **a** *the (letter) a,* **la hache** *the h,* **La Haya** The Hague.

156. CONTRACTION OF THE DEFINITE ARTICLE

1. See Sec. **3.**
2. **El** does not contract with **a** and **de** when the definite article forms part of a name of a place or the title of literary and artistic works, and commercial establishments and brands.

La finca de "El Encinar" pasó del padre al hijo.	*The estate of "El Encinar" passed from father to son.*
Fueron a El Escorial.	*They went to the Escorial.*

157. USES OF THE DEFINITE ARTICLE

1. The definite article is used more frequently in Spanish than in English. For the most important uses, see Secs. **7, 73.** The definite article is also used—in contrast to English: (*a*) with the names of all rivers and mountains (these are invariably masculine), (*b*) with the names of certain countries and cities, forming, especially in the case of certain cities, an integral part of the name, (*c*) in apposition with personal pronouns, expressed or implied, (*d*) with nouns of weight and measure, (*e*) in equivalents of set adverbial phrases in English.

a.	**los Alpes**	*the Alps*
	El Guadalquivir	*the Guadalquivir*
	el Guadarrama	*the Guadarrama (Mountains)*
	el Misisipí	*the Mississippi*
	los Pirineos	*the Pyrenees*
b.	**la Argentina**	*Argentina*
	el Brasil	*Brazil*
	el Canadá	*Canada*
	la Florida	*Florida*
	la Habana	*Havana*
	el Japón	*Japan*
	el Paraguay	*Paraguay*
	el Perú	*Peru*
	el Uruguay	*Uruguay*
		(see Appendix, Sec. **273**)
c.	**(Nosotros) los españoles preferimos un desayuno ligero.**	*We Spaniards prefer a light breakfast.*

NOTE. In such cases the pronoun may be omitted: **A los hombres no nos gusta ir de compras** *We men do not like to go shopping.*

d.	**Estas naranjas se venden a treinta pesos la docena.**	*These oranges sell for thirty pesos a (the) dozen.*
	Le costó la tela noventa pesos el metro.	*The fabric cost her ninety pesos a meter.*
e.	**ir a la escuela (la iglesia, la cama, la cárcel)**	*to go to school (church, bed, jail)*
	a las mil maravillas	*wonderfully, perfectly*

2. In contrast to the English usage the article is omitted in Spanish before the numerical designations of rulers and popes.

Isabel Segunda *Elizabeth the Second,* **Juan Carlos Primero** *John Charles the First,* **Juan Veintitrés** *John the Twenty-Third.*

EJERCICIO

Póngase el artículo definido en los espacios donde sea necesario:

1. Vamos a aprender _____ portugués.
2. El pan se vende a veinte pesos _____ kilo.
3. El año pasado cruzamos _____ Andes cuando fuimos de _____ Chile a _____ Argentina.
4. A _____ hispanos les encanta hablar por hablar.
5. _____ Montevideo, _____ Cairo y _____ Nueva York son ciudades pintorescas.
6. Muchos cubanos que han venido de _____ Habana, ahora viven en ____ Miami en _____ Florida.
7. Alfonso _____ Trece fue un rey de España.
8. _____ Canadá y _____ Haití son países de _____ habla francesa.
9. (Vosotros) _____ norteamericanos os preocupáis demasiado por la salud.
10. _____ Perú y _____ Ecuador reclaman el mismo territorio.
11. _____ plátanos cuestan treinta pesos _____ docena.
12. _____ democracia es un ideal en muchos países.
13. _____ domingos vamos a _____ iglesia.
14. Don Quijote y Sancho Panza son símbolos de _____ humanidad.
15. _____ pasearse es un placer.
16. ¿Vas a ponerte _____ corbata?
17. _____señorita Martínez tiene _____ ojos negros y _____ pelo castaño.
18. _____ general Díaz fue jefe de estado.
19. _____ hambre es la mejor salsa.

---

158. THE INDEFINITE ARTICLE AND ITS EQUIVALENTS (SEC. 9)

1. **Uno** always retains (*a*) some of its basic numerical value (*one*). As a consequence, it is used much less frequently than the English indefinite article, which is (*b*) usually translated in Spanish by the omission of the article, or (*c*) occasionally by the definite article. English speakers have to make a special effort not to use the indefinite article except where it is required.

a. **Tiene un hoyuelo en la barbilla.**	*She has a (i.e., one) dimple in her chin.*
b. **Llevaba bastón y sombrero.**	*He was carrying a cane and a hat.* (**Un bastón** *would mean* one cane).
¿Tiene Ud. fósforos?	*Have you a match? (i.e., any matches?)*
Salió sin abrigo.	*He left without an overcoat.*

NOTE. The omission of the article after prepositions is especially frequent.

    c. **Tengo la garganta mala.**   *I have a* (i.e., my) *sore throat*

NOTE. A similar use of the definite article occurs in the type: **tiene el pelo negro y los ojos azules** *she has black hair and blue eyes.*

    2. **Uno**—as a consequence of the preceding—is normally not used with the indefinites **otro** *another,* **cierto** *a certain,* **tal** *such a,* and **semejante** *such a* (see Sec. **205.3**).

    Déme otra taza de café, haga el   *Give me another cup of coffee, please.*
      favor.
    En cierto pueblo de Aragón . . .   *In a certain town of Aragon . . .*

NOTE. In spite of its numerical value, **uno** is not used with **ciento** *one hundred* or **mil** *one thousand* (see Sec. **207.1 d, e**).

EJERCICIO

Póngase el artículo indefinido en los espacios donde sea necesario:
1. Mi tío es _____ ingeniero.
2. Entró jadeante sin _____ sombrero ni _____ chaqueta.
3. Linares es _____ ciudad.
4. Ayer nos encontramos con _____ cierto señor Zubizarreta que es _____ catedrático.
5. ¿Tiene Ud. _____ cigarrillos?
6. Bilbao es _____ ciudad industrial.
7. Nos contó algo de _____ otro profesor, _____ buen amigo suyo.
8. Nunca había oído _____ tal cosa en la vida.
9. El primer ministro es _____ católico democrático.
10. Más de _____ mil turistas fueron a la fiesta.
11. No tengo _____ enemigos.
12. El cantante tenía _____ cicatriz en la cara.
13. La criada era _____ andaluza muy joven.
14. La señorita llegó en _____ taxi.

Traducción 14A

    1. Hunger is a bad adviser.
    2. García Gutiérrez is the author of *El Trovador.*
    3. You Americans are not as fond of talking as we are.
    4. His oldest son enters college next fall.
    5. This store sells wholesale.
    6. We always pay cash.

7. Pope Clement VII and King Henry VIII were contemporaries.
8. Don't go out without an umbrella.
9. I don't have a pen.
10. She had a headache.
11. He doesn't have a telephone in his house.
12. I have very cold hands.
13. They have bought a country house in Florida.
14. We don't have a fireplace in our apartment.
15. Miss Helen went to church and then home.
16. Painting is one of the fine arts.
17. Fish is more expensive than meat.
18. There are some mines in Andalusia which produce silver, copper, and mercury.
19. Uruguay and Paraguay are on the same continent as Peru.
20. The Andes separate Chile from Argentina.
21. The Amazon is larger than the Plate.
22. Don Miguel is Dr. Gutiérrez's uncle. He is a Catholic and a Republican.
23. This food hasn't any salt.
24. We wanted to rent the house, but it doesn't have a garage.
25. A certain day, when I was in the country . . .
26. The dog has long legs and a short tail.
27. Green fruit is not good to eat.
28. Gold weighs more than iron.
29. Girls like to study more than boys.
30. What language is he speaking, Catalan or Portuguese?
31. Do you like Spanish bread?
32. Open your mouth and close your eyes.
33. He forgot (left forgotten) his briefcase.
34. Bring your notebooks to class.
35. Take your overcoat with you.
36. Mrs. Gómez's purse was stolen.
37. Our patience was exhausted.
38. Have (take) another cigar.
39. Have you ever seen such a blockhead?
40. Such ignorance left us amazed.
41. Veal sells at sixty pesos the half kilo.

II

159. OTHER USES OF THE DEFINITE ARTICLE

The definite article is also used (*a*) with proper and geographical names modified by an adjective, (*b*) in referring to feminine celebrities, and with the given names of women, in popular and colloquial style, and (*c*) with infinitives (in a general sense) and noun clauses (Sec. **107**).

a. **La España democrática** *democratic Spain,* **el Reino Unido** *the United Kingdom,* **la Rusia Soviética** *Soviet Russia,* **el amigo Manso** *(our) friend Manso,* **la pobre Rita** *poor Rita.*

b. **La Pardo Bazan** *(Mrs.) Pardo Bazan,* **la Mistral** *(Ms.) Mistral,* **la Pepa** *Jo.*

c. **El casarse es algo serio.** *Getting married is something serious.*

160. OMISSION OF THE ARTICLE (*CONTINUED*)

In general, the omission of the article gives to the expression the effect of a single concept, which in many cases acquires a generic and rhetorical value.

Perdió casa, fortuna y familia en aquel desastre.	*He lost his home, his fortune, and his family (everything) in that disaster.*
Casa y cortijo pertenecían a D. Juan.	*The house and the farm (together) belonged to Don Juan.*
Perro que ladra no muerde.	*A barking dog doesn't bite.*
Con paciencia de bestia sumisa.	*With the patience of a long-suffering beast.*

EJERCICIO

Póngase el artículo definido en los espacios donde sea necesario:

1. Hay mucha industria en _____ Italia septentrional.
2. Se enfermó _____ pobre Carlos.
3. _____ año pasado estudiamos _____ Europa medieval.
4. _____ Matute y otros novelistas han contribuido a _____ literatura española contemporánea.
5. Raquel leyó algo de la historia de _____ México.
6. Muchos oficiales criollos participaron en la liberación de _____ América.
7. No podemos olvidar la importancia de _____ China comunista.
8. A _____ buen entendedor, pocas palabras.

---

161. OTHER USES OF THE INDEFINITE ARTICLE

1. When a predicate noun denoting a social, political, religious, or occupational group is used (*a*) without the indefinite article (Sec. **9**), the predicate noun functions as an adjective denoting a general class, such as **rico, pobre, joven, viejo.** (Actually, the large majority of such predicate nouns [e.g., **español, médico, militar, católico, socialista**—including all nouns ending in **-ista**] are originally adjectives.) But when such a predicate noun is used (*b*) with the indefinite article, some numerical value is present (i.e., **un, una** are understood to mean *one*) and the predicate functions as a noun.

a. **Es rico.**	*He is (a) rich (man).*
Es cobarde.	*He is cowardly (a coward).*
Es médico.	*He is a doctor.*
Es artista.	*He is an artist (by profession).*
b. **Es un artista.**	*He is an artist (by temperament).*
Es un cobarde.	*He is a (real) coward.*

NOTE. Special emphasis is given by the use of the indefinite article in these examples.

2. The same principles hold true when the predicate noun has adjectival modifiers. If the predicate as a whole forms a general class concept, (*a*) the indefinite article is omitted. If the adjectival modifier serves to distinguish the noun from others of its class, (*b*) the indefinite article is employed.

a. **Es buen sastre.**	*He is a good tailor (differentiation is not stressed).*
Es mala persona.	*He is a bad sort (actually the equivalent of* **es malo.***)*
Es médico de fama.	*He is a well-known doctor (general group).*
b. **Es un sastre muy bueno.**	*He is a very good tailor (differentiated from others).*
Es un chileno que conocí en San Luis.	*He is a Chilean I met in St. Louis.*

NOTE. Augmentative and diminutive suffixes function as adjectival modifiers with differentiating force: **es un pintorzuelo** *he is an (inferior) painter.*

3. When **uno** is used with **cierto** and **tal,** they become more specific in value.

Cierto hombre.	*A certain (indefinite) man.*
Un cierto sabor.	*A special flavor.*
Tal cosa.	*Such a thing.*
Un tal Gómez.	*A certain Gómez.*

EJERCICIO

Póngase el artículo indefinido donde sea necesario en los espacios:
1. Mi primo era _____ novelista, pero no era _____ novelista muy conocido.
2. Es _____ buen profesor, a pesar de sus defectos.
3. Antonio Goicoechea es _____ vasco que vive en Guernica.
4. Me dijo que era _____ valiente.
5. No puedes admitir que es _____ poeta (by profession).

162. EMPHATIC USES OF *UNO*

Uno is used in exclamatory and elliptical expressions with the force of the English *such* (colloquially *some*).

¡Había una (enormidad) de gente!	*There was such a crowd! ("some" crowd!)*
¡Tiene unos ojos! (más bonitos)	*She has such eyes!*

163. USE OF THE ARTICLE IN APPOSITIONAL PHRASES

(*a*) The definite article is used when the appositional or parenthetical phrase supplies information regarded as already familiar to the listener; (*b*) the indefinite article is omitted when the parenthetical fact is regarded as necessary to identify the noun; (*c*) the indefinite article is used only when the parenthetical information is stressed.

a.	**Platón, el filósofo griego**	*Plato, the Greek philosopher (well-known fact)*
b.	**Francisco Suárez, teólogo jesuita**	*Francisco Suárez, a Jesuit theologian (unstressed identification)*
c.	**Humberto Eco, un estudioso italiano**	*Humberto Eco, an Italian scholar (stressed identification)*

164. FURTHER USES OF THE NEUTER ARTICLE

(See Sec. **10, 78, 126.**) The neuter article **lo** is used (*a*) with adverbs in expressions of sufficiency and possibility, (*b*) with adverbs and adjectives to form prepositional phrases, and (*c*) with **de** in prepositional phrases (see Sec. **78**).

a.	**lo antes (mas pronto) posible**	*as soon as possible*
	lo bastante para vivir	*enough to live (on)*
b.	**a lo lejos**	*in the distance*
	a lo largo de la costa	*along the coast*
	a lo gitano	*in gypsy style*

NOTE. This latter construction can be extended to nouns used adjectivally: **a lo siglo dieciocho** *in the eighteenth century style (spirit)*, **a lo Napoleón** *Napoleonic (in spirit)*. Contrast with the more specific **a la (manera) española** *in the Spanish fashion*: **Chocolate a la española** *(made according to the Spanish recipe)*.

Traducción 14B

1. Southern Spain produces wheat, grapes, and olives.
2. (Miss) Streep, (Miss) Close, and other movie actresses were staying in that hotel.
3. Typewriting tires me a great deal.
4. His cousin Elizabeth is a piano teacher.
5. My roommate is a (real) artist.
6. He is a brave (man).
7. He was a good father and a good citizen.
8. He is a bad carpenter.
9. She is a woman of great influence.
10. This girl is silly.
11. A certain Don Raimundo has been here to see you.
12. He says such things!
13. There was "some" shooting!
14. Darío, the famous Nicaraguan poet, died in poverty.
15. Havana, the capital of Cuba, has a magnificent harbor.
16. We arrived at Marbella, a town near Málaga.
17. Mrs. Soler, a councilwoman, invited us to dinner.
18. We live here in student fashion.
19. Do you like rice Valencian style?
20. First of all let us have breakfast and then we'll talk.
21. She was talking in a low voice.
22. He is fifty years old at the utmost.
23. Evidently we will have to stay here.
24. I have "some" appetite!
25. The master and the servant sat at the same table.
26. I do not know her (well) enough to invite her.
27. He wrote the letter as (the) best he could.
28. He replied with the haughtiness of an old aristocrat.

III

Verbos y Modismos

Quedar *to remain, be (have) left, turn out, fit, become, etc.:* **quedar en** *to agree to;* **quedar bien (mal)** *to do well (badly);* **quedarse** *to stay, be (stressing result with participles and adjectival phrases);* **quedarse con** *to keep (retain),* **quedarse sin** *to lose.*

1. Most of the guests had gone; only a few intimate friends were left.
2. Whatever is left will be for the poor.
3. He has nothing left (is left to him) of his immense fortune.
4. (There) remain a few details to (**por**) be finished.

5. Will you be much longer (have much left)?—No, I (will) finish right away.
6. We have "gotten in wrong" with (**quedar mal con**) those gentlemen.
7. He passed (**quedar bien en**) the examination.
8. They became (result) great friends.
9. How (**¿en qué?**) did (has) the argument turn out?
10. We agreed to meet (**vernos**) on the following day.
11. He went off to Arequipa and we stayed in Lima.
12. Why don't you stay a few (**unos**) days with us?
13. Walk a little faster; don't lag (stay) behind.
14. I was astonished.
15. They remained silent.
16. Clean it with this and it will be like new.
17. He became blind.
18. Do you like it? Then keep it.
19. If you lend him a book he (will) keep it.
20. He lost his voice (became voiceless).
21. Sincerely yours (**Quedo suyo afectísimo**).

Seguir (Secs. **228, 229**) *to follow, continue, keep on (followed by the present participle), be still (in an act or state).*

1. We will follow the course of the river.
2. Let's keep on going (**adelante**).
3. Continue reading.
4. We (impersonal with **se**) can't keep on this way.
5. We are still without news of him (his).
6. He is still as amusing as ever.
7. The strike is still (on).
8. He still has (**sigue con**) his cough.

Tema

Escriba Ud. un párrafo de unas ciento setenta y cinco palabras sobre la ciudad favorita de Ud. Conteste las preguntas siguientes:

1. ¿Dónde se halla esta ciudad?
2. ¿Cómo es la región en que se halla?
3. Describa Ud. lo más notable de su apariencia física, su historia, etc.
4. ¿Cómo son los habitantes?
5. ¿Tiene esta ciudad alguna importancia histórica?
6. ¿Qué es lo que más le gusta de esta ciudad?
7. ¿Viviría Ud. allí si pudiera o sólo le gusta para visitar?
8. ¿Qué debe tener una ciudad para que sea un buen lugar para vivir?

Escriba Ud. este párrafo en sus propias palabras y utilice por lo menos cinco de los verbos y expresiones de la sección Verbos y Modismos.

NOUNS

I

165. GENDER OF NOUNS

1. See Sec. **2.**
2. Nouns of Greek origin ending in **-a** (usually **-ma**) are masculine (for longer list, see Sec. **274**).

el poema	*poem*	**el tema**	*theme*
el drama	*drama*	**el telegrama**	*telegram*
el mapa	*map*	**el panorama**	*panorama*

NOTE. Nouns ending in **-ista** are masculine or feminine according to their meaning: **el (la) novelista, el (la) violinista.**

3. Nouns ending in **-ad, -ud, -ie, -ción (-sión),** and **-umbre** are feminine. Such nouns are usually abstract or collective in meaning.

la ciudad	*city*	**la especie**	*species, kind*
la libertad	*liberty*	**la nación**	*nation*
la juventud	*youth*	**la muchedumbre**	*multitude*

4. Many nouns denoting male beings have a corresponding feminine form in **-a.** (See, however, Sec. **2.3.**)

el tío	*uncle*	**la tía**	*aunt*
el abogado	*lawyer*	**la abogada**	*lawyer*
el general	*general*	**la generala**	*general's wife*

Certain nouns vary in meaning according to whether they are masculine or feminine.

el cura	*priest*	**la cura**	*cure*
el capital	*capital (money)*	**la capital**	*capital (city)*
el orden	*order (arrangement)*	**la orden**	*order (command, rule)*

NOTE. **Arte** is masculine in the singular and feminine in the plural: **el arte moderno** *modern art*, **las bellas artes** *the fine arts*. **Mar** may be either masculine or feminine. **El mar** usually is more concrete, simply designating the sea, while **la mar** is more poetic and may be used figuratively, e.g., **la mar de gente** *crowd of people*. The feminine of many nouns must be learned by use.

el actor	*actor*	**la actriz**	*actress*
el conde	*count*	**la condesa**	*countess*
el emperador	*emperor*	**la emperatriz**	*empress*
el marido	*husband*	**la esposa**	*wife*
el yerno	*son-in-law*	**la nuera**	*daughter-in-law*

7. Phrases used as nouns are usually masculine. They may be (*a*) infinitives (Sec. **108.2**), (*b*) verb phrases (Sec. **174.2**), (*c*) other set phrases.

a. **el deber**	*duty*	**el poder**	*power*
b. **el pagaré**	*I.O.U., promissory note*	**el pésame**	*condolence*
un no sé qué	*a certain something*	**el cúmplase**	*approval; decree*
c. **el visto bueno** (Vo. Bo.)	*approval*	**la enhorabuena**	*congratulations*

EJERCICIO

Póngase el artículo en los espacios:

_____ clima, _____ bondad, _____ costumbre, _____ periferia, _____ idioma, _____ costumbre, _____ atleta, _____ merced, _____ problema, _____ síntoma, _____ telegrama, _____ vanidad, _____ poeta, _____ dilema, _____ superficie, _____ cometa, _____ pesadumbre, _____ virtud, _____ sistema.

166. PLURAL OF NOUNS

1. See Secs. **4, 5.**

2. Nouns ending in accented vowels—except **é**—add **-es** to form the plural.

el bajá	*pasha*	**los bajaes**	**la o**	*(letter) o*	**las oes**
el rubí	*ruby*	**los rubíes**	**el tisú**	*tissue*	**los tisúes**

EXCEPTIONS: **el papá** *dad* **los papás; la mamá** *mom* **las mamás; el esquí** *ski* **los esquís** *skis*

3. Nouns ending in **-é** add *-s* to form the plural.

el pie	*foot*	**los pies**	**el café**	*coffee*	**los cafés**

EXCEPTION: **las ees** *the e's* (all letters of the alphabet are feminine).

4. The following words shift their accent in the plural:

el carácter	**los caracteres**	*characters*
el régimen	**los regímenes**	*régimes, diets*

5. The following are unchanged in the plural: (*a*) patronymics with final unaccented syllable ending in **-z,** (*b*) nouns with final unaccented syllable in **-s,** (*c*) a few Latinisms.

a.	**los Fernández**	*the Fernandezes*
b.	**las crisis**	*(the) crises*
	los lunes	*(the) Mondays*
c.	**los déficit**	*the deficits*

NOTE. A few foreign importations drop a final consonant to form the plural: **el lord, los lores** *lords.* The majority, however, are regular: **el chófer, los chóferes** *chauffeurs,* **el mitin, los mítines** *(political) meetings.* In some cases the foreign plural forms are retained: **los clubs** *clubs,* **los complots** *conspiracies,* **los jerseys** *sweaters,* **los suéters** *sweaters,* **los smokings** *tuxedos,* **los esnobs** *snobs,* plus many more less-integrated Anglicisms like *films, flirts, gangsters, cocktails, gentlemen,* etc.

167. DISTRIBUTIVE PLURAL AND GENERIC SINGULAR

1. The masculine plural of personal nouns may be used to designate both the male and female members of a pair (or group) possessing equal natural, hereditary, or occupational standing.

los hermanos	*brothers, brother(s) and sister(s)*
los señores Peña	*Mr. and Mrs. Peña*
los padres	*parents*
los reyes	*the king and queen*
But: **el doctor Núñez y señora**	*Dr. and Mrs. Núñez*

2. With parts of the body and articles of clothing, Spanish chooses between the generic singular and the distributive plural according to the exact shade of meaning involved.

Todos levantaron la mano.	*All raised their hand. (Each raised one hand.)*
Todas levantaron las manos.	*All raised their hands. (Each raised both hands.)*
Las mujeres, con la mantilla puesta . . .	*The women, wearing the (typical) mantilla . . .*
Las mujeres, con las mantillas puestas . . .	*The women, wearing their mantillas . . .*

3. The same distinction applies to the use of singular or plural verbs with collective nouns.

La mayor parte llegó (llegaron) tarde.	*The majority arrived late.*
La mayor parte de los estudiantes se había(n) marchado ya.	*Most of the students had already left.*

EJERCICIO

Cámbiense las frases siguientes según el modelo: **Andrés es el hermano y Pilar es la hermana.** → **Andrés y Pilar son hermanos.**

1. El rey era Fernando y la reina era Isabel.
2. La señorita Arregui es profesora y el señor Alcalá es profesor.
3. Margarita es mi prima y Jorge es mi primo.
4. Mi tío vive en Zaragoza y mi tía vive allí.
5. Eduardo era el hijo de doña Gertrudis y Lupe era su hija.

Pónganse el singular o el plural de las palabras entre paréntesis en el espacio:

6. Vamos a ponernos _____ (el sombrero).
7. Se quitaron _____ (el zapato).
8. Se pusieron _____ (la corbata) y _____ (el guante).
9. Abren _____ (la boca) y comienzan a reír.
10. Hemos perdido _____ (la camisa).

168. PERSONAL *A* (*CONTINUED*)

    1. See Secs. **6, 99, 118.**

    2. The use of the personal **a** gives to any noun the qualities of (*a*) definiteness and individuality, or (*b*) personification. Conversely, its absence has the opposite effect. Its use with numerals and the indefinites **uno, otro, ninguno, todo, cualquiera,** etc., follows this principle.

a. **Busco a un amigo.**	*I am looking for a (definite) friend.*
Busco un amigo.	*I am looking for a (any) friend.*
He encontrado otro chófer.	*I have found another chauffeur (undifferentiated).*
He encontrado a mi chófer.	*I have found my chauffeur (definite).*
He encontrado a otro amigo.	*I have met another (definite) friend.*
b. **amar a la virtud y aborrecer al vicio**	*to love virtue and hate vice*
Llaman resignación a su cobardía.	*They call their cowardice resignation.*

NOTE. The personal **a** is not used with geographical names accompanied by the definite article: **atravesó el Ebro** *he crossed the Ebro,* **he visto la Coruña** *I have seen la Corunna.*

    3. The personal accusative is not used with **tener,** except as an idiomatic equivalent to the verb *to be.*

Tengo tres hermanos.	*I have three brothers (brothers and sisters).*
But: **Tengo a un hermano en México.**	*I have a brother in Mexico. (One of my brothers is in Mexico.)*
Ahí tiene Ud. al señor Salas.	*There is Mr. Salas.*

EJERCICIO

Pónganse **a** delante de los objetos donde es necesario, reemplazando las palabras subrayadas con las palabras entre paréntesis:

1. Veo <u>el tranvía</u> pero no veo <u>a Manolo</u>.
2. Saludaron <u>a la muchacha</u>.
3. ¿Han visto Uds. <u>la televisión</u>?

(el taxi, el chófer, el jardín, el jardinero, la bailarina, su hija, Carlos, sus amigos, la bandera, los soldados, el jefe, el turista, mi perro, su caballo, nuestro obispo, los periodistas).

---

169. COMPOUND NOUNS

    One of the outstanding characteristics of English is the ease with which two or more nouns may be combined to form compounds, such as *railroad, egghead, stock market, aversion therapy, language laboratory,* etc. To form similar compounds Spanish is (*a*) usually compelled to resort to prepositional phrases, chiefly with **de** and **para,** although (*b*) a few genuine compounds of the type **ferrocarril** *railroad* exist.

a.	**la máquina de coser**	*sewing machine*
	la bolsa de valores	*stock market*
	abrigos para señoras	*ladies' coats*
	neumático de repuesto	*spare tire*
	el plan de abastecimiento de aguas	*water supply project*
	la compañía de seguros contra incendios	*the fire insurance company*
b.	**la radiodifusión**	*broadcasting*
	el electromagnetismo	*electromagnetism*
	el telerreceptor	*television receiver*
	la videocasetera	*video cassette recorder*

NOTE. Abbreviations, such as **la radio** *radio* for **radiotelefonía, la mecano** *typist* for **mecanógrafa** retain their original gender.

EJERCICIO

Contéstense:
1. ¿Qué es una estación donde venden gasolina? (Es una estación de gasolina.)
2. ¿Qué es un vaso del que bebemos agua? (Es un vaso para agua.)
3. ¿Qué es un asilo donde viven los huérfanos?
4. ¿Qué es una máquina que sirve para escribir?
5. ¿Qué es un agente que da publicidad?
6. ¿Qué es un campamento donde encierran a los prisioneros?
7. ¿Qué es una compañía que opera los tranvías?
8. ¿Qué es una declaración en la que se notan los ingresos?
9. ¿Qué es una fábrica donde hacen muebles?
10. ¿Qué es un hombre que se dedica a los negocios?
11. ¿Qué es un hombre que se dedica a la ciencia?

170. DIMINUTIVES AND AUGMENTATIVES

Spanish, in contrast with English, has great freedom in the formation of diminutives and augmentatives. The more frequent (*a*) diminutive suffixes are: **-ito (-cito, -ecito), -in,** and **-illo (-cillo, -ecillo),** which imply small size or affectionate interest. The more frequent (*b*) augmentative suffixes are **-ón, -ote,** and **-azo,** which imply large size or comic effect. (*c*) Diminutives may be added to other parts of speech besides nouns and adjectives (see Sec. **183**).

a.	caballo	*horse*	caballito	*little horse*
	chico	*small (boy)*	chiquito	*"kid"*
	viejo	*old (man)*	viejecito	*(nice) old man*
	joven	*young (man)*	jovencito	*youngster*

NOTE 1. The suffix **-illo** generally implies a more subjective attitude than **-ito.** For general principles concerning the formation of diminutives, see Appendix, Secs. **275–277.**

b.	mujer	*woman*	mujerona	*large woman*
	perro	*dog*	perrazo	*big dog*
	pájaro	*bird*	pajarote	*big bird*

NOTE 2. These forms are especially characteristic of colloquial speech, diminutives being used much more than augmentatives. They are very frequent with proper names: **Mariquita** (María), **Manolito** (Manuel), **Dolorcitas** (Dolores), and with adjectives and adverbs (Sec. **183**).

c.	cerquita	*very near*	adiosito	*bye-bye*

EJERCICIO

Fórmense los diminutivos de las palabras siguientes: mesa, cuchara, libro, casa, mano, solo, amigo, perro, gato, muchacha, ventana, peseta, hombre, dolor, jardín.

171. GENDER OF CITIES AND COUNTRIES

Names of countries and cities are feminine when they end in **-a;** otherwise they are usually masculine.

la romántica Granada   *romantic Granada*
el montañoso Chile   *mountainous Chile*

NOTE. Even when the name of a city is feminine **todo, medio, un(o)** may be used to refer to the population rather than to the area: **todo Barcelona** *all Barcelona.*

172. ABSTRACT NOUNS WITH CONCRETE MEANING

Spanish frequently uses abstract nouns to denote specific manifestations of the abstract idea.

Eso es una locura.   *That is a crazy idea* (or act).
Las ridiculeces de este señor.   *The absurd notions* (or acts) *of this gentleman.*

Los disparates de aquella gente.	*The nonsense of those people (nonsensical acts.)*
Me dio muy buenos consejos.	*He gave me very good advice.*

173. PERSONAL *A* (*CONTINUED*)

The personal **a** (*acusativo personal*) may be (*a*) used or (*b*) omitted in the interests of clearness. It is (*a*) used with non-personal objects in order to distinguish the object from the subject, and (*b*) may be omitted with personal objects in order to distinguish the direct from the indirect object.

a.	**A la primavera sigue el verano.**	*Summer follows spring.*
b.	**Le mandé mi secretario a mi socio.**	*I sent my secretary to my partner.*

Traducción 15A

1. The general's wife is a very charming woman.
2. Two sisters of Charity were in the street car.
3. You can't see the Azores Islands on this map.
4. The fruit orchard belonged to the mayor of the town.
5. The postman kicked the gardener's dog.
6. Days of happiness are short.
7. The boys of the town serve as guides to tourists.
8. The Catholic Sovereigns are buried in Granada.
9. Mr. and Mrs. Aguilar are my friend's parents.
10. Yesterday I visited my uncle and aunt.
11. They have a nice little house near the river.
12. He went to the city to see his niece.
13. The robber killed a policeman.
14. The prisoner bribed the guards.
15. He was made knight of the Order of "Isabel la Católica."
16. The students raised their hands.
17. They all took off their hat(s) on entering the church.
18. We put on our overcoats and left.
19. Only fifty per cent of the workers went on (to the) strike.
20. That is the man to whom I sold my car.
21. The chief was scolding someone.
22. The orphan asylum is near a furniture factory.
23. I don't want to see anybody.
24. The colors of this steamship company are blue and white.
25. All the cars have six-cylinder engines.
26. All sorts of things are sold in the store: typewriters, safety razors, ladies' silk stockings, children's clothes, writing paper.
27. What a huge man!
28. You have a very cute little daughter.

29. My mother is sick (use **tener**).
30. We saw many women working in the fields.
31. He called his children to his deathbed.
32. There you have the book you were looking for.
33. He admires England.
34. We visited all our friends.
35. My feet ache.
36. This street is full of cafés.
37. We saw the parade of the Moroccan troops.
38. I called the taxi driver a liar.

II

174. COMPOUND NOUNS (*CONTINUED*)

1. A special class of compounds in Spanish is that formed by combining the third person singular of the present indicative and a complement, usually a plural noun, e.g., **el matamoscas** *fly swatter* (cf. English compounds like *breakfast, breakwater, cutthroat, sawbones,* etc.). There are hundreds of these compounds in Spanish and new ones can be formed at any time. They are frequently characteristic of popular speech, and are usually masculine. Many of these compounds are used to indicate (*a*) instruments or gadgets, (*b*) occupations, (*c*) inferior or despised representatives of certain occupations, (*d*) persons with annoying characteristics.

a.	**el cuentakilómetros**	odometer; speedometer
	el lanzacohetes	rocket launcher
	el paraguas	umbrella
	el paracaídas	parachute
	el portaequipajes	baggage rack
	el sacacorchos	corkscrew
	el salvavidas	life preserver
b.	**el guardagujas**	switchman
	el lavacoches	car washer
	el limpiabotas	bootblack
	el quitamanchas	spot remover (dry cleaner)
c.	**el matasanos**	quack doctor
	el chupatinta	office worker
	el buscapleitos	shyster lawyer
	el manchacuartillas	hack writer
d.	**el aguafiestas**	killjoy
	el correfaldas	skirt chaser
	el papanatas	simpleton
	el perdonavidas	bully
	el quitamotas	flatterer
	el sábelotodo	know-it-all

2. Other verb phrases and set phrases may be used as compound nouns. These, too, are usually masculine (see Sec. **165**).

el hazmerreír	*laughing-stock*
el acabose	*chaos*
dimes y diretes	*bickering*
el qué dirán	*gossip, public opinion*

NOTE. In compounds an original initial **r** is written **rr** to reflect the pronunciation, e.g., **prerromanticismo, iberorrománico, telerrecepción, puertorriqueño,** etc.

3. The noun is occasionally used as an adjective in set appositional phrases, especially with proper names. In this construction the nouns **color, tipo,** or **marca** are often expressed or understood.

una esposa modelo	*a model wife*
un camión Ford	*a Ford truck*
una novela tipo Walter Scott	*a novel of the Walter Scott type*
un sombrero hongo	*a Derby hat*
un automóvil color cereza	*a cherry-colored automobile*
una carroza siglo dieciocho	*an eighteenth century (style) carriage*
el hombre masa	*"mass-man"*

4. Very rarely two nouns are combined without one being considered an adjective.

la casatienda	*store and home in the same building*
el papel moneda	*paper money*
el maestrescuela	*schoolmaster*
la hoja-bloque	*souvenir sheet of postage stamps*

EJERCICIO

Contéstense:
1. ¿Qué es un instrumento que apaga los incendios? (Es un apagaincendios.)
2. ¿Qué es un instrumento que corta tubos? (Es un cortatubos.)
3. ¿Qué es una cosa que cubre los platos?
4. ¿Qué es un hombre que cata los vinos?
5. ¿Qué es una caja en que se guardan joyas?
6. ¿Qué es un hombre que guarda un puente?
7. ¿Qué es un instrumento que limpia el parabrisas de un automóvil?
8. ¿Qué es un instrumento para matar las moscas?
9. ¿Qué es una cosa que sirve para pisar los papeles?

175. SUFFIXES

Suffixes play an important part in word formation in Spanish. The following uses of suffixes are worthy of note:

(*a*) the diminutive suffixes **-ete, -cete, -ecete; -uelo, -zuelo, -ezuelo** indicate a depreciative or contemptuous attitude on the part of the speaker.

(*b*) **-ote, -ejo, -ajo, -aco, -acho, -uco,** and **-ucho** give a stronger depreciative or contemptuous force (for a list of depreciative suffixes see Appendix, Sec. **277**).

(*c*) the suffix **-ada** indicates capacity (cf. English *-ful*),

(*d*) **-ada** and **-azo** indicate a wound or blow,

(*e*) **-al, -ar, -eda** indicate a collection or group,

(*f*) **-dor** (cf. English *-or*) one who performs a certain action,

(*g*) **-ero** (cf. English *-er*) one engaged in a certain occupation,

(*h*) **-ería** a place where certain business or work is carried on,

(*i*) **-ista** one who engages in a certain profession or occupation, or is the adherent of a doctrine (cf. English *-ist*),

(*j*) **-ismo** a doctrine or ideology (cf. English *-ism*).

a.	**el vejete**	*old man*
	el mozuelo	*youngster*
b.	**el caballejo**	*nag, hack*
	la casucha	*small, ill-kept house*
	el perrote	*big, clumsy dog*
c.	**una cucharada**	*a spoonful*
	una manada	*a handful—herd*
d.	**la puñalada**	*dagger thrust*
	un balazo	*a bullet wound, shot*
	un portazo	*a door slam*
	un cañonazo	*a cannon shot*
e.	**el arenal**	*sandbank*
	el pinar	*pine grove*
	una arboleda	*a clump of trees*
	una alameda	*poplar grove; tree-lined walk, mall*
f.	**el cobrador**	*collector*
	el vencedor	*winner, conqueror*
g.	**el librero**	*book seller*
	el portero	*doorman; janitor*

NOTE. A few common formations have a syllable between the base word and the suffix: **carnicero** *butcher*, **panadero** *baker*.

h.	**la zapatería**	*shoe store*
	la herrería	*iron works, smithy*

i. **la modista**	*dressmaker*
el cuentista	*story writer*
el militarista	*militarist*
el separatista	*separatist*
j. **el centralismo**	*centralism*
el marxismo	*Marxism*

EJERCICIO

Contéstense, poniendo las palabras entre paréntesis en lugar de las palabras subrayadas:
1. ¿Qué es <u>un rey</u> despreciable?—Es un <u>reyezuelo</u>. (pintor, autor, mujer, dictador)
2. Si uno le da a Ud. un golpe con <u>un bastón</u>, ¿qué le da?—Me da <u>un bastonazo</u>. (botella, pelota, flecha)
3. ¿Qué es un hombre que <u>vende cosas de papel</u>?—Es <u>papelero</u>. (hace alfombras, hace pan, hace pasteles, hace la comida en la cocina)
4. ¿Qué es una tienda donde <u>venden papel</u>?—Es una <u>papelería</u>. (botones, sombreros, ropa, leche, muebles)
5. ¿Qué es un hombre que <u>trabaja</u>?—Es <u>trabajador</u>. (vende, acomoda a los espectadores en un teatro, alista reclutas para el ejército, doma caballos, educa, habla mucho, engaña, mata el toro en una corrida)
6. ¿Qué es una persona que <u>pertenece a la izquierda</u>?—Es <u>izquierdista</u>. (pertenece a la derecha, cree en el centralismo, cree en el comunismo, trabaja con la electricidad, es notado por su egoísmo)

Traducción 15B

1. He gave me good advice (pl.).
2. You are driving me crazy with your impatient (outbursts).
3. I have very good friend(ships) here.
4. That was a rash act.
5. That bootblack used to own a shoe store in this town.
6. My hands are full of scratches.
7. He always wears a brown (coffee color) derby.
8. What a beautiful oak grove!
9. I have to buy something in the hardware store.
10. Our landlord is a very generous man.
11. He hit the pickpocket with his cane.
12. That poor, old, wrinkled woman is a chestnut vender.
13. Is there a pastry shop on this street?—Yes, there is one between the dairy store and the dry cleaner's.
14. I had to nudge him to keep quiet.
15. This is a vile, low newspaper.

16. We prefer a foreigner to a native.
17. The committee discussed the problem of the unemployed.
18. He was the laughing-stock of the neighborhood.
19. This section (of the town) has a certain something which I like very much.
20. Paris is called the City (of) Light.
21. I introduced my friend to the young lady.
22. His speech preceded mine.
23. Toledo, the Museum City of Spain.
24. He does that for fear of public opinion.
25. Where is the loudspeaker?
26. The play is a historical drama of the Calderón type.
27. He wore a canary-colored tie.
28. She has tiny little feet.
29. What an awful temper he has!
30. She is a great actress.
31. Let us take this narrow little path.

III

Verbos y Modismos

Ir (Sec. **249**) *to go;* **irse** *to go away, go on;* **¡Vaya!** *Come on now! (coaxing), What a . . . (approval or disapproval),* etc.

1. This road leads to (the) town.
2. When is he going (away)?
3. Let's see.
4. I'll (go to) see.
5. No, don't say anything to him, lest you (don't go to) make him angry.
6. What can we do about it (**le**)?—It can't be helped.
7. What do you mean he is (**¿Que va a ser . . . ?**) rich?
8. He was (went) looking for it everywhere.
9. I am arranging the apartment.
10. They all went (along) very happy.
11. You are very silent.
12. His affairs are not going very well (for him).
13. How are (goes it with) you?
14. This hat looks very well on you.
15. It annoys me to have to go shopping.
16. I have nothing at stake. (**A mi no me va nada en ello.**)
17. Don't pay any attention to him; that is not meant (**no va**) for you.
18. Don't go away without seeing (talking to) me.
19. Let's get out of here.

20. All his money goes (**se le va**) for (**en**) books.
21. Come now, come now, don't get angry.
22. What a silly answer!

Tardar *to be (take) long (in).*

1. We are waiting for you. Don't be long.
2. How long does it take to go (**se tarda**) from Santiago to Valparaíso?—It takes (**tardar** pl.) about three hours.
3. It took him a long time (**mucho**) to (**en**) do it.

ADJECTIVES

I

176. GENDER OF ADJECTIVES

1. See Sec. **11.**

2. Adjectives (including those used as nouns) which end in **-án, -ón,** or **-ín** add **a** to form the feminine, and lose the written accent.

burlón	**burlona**	*mocking*
encantador	**encantadora**	*charming*
chiquitín	**chiquitina**	*tiny (person)*
holgazán	**holgazana**	*lazy (person)*

EXCEPTION: The comparative–superlatives **mejor, peor, mayor, menor** (see Sec. **196**) and the adjectives **interior, exterior, anterior, posterior, inferior, superior** are invariable. The sole exception is the noun **superiora** *Mother Superior.*

3. Adjectives (and nouns) ending in the suffixes **-ete, -ote** (derogatory), form the feminine by changing the final **-e** to **-a.**

feote	**feota**	*ugly*
pesadote	**pesadota**	*heavy, boring*
pobrete	**pobreta**	*wretch*

4. A few adjectives ending in **-a,** including those formed with the suffix **-ista,** are invariable.

el arte indígena	*the native art*
el partido socialista	*the Socialist party*

177. PLURAL OF ADJECTIVES

See Sec. **4.**

178. SHORTENED ADJECTIVES

See Sec. **13.**

179. AGREEMENT OF ADJECTIVES

1. See Sec. **12.**

2. An adjective modifying two or more nouns of different gender is (*a*) masculine, if plural, (*b*) if singular, in agreement with the nearest noun.

a. **El chófer y la cocinera eran muy divertidos.**	*The chauffeur and the cook were very amusing.*
Árboles, casas y puentes fueron arrasados por la riada.	*Trees, houses, and bridges were carried away by the flood.*
b. **Se portó con toda justicia y decoro.**	*He acted with thorough justice and decorum.*

NOTE. The singular adjective is used when the two nouns form a single concept, as in the previous example.

EJERCICIO

Pónganse las formas correctas de los adjetivos entre paréntesis en los espacios:
1. Elena y Concha son muchachas _____. (hablador, mandón, superior)
2. Los jefes se portaban de manera _____. (burlón, juguetón)

---

180. POSITION OF ADJECTIVES

1. Determinative adjectives (articles, demonstratives, possessives, and indefinites) usually precede the noun they modify (see Sec. **14**). When they are especially stressed or used with differentiating force, they follow.

un amigo mío	*a friend of mine*
el hombre aquel	*that man*

sin dificultad alguna	*without any difficulty*
un hombre cualquiera	*an ordinary man*
la lección primera	*the first lesson (used as a title)*
Felipe Segundo	*Philip the Second (and so all titles)*

2. When the descriptive adjective differentiates, distinguishes, or in any way sets apart the noun it modifies, and thus is stressed, it follows the noun. Since most descriptive adjectives do indeed distinguish their nouns from other nouns and are therefore stressed, they normally follow the noun.

When the idea of differentiation is neither present nor stressed, the descriptive adjective precedes the noun. This usually occurs when the adjective denotes a non-distinctive characteristic of the noun.

Putting a descriptive adjective in front of a noun also tends to be more characteristic of poetic, literary style. Ordinary prosaic, conversational style rarely puts descriptive adjectives before the noun.

Viven en la casa amarilla.	*They live in the yellow house (differentiation).*
las blancas casas del pueblo andaluz	*the white houses of the Andalusian town* (most Andalusian houses are white, so white is non-distinctive.)
sus parientes ricos	*his rich relatives* (those who are rich, distinguished from those who are not rich.)
sus ricos parientes	*his rich relatives* (all known to be rich)
la España septentrional	*Northern Spain*
la Argentina meridional	*Southern Argentina*
la meridional España y la septentrional Argentina	*southerly Spain and northerly Argentina* (epithets)

NOTE 1. In general, the differentiating position of the adjective in Spanish corresponds to the heavy stress (and pause) in English: **sus parientes ricos** *his RICH relatives* **sus ricos parientes** *his rich relatives* (relatively unstressed).
NOTE 2. Some adjectives are so commonly used that they have relatively little differentiating force and are far more likely to go in front of the noun in the unstressed position: **bueno, malo, famoso.**

3. As a consequence, certain adjectives have different meanings depending on whether they precede or follow the noun. (For a longer list see Appendix, Sec. **271.**)

un pobre hombre	*an unfortunate man*
un hombre pobre	*a poor (indigent) man*
un discurso muy valiente	*a courageous speech*
¡Valiente discurso!	*What a speech!*
el español medio	*the average Spaniard*
medio español	*one-half Spanish*

EJERCICIO

Contéstense según el modelo: ¿Qué es un hombre desgraciado? (pobre)—Es un pobre hombre. ¿Qué es un hombre que no tiene dinero y pocas esperanzas de tenerlo?—Es un hombre pobre.

1. (viejo) ¿Qué es un amigo que conocemos desde hace mucho tiempo?
   ¿Qué es un amigo que tiene muchos años?
2. (nuevo) ¿Qué es un coche que acaba de salir de la fábrica?
   ¿Qué es un coche que acabamos de comprar?
3. (único) ¿Qué es una pintura que no tiene igual?
   ¿Qué es una pintura que tengo, si tengo una sola?
4. (alto) ¿Qué es un oficial del gobierno en una posición muy elevada?
   ¿Qué es un oficial que mide dos metros de altura?
5. (grande) ¿Qué es un libro de dimensiones extraordinarias y que pesa mucho?
   ¿Qué es un libro clásico de alta calidad?
6. (cierto) ¿Qué es un informe ordinario sobre algo?
   ¿Qué es un informe que nos da datos absolutamente seguros?
7. (antiguo) ¿Qué es una residencia que antes era del rey?
   ¿Qué es una residencia que se construyó en la Edad Media?

4. When a noun is modified by two or more descriptive adjectives each is placed (*a*) according to the preceding principles. If (*b*) both adjectives precede or follow they are connected with **y,** unless (*c*) one of the two adjectives is so closely related to the noun as to form with it a concept equivalent to a compound noun.

a.	**Velázquez y Goya son dos famosos pintores españoles.**	*Velazquez and Goya are two famous Spanish painters.*
b.	**una habitación grande y clara**	*a large, light room*
	las estrechas y misteriosas calles de Toledo	*the narrow and mysterious streets of Toledo*
c.	**el arte gótico español**	*Spanish Gothic art*

EJERCICIO

Pónganse dos de los adjetivos entre paréntesis con los sustantivos subrayados:

1. En Toledo se ven casas. (antiguo-pintoresco; famoso-antiguo; grande-medieval)
2. Cerca de Madrid hay montañas. (alto-verde; grande-empinado; seco-rocoso)
3. En Segovia conocí a unas muchachas. (bonito-español; simpático-atractivo; hermoso-hablador)
4. Fuimos a un hotel. (moderno-grande; viejo-pequeño; lujoso-turístico)
5. Miguel estudió las culturas. (francés-italiano; americano-indio)

181. ADJECTIVES USED AS NOUNS

1. In Spanish, adjectives—and participles—are used as nouns when the noun they modify is deleted (see Secs. **67, 68**). English often supplies the nouns *man, woman,* or the pronoun *one.*

los vivos y los muertos	*the living and the dead*
la casa blanca y la amarilla	*the white house and the yellow one*
los versados en aquella ciencia	*those versed in that science*
los casados	*married people*

2. Predicate adjectives and participles are often used in Spanish as equivalent to adverbs or adverb phrases in English.

Vivían contentos.	*They lived contentedly.*
Corrimos veloces.	*We ran swiftly.*
Gritaron asustadas.	*They shouted in alarm.*

182. ADJECTIVE PHRASES

Spanish usually has recourse to prepositional phrases to render (*a*) adjectives of material, (*b*) the adjectival element in compounds of the type *sewing machine* (see Sec. **169**).

a.	**un banco de piedra**	*a stone bench*
	un reloj de plata	*a silver watch*
b.	**la telegrafía sin hilos**	*wireless telegraphy, radio*
	una espada con puño de oro	*a gold-hilted sword*
	un sombrero de ala ancha	*a broad-brimmed hat*

183. DIMINUTIVES

Diminutive endings may be used to strengthen adjectives, participles, and adverbs, especially in popular speech (see Sec. **170**).

Vuelvo en seguidita.	*I am coming right back.*
Hagámoslo ahorita.	*Let's do it right now.*
El problema es dificilillo.	*The problem is a bit difficult.*
Entraron callandito.	*They came in very quietly.*
El niño estaba dormidito.	*The child was sleeping sweetly.*

Traducción 16A

1. She is a dreamer.
2. The landlady of the boardinghouse was a very thrifty woman.
3. This theater always presents the best pictures.
4. The dean and his wife were very courteous to us.
5. That child (fem.) is (an) awful (**muy**) cry-baby.
6. How handsome and healthy-looking she is.
7. The silk stockings were very inferior to the ones she bought the last time.
8. She belongs to one of the feminist associations.
9. Did you see him?—Whom?—That fellow who was looking for you.
10. The joke was not a bit funny.
11. The costumes and the scenery are splendid.
12. The high mountains of northern Spain are covered with snow the greater part of the year.
13. Her black eyes and dark complexion made her pass for a Spanish woman.
14. The comical adventures of Don Quixote have inspired many great writers.
15. The blind man plays the piano in a downtown café.
16. The blue Mediterranean bathes the Valencian coast.
17. That yellow building is the town hall; the doorway is a good example of plateresque art.
18. The immense plains of Texas resemble greatly the landscape of central Spain.
19. Napoleon died in the remote island of Saint Helena.
20. Merry England, green Ireland, sweet France, and wide Castile have been sung by many poets.
21. Mr. and Mrs. Moncada have a fine collection of old tapestries. Their house is a real antique shop.
22. The excessive speed of the car was the cause of the collision.
23. Vast Russia is a country half European, half Asiatic.
24. Gothic architecture is the most glorious expression of the Middle Ages.
25. The comedy has three principal characters: a wealthy businessman, a clever stenographer, and a very funny newspaperman who comes to the office.
26. I want you to meet my new partner, Mr. Galindo.
27. It was a dark moonless night. After various incidents we finally arrived at the inn.
28. This blessed fireplace never works.
29. What a predicament!
30. Poor old man!
31. Cadiz and Malaga are the most ancient Spanish cities.
32. He is a tall, thin man with a blond mustache.
33. The solitary and melancholy moon shed its dim light on the rough stones of the old castle.
34. We were the last ones to (**en**) arrive.
35. Those favored by fortune seldom think of the less fortunate.
36. They were talking excitedly.
37. Have you any chewing gum?

38. Some of my traveling companions were Europeans; others, Americans.
39. I don't like fresh-water fish.
40. It was very cold. I had a couple of woolen blankets on my bed.
41. Let's go slowly (diminutive).
42. They were waiting for me impatiently.
43. She is a very pretty little English girl.

II

184. AGREEMENT OF ADJECTIVES

When two or more adjectives modify a plural noun in a distributive sense, they remain in the singular.

los tomos primero y segundo	*the first and second volumes*
las literaturas francesa y española	*French and Spanish literatures*

185. SHORTENED ADJECTIVES (*CONTINUED*)

Santo is not shortened before names beginning with **To-** or **Do-.**

Santo Tomás	*Saint Thomas*
Santo Domingo	*Saint Dominic*

(The forms **San Tomás, San Tomé, San Domingo,** etc. are occasionally found as relics of a former usage.)

186. ADJECTIVES USED AS NOUNS (*CONTINUED*)

Spanish uses the adjective as a noun—in contrast to English—in the following constructions: (*a*) in partitive and superlative expressions of the type *one of the . . . and of the . . . kind* (sort, etc.), and (*b*) in appositional phrases introduced by **de.** This latter construction is much more frequent in Spanish than in English, and may be extended to nouns.

a. **una calle de las céntricas**	*one of the central streets*
un amigo de los que tengo en España	*one of the friends I have in Spain*
vino del más caro	*wine of the most expensive kind*
de lo mejor y más granado	*of the best and most select kind*

NOTE. This construction is often used as equivalent to the absolute superlative: **una noche de las más hermosas** *a most beautiful night.*

Cámbiense las frases siguientes según el modelo: **Pasan por una calle de las calles céntricas.** → **Pasan por una calle de las céntricas.**

1. Fuimos a visitar un castillo de los castillos más antiguos.
2. El guardia era un hombre de los hombres que parecen ser parte del país.
3. Nos mostró un libro medieval de los libros que tenía en un aposento.
4. Luego nos invitó a probar un vino del vino típico de la región.
5. Regresamos por unas montañas de las montañas altas de la región.

b. **el bueno de D. Diego**	*good old D. Diego*
la tonta de mi suegra	*that fool of a mother-in-law of mine*
¡qué egoísmo de hijo!	*what a selfish son!*

Cámbiense las frases siguientes según el modelo: **Mi suegro es tonto y no sabe nada.** → **El tonto de mi suegro no sabe nada.**

1. Román es pobre y tiene que trabajar todo el día.
2. La vecina es chismosa y repite todo lo que oye.
3. Mi tío era un santo y no podía creer mal de nadie.
4. Carlos es un idiota y va a estropearlo todo.
5. La muchacha es un encanto y roba todos los corazones.

187. POSITION OF ADJECTIVES (*CONTINUED*)

1. Since the position of the adjective is so flexible in Spanish, it is frequently employed as a rhetorical or stylistic device. Any displacement of the adjective from its normal position gives it a rhetorical or emotional stress, in short, a subjective value.

¡Terrible vicio es la ingratitud!	*Ungratefulness is a terrible vice!*
Asomaba el sol por el hispano horizonte.	*The sun was rising over the Spanish horizon.*
Una mirada de sus negros ojos y estoy perdido.	*A glance from her black eyes and I am lost.*
el dulce, amoroso, romántico canto del ruiseñor	*the sweet, amorous, romantic song of the nightingale*
la inglesa costumbre de tomar el té	*the English custom of having tea*
Paseaba dedicado a sus nocturnas meditaciones.	*He strolled along, wrapped up in his nocturnal meditations.*
Interrumpió su oficinesca labor.	*He interrupted his bureaucratic labors.*
Sus fieros bigotes y enorme nariz producían cómico contraste.	*His fierce mustache and his enormous nose produced comic contrast.*

188. SUMMARY OF ADJECTIVE POSITION

POST-POSITION	PRE-POSITION
Differentiation	No differentiation
Divided concept	Single (undivided) concept
Objective value	Subjective value (preconception; rhetorical, lyric, comic, etc., effect).

189. COMPOUND ADJECTIVES

There are two general patterns for the formation of compound adjectives in Spanish: (*a*) the double adjective, the first part of which takes the Latin form ending in **o,** and (*b*) those compounded of a noun and adjective, in which the connecting vowel is **i.**

a.	**anglosajón**	*Anglo-Saxon*
	hispanoamericano	*Hispanic American*
	francoitaliano	*Franco-Italian*
	políticorreligioso	*politico-religious*
b.	**ojinegro**	*black-eyed*
	verdinegro	*black-green*
	puntiagudo	*sharp-pointed*

190. PREFIXES

The intensifying prefixes **re- (rete-, requete-)** and **archi-** are used colloquially with adjectives and participles: **re-** (etc.) is also used with adverbs.

¡Qué rebonito!	*How awfully cute!*
una cosa archisabidísima	*something absolutely everybody knows*
Habla muy requetebién.	*He is a perfectly marvelous speaker.*

Traducción 16B

1. The nineteenth and twentieth centuries are the most interesting in human history.
2. It was a sailboat of the sort that is seen in the Mediterranean.
3. We went to one of those (country) town fairs.
4. This is one of the best of his descriptions.
5. He gave him a good, sound scolding.
6. The (old) gossip of a cook . . .
7. Poor D. Alejandro!

8. What a silly (noun) article!
9. What a charming (noun) girl!
10. It was a marvelous (noun) landscape.
11. The lonely, distant barking of a dog added a mysterious note to the scene.
12. The burning African sun blinded the weary travelers.
13. He has the disagreeable habit of talking in a very loud voice.
14. The wounded animal gave a sad cry.
15. This is an incredible thing (reverse order).
16. Those were unforgettable days.
17. Who is that red-haired (girl)?
18. Medieval Hispano-Arabic literature was very rich in scientific and philosophic works.
19. The musical murmur of the pine trees calmed our spirits.
20. As we rested, we listened to the animated and graceful rhythm of Spanish folk music.
21. The repeated visits of his insistent creditors began to worry him.
22. The sweet, juicy, golden oranges of Valencia always remind me of my trip to the Levant.
23. The peasant wiped his sweaty brow.
24. In a quiet little town of the province, far from the noisy and feverish bustle of the city, not long ago there lived a strange old man.

III

Verbos y Modismos

Venir (Sec. **263**) *to come, suit, agree.* **¡Venga!,** *Let's have it! Give (bring) it here!*

1. Don't come to me with gossip!
2. Come around (here) whenever you can!
3. It has to be done, come what may (come).
4. What is that for? (**¿a qué viene eso?**)
5. The news is in (comes in) today's paper.
6. He is (comes) very sick.
7. They were (came away) enthusiastic over (**con**) the speech.
8. He came in (**de**) uniform.
9. I have been telling you so for (**hace**) a long time.
10. Your present suits me to a T (**al pelo**).
11. Shake! (**¡Venga esa mano!**)
12. Give the money (here).
13. It amounts to (**viene a ser**) the same (thing).
14. That's beside the point (**no viene a cuento**).
15. His family had come down in the world (**venir a menos**).

Traer(se) (Sec. **261**) *to bring (with), carry (with), have.*

1. Bring me the coffee at once.
2. I didn't bring my bathing suit with me.
3. Bring your brother along.
4. They brought orders from the governor.
5. Does the dictionary have this word?
6. His conduct has me very worried.
7. The result doesn't worry me at all (**me trae sin cuidado**).
8. This problem is a real one (**se las trae**).
9. Do you have any money?

Constar (impers.) *to be known (clear) to one; appear* **constar de** *to consist of, be composed of.*

1. I want it known (let it be clear) that this plan is not mine.
2. I know (impers.) he is in Madrid.
3. The volume consists of some 400 pages.
4. These sentences are not in the last edition.

Tema

En unas doscientas palabras describa Ud. lo que Ud. entiende por la palabra "industrialización." En su respuesta conteste las preguntas siguientes:

1. ¿Qué se necesita para que un país se industrialice?
2. ¿Cuáles son algunos de los efectos en la vida pública, en la educación, en los medios de transporte, en la vida privada?
3. ¿Qué significamos cuando decimos que un país está atrasado o que es un país subdesarrollado?
4. ¿Es la industrialización una señal del progreso?
5. ¿Qué entiende Ud. por el progreso?

ADVERBS AND EXPRESSIONS OF COMPARISON

I

191. FORMATION OF ADVERBS AND ADVERBIAL PHRASES

1. Adverbs of manner are formed by suffixing **-mente** (compare the English suffix *-ly*) to the feminine singular of adjectives (Sec. **16**). When two or more adverbs in **-mente** are connected by a conjunction, **-mente** is added only to the last adjective.

Trabajaba lenta y pacientemente.	*He worked slowly and patiently.*
Le contestó amable, pero enérgicamente.	*She answered him courteously but firmly.*

2. Equivalent to adverbs in **-mente** are adverbial phrases formed by (*a*) the preposition **con** (or **sin**) + noun and (*b*) the phrase **de una manera (modo)** + adjective.

a.	**Viene a vernos con frecuencia.**	*He comes to see us frequently.*
b.	**Habla de una manera muy confusa.**	*He talks in a very confused way.*

192. POSITION OF ADVERBS

Adverbs usually stand close to the verb they modify. They come first in the sentence much more frequently in Spanish than English.

Pronto sabremos el resultado.	*We shall soon find out the results.*
Después hablaremos de eso.	*We will talk about that later.*
Abajo está su hermano.	*Your brother is downstairs.*

193. SPECIAL USES OF CERTAIN ADVERBS

1. **Ahora** means (*a*) *now, while;* **ya** may mean (*b*) *now* or *already*—with present tenses, (*c*) *already* or *just*—with past tenses, (*d*) *later*—with future tenses. (*e*) **ya** is used colloquially to indicate to someone that one understands or agrees with what is being said.

a.	**Ahora viven en México.**	*They are now living in Mexico.*
b.	**Ya vienen los bomberos.**	*The firemen are coming now.*
	Ya están aquí.	*They are already here.*
c.	**Ya se lo he dicho.**	*I have already told him.*
	Ya he terminado.	*I have just finished.*
d.	**Ya se lo contaré a Ud.**	*I will tell you later.*
	Ya verá Ud.	*You'll see.*
e.	**Tenemos que hacer lo que quiere. En fin, se trata de un amigo.— Ya, ya.**	*We have to do what he wants. After all, he's a friend.—Of course.*
	Soy representante de la editorial.—¡Ah, ya!	*I'm a representative of the publishing house.—Oh, yes.*

NOTE. **Ya no** *no longer:* **ya no viven aquí** *they no longer live here.*

2. **Todavía** and **aún** mean *yet, still.*

¿Todavía están Uds. aquí?	*Are you still here?*
No estoy bien aún.	*I am not well yet.*

NOTE. **Seguir** (Sec. **133**) is often used in this sense: **sigue enfermo** *he is still sick.*

3. Equivalents of *then.*

Entonces means (*a*) *then* in the sense of *at that moment* or *in that case;* **pues** (or **pues entonces**) means (*b*) *well then, in that case,* but **luego** means (*c*) *immediately afterwards* or *consequently;* **después** (*d*) is *afterwards* (more general).

a.	**Entonces oímos un gran ruido.**	*Then (at the moment) we heard a great noise.*
	No me gusta ese ejemplo.— (Pues) entonces busca otro.	*I don't like that example.—Well then, find another.*

b. **Pues no lo encuentro.**	*But I don't (can't) find it.*
c. **¿No resulta? Luego dejémoslo.**	*Doesn't it work? Then (therefore) let's abandon it.*
Luego salieron a la calle.	*Then (thereupon) they went out.*
d. **Después se fueron al teatro.**	*And afterwards they went to the theater.*

4. The noun **tiempo** *time* is usually expressed in Spanish as the equivalent of the English *long (time)* and related expressions.

¿Se queda Ud. aquí (por) mucho tiempo?	*Are you going to be here long?*
más tiempo	*longer*
demasiado tiempo	*too long*
¿cuánto tiempo?	*how long?*

But: **hace poco** *a short while ago, (for) a short time*

NOTE. **Un (mucho) rato** *a (long) while* (duration not exceeding a few hours) is similarly used: **¿Lleva Ud. aquí mucho rato?** *Have you been here long?* **No, hace un ratito.** *No, just a short while.* Used without the article, it implies a longer time: **Hace rato que no viene por acá.** *She has not come around for a while.*

194. THE GENERAL OR ABSOLUTE SUPERLATIVE

An indefinite or general degree of superlativeness, corresponding to the English *a* (not *the*) *most, very, highly, exceedingly,* is expressed in Spanish by suffixing **-ísimo, -ísima** to adjectives and adverbs. This usage is very frequent in Spanish. **Muchísimo** (not **muy mucho**) is the regular form for *very much.*

unos montes altísimos	*some very high mountains*
una función aburridísima	*a most tiresome performance*
lentísimamente	*most (exceedingly, very) slowly*

NOTE. Adjectives and adverbs ending in **-co, -go,** and **-z** show the necessary orthographic changes: **cerquísima** *very near,* **larguísimo** *very long,* **felicísima** *most happy;* those ending in **-ble** insert **i** between the **b** and the **l: noble, nobilísimo.**

195. THE SPECIFIC OR COMPARATIVE SUPERLATIVE

The definite or specific comparison of superiority or inferiority between two or more members of the same class is rendered in Spanish by placing the adverbs **más** *more, (the) most,* and **menos** *less, (the) least* before adjectives and adverbs.

Ella es más lista que él.	*She is more clever than he.*
Él es el menos inteligente de la familia.	*He is the least intelligent in the family.*
Iban más de prisa que nosotros.	*They were going faster than we.*

EJERCICIO

Combínense las frases siguientes según el modelo: **María es lista pero Luis es más listo.** → **Luis es más listo que María.**

1. Paco es rico, pero Rafael es más rico.
2. Nuestra destinación está lejos, pero la suya está más lejos.
3. Este país está atrasado, pero aquel país está más atrasado.
4. El texto de José es interesante, pero nuestro texto es más interesante.

Reemplácense las palabras subrayadas con las palabras entre paréntesis:

5. Jorge[a] es el más inteligente[b] de la clase[c].

    a. (Josefa, tú y Carlos, Roberto, las dos amigas)

    b. (rico, divertido, serio, alegre)

    c. (familia, mundo, grupo, escuela)

---

196. IRREGULAR FORMS OF THE COMPARATIVE

The following forms show irregularities:

mucho—más	*more, (the) most*
poco—menos	*less, (the) least*
bueno, bien—mejor	*better, (the) best*
malo, mal—peor	*worse, (the) worst*
grande—más grande or **mayor**	*larger, (the) largest; older, (the) oldest*
pequeño—más pequeño or **menor**	*smaller, (the) smallest; younger, (the) youngest*

Más grande and **más pequeño** refer strictly to size, while **mayor** and **menor** usually, although not exclusively, refer to age (of persons).

Habla inglés mejor que yo.	*He speaks English better than I.*
Su mujer es mayor que él.	*His wife is older than he.*

NOTE. **Más bien** means *rather*. **Más** (with **gustar**) also means *better*.

197. USES OF *QUE* AND *DE* IN COMPARISONS

1. *Than* introducing a phrase or clause not containing a finite verb is rendered (*a*) by **que,** or (*b*) by **de** before numerals.

a. **Más vale reír que llorar.**	*It is better to laugh than to cry.*
b. **Este cuadro vale más de cinco mil dólares.**	*This picture is worth more than five thousand dollars.*

NOTE. **No . . . más que** = *only* (with verb expressed): **no tiene más que doce años** *he is only twelve years old.* It may replace **sólo** or **solamente,** except when the verb is not expressed.

EJERCICIO

Reemplácense las palabras subrayadas con las palabras entre paréntesis: **Alberto gastó*ᵃ* mas (menos) de cien dólares*ᵇ*.**
a. (ganar, perder, tener)
b. (mil pesetas, cincuenta pesos, quinientos francos)

---

2. But when the *than* clause contains a finite verb, *than* is rendered in Spanish by the full forms (*a*) *than what* **de lo que** or (*b*) *than that (those, the ones) which* **del que, de la que,** etc. **De lo que** is used when the antecedent is an adjective or adverb; the inflected forms are used when it is a noun.

a. **Las dificultades eran más serias de lo que habíamos creído.**	*The difficulties were more serious than we had thought.*
Tiene más de lo que necesita.	*She has more than she needs.*
Tiene más de lo (que es) necesario.	*She has more than (what is) necessary.*
b. **El asunto tiene más dificultades de las que habíamos previsto.**	*The affair has more difficulties than (the specific ones which) we had foreseen.*

3. In superlative expressions, Spanish uses **de** where English uses *in.* In this type of sentence **mejor, peor, mayor,** and **menor,** like **bueno, malo,** etc., always precede the nouns they modify, except when they stress differentiation.

Es el peor estudiante de la clase.	*He is the worst student in the class.*
la mayor alegría de su vida	*the greatest joy in your life*
But: **mi hija menor**	*my youngest daughter*

EJERCICIO

Pónganse las palabras entre paréntesis en lugar las palabras subrayadas:
Mi padre nos dio más <u>libros</u>*ᵃ* de los que <u>queríamos</u>*ᵇ*.
a. (dinero, pesetas, carne, pesos)
b. (pedir, hacernos falta, anticipar)

---

198. COMPARISONS OF EQUALITY

Comparisons of equality are rendered by **tanto** and **como** according to the following scheme: (*a*) **tanto como** *as much as* after verbs, (*b*) **tan . . . como** *so, as . . . as* with adjectives and adverbs, (*c*) **tanto** (inflected) **. . . como** *as much (many) . . . as* with nouns, expressed or understood.

a.	**Gasta tanto como gana.**	*He spends as much as he earns.*
b.	**Es tan generoso como su padre.**	*He is as generous as his father.*
	tan pronto como sea posible	*as soon as possible*
c.	**Este piso tiene tantas habitaciones como el otro.**	*This apartment has as many rooms as the other one.*

EJERCICIO

Reemplácense las palabras subrayadas con las palabras entre paréntesis:
1. Aquella iglesia*ᵃ* no es tan grande*ᵇ* como la otra.
    a. (casa, museo, pueblo, lugar)
    b. (antiguo, interesante, pintoresco, hermoso)
2. A mí me hace falta tanto dinero como a Ud.
    (plata, libertad, suerte, pesos, vino)
3. Tomás toca la guitarra tan bien como los gitanos.
    (mal, admirablemente, delicadamente, seriamente)

Traducción 17A

1. We were all talking rapidly and heatedly.
2. He expressed himself very accurately.
3. Then she entered noiselessly.
4. We are going to the fair tomorrow.
5. I have all my books upstairs.
6. Have you seen many plays this season?—Not as many as I should like.
7. The show has already begun.
8. What are you going to do now?
9. The parade is starting now.
10. Are you coming with us?—No, I can't now. I'll see you later in the café.
11. Are you still living in the same house?—Yes, we haven't moved yet.
12. I don't want to stay too long in this town.—Well, then, we will leave whenever you want.
13. Have you been here long?—Only ten minutes.
14. It was an extremely hot day.
15. This desk is larger than mine.
16. My brother is (a) better mechanic than I.
17. He likes cats better (**más**) than dogs.
18. I have paid more for the furniture than it is worth.

19. He has more than five thousand dollars (of) income.
20. There are more students in the course than we had anticipated.
21. He buys more books than he can read.
22. In the morning we went to the bank, then to the consulate, and afterwards to the station.
23. He no longer writes to us.
24. These mountains are not so high as those in the West.
25. They have only a daughter.
26. She is younger than her sister.
27. She is as kind as (she is) intelligent.
28. She has the (**unos**) blackest eyes!
29. There were more than one hundred guests at the wedding.
30. The weather was exceedingly fine.

II

199. SPECIAL USES OF CERTAIN ADVERBS (*CONTINUED*)

Adverbial phrases of time and direction usually follow nouns. The English **-wards** is usually rendered by **hacia** + adverb. (Occasionally **para** is also found.)

años después	*years after(wards)*
calle abajo	*down the street*
hacia atrás	*backward*
hacia aquí	*this way (towards here)*
hacia adelante	*forward*
para adelante	*forward*
cuesta arriba	*up (the) hill*

EJERCICIO

Pónganse las palabras entre paréntesis en los espacios en las frases siguientes:
1. El viejo seguía _____ .
2. Los guardias corrieron _____ .
3. Alfredo fue _____ .
(hacia adelante, para atrás, hacia abajo, calle abajo, cuesta arriba, hacia aquí)

---

2. Adverbial phrases of manner may be formed (*a*) by **a la** + feminine adjectives of nationality (Sec. **164**) and (*b*) by **a** + the feminine plural of adjectives and participles.

a. **a la francesa**	*in the French style*
b. **a ciegas**	*blindly*
a sabiendas	*wittingly*
a gatas	*on all fours*
a escondidas	*on the sly*
a hurtadillas	*stealthily*
a oscuras	*in the dark*
a solas	*alone*
a pie juntillas	*with feet together; firmly*
(a pie juntillo,	
a pies juntillos)	

EJERCICIO

Pónganse las palabras entre paréntesis en lugar de las palabras subrayadas:
Me gusta la <u>carne</u>*ᵃ* a la <u>francesa</u>*ᵇ*.
a. (el chocolate, la ensalada, el postre, el pescado)
b. (española, italiana, alemana, mexicana)

---

3. Certain adverbs may be used as nouns.

en aquel entonces	*at that time*
el por qué	*the reason why*
el cómo	*the "how" of it*

4. **Recientemente** *recently, newly* is shortened to **recién** before past participles.

el recién llegado	*the newcomer*
los recién casados	*the newlyweds*

200. INTENSIFICATION

Following are some of the more frequent means of intensifying words and phrases in Spanish: (*a*) by the adverbs **ya, mismo, bien, tan,** and **puro;** (*b*) by repetition of adverbs; (*c*) by the absolute superlative and, in colloquial speech, by the diminutive of adverbs; (*d*) by introducing phrases with **si** (Sec. **123.3**), **que, sí que,** or **es que.**

a. **¡Ya caigo!**	*I see!*
¡Ya lo creo!	*I should say so!*
ahora mismo	*right now*
ayer mismo	*just yesterday*
¡Y ellos tan contentos!	*And weren't they happy!*
No me puedo mover de puro cansado.	*I can't move for sheer exhaustion.*

b. **casi casi**   *almost*
   así así   *so-so*

c. **lejísimo**   *very far*
   en seguidita   *right away*
   ¡callandito!   *hush! hush!*

d. **¡Si ya lo sé!**   *Why, of course, I know it!*
   ¡Que no he sido yo!   *(I insist) it wasn't me!*
   ¡Entonces sí que nos lucíamos!   *We certainly would be in a fix then!*
   ¡Eso sí que no!   *Not that, by any means!*
   ¿Es que no le gusta?   *But don't you really like it?*
   ¡Basta ya!   *Enough is enough!*

NOTE. In Spanish America **no más** is frequently used as an intensifier (*just, right*): **¡Pase Ud. no más!** *Come (go) right in!*

EJERCICIO

Intensifíquense las palabras subrayadas según el modelo: **Vamos ahora.** →
Vamos ahora mismo. Trabajamos mucho. → **Sí que trabajamos mucho.**

1. Nos vio y <u>entonces</u> empezó a correr.
2. Margarita <u>habla</u> mucho.
3. Fui a verlo <u>ayer</u>.
4. No <u>fue</u> él quien lo hizo.
5. Me llamó <u>aquí</u>.

---

201. ABSOLUTE SUPERLATIVE (*CONTINUED*)

There are certain irregular forms of the absolute superlative, relics of the original Latin. (For a complete list, see Appendix, Sec. **271**)

202. THE COMPARATIVE (AND SUPERLATIVE) (*CONTINUED*)

1. No formal distinction exists in Spanish between the comparative and superlative degrees. The context suffices to show the meaning. The definite article is used only when necessary for the meaning, i.e., in certain cases of apposition.

el hombre de más mérito   *the man of most merit*
¡Pero yo . . . criatura más inútil! *But I am such a (the most) useless*
                                        creature!

mi hija la menor   *My younger—or youngest—daughter*
                                        (lit., my daughter the youngest one of
                                        the lot).

2. The following special uses should be noted: (*a*) **más bueno** and **más malo** are used when moral qualities are involved, (*b*) they may also be used as substitutes in exclamations for the absolute superlative; (*c*) **lo** is used with the superlative of adverbs when followed by an expression of possibility; (*d*) *most of* is either **la mayor parte de** or **los (las) más de** (see Sec. **167**); (*e*) **nada más** is used colloquially as equivalent to **no más . . . que.**

a.	**Es más bueno que el pan.**	*He is as good as gold.*
	Es más malo que Barrabás.	*He is more wicked than Barabbas.*
b.	**¡Es el (un) hombre más bueno!**	*He is such a kind man!*
c.	**lo más pronto posible**	*as soon as possible*
d.	**La mayor parte (los más) de los turistas desembarcaron en Cádiz.**	*Most of the tourists landed in Cadiz.*

NOTE. **Los más** may also be used adjectivally: **las más veces** *most of the time.*

e.	**Tiene doce años nada más.**	*He is only twelve years old.*

NOTE. In Spanish America the colloquial form is **no más,** which is used very frequently.

203. THAN (*CONTINUED*)

1. The **de lo que, del que,** etc., construction offers the following special cases: (*a*) **de lo que** may be used instead of the inflected forms in order to impart an indefinite value to the noun antecedent; (*b*) if the antecedent of **el que** is the subject, not the object, of the preceding verb, **que,** not **de,** is used for *than*; (*c*) sometimes especially in colloquial and proverbial expressions, **que** alone is used, if the two finite verbs are directly contrasted. (These forms are used instead of simple **que** when the finite verb is expressed because **que** cannot function both as the conjunction *than* and as the relative pronoun object of the verb, since the relative cannot be omitted, as in English.)

a.	**Este asunto tiene más importancia de lo que se creía.**	*This matter is of more importance than was thought.*
b.	**Este plan ofrece más ventajas de las que se ven.**	*This plan offers more advantages than can be seen.*
	Este plan ofrece más ventajas que el que nos propuso ayer.	*This plan offers more advantages than the one which you proposed yesterday.*
	Esta revista es más interesante que la que leímos ayer.	*This magazine is more interesting than the one we read yesterday.*
c.	**Pescador de caña, más pierde que gana.**	*The man who fishes with a rod loses more than he gains.*
	Peor está que estaba.	*She's worse off than she was before.*

2. **Que que** *than that* may be (*a*) amplified to **que el que** or **que no que,** or (*b*) reduced to simple **que** (since both **que's** are conjunctions).

a. **Es mejor que lo piense que que** (or **que el que, que no que**) **lo diga.**	*It's better for you to think so than to say so.*

NOTE. **Que no que** is used only when direct contrast is involved, as above.

b. **¡Qué más quisiera yo que me dejaran la criatura!**	*What more could I ask for than that they should let me have the child?*

204. *TANTO, CUANTO,* AND OTHER EXPRESSIONS OF COMPARISON

1. Following are some special uses of **tanto, cuanto,** and related forms: (*a*) **tanto** (not **tan**) is used with comparatives, (*b*) **tan** may be omitted in combination with **como,** (*c*) *as, like,* is **como,** while the same *as, just like* is **lo mismo que, igual que,** (*c*) **tanto como** is occasionally replaced by **tanto cuanto,** (*e*) **cual** is found for **como** only in archaic or poetic style.

a. **Tanto peor para ellos.**	*So much the worse for them.*
b. **Es claro como el agua.**	*It is (just as) clear as water.*
c. **El enfermo está lo mismo que ayer.**	*The patient is just the same as yesterday.*
d. **Gasta tanto cuanto gana.**	*He spends as much as (all that) he earns.*
e. **Su frente cual borrascoso cielo . . .**	*His brow, like a tempestuous sky . . .*

2. (*a*) **The more . . . the more** is expressed in Spanish by **cuanto más . . . (tanto) más,** (*b*) *more and more* by **cada vez más,** and (*c*) *all the more . . . because* by **tanto más . . . cuanto que.**

a. **Cuanto más se habla, menos se piensa.**	*The more one talks, the less one thinks.*

NOTE. **Mientras** may be substituted for **cuanto: mientras más estudio, más aprendo** *the more I study, the more I learn.*

b. **Estaba cada vez más preocupado.**	*He became more and more worried.*
Hablaba cada vez más confusamente.	*He spoke more and more confusedly.*
Andaba cada vez más lentamente.	*He walked slower and slower.*
c. **Es Ud. injusto para con él, tanto más cuanto que no sabe Ud. nada de cierto.**	*You are all the more unjust toward him, the more so since you know nothing for certain.*

3. **Tanto ... como** is often the equivalent of the English expression using *both ... and.*

Tanto los padres como los tíos acompañaron a las niñas a misa.	*Both the parents and the aunts and uncles accompanied the girls to mass.*

Traducción 17B

1. She was walking uphill.
2. I had seen her two weeks before.
3. We were going half and half in the purchase.
4. I don't know her name; they simply call her Encanto.
5. Here we have a few books just published.
6. I will surely write to her tomorrow.
7. Her hair seemed blue from sheer black(ness).
8. The bullring is quite near.—Well, then, let's go on (**a**) foot.
9. That certainly would be difficult.
10. Unless the express is late, we are going to miss it.—Then we certainly shall miss it.
11. She has gone (refl.) to live in the country as far as possible away from business.
12. She has more pride than it seemed.
13. This map has more details than the one I have just bought.
14. It is better for her to stay than to come with us.
15. If she doesn't want to accept, so much the worse for her.
16. She is [as] tame as a lamb.
17. Everything was the same as when she left.
18. The more I hear this music, the more I like it.
19. The more you think about it, the more difficult it will seem to you.
20. She is getting fatter and fatter.—Well, I haven't noticed it.
21. The sea was getting rougher and rougher.
22. I think all this is inopportune, all the more because we haven't been invited to express our opinion.
23. The apartment is much larger than the one we had last year.
24. The morning train doesn't make as many stops as the evening train.
25. This bulb doesn't give as much light as the other one.
26. Both your friends and my friends will attend the party.

III

Verbos y Modismos

Llevar *to take (to), bear, wear, have, be (indicating duration of time);* **llevarse** *to take away, carry off, get along together, buy.* (**Llevar** implies **ir,** traer *implies* **venir,** while **tomar** implies either *reception* or *choice.*)

1. Take me to the circus!
2. He has taken my overcoat (away) with him.
3. The flood carried away the bridge.
4. She leads a very healthful life.
5. He was wearing a top hat and (carrying) a cane.
6. The job took her two hours.
7. The author has already written two acts.
8. How many years have you been here?
9. My brother is (**me lleva**) four years (older than I).
10. She carried out (**a cabo**) the orders of the general.
11. You are always opposing (**llevar la contraria**) me.
12. The two get along very well together.
13. She was greatly disappointed (**Llevar un gran chasco**).

Subir *to go (come, carry, bring, take, put) up, rise, get on (a train, bus,* etc.); **bajar** *to go (come, carry, bring, take, put) down, lower, get off (a train, bus,* etc.). (Note that these two verbs [also **entrar**] are both transitive and intransitive.) (When used intransitively and without adverb complement, **subir arriba** and **bajar abajo** are heard colloquially.)

1. Go up (down) to my room and bring me my hat.
2. The price of commodities has gone up (come down) recently.
3. Please tell them to bring (up, down, in) my breakfast.
4. We will have to (impers.) call a porter to carry (bring, take) our baggage (up, down).
5. This year they have raised (lowered) her (the) salary (for her) twice.
6. We must get on (off) the (**al, del**) train now.
7. The tide is coming in (going out).
8. She climbed the tower to see the view.
9. Success has gone to her (**subírsele**) head.
10. Lower your voice(s); there is someone (**un**) sick in the house.

18 INDEFINITES AND NUMERALS

I

205. INDEFINITES

Following are the more common indefinites in Spanish:

1. **alguien, alguno, algo; nadie, ninguno, nada**—see Secs. **98, 99.**
2. **Mucho** *much* (sing.), *many* (pl.), and **poco** *little* (sing.), *few* (pl.) are both adjectives and pronouns. *A little (of)* is **un poco (de).** *Very much (many)* is **muchísimo(s).** These forms are likewise used as adverbs. **Muy** is used as the intensifier before adverbs and adjectives. *Too, too much (many)* is **demasiado.**

Tengo muchos libros, pero pocos buenos.	*I have many books but few good ones.*
Tenía poco dinero, pero mucha suerte.	*He had little money but a great deal of luck.*
Deme Ud. un poquito de eso.	*Give me a little of that.*
Es demasiado caro.	*It is too expensive.*

NOTE. **Mucho,** not **muy,** is used when it stands alone: **¿Está muy ocupado?—Sí, mucho.** *Is he very busy?—Yes, very.*

3. **Otro** *another, other, else,* and **tal** *such (a)* are both adjectives and pronouns, but **cierto** *a certain* and **semejante** *such (a)* are always adjectives.

225

otra vez	*another time, again*
otra cosa	*another thing, something else*
¿Qué dicen los otros?	*What do the others say?*
esto y lo otro	*this and that (other thing)*

NOTE. *Nothing else* is **nada más.** *The others,* in the sense of *the rest, the remaining* is **los (las, lo) demás, los restantes.**

No hay tal cosa.	*There is no such thing.*
cierta persona de influencia	*a certain influential person*
¿Ha visto semejante majadero?	*Have you ever seen such an annoying person?*
una cosa cierta	*a sure thing*
una locura semejante	*such madness*

NOTE. The indefinite article is used with **cierto** and **semejante** when they follow the noun.

4. **Cada** *each* is an invariable adjective, but **ambos** (or **los dos**) *both* and **todo** *every, all* are both adjectives and pronouns. *Everybody* is **todo el mundo** and *everything* is **todo** (neuter). **Todo** in the sense of *all* requires the definite article between it and the noun; when **todo** is direct object of the verb the pronoun **lo** must also be used.

cada semana	*each week*
cada uno, cada cual	*each one*
Esto basta para los dos.	*This is enough for both (of us).*
Tiene ambas piernas rotas.	*He has both legs broken.*
todos los hombres, todo hombre	*any (every) man, each man*
todas las mujeres, toda mujer	*all the women, each (any) woman*
todo el día	*all day (long)*
Hay para todos.	*There is enough for all.*
Lo tengo todo aquí.	*I have everything here.*

NOTE. In translating *every* in time expressions, **todos** is collective and **cada** is distributive and more emphatic: **cada noche** *every night* (i.e., *night after night*), **todas las noches** *every night* (i.e., *all the nights*). The latter construction is the more frequent.

5. **Cualquiera** *any, anyone, anybody (whatsoever, at all)* is both adjective and pronoun. It loses its final **-a** when it precedes; when it follows, the indefinite article is used with the noun. The plural is **cualesquier(a).**

cualquier cosa	*anything (at all)*
una persona cualquiera	*anybody (at all)*
¿Cuál prefiere Ud.?—Cualquiera.	*Which one do you prefer?—Any one.*
Eso cualquiera lo sabe.	*Anybody knows that.*

NOTE. The ordinary English pronoun *whatever* is either **lo que** (with subjunctive) or **cualquier cosa que** (emphatic): **haré lo que (cualquier cosa que) Ud. me diga** *I will do whatever (thing) you say.* The **que** is always required to introduce the following clause. The indicative is used when the meaning requires it: **cualquier cosa que hace, la hace bien** *whatever thing he does, he does well.*

      6. *Somewhere, anywhere,* is **alguna parte;** *nowhere* **ninguna parte;** *everywhere* **todas partes.** Note that in Spanish the proper preposition must always be used with these forms.

La encuentro en todas partes.	*I meet her everywhere.*
No voy a ninguna parte.	*I am not going anywhere.*

NOTE. In conversation especially, **lado** and **sitio** are sometimes used instead of **parte.**

Pónganse las palabras entre paréntesis en lugar de las palabras subrayadas, haciéndose los cambios necesarios.
1. Tiene <u>bastantes</u> libros. (pocos, muchos, demasiados)
2. No me traiga Ud. <u>tales</u> cuentos. (semejante, este)
3. <u>Todas</u> las tardes trabajo en la biblioteca. (cada, cualquier, mucho)
4. A él le gusta <u>cualquier</u> cosa. (todo, mucho, tal, poca)
5. Las llaves estarán en <u>alguna</u> parte. (ninguno, todo, cualquier)
6. Todo el <u>día</u> jugamos al tenis. (tarde, mañana, semana)

---

206. THE PARTITIVE OR APPOSITIONAL *DE*

      In certain set expressions with the verbs **haber** and **tener,** a partitive or appositional **de** is introduced between the indefinites **algo, mucho, nada, ¿qué?, lo que,** and the adjective which follows.

¿Qué hay de nuevo?—Nada de particular.	*What's up?—Nothing special.*
Tiene algo (mucho) de inglés.	*He has something (a great deal) of the Englishman about him.*
lo que hay de drámatico en ello	*the dramatic elements in the matter*

NOTE. A similar expression is **hay de todo** *there are all kinds.*

Pónganse las palabras entre paréntesis en lugar de la palabra subrayada: Hay <u>algo</u> de interés en este asunto. (poco, mucho, nada, ¿qué?)

207. NUMERALS

For a list of the cardinal and ordinal numerals, see Sec. **279.**

1. The following peculiarities of the cardinal numbers are to be noted:

(*a*) the composite forms (**dieciséis, veintiuno,** etc.) are more frequent in rendering 16 through 19, 21 through 29, while the compound forms (**treinta y uno,** etc.) prevail from 31 on;

(*b*) three of the hundreds are irregular forms **quinientos, setecientos,** and **novecientos;**

(*c*) **veintiuno, treinta y uno,** etc., and **doscientos, trescientos,** etc., are inflected for gender;

(*d*) **un(o)** is omitted before **cien(to)** and **mil;** but

(*e*) not before **millón** *million,* which, like **par** *pair, couple,* and **docena** *dozen,* is a noun and is used with **de.**

a.	**veintidós hombres y treinta y tres mujeres**	*22 men and 33 women*

NOTE. A written accent is required on **dieciséis, veintidós, veintitrés,** and **veintiséis.**

b.	**Lo vendí en dos mil quinientas pesetas.**	*I sold it for 2500 pesetas.*
c.	**veintiuna páginas**	*21 pages*
	novecientas libras	*900 pounds*
d.	**cien soldados**	*100 soldiers*
	¡Mil gracias!	*A thousand thanks!*
	ciento cincuenta páginas	*150 pages*

NOTE. In colloquial speech **cien** is heard as a noun: **tengo unos cien** *I have about 100.*

e.	**quinientos millones de pesos**	*500,000,000 pesos*
	un millón de dólares	*a million dollars*

EXCEPTIONS: **millón y medio** *a million and a half;* **miles de personas** *thousands of people.*

2. The ordinals are inflected for gender and number. Above *tenth* they are usually replaced by the cardinals. Both ordinals and cardinals follow the noun if they indicate an individual member of an established series.

Leí las cien primeras páginas.	*I read the first hundred pages.*
Leí hasta la página ciento once.	*I read as far as page 111.*
Felipe Segundo; Alfonso Doce	*Philip II; Alfonso XII*
el capítulo segundo	*the second chapter*

3. In dates the cardinals are regularly used with one exception: **primero.** In writing full dates the preposition **de** may be omitted.

¿Cuál es la fecha de hoy?	*What date is today?*
¿Qué fecha es hoy?	
¿A cuántos estamos?	
Hoy es el cinco de se(p)tiembre.	*Today is the 5th of September.*
Estamos a cinco de se(p)tiembre.	
But: **el primero de marzo**	*the first of March*
15 (de) septiembre (de) 1999.	*September 15, 1999.*

NOTE. In oral dates and in counting **mil** is always used: **mil cuatrocientos noventa y dos** 1492.

EJERCICIO

Léanse el párrafo siguiente y después contéstense las preguntas: Ramón acaba de recibir 2.500 pesos de su padre. Luego vendió a su amigo Diego tres libros que ya no quería, a 250 pesos cada uno. En la Caja de Ahorros tenía depositados 4.795 pesos. Por la tarde fue al centro a comprar un regalo para su novia. Quería comprar a plazos un collar de perlas por 3.100 pesetas y dejó como depósito 900 pesos. Al salir de la tienda vio que le habían multado en 150 pesos por haber estacionado su auto en una zona donde se prohibe estacionar los coches.

1. ¿Cuánto dinero recibió por los libros?
2. ¿Cuánto tenía después de venderlos?
3. ¿Cuánto tenía después de hacer el primer pago por el collar?
4. Al fin del día, ¿cuánto dinero tenía?
5. ¿Cuánto debía Ramón?

Contéstense:

6. ¿Qué fecha es hoy? ¿A cuántos estamos?
7. ¿Cuál es la fecha del cumpleaños de Ud.?
8. ¿Cuál es la fecha del nacimiento de su padre?

Traducción 18A

1. They were walking very slowly.
2. Give me a little water.
3. They have many relatives in Havana.
4. Do you like this necklace?—Very much.
5. Let's talk about something else.
6. Ring again.
7. Do you want anything else?—No, thanks, nothing else.
8. Don't come to me with such stories.

9. I'll send you the check every month or if you prefer, every other month.
10. Each time the telephone rings, I have to go downstairs to the living room.
11. She has been playing tennis the whole morning.
12. She works every afternoon in the library.
13. She is satisfied with anything.
14. I'll bet you anything.
15. She'll arrive here any day.
16. This train doesn't stop anywhere until we get to Madrid.
17. The key must be here somewhere.
18. Have you any cigarettes left?—Yes, I have some.
19. Buy me (some) sugar and (some) coffee at the store.
20. Which one do you want?—Any one.
21. Come to see us any evening.
22. She has something of (the) poet (about her).
23. The little there is (in the way) of dialogue is the best thing in the book.
24. We translated the first two hundred lines without making a single mistake.
25. She had some five hundred dollars left after paying a few bills.
26. The feast of St. John is the 24th of June.

II

208. INDEFINITES (*CONTINUED*), EXCEPT THOSE OF QUANTITY

1. (*a*) **Otro** usually precedes other adjectives, except **alguno;** (*b*) **ajeno** *of others, other people*'s is the possessive corresponding to **otro;** (*c*) **sendos (pl.)** is the distributive adjective corresponding to **cada uno.** It is rarely used. (*d*) **uno y otro (ni uno ni otro)** *both, either (neither)* are distributive, referring to a pair.

a. **esto y otras muchas cosas**	*this and many other things*
otros cien soldados	*another hundred soldiers*
algún (que) otro	*some (one or) other*
Viene por aquí alguna que otra vez.	*He drops in once in a while.*
b. **lo propio y lo ajeno**	*one's own property and that of others*
c. **Los dos ancianos, sentados en sendas mecedoras . . .**	*The two old men, each seated in a rocking chair . . .*
d. **una y otra ribera del río**	*both (either) bank(s) of the river*
ni uno ni otro partido	*neither (of the two) party(ies)*

2. In colloquial speech (*a*) **cada** has acquired an iterative and emphatic value and (*b*) **cualquiera** has taken on negative force.

   a. **¡Le dio cada golpe!**   *He gave him such a beating! (blow after blow)*

       ¡Oye uno cada historia!   *One hears all kinds of stories!*

       ¡Metiste cada pata!   *You really put your foot in it!*

   b. **¡Cualquiera le hablaba!**   *Nobody could talk to him.*

NOTE. **Un cualquiera (pl. unos cualquieras)** is *an ordinary person, a nobody.*

    3. Similar to **cualquiera** in meaning and form, but much less frequently used are the very emphatic (*a*) **quienquiera** *whoever,* (*b*) **dondequiera** *wherever* (*c*) **cuandoquiera** *whenever,* and (*d*) **comoquiera que** *since, as* (see also **siquiera,** Sec. **103**). The **que** must be used to introduce the following clause, which takes the indicative or the subjunctive according to the rules for adjective clauses.

   a. **Diga, a quienquiera que sea, que**   *Tell whomever it may be that I am not at*
       no estoy en casa.   *home.*

NOTE. *Whoever* is ordinarily **el que (quien)** followed by the subjunctive (see Sec. **118**). *Whoever* in the sense of *every one who* is **todo el que: todo el que se encuentre en esas circunstancias** *whoever finds himself in that situation.*

   b. **por dondequiera que vamos**   *wherever we (do) go*
       por dondequiera que vaya   *wherever he goes (may go)*
   c. **cuandoquiera que lo necesite**   *whenever you (may) need it*
       Tráigalo comoquiera que esté.   *Bring it just as it is (may be).*

    4. Both (*a*) **un tal** *a certain* and (*b*) **el tal** *the aforesaid* are used of persons, (although **el tal** may be used in humorous style referring to things). (*c*) **dicho** or **el referido** *said* and **determinado (a)** *certain* (known but unmentioned) are used of both persons and things; (*d*) **un no sé qué de** means *a certain (indefinable) air (or quality) of.*

   a. **Hablamos con el dueño del**   *We had a conversation with the owner of*
       garaje, un tal D. Facundo.   *the garage, a certain Don Facundo.*
   b. **El tal señor era un hombre de**   *The aforesaid gentleman was a very ill-*
       muy mal humor.   *humored man.*
   c. **dicha señora**   *the said lady*
       los referidos artículos   *the above-mentioned articles*
       Anoche nos refirió determinada *Last night a certain party told us . . .*
       persona . . .
   d. **Esta música tiene un no sé qué**   *This music has a certain exotic quality.*
       de exótico.

    5. Spanish possesses the following characteristic indefinite pronouns referring to persons: **Fulano** *Mr. So-and-so,* which may be used as a noun, and **Zutano, Mengano,** and **Perengano,** which are used only in series after Fulano.

don Fulano de Tal y don Mengano de Cual	*John Doe and Richard Roe*
Fulano, Zutano y Mengano	*Tom, Dick, and Harry*
¿Quién es ese fulano?	*Who is that fellow?*

EJERCICIO

Pónganse las palabras entre paréntesis en lugar de las palabras subrayadas:
1. Ayer vimos la catedral y muchas otras <u>cosas</u>. (iglesias, lugares, puntos de interés)
2. Algún que otro <u>muchacho</u> venía a saludarnos. (mujer, turista, guía, amigo)
3. El tal*ª* <u>sujeto</u>*ᵇ* venía preparado a reñir.
   a. (dicho, referido)
   b. (señor, guardia, mujer)
4. ¿Conoce Ud. a Fulano, el que <u>fue a América</u>? (mató a su mujer, ganó el premio gordo en la lotería, vivía en la otra calle)

209. INDEFINITE EXPRESSIONS OF QUANTITY

1. In general, it may be said that the Spanish indefinites present more precise shades of meaning than their English equivalents (compare the different ways of rendering the vague and general English *some, any, certain, such, said,* etc.). This is especially true of indefinite expressions of quantity such as (*a*) **unos, unos cuantos, algunos,** and **varios,** (*b*) **unos pocos, un poco (poquito) de, un (algún) tanto, bastante.**

a. **Conocimos a unos españoles.**	*We met some Spaniards (very general).*
Conocimos a unos cuantos españoles.	*We met some (a small number of) Spaniards.*
Conocimos a algunos españoles.	*We met some (a few) Spaniards.*
Conocimos a varios españoles.	*We met several Spaniards.*

NOTE. There is a decreasing order of definiteness in the above examples.

b. **¿Tiene Ud. muchos libros en su despacho?—Unos pocos.**	*Do you have many books in your study?—Just a few.*
Écheme un poquito más de café.	*Pour me a little more coffee.*
El artículo era un tanto insolente.	*The article was a bit (somewhat) insolent.*
Suspendieron a bastantes.	*Quite a few were flunked.*

NOTE. In certain expressions **cuatro** (and less frequently **dos**) is used with indefinite value: **¡Señorito, cuatro palabras nada más!** *Please, sir, just a few words.* **Dos palabras al lector** *Preface (a few words to the reader).*

2. Indefinite expressions of collective meaning are **una porción de** *some, a number of,* **(una) gran parte, (un) gran número** *a great many,* **una serie de** *a series (collection) of.*

He comprado una porción de cosas antiguas.	I have bought a number of antiques.
En el andén había un gran número de extranjeros.	A great many foreigners were on the platform.
Gran parte de los pasajeros perecieron en el naufragio.	A great many of the passengers perished in the shipwreck.
¡Qué serie de disparates!	What a bunch of nonsense!

NOTE. **Una barbaridad, la mar,** and similar expressions are used colloquially:

Me gustó una barbaridad (la mar).	I liked it immensely.
Tiene la mar de gracia.	It's awfully funny.
una barbaridad de gente	an awfully large crowd

3. **Tanto** and **mucho** may be used collectively in the singular (see Sec. **167.2**).

| No se podía andar con tanto automóvil y tanto autobús. | You couldn't walk for the number of automobiles and buses. |
| Hay mucha piedra por aquí. | There is an abundance of stone(s) around here. |

4. **Cosa** is used in several indefinite expressions:

(a) **una cosa** (also **alguna, ninguna cosa**) as emphatic equivalents of **algo** (or **nada**);
(b) **gran cosa** (in negative sentences) as an emphatic variant of **poco;**
(c) **cosa de,** about, approximately, some.

a. **Voy a decirle una cosa.**	I'm going to tell you something.
b. **No me importa gran cosa.**	It makes but little difference to me.
c. **Tengo cosa de cuatrocientos dólares en el banco.**	I have about (some) 400 dollars in the bank.

5. Other expressions of approximation are **unos** some, **cerca de** about, around; **como** about, as if; **(poco) más o menos,** approximately, more or less; **y pico** a little over (after). **A eso de** about and **sobre** around are used only of time.

Un hombre de unos cuarenta años.	
Un hombre como de cuarenta años.	A man about forty years old.
Un hombre de cuarenta años, (poco) más o menos.	
Tiene cerca de un millón.	He has almost (close to) a million.
La finca tiene ciento y pico de hectáreas.	the estate contains a little over a hundred hectares.
Vino a eso de (sobre) las ocho.	He came around eight o'clock.

NOTE. **Tantos** may be added to **veinte** *twenty* (up to **noventa**) to express approximation: **tiene treinta y tantos años,** *she is thirty something.*

EJERCICIO

Pónganse las palabras entre paréntesis en lugar de las palabras subrayadas:
1. Aprendí <u>unas</u> palabras de francés. (algunas, unas cuantas, varias, bastantes, unas pocas, cuatro)
2. Había <u>una porción</u> de cuadros interesantes en la tienda. (gran número, una serie, una barbaridad)
3. Esta es mucha <u>casa</u> para mí. (automóvil, trabajo, dinero)

---

210. NUMERALS (*CONTINUED*)

1. English *half* is (*a*) as a noun, **la mitad (de)** (*b*) as an adjective, **medio** (with no accompanying article).

a. **Perdí la mitad de mi dinero.**	*I lost half my money.*
b. **media docena**	*a half dozen*
año y medio	*a year and a half*
a las cinco y media	*at half past five*

NOTE. **Medio** may also mean *average,* although **promedio** is also used; **el hombre medio** *the average man.* (*Average* as a noun is **media.**) **Medio** is also used adverbially: **medio muertos** *half dead (pl.),* **está a medio hacer** (or **hecho a medias**) *it is half done.* **Medio** as a noun means *middle:* **en medio de la calle** *in the middle of the street.* It must not be confused with **medio** *means.*

2. Arithmetical fractions have cardinals as numerator and ordinals as denominator. In non-technical language the construction with **parte** is usually employed.

Seis es dos tercios de nueve, pero la mitad de doce.	*Six is two-thirds of nine, but just half of twelve.*
Perdí la tercera parte de mi dinero.	*I lost a third of my money.*

3. Collectives are usually formed by the suffixes **-ena** and **-ar.** In some cases these collectives have an indefinite value.

docena	*dozen*
una decena, veintena, centena	*some ten, twenty, hundred*
La huerta tiene un centenar de manzanos.	*The orchard has about a hundred apple trees.*

4. For expressions of price, rate, and measure, see Secs. **157d, 211.2c.**
Time and rate are usually expressed by adjectives.

seis pesos diarios (por día)   *six pesos a day*
Also **semanales (por** or **a la semana), mensuales (al mes),** and **anuales (al año)**

NOTE. In expressions of amount, size, or price **ser** is usually followed by **de:**
el precio *(total)* **será de unos doscientos dólares** *the (total) price will be around two hundred dollars.*

5. Dimensions may be expressed according to the following scheme of possibilities:

La torre tiene   **una altura de cien metros.**
La torre es de   **cien metros de altura** (or **de alto**).   *The tower is 100 meters high.*

El tamaño que busco es cuatro centímetros de largo por tres de ancho.   *The size I want is four centimeters high by three wide.*

EJERCICIO

Contéstense en frases completas:
1. Gregorio tenía dieciocho libros y vendió la tercera parte de ellos. ¿Cuántos le quedaban?
2. Ana tenía veinticuatro pesos y gastó la mitad de ellos. ¿Cuántos tenía entonces?
3. Un rascacielos tiene 900 metros de altura. ¿Cuántos metros hay en la cuarta parte? ¿En la quinta parte? ¿En la sexta parte?
4. Felipe gana 1.750 pesos cada semana y trabaja cinco días a la semana. ¿Cuánto gana por día? Si trabaja siete horas por día, ¿cuánto gana por hora? ¿Cuánto gana al mes? ¿Al año?
5. Varios amigos hacen una colección de libros usados para venderlos. Uno da cincuenta libros de a un dólar cada uno, otro da sesenta y cinco libros de a dos dólares cada uno, y un tercer amigo da cinco libros de a tres dólares y medio cada uno. ¿Cuánto recibirán por todos los libros? Si dividen el dinero igualmente, ¿cuánto recibirá cada amigo?

Traducción 18B

1. He always keeps other people's books.
2. I have told you time and again not to do it.
3. They drew their pistols (each one had a pistol).
4. He used to give (**echar**) her such sermons!

5. She gave him such looks!
6. She wears such (big) hats.
7. Whoever has said that, doesn't know what he is talking about.
8. Wherever you go, you will find good friends.
9. Last night I met a certain D. Gregorio, a countryman of yours.
10. The said town is about twenty-two miles from Cordova.
11. The whole scene had the tone of a painting by (of) Goya.
12. We saw each other a few times.
13. There were several errors in a few (small number of) pages.
14. It was an informal dinner. A few (**cuatro**) friends, that was all.
15. Where do you keep the back numbers of *La Prensa?*—There you have a few, the rest are on the shelf.
16. Drop (**poner**) me a line (**unas letras**).
17. I have a great many things to discuss with you.
18. These people are awfully serious.
19. She was about sixty years old when she died.
20. We arrived a little after nine o'clock.
21. We made an average of fifty-five kilometers an (by) hour.
22. We will leave Algeciras at half past one.
23. The average monk cares little for money.
24. The Mulhacén in (the) Sierra Nevada is over three thousand meters high.
25. There were about one hundred people on the beach.
26. I have translated a fourth of the lesson.
27. The lake is more than three kilometers wide.

III

Verbos y Modismos

Salirse (Sec. **258**) *to leave (intrans.), come out, go out, turn out,* etc.

1. I am leaving tomorrow for Europe.
2. What time does the airplane leave?
3. The servant told us that the master and mistress had gone out for a (**de**) walk.
4. Come out to the window.
5. How are we going to get out of the difficulty?
6. They all came out unhurt.
7. You are the one who will be the loser (**salir perdiendo**).
8. She came forth with a silly remark.
9. How (**¿por dónde?**) do you (indef.) get out of this building?
10. She is very headstrong; she always gets her own way.
11. Most all the students passed the examinations.
12. This pitcher leaks.
13. The deal did not turn out right (**bien**) for her.

14. The photographs have turned out very well.
15. Her hair has turned gray (**salirle canas**).
16. Two contracts have turned up for us today.
17. A wheel came off (**salírsele**) the car.
18. She took off like a shot (**salir disparado; como alma que lleva el diablo**).

Entrar *to enter, come in, bring in, get (afraid, sleepy,* etc.)

1. Four steamers have entered (in) the port.
2. Come in this way.
3. This key does not fit.
4. Have (**que**) them bring my breakfast in.
5. I see he doesn't understand (**entrarle**).
6. I am getting sleepy (noun).
7. We became afraid.
8. Flies do not enter a closed mouth.

Ocurrir *to occur, happen;* **ocurrírsele a uno** *to come to one's mind.*

1. What's the matter (goes on)?—An accident has occurred.
2. Let this not happen again.
3. Many things happened to us on the trip.
4. I have an idea.
5. He thinks of very amusing things (to say).

19 PREPOSITIONS AND CONJUNCTIONS

I

211. SIMPLE PREPOSITIONS

The most frequently used are **de, a, en, con, por,** and **para.** The following brief treatment of each (except **por** and **para;** see Secs. **107, 109**), is, of course, far from complete. Students must be acutely aware that the use of prepositions is largely idiomatic in every language and it is rare that one can translate every English preposition by a given Spanish one.

1. **De** has a very wide range of uses. It corresponds, in general, to the English (*a*) *from, of* (except as dative of separation; Sec. **53**), (*b*) *with* or *in* (in the sense of *from, of, with regard to*), and (*c*) *as* (in the capacity of). It is used (*d*) in many adverbial expressions.

a.	**Soy de Madrid.**	*I am from Madrid.*
	abrigo de piel	*fur coat*
	el dueño de la casa	*the owner of the house*
	máquina de escribir	*typewriter*
But:	**Se lo robaron al viejo.**	*It was stolen from the old man.*
b.	**loco de alegría**	*mad with joy*
	el hombre de la capa	*the man with (in) the cloak*
	vestido de negro	*dressed in black*
	ciego del ojo derecho	*blind in the right eye*

238

c.	**vestido de paisano**	*dressed as a civilian*
	adornado de azul	*trimmed in blue*
	Servía de guía.	*He served as a guide.*
	Estuvo allí de embajador.	*He was there as ambassador.*
d.	**de buena gana**	*willingly*
	de oídas	*on hearsay*
	de prisa	*rapidly*

2. **A** also has a very wide range of uses. It corresponds, in general, (*a*) to the English *to, at,* denoting motion or direction, or location in space or time with reference to motion or direction. **A** also expresses (*b*) manner, (*c*) price or rate, (*d*) *on* or *in* (in the sense of *to, at, like*).

a.	**Llegó a Barcelona.**	*He arrived at (in) Barcelona.*
	Echó a correr.	*He started to run.*
	a la derecha	*to (on) the right*
	a dos kilómetros de aquí	*two kilometers from here*
	asomado a la puerta	*standing at (looking out of) the door*
	sentado a la mesa	*seated at the table*
	a las dos de la tarde	*at two o'clock in the afternoon*
b.	**a la francesa** (see Sec. **164**)	*in the French style*
	poco a poco	*little by little*
	a toda prisa	*in all haste*
c.	**a peso el kilo**	*at a peso a (the) kilo*
	a cincuenta kilómetros por hora	*at 50 km. an hour*
d.	**a la mañana siguiente**	*on the following morning*
	a bordo del vapor	*on board the steamer*
	al contrario	*on the contrary*
	a gatas (Sec. **199.2**)	*on all fours*
	a tiempo	*on (in) time*
	a su alcance	*within his reach*
	a su servicio	*at (in) his (her) service*

3. **En** corresponds in general (*a*) to English *in* or *at* (place where or state in which), (*b*) to English *in* = *within* (time and place), (*c*) to English *into* (after certain verbs), (*d*) to English *on*.

a.	**en Buenos Aires**	*in Buenos Aires*
	en casa	*at home*
	en mangas de camisa	*in shirt sleeves*

NOTE. In translating English *at,* **en** indicates rest; **a** motion:

Llegamos al hotel.	*We arrived at the hotel.*
Estamos en casa.	*We are at home.*

b.	**en el verano**	*in (the) summer*
	en dos semanas	*in two weeks*

NOTE. *Within* is **dentro de:**

dentro de la casa	*inside the house*
dentro de poco tiempo	*within a short while*
c. **Entramos en la casa.**	*We entered the house.* (Also with **meter, penetrar, introducir,** etc.)
d. **en la mesa**	*on the table*
en la isla	*on the island*

4. **Con** corresponds, in general, (*a*) to the English *with* (accompaniment, instrument, manner); (*b*) it occasionally has concessive force (see Sec. **108.5c**).

a. **Estaba en el café con sus amigos.**	*He was in the café with his friends.*
Lo he visto con mis propios ojos.	*I have seen it with my own eyes.*
con rapidez	*rapidly*
b. **Con todo su dinero, no tenía un solo amigo.**	*With (in spite of) all his money, he did not have a single friend.*

5. For a list of the more common verbs construed with prepositions see Appendix Sec. **269.**

EJERCICIO

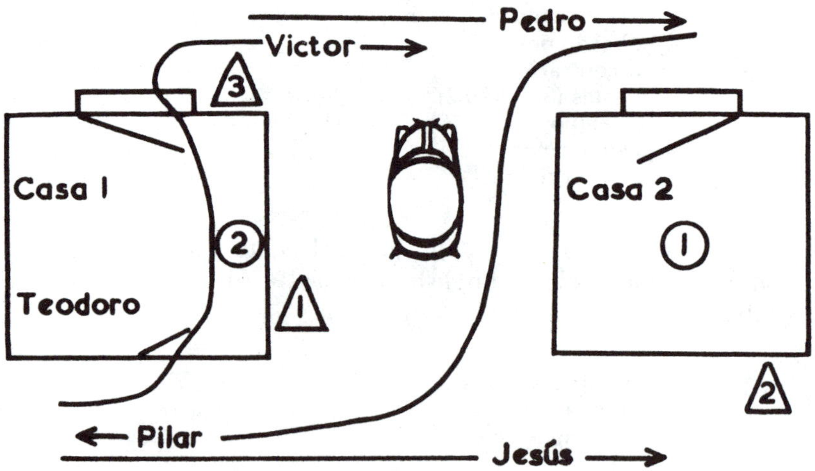

He aquí dos casas vistas desde el aire.
Contéstense:

1. ¿Dónde está el autómovil?
2. ¿Dónde está Teodoro?
3. ¿Dónde está el círculo número 1?

4. ¿Dónde está el círculo número 2?
5. ¿Dónde está el triángulo número 1?
6. ¿Dónde está el triángulo número 2?
7. ¿Dónde está el triángulo número 3?

212. COMPOUND PREPOSITIONS

Compound prepositions are usually formed (*a*) chiefly from adverbs and adverbial phrases by the addition of **de,** (*b*) sometimes from adjectives, participles, and nouns, by the addition of **a.**

a.	**antes de**	*before (time, order)*
	cerca de	*near*
	debajo de	*under*
	delante de	*before, in front of (place)*
	dentro de	*within*
	después de	*after (time, order)*
	detrás de	*behind, after (place)*
	encima de	*over, on top of*
	fuera de	*outside of*
b.	**conforme a**	*according to*
	(con) respecto a	*with respect (regard) to*
	en frente de	*opposite, facing*
	frente a	*opposite*
	junto a	*close to, beside*
	tocante a	*touching, concerning*

NOTE 1. *In front of* is normally translated as **delante de.**
NOTE 2. The adverbs **abajo, afuera,** and **adentro** (+ **de**) are heard in colloquial speech used as prepositions.

213. COORDINATE ("JOINING") CONJUNCTIONS

The coördinate conjunctions are:

(*a*) **y** *and* (**e** before words beginning with **i** or **hi**)
(*b*) **o** *or* **u** (before words beginning with **o** or **ho**) and **ni** *nor* (see Sec. **103**)
(*c*) **pero** *but* (*nevertheless*)
(*d*) **sino** *but* (*on the contrary*—direct contrast to preceding negative)

a. **España e Italia**	*Spain and Italy*
madre e hija	*mother and daughter*

EXCEPTIONS: Before the diphthong **ie: sangre y hierro** *blood and iron;* at the beginning of questions and exclamations: **¿y Isabel?** *and what about Isabel?*

b. **siete u ocho**	*seven or eight*
mujer u hombre	*man or woman*
c. **El pueblo es grande, pero sucio.**	*The town is large, but dirty.*
No queríamos ir, pero fuimos.	*We didn't want to go, but we went.*

NOTE. **Mas** *but* (equivalent to **pero**) is archaic and rhetorical.

d. **No parece española sino inglesa.**	*She doesn't look Spanish, but English.*
No les gusta salir sino quedarse en casa.	*They don't like to go out, but to stay home.*

NOTE. When two finite verbs are directly contrasted, **sino que** is used:

No hace falta que venga sino que escriba.	*It isn't necessary for him to come, but to write.*

But in the sense of *only* is either **no . . . más que** (Sec. **197**) or **no . . . sino:**

No hace (nada) sino comer y dormir.	*He does nothing except eat and sleep.*

214. SUBORDINATE CONJUNCTIONS

1. (*a*) The simple subordinate conjunctions are:

que	*that*
como	*as, since (causal)*
cuando	*when*
mientras (que)	*while*
pues (que)	*for, since (cause)*
si	*if*

a. **Como no sé alemán, no pude hacerme entender.**	*Since (as) I don't know German I couldn't make myself understood.*

(*b*) The compound subordinate conjunctions are usually formed by adding **que** to adverbs, prepositional phrases, and prepositions, chiefly the latter (see Sec. **119**).

b. **antes (de) que**	*before (time)*
así que	*as soon as, so that*
aunque, bien que	*although*
(en) caso (de) que	*in case*
con tal (de) que	*provided*
desde que	*since (time)*
después (de) que	*after (time)*
hasta que	*until*
luego que	*as soon*
a medida que	*(according, in proportion) as, at the same time as*
mientras (que)	*while, as*
de modo (manera, suerte, forma) que	*so that*
para que, a fin de que	*in order that*
puesto que	*for, since (cause)*
sin que	*without*
ya que	*now that, since (cause)*

2. **Que** *that* is ordinarily not omitted in noun clauses, and is even required after verbs of saying and thinking when followed by **sí** or **no** or when used parenthetically.

Creo que sí.	*I think so.*
Dice que no.	*He says not (no).*
¡Ya lo creo que sí!	*I should certainly say so!*
Fue a casa, me parece que por su abrigo.	*He went home for his overcoat, I think.*

Traducción 19A

1. The city of Granada was the last capital of the Moors in Spain.
2. Fashionable beaches are found in Yucatán.
3. A velvet rug covered the floor.
4. The girl on the beach with the red hair was wearing a bikini.
5. He dressed in (a) tuxedo.
6. The child turned pale from fear.
7. I have a mahogany table.
8. He was blind with rage.
9. I have him here as secretary.
10. He died of hunger.
11. I know the book by heart.
12. I have received a letter from your cousin.
13. We went out to the street.
14. Turn to the left.
15. They started to laugh.

16. The steamship was going at full speed.
17. She likes to ride horseback.
18. He finished the short story in three days.
19. I will see you at the office.
20. I will be there within half an hour.
21. They entered the cathedral.
22. I met her on the boat.
23. I cannot eat this with a fork.
24. In spite of all that I can't make up my mind to buy it.
25. Put the lights out before you go to bed.
26. There is an avenue of trees in front of the house.
27. We all sat around the bonfire.
28. The station is far from the village.
29. We haven't decided anything in regard to that matter.
30. He doesn't know how to swim, but he wants to learn.
31. She does nothing but read.
32. Her eyes aren't black, but blue.
33. He didn't say that he didn't want to, but that he couldn't.
34. I will tell him when I see him.
35. Stay here until we come back.
36. We'll wait for you provided you don't take long.
37. His ambitions and ideals are exceptional for someone his age.
38. The *Poem of El Cid* has a great literary and historical importance.
39. Do you think he will be successful?—I hope so.
40. I'll change it, since you insist.

II

215. SIMPLE PREPOSITIONS (*CONTINUED*)

(*a*) The English **for** is sometimes rendered by **a** (in the sense of **por** or **hacia**);

(*b*) **en** is sometimes used to express estimate or price;

(*c*) **sin** sometimes corresponds to the English prefix *un-* or suffix *-less;*

(*d*) **hasta** means *as far as, even;*

(*e*) **cuando** and **mientras** are occasionally used as prepositions;

(*f*) **según** may be used as an adverb.

a. **su amor a la patria**	*his love for his country*
b. **Lo tasaron en cien mil pesos.**	*They appraised it at 100,000 pesos.*
Lo compramos en un dólar.	*We bought it for a dollar.*
c. **una noche sin luna**	*a moonless night*
un hombre sin cultura	*an uncultured man*
d. **Esto lo saben hasta los niños de pecho.**	*Even babes in arms know this.*

e. **cuando la visita del Presidente**	*at the time of the President's visit*
f. **¿Piensas contestar?—Según.**	*Do you intend to answer?—That depends.*

EJERCICIO

Pónganse las palabras entre paréntesis en lugar de las palabras subrayadas:
1. El coche[a] lo vendí[b] en 70.000 pesos.
   a. (los muebles, la ropa, los trajes de luces, los tres toros)
   b. (comprar, obtener)
2. Conoció a su mujer cuando la fiesta nacional. (la exposición internacional, la huelga general, la caída del dictador, la muerte del jefe)

---

216. COMPOUND PREPOSITIONS (*CONTINUED*)

Note the following peculiarities:

(*a*) **por** and **de** combine with other prepositions after verbs of motion;

(*b*) **para con** as equivalent of the English *to, towards* (i.e., attitude towards persons);

(*c*) **de a** in adjectival phrases of set price, manner, or size.

a.	**Los trenes pasan por debajo del río.**	*The trains go under the river.*
	Un hombre salió de entre los árboles.	*A man came out from among the trees.*
b.	**las atenciones que tuvo para conmigo**	*his kindness to (towards) me*
c.	**puros de a diez pesos**	*ten peso cigars*
	los de a caballo y los de a pie	*those on horseback and those on foot*

EJERCICIO

En los dibujos del Ejercicio (**p. 240**), contéstense:
1. ¿Por dónde va Jesús?
2. ¿Por dónde va Víctor?
3. ¿Por dónde va Pedro?
4. ¿Por dónde va Pilar?

Pónganse las palabras entre paréntesis en lugar de las palabras subrayadas:
5. Le sorprendió la actitud[a] para con sus padres[b].
   a. (atenciones, falta de respeto, desprecio)
   b. (hermanos, profesores, amigos)

217. DISTINCTIONS BETWEEN RELATED PREPOSITIONS

The following groups of related prepositions require careful differentiation:

(*a*) **antes de** refers to time and order, **delante de** to place, and **ante** means in the presence of;

(*b*) **bajo** is used figuratively, **debajo de** literally;

(*c*) **cerca de** refers to location or approximation, **acerca de** means *about, concerning;*

(*d*) **desde** and **hasta** are used both of time and place;

(*e*) **después de** refers to time, **detrás de** to position and **tras** to succession;

(*f*) **en** is usually *on*, **sobre** *upon, above,* and **encima de** *on top of, above, over.* **Sobre** also means *concerning* and *in addition to.*

---

a. **antes de salir**	*before leaving*
delante de la casa	*before (in front of) the house*
ante el tribunal	*before the court*
b. **debajo de la mesa**	*under the table*
bajo un cielo estrellado	*under a starry sky*
c. **cerca del pueblo**	*near the town*
cerca de dos mil	*nearly, about 2,000*
acerca del caso	*concerning the matter*
d. **desde aquí**	*from this point*
desde aquí en adelante	*from now on*
hasta la esquina	*as far as (up to) the corner*
hasta mañana	*until tomorrow*
e. **después de cenar**	*after supper*
detrás del Ayuntamiento	*behind the City Hall*
tras la tormenta viene la calma	*after the storm comes fine weather*
uno tras otro	*one after another*
f. **en la pared**	*on the wall*
sobre la mesa	*upon the table*
encima de la cómoda	*on top of the dresser*
Sobre (por encima de) el interés personal está el deber.	*Duty is above personal gain.*
sobre el asunto	*about the affair*
Sobre no tener salud, no tiene dinero.	*In addition to having bad health, he has no money.*

NOTE. The adverbs **delante, encima,** etc., are used instead of the corresponding prepositions when the object of the latter would be a personal pronoun:

la casa que tenía delante	*the house which was (I had) in front of me*
El árbol le cayó encima.	*The tree fell on top of him.*

NOTE. See the use of the indirect object pronoun of reference **le** in the second example. No such pronoun is required in the first because the person concerned is the subject of the verb.

218. COORDINATE CONJUNCTIONS (*CONTINUED*)

Y, when beginning a question or an exclamation, is frequently the equivalent of English *what about . . . ? what do you think of . . . ?* etc.

Pero, ¿y usted?	*But, what about you?*
¡Y los tíos sin saber nada!	*Just think of it! Aunt and Uncle didn't know a thing.*

NOTE. **Pero** may be used in repetitions for emphasis: **¡Muy bien, pero que muy bien!** *Very well, very well indeed!*

219. SUBORDINATE CONJUNCTIONS (*CONTINUED*)

Como, cuando, and **si** clauses—and other indirect questions—may be construed as noun clauses and be introduced by prepositions or the article **el** (see Secs. **104.5; 108.1**).

Me enteré de cómo ocurrió.	*I learned how it happened.*
En cuanto a si acepta o no . . .	*As to his accepting or not . . .*
No me explico el por qué de todo eso.	*I can't understand the reason for all that.*

NOTE. **Como** in certain cases loses most of its interrogative force and becomes equivalent to **que** (compare English *how = that*), in which case it has no written accent:

Me habló de como había cambiado de opinión.	*He told about how he had changed his mind.*

220. SPECIAL CONSTRUCTIONS WITH QUE

1. **Que** introducing a noun clause after verbs of saying or requesting is occasionally omitted, chiefly (*a*) in correspondence and (*b*) to avoid the juxtaposition of several **que**'s.

a.	**Le ruego se sirva informarme.**	*I beg you please to inform me.*
b.	**¡Las cosas que supongo te habrá dicho!**	*The things I suppose he has told you!*

2. Similar to the use registered in Sec. **214.2, que** is widely employed as a connective (for which there is no equivalent in English) carrying the force of an expression of affirmation: (*a*) after any word or phrase of exclamation or asseveration, expressed or implied, (*b*) before the answer to a question beginning with **¿qué?** (*c*) as an intensifier to introduce exclamations or commands.

a.	**¡Claro que lo hará!**	*Of course he'll do it.*
	La señorita, que vayas en seguida.	*The mistress wants you to come right away.*

NOTE. A further extension of this use may be seen in the introductory conjunctions of the type used in coordinate or pseudo-principal clauses:

ahora que	*now that*
sólo que	*only, but*
por cierto que	*to be sure*
de aquí que	*hence*
sobre que	*besides*

Acabo de ver a D. Jorge—por cierto que no me dijo nada del asunto.	*I have just seen D. Jorge—to be sure, he said nothing about the matter.*
b. **¿Qué ha dicho?—Que te presentes en seguida.**	*What did he say?—For you to come at once.*
c. **¡Que me matan!**	*They are killing me!*
¡Que vienen ahora!	*They're coming now!*
¡Que sí!	*Yes, indeed!* (in answer to a negative statement)

3. In other cases the general connective **que** has the force of a mild causal conjunction equivalent to the English *for, as.* This **que** is particularly frequent after exclamations and imperatives.

Vamos, que ya son las seis.	*Come along, it's already six o'clock.*
Abra Ud. la ventana, que hay mucho humo aquí.	*Open the window, (for) there is (too) much smoke here.*

NOTE. The relative **que** is similarly used as a loose connective (see Sec. 94).

4. The general connective **que** occasionally has the value of (*a*) result, (*b*) purpose (equivalent of **para que, a fin de que, de modo que**), (*c*) manner. (Of course, **que** by itself has no meaning of cause, result, purpose, manner, concession, etc. It is the context which imparts the special meaning to the general connective.) This latter type of **que** is also used (*d*) as an intensifier in repetitions.

a. **¿Dónde estás que no te veo?**	*Where are you, (that) I don't see you?*
b. **Acércate que te oiga mejor.**	*Come closer so I can hear you better.*
c. **Escribe que da gusto.**	*He writes splendidly.*
d. **¡Mejor que mejor!**	*So much the better!*
Venía silba que silba.	*He came along whistling merrily.*
Estaban fuma que (te) fuma.	*They were smoking incessantly.*

NOTE. In these expressions the graphic verbs **estar, ir,** etc., are either expressed or implied. A similar use of the intensifying repetition may be seen in the rare construction **en llegando que llegó (llegue)** *as soon as he arrived (arrives)* and **llegado que hubo** (see Sec. **133**) types.

221. CORRELATIVE CONJUNCTIONS

Following are some of the more usual correlatives:

apenas . . . cuando	*scarcely . . . when*
así . . . como	*both . . . and*
lo mismo . . . que	*both . . . and (as well as)*
ni . . . ni	*neither . . . nor (see Sec. 103)*
no bien . . . (cuando)	*no sooner . . . than, as soon as*
o (bien) . . . o (bien)	*either . . . or*
ya . . . ya **sea . . . sea**	*whether . . . or (see Sec. 117)*
tanto . . . como	*both . . . and*
Apenas había salido él cuando llegó ella.	*He had scarcely left when she arrived.*
No bien nos acercamos cuando comprendimos la causa del tumulto.	*As soon as we drew near we understood the cause of the uproar.*
Lo mismo el padre que el hijo son buenos músicos.	*Both father and son are good musicians.*

NOTE. In conversation **que** may be used as a substitute for correlative **ora, ya, sea,** etc.:

Cuando uno sale de noche es para algo divertido, que el café, que el teatro, que los amigos . . .	*When one goes out at night it is for entertainment: the café, the theater, friends, etc.*

Traducción 19B

1. They got the cat out from under the car.
2. We passed behind the factory.
3. His name appeared in letters a foot high.
4. Under Philip II El Escorial was built.
5. There is a large square in front of the church.
6. I will do it before I go out.
7. The case was discussed before the board of directors.
8. They live near us.
9. Do you know anything about this?
10. I will accompany you as far as the station.
11. I will wait for your reply until next week.
12. I can't see it from here.

13. After some unsuccessful experiment . . .
14. I will let you know after consulting with my partner.
15. I have left my gloves on the counter.
16. It is (**hace**) five degrees below zero.
17. There was a bronze figure on top of the bookcase.
18. (Be sure you) don't fail to write.
19. She plays the piano (in such a way) that it is glorious to hear (**que da gloria**).
20. I had no sooner arrived at the hotel than I received your telegram.
21. He writes a great deal in Spanish as well as in English.
22. And (there) I (was) without a penny.
23. She sings very well indeed.
24. Find out if (the) dinner is ready.
25. They told us how the flood had destroyed everything.
26. Please (I request you to) answer at your earliest convenience.
27. (I should like you to) write to me often.
28. These oranges surely are good.—They certainly are.
29. Go to the kitchen and (tell) them to make some sandwiches for us.
30. What did he say?—(He said) he would give it to us tomorrow.
31. Don't be long; I am in a hurry.
32. They were talking and talking.

III

Verbos y Modismos

Pasar *to pass (by, through, along, in, to, for), spend, happen, suffer,* etc.;
pasarse *to pass (off, beyond), surpass,* etc.

1. Some policemen passed on bicycles.
2. Shall we go through this town?
3. We spent the morning playing golf.
4. We have had a splendid time in Viña del Mar.
5. What is the matter?
6. What happens is that we have a puncture.
7. What is the matter with you?
8. He went by (**de largo**) without speaking to me.
9. The bullet pierced the wall.
10. We ordered a couple of soft-boiled (**pasados por agua**) eggs.
11. Come in.
12. They went into the office.
13. Send me the bill at the end of the month.
14. Stop by (**por**) my house this afternoon.
15. He has suffered many hardships in his youth.

16. I cannot stand for such a thing.
17. He passed for a man of great influence.
18. Let us skip over (**pasar por alto**) his defects.
19. Let it pass this time but let it not be repeated.
20. We have missed (gone beyond) our (**de**) station.
21. Have you gotten over (has it passed off) your headache?
22. He was too smart (**pasarse de listo**).
23. I can't do without my pipe.
24. This fruit is spoiled (condition).

Tratar *to treat, address (by pronoun or title), speak to, be intimate with;* **tratar de** *to deal with, to try to,* **tratarse de** *to be a question of,* etc.

1. They treated me as (one) of the family.
2. The children addressed their grandparents as (**de**) **Ud.** and their parents as (**de**) **tú.**
3. Do you know the mayor?—I know him, but not to speak to.
4. The two families did not speak to each other.
5. Try to convince him.
6. The board of directors dealt with various matters.
7. That's not the point.

Valer (Sec. **262**) *to be worth, be of avail,* etc.; **valerse de** *to avail oneself of, make use of.*

1. How much is this worth?
2. Excuses are of no avail.
3. It is not worth while (**la pena**) to stay here a week.
4. He makes use of all kinds of tricks to get what he wants.
5. This time the prestige of his name will not help him.
6. His scientific work has brought him the Nobel Prize.
7. God help me!
8. Don't say anything. It is best (**más vale**) to keep quiet.
9. It would be better for you to mind your own business (**ocuparse de lo suyo**).
10. It is not that nor anything like it (**cosa que lo valga**).
11. There is no but about it (**no hay pero que valga**).
12. He is a young lawyer of great promise (**que vale mucho**).

Caber (Sec. **235**) *to be contained (in), be room for (in), fit into, hold, be possible.*

1. There is not (enough) room for me in this bed; it is too narrow.
2. One of us will have to stay ashore; there is not (enough) room for all of us.
3. How many people does this bus hold?
4. It is possible to indicate other reasons besides the ones already mentioned.
5. I have no doubt (**no cabe duda**) that things happened that way.

Cumplir(se) *to carry out, fulfill, reach one's birthday;* **cumplir con** *to perform (one's duty), keep (one's promise).*

1. The order has not been carried out.
2. His hopes were not fulfilled.
3. Isabel is just twenty years (old); yesterday was her birthday.
4. Let us do our duty.
5. I am going to live up to what (I) promised.
6. Let's not stand on (**andar con**) ceremony (**cumplidos**).
7. He is a very polite person.

Faltar *to be lacking, fail,* etc.

1. Here is the baggage, three pieces (**bultos**); one is missing.
2. He lacks two months of (**para cumplir**) twenty-one (years).
3. I am five dollars short; I must have lost a bill.
4. I (will) expect you at five o'clock; don't fail.
5. Don't miss the (**al**) banquet.
6. You will stay to dinner (dine) with us, will you not?—I should say so! Of course! (**¡No faltaba más!**)
7. After we had waited for several hours, the mechanic told us he couldn't fix the car until the next day. That was the last straw! (**¡No faltaba más!**).

Bastar *to suffice, be enough (for), have enough (with);* **bastarse** *to be self-sufficient.*

1. He is so ambitious that nothing satisfies (suffices) him.
2. The arrival of the police was enough to quell the riot.
3. How many actors do we have (count with)? (With) five.—That's (they are) not enough.
4. That's enough (**Basta de**) talk (**discusión**).
5. It should be enough for (let it suffice) you to know that there will be no meeting.
6. Here are the stamps, take all you want.—One is enough (I have enough with one).
7. Your saying so is enough for me (I have enough with, etc.).
8. One must be self-sufficient (to oneself).

Sobrar *to be (have) more than enough, left over, superfluous,* etc.

1. With his income he has more than enough to live well.
2. I have two tickets left over for this evening's performance. Do you want them?
3. How many are there?—Twelve.—Then that's two too many.
4. There is more than enough time.

Acabar *to finish, end, be over;* **acabar de** *to finish, have just;* **acabarse** *to give out, be finally over.* (**Terminar** [and **concluir**] may be used in sentences 2–8.)

1. This book has just been published.
2. Wait a moment, I (will) finish right away.
3. Finish dressing and we will go out together.
4. He ended by (**por**) going to sleep.
5. Our provisions gave out.
6. Is the writing paper all gone?
7. It's all over now (**¡Ya se acabó!**).
8. No more (**se acabaron**) foolishness (pl). (Get) to work!
9. This is the limit (**el acabóse**)!
10. He died and was buried and that was all there was to that (**y sanseacabó**).

Temas

A. Escriba Ud. un párrafo sobre una visita real o imaginaria a un viejo castillo. Empiece con las frases siguientes: "La solitaria y melancólica luna derramaba su débil luz sobre las toscas piedras del castillo. El lejano ladrar de un perro añadía una nota de misterio a la escena."

B. Describa Ud. un viaje por las montañas. Empiece con la frase siguiente: "Las montañas de la España septentrional están cubiertas de nieve la mayor parte del año."

C. Describa Ud. un personaje raro. Empiece con las frases siguientes: "En un pueblecito tranquilo de la provincia lejos del ruidoso y febril bullicio de la ciudad, hace poco que vivía un viejo loco. ¡Pobre de don Alejandro!"

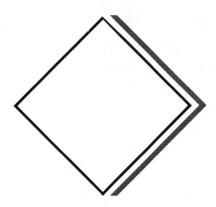

APPENDIX

VERBS

REGULAR VERBS

222. SIMPLE TENSES

INFINITIVE

hablar *to speak* vender *to sell* vivir *to live*

PRESENT PARTICIPLE

hablando vendiendo viviendo

PAST PARTICIPLE

hablado vendido vivido

INDICATIVE MOOD

Present

hablo	vendo	vivo
hablas	vendes	vives
habla	vende	vive
hablamos	vendemos	vivimos
habláis	vendéis	vivís
hablan	venden	viven

Imperfect

hablaba	vendía	vivía
hablabas	vendías	vivías
hablaba	vendía	vivía
hablábamos	vendíamos	vivíamos
hablabais	vendíais	vivíais
hablaban	vendían	vivían

Preterit

hablé	vendí	viví
hablaste	vendiste	viviste
habló	vendió	vivió
hablamos	vendimos	vivimos
hablasteis	vendisteis	vivisteis
hablaron	vendieron	vivieron

Future

hablaré	venderé	viviré
hablarás	venderás	vivirás
hablará	venderá	vivirá
hablaremos	venderemos	viviremos
hablaréis	venderéis	viviréis
hablarán	venderán	vivirán

Conditional

hablaría	vendería	viviría
hablarías	venderías	vivirías
hablaría	vendería	viviría
hablaríamos	venderíamos	viviríamos
hablaríais	venderíais	viviríais
hablarían	venderían	vivirían

Imperative (intimate)

habla	vende	vive
hablad	vended	vivid

SUBJUNCTIVE MOOD

Present

hable	venda	viva
hables	vendas	vivas
hable	venda	viva
hablemos	vendamos	vivamos
habléis	vendáis	viváis
hablen	vendan	vivan

Past, -ra Form

hablara	vendiera	viviera
hablaras	vendieras	vivieras
hablara	vendiera	viviera
habláramos	vendiéramos	viviéramos
hablarais	vendierais	vivierais
hablaran	vendieran	viviera

Past, -se Form

hablase	vendiese	viviese
hablases	vendieses	vivieses
hablase	vendiese	viviese
hablásemos	vendiésemos	viviésemos
hablaseis	vendieseis	vivieseis
hablasen	vendiesen	viviesen

Future

hablare	vendiere	viviere
hablares	vendieres	vivieres
hablare	vendiere	viviere
habláremos	vendiéremos	viviéremos
hablareis	vendiereis	viviereis
hablaren	vendieren	vivieren

223. COMPOUND TENSES OF *HABLAR, VENDER, VIVIR*

PERFECT INFINITIVE	PERFECT PARTICIPLE
haber hablado, vendido, vivido	**habiendo** hablado, vendido, vivido

INDICATIVE MOOD

Present Perfect
he hablado, vendido, vivido
has hablado, vendido, vivido
ha hablado, vendido, vivido
hemos hablado, vendido, vivido
habéis hablado, vendido, vivido
han hablado, vendido, vivido

Pluperfect
había hablado, vendido, vivido
habías hablado, vendido, vivido
había hablado, vendido, vivido
habíamos hablado, vendido, vivido
habíais hablado, vendido, vivido
habían hablado, vendido, vivido

Preterit Perfect
hube hablado, etc.

Future Perfect
habré hablado, etc.

Conditional Perfect
habría hablado, etc.

SUBJUNCTIVE MOOD

Present Perfect
haya hablado, etc.

Pluperfect
hubiera hablado, etc.
hubiese hablado, etc.

Future Perfect
hubiere hablado, etc.

224. PROGRESSIVE TENSES

These tenses are formed regularly with **estar** (**ir,** etc., Secs. **10, 132**) and the invariable present participle.

225. PASSIVE VOICE

The passive voice is formed regularly with **ser** and the inflected past participle (Sec. **148**). In the compound tenses **sido** is invariable: **habían sido castigadas** *they (fem.) had been punished.*

Radical (or stem-) changing verbs

(Radical-changing verbs are indicated as such in the Vocabulary. They must be learned by observation.)

226. CLASS I (*CONTAR–PERDER*) TYPE

There are three classes of radical (or stem-) changing verbs in Spanish. Class I comprises verbs of the first (**-ar**) and second (**-er**) conjugations, in which the stem-vowels **e** and **o** change when stressed to **ie** and **ue** respectively. These changes occur only in the present tenses (indicative and subjunctive) throughout the singular and in the third person plural, and in the intimate imperative, singular.

contar *to tell*

PRES. IND.   cuento, cuentas, cuenta, contamos, contáis, cuentan
PRES. SUBJ.   cuente, cuentes, cuente, contemos, contéis, cuenten
IMPERATIVE   cuenta, contad

perder *to lose*

PRES. IND.   pierdo, pierdes, pierde, perdemos, perdéis, pierden
PRES. SUBJ.   pierda, pierdas, pierda, perdamos, perdáis, pierdan
IMPERATIVE   pierde, perded

227. CLASS II (*SENTIR–DORMIR* TYPE)

This class comprises verbs of the third (**-ir**) conjugation in which the stem-vowels **e** and **o** not only change when stressed to **ie** and **ue** respectively, but also to **i** and **u** respectively in the present participle, the first and second persons plural of the present subjunctive, the third person singular and plural of the preterit, and throughout the past subjunctive (both forms) and the future subjunctive.

sentir *to feel*

PRES. IND.   siento, sientes, siente, sentimos, sentís, sienten
PRES. SUBJ.   sienta, sientas, sienta, sintamos, sintáis, sientan
IMPERATIVE   siente, sentid
PRES. PART.   sintiendo
PRETERIT   sentí, sentiste, sintió, sentimos, sentisteis, sintieron
PAST SUBJ.   (**-ra**) sintiera, etc.   PAST. SUBJ.   (**-se**) sintiese, etc.
FUT. SUBJ.   sintiere, etc.

dormir *to sleep*

PRES. IND.   duermo, duermes, duerme, dormimos, dormís, duermen
PRES. SUBJ.   duerma, duermas, duerma, durmamos, durmáis, duerman
IMPERATIVE   duerme, dormid
PRES. PART.   durmiendo
PRETERIT   dormí, dormiste, durmió, dormimos, dormisteis, durmieron
PAST SUBJ.   (**-ra**) durmiera, etc.   PAST SUBJ.   (**-se**) durmiese, etc.
FUT. SUBJ.   durmiere, etc.

228. CLASS III (*PEDIR* TYPE)

This class comprises verbs of the third (**-ir**) conjugation in which the stem-vowel **e** changes to **i** both when stressed and in all cases indicated in Class II.

pedir *to ask for*

PRES. IND. pido, pides, pide, pedimos, pedís, piden
PRES. SUBJ. pida, pidas, pida, pidamos, pidáis, pidan
IMPERATIVE pide, pedid
PRES. PART. pidiendo
PRETERIT pedí, pediste, pidió, pedimos, pedisteis, pidieron
PAST SUBJ. (**-ra**) pidiera, etc. PAST SUBJ. (**-se**) pidiese, etc.
FUT. SUBJ. pidiere, etc.

229. ORTHOGRAPHIC-CHANGING VERBS

Many verbs present certain regular changes in orthography (spelling) in order to reflect the pronunciation accurately.

1. Verbs ending in **-car** and **-gar** change **c** and **g** to **qu** and **gu** respectively before **e** (i.e., in the first person preterit and throughout the present subjunctive).

buscar *to look for*

PRETERIT **busqué,** buscaste, buscó, buscamos, buscasteis, buscaron
PRES. SUBJ. **busque, busques, busque, busquemos, busquéis, busquen**

llegar *to arrive*

PRETERIT **llegué,** llegaste, etc.
PRES. SUBJ. **llegue, llegues,** etc.

2. Verbs ending in **-guar** change **gu** to **güe** before **e** (in the same cases as in 1).

averiguar *to find out, ascertain*

PRETERIT **averigüé,** averiguaste, etc.
PRES. SUBJ. **averigüe, averigües,** etc.

3. Verbs ending in **-zar** change **z** to **c** before **e** (in the same cases as in 1).

empezar *to begin*

PRETERIT **empecé,** empezaste, etc.
PRES. SUBJ. **empiece, empieces,** etc.

4. Verbs ending in **-cer** or **-cir** preceded by a consonant change **c** to **z** before **a** and **o** (i.e., in the first person present indicative and throughout the present subjunctive).

convencer   *to convince*

PRES. IND.   **convenzo,** convences, convence, etc.
PRES. SUBJ. **convenza, convenzas, convenza,** etc.

5. Verbs ending in **-ger** and **-gir** change **g** to **j** before **a** and **o** (i.e., in the same cases as in 4).

dirigir   *to direct*

PRES. IND.   **dirijo,** diriges, etc.
PRES. SUBJ.   **dirija, dirijas,** etc.

6. Verbs in **-guir** change **gu** to **g** before **a** and **o** (in the same cases as 4).

seguir   *to follow*

PRES. IND.   **sigo,** sigues, sigue, seguimos, seguís, siguen
PRES. SUBJ.   **siga, sigas,** etc.

7. Verbs whose stems end in **ll** or **ñ** drop the **i** of the diphthongs **ie** and **io.**

reñir   *to scold, quarrel*

PRES. PART.   **riñendo**
PRETERIT   reñí, reñiste, **riñó,** reñimos, reñisteis, **riñeron**
PAST SUBJ.   **(-ra) riñera,** etc.
PAST SUBJ.   **(-se) riñese,** etc.
NOTE. All verbs in **-eñir** are radical-changing (Class III).

bullir   *to bubble, boil*

PRES. PART.   bu**llendo**
PRETERIT   bullí, bulliste, **bulló,** bullimos, bullisteis, **bulleron**
PAST SUBJ.   **(-ra) bullera,** etc.
PAST SUBJ.   **(-se) bullese,** etc.

8. **Oler** *to smell* is a radical-changing verb of Class I. Wherever the diphthong **ue** appears initially, the form in which it appears is written with **h-.**

PRES. IND.   **huelo, hueles, huele,** olemos, oléis, **huelen**
PRES. SUBJ.   **huela, huelas, huela,** olamos, oláis, **huelan**
IMPERATIVE   **huele,** oled

9. **Errar** *to err,* and any radical-changing verb in which the diphthong **ie** appears initially, spells the diphthong **ye-.** (See **erguir,** Sec. **244.**)

PRES. IND. **yerro, yerras, yerra,** erramos, erráis, **yerran**
PRES. SUBJ. **yerre, yerres, yerre,** erremos, erréis, **yerren**
IMPERATIVE **yerra,** errad

230. VERBS OF THE -ER AND -IR CONJUGATIONS WHOSE STEM ENDS IN A VOWEL

Verbs like **creer, leer,** etc. always spell the unstressed **i** with the letter **y.** Stressed **i** always bears the written accent.

creer *to believe, think*

PRES. PART. cre**yendo** PAST PART. creído
PRETERIT creí, creíste, **creyó,** creímos, creísteis, **creyeron**
PAST SUBJ. (**-ra**) **creyera,** etc.
PAST SUBJ. (**-se**) **creyese,** etc.
NOTE. **Oír** (Sec. **251**), and **caer** (Sec. **236**), and their compounds show the above changes.

231. VERBS IN *-EÍR* ARE RADICAL-CHANGING VERBS OF CLASS II (*PEDIR* TYPE)

Stressed **i** always bears the written accent. Two contiguous **i**'s are reduced to one.

reír *to laugh*

PRES. PART. riendo PAST PART. reído
PRES. IND. **río, ríes, ríe,** reimos, reís, **ríen**
PRETERIT reí, reíste, rió, reímos, reísteis, **rieron**
IMPERATIVE ríe, reíd
PRES. SUBJ. **ría, rías, ría, riamos, riáis, rían**
PAST SUBJ. (**-ra**) **riera,** etc.
PAST SUBJ. (**-se**) **riese,** etc.

IRREGULAR VERBS

232. PRINCIPAL AND DERIVED PARTS

1. Certain forms of the Spanish verb are known as the "principal parts" because it is possible to derive all of the forms of the verb if one starts with these forms. With regular verbs, it is possible to begin with the infinitive and derive all the forms of a verb. Thus the vowel preceding the **-r** of the infinitive is found preceding the personal endings in the present indicative, except before

the **-o** of the first person singular of the present indicative, e.g. **habl-a-mos, vend-e-mos, viv-i-mos.** (It scarcely needs to be pointed out that in the second [**-er**] conjugation, and the third [**-ir**] conjugation, the characteristic or thematic vowel appears only in the first and second plural of the present indicative, and all other tenses are identical in form with both conjugations.

With irregular verbs, on the other hand, it is usual for one particular tense or mood form to be irregular in form so that if one knows the "principal parts" almost all other moods and tenses may be derived, according to the scheme printed below. The principal parts are the infinitive, the present participle, the past participle, the present indicative-first person singular, and the preterit. Only in the case of some irregular futures and conditionals and intimate imperatives do the principal parts fail to give the correct form. These forms, therefore, must be learned separately. Consequently the student will find it very useful to know these forms when learning the conjugation of irregular verbs. The following illustration taken from Sec. **247** shows how the various forms are made.

INFINITIVE	PRES. PART.	PAST PART.	PRES. IND.	PRETERIT
hacer	**haciendo**	**hecho**	**hago**	**hice**

IMPERFECT IND.	PROGRESSIVE TENSES	COMPOUND TENSES	PRES. SUBJ.	PAST SUBJ.
hacía	**estoy,** etc. **haciendo**	**he,** etc. **hecho**	**haga,** etc.	**hiciera** **hiciese**

FUTURE			IMPERATIVE	
haré			**haz** **haced**	

CONDITIONAL				FUT. SUBJ.
haría				**hiciere**

2. In the preceding table, all forms except **haré, haría,** and **haz** are derived regularly from the principal parts. Consequently, in the following synopses of Spanish irregular verbs, only the principal parts and those forms not regularly derived from them are given. No separate mention is made of the conditional (which is always similar to the future) nor of the past and future subjunctive unless these forms show special irregularities. The irregular forms, together with radical-changing forms and orthographic changes, are printed in boldfaced type.

The irregular preterit forms of the **tuve** type all have the same endings, which, it should be noted, are not stressed in the first and third, singular forms:

	-e	**-imos**	
	-iste	**-isteis**	
	-o	**-ieron**	
e.g.	**tuve**	**tuvimos**	
	tuviste	**tuvisteis**	
	tuvo	**tuvieron**	

233.

andar to walk, go

PRIN. PARTS andar, andando, andado, ando, **anduve**

234.

asir to seize

PRIN. PARTS asir, asiendo, asido, **asgo,** así
PRES. IND. **asgo,** ases, ase, asimos, asís, asen
PRES. SUBJ. **asga, asgas,** etc.

235.

caber to be contained in, fit

PRIN. PARTS caber, cabiendo, cabido, **quepo, cupe**
PRES. IND. **quepo,** cabes, cabe, cabemos, cabéis, caben
PRES. SUBJ. **quepa, quepas,** etc.
FUT. IND. **cabré, cabrás,** etc.
PRETERIT. **cupe, cupiste, cupo, cupimos, cupisteis, cupieron**

236.

caer to fall

PRIN. PARTS caer, **cayendo,** caído, caigo, caí
PRES. IND. **caigo,** caes, cae, caemos, caéis, caen
PRES. SUBJ. **caiga, caigas,** etc.
PRETERIT caí, caíste, **cayó,** caímos, caísteis, **cayeron**
PAST SUBJ. **cayera,** etc.; **cayese,** etc.
FUT. SUBJ. **cayere,** etc.

237.

concluir to conclude

(All verbs whose infinitive ends in **-uir** [except **-guir** and **-quir**] and **-üir** insert **y** between the **u** and the ending in the singular and third person plural of the present tense and the familiar imperative. Unstressed **i** is also spelled **y** in other forms [see Sec. **230**].)

PRES. PART. **concluyendo** PAST PART. concluido
PRES. IND. **concluyo, concluyes, concluye,** concluimos, concluís, **concluyen**
PRETERIT **concluí,** concluiste, **concluyó,** concluimos, concluisteis, **concluyeron**
IMPERATIVE **concluye,** concluid
PRES. SUBJ. **concluya, concluyas,** etc.
PAST SUBJ. **(-ra) concluyera,** etc.
PAST SUBJ. **(-se) concluyese,** etc.

238.

conducir   *to conduct*

(All verbs in **-ducir** are conjugated similarly.)

PRIN. PARTS   conducir, conduciendo, conducido, **conduzco, conduje**
PRES. IND.   **conduzco,** conduces, conduce, conducimos, conducís, conducen
PRES. SUBJ.   **conduzca, conduzcas,** etc.
PRETERIT   **conduje, condujiste, condujo, condujimos, condujisteis, condu-jeron**
PAST SUBJ.   **condujera,** etc.; **condujese,** etc.
FUT. SUBJ.   **condujere,** etc.

239.

conocer   *to know, be acquainted with*

(All verbs in **-ecer, -ocer, -ucir** insert **z** before **c** in the first person present indicative and throughout the present subjunctive.)

PRES. IND.   **conozco,** conoces, conoce, etc.
PRES. SUBJ.   **conozca, conozcas, conozca,** etc.

NOTE. Irregular verbs in **-ducir** (Sec. **238**) show the above changes, but **hacer, decir, cocer, mecer,** and their compounds do not.

240.

continuar   *to continue*

(Verbs in **-uar,** except **-guar,** regularly have stress, and a written accent, on the **u** throughout the singular and in the third person plural of the present tense.)

PRES. IND.   **continúo, continúas, continúa,** continuamos, continuáis, **continúan**
PRES. SUBJ.   **continúe, continúes, continúe,** continuemos, continuéis, **continúen**
IMPERATIVE   **continúa,** continuad

241.

dar *to give*

PRIN. PARTS   dar, dando, dado, **doy, di**
PRES. IND.   **doy,** das, da, damos, dais, dan
PRES. SUBJ.   **dé,** des, **dé,** demos, deis, den
PRETERIT   **di, diste, dio, dimos, disteis, dieron**
PAST SUBJ.   **diera,** etc.; **diese,** etc.

242.

decir *to say, tell*

PRIN. PARTS   decir, **diciendo, dicho, digo, dije**
PRES. IND.   **digo, dices, dice,** decimos, decís, **dicen**
PRES. SUBJ.   **diga, digas,** etc.
IMPERATIVE   **di,** decid
PRETERIT   **dije, dijiste, dijo, dijimos, dijisteis, dijeron**
PAST SUBJ.   **dijera,** etc; **dijese,** etc.
FUT. IND.   **diré, dirás,** etc.

243.

enviar *to send*

(Some other verbs ending in **-iar** stress the **i** through the singular and the third person plural of the present tense.)

PRIN. PARTS   enviar, enviando, enviado, **envío,** envié
PRES. IND.   **envío, envías, envía,** enviamos, enviáis, **envían**
PRES. SUBJ.   **envíe, envíes, envíe,** enviemos, enviéis, **envíen**
IMPERATIVE   **envía,** enviad

244.

erguir *to raise, lift up*

PRIN. PARTS   erguir, **irguiendo,** erguido, **yergo (irgo),** erguí
PRES. IND.   **yergo, yergues, yergue,** erguimos, erguís, **yerguen**
(alternate)   **irgo, irgues, irgue,** erguimos, erguís, **irguen**
PRES. SUBJ.   **yerga, yergas, yerga, irgamos, irgáis, yergan**
(alternate)   **irga, irgas, irga, irgamos, irgáis, irgan**
PRETERIT   erguí, erguiste, **irguió,** erguimos, erguisteis, **irguieron**

245.

estar   *to be*

PRIN. PARTS   estar, estando, estado, **estoy, estuve**
PRES. IND.   **estoy, estás, está,** estamos, estáis, **están**
PRES. SUBJ.   **esté, estés, esté,** estemos, estéis, **estén**
PRETERIT   **estuve, estuviste, estuvo, estuvimos, estuvisteis, estuvieron**
IMPERATIVE   **está,** estad

246.

haber   *to have* (impers. *to be*)

PRIN. PARTS   haber, habiendo, habido, **he, hube**
PRES. IND.   **he, has, ha** (impers. **hay**), **hemos,** habéis, **han**
PRES. SUBJ.   **haya, hayas,** etc.
PRETERIT   **hube, hubiste, hubo, hubimos, hubisteis, hubieron**
FUT. IND.   **habré, habrás,** etc.

247.

hacer   *to do, make*

PRIN. PARTS   hacer, haciendo, **hecho, hago, hice**
PRES. IND.   **hago,** haces, hace, hacemos, hacéis, hacen
PRES. SUBJ.   **haga, hagas,** etc.
IMPERATIVE   **haz,** haced
PRETERIT   **hice, hiciste, hizo, hicimos, hicisteis, hicieron**
FUT. IND.   **haré, harás,** etc.

248.

inquirir   *inquire*

PRIN. PARTS   inquirir, inquiriendo, inquirido, **inquiero,** inquirí
PRES. IND.   **inquiero, inquieres, inquiere,** inquirimos, inquirís, inquieren
PRES. SUBJ.   **inquiera, inquieras, inquiera,** inquiramos, inquiráis, **inquieran**
IMPERATIVE   **inquiere,** inquirid

249.

ir   *to go*

PRIN. PARTS   ir, **yendo,** ido, **voy, fui**
PRES. IND.   **voy, vas, va, vamos, vais, van**

PRES. SUBJ. **vaya, vayas,** etc.
IMPERATIVE **ve,** id
IMPERF. IND. **iba, ibas,** etc.
PRETERIT **fui, fuiste, fue, fuimos, fuisteis, fueron**
PAST SUBJ. **fuera,** etc.; **fuese,** etc.

250.

jugar *to play* (a game)

PRIN. PARTS jugar, jugando, jugado, **juego, jugué**
PRES. IND. **juego, juegas, juega,** jugamos, jugáis, **juegan**
PRES. SUBJ. **juegue, juegues, juegue,** juguemos, juguéis, **jueguen**
IMPERATIVE **juega,** jugad
PRETERIT **jugué,** jugaste, jugó, jugamos, jugasteis, jugaron

251.

oír *to hear*

PRIN. PARTS oír, **oyendo, oído, oigo,** oí
PRES. IND. **oigo, oyes, oye,** oímos, oís, **oyen**
PRES. SUBJ. **oiga, oigas,** etc.
IMPERATIVE **oye** oíd
PRETERIT **oí, oíste, oyó, oímos, oísteis, oyeron**
PAST SUBJ. **oyera,** etc.; **oyese,** etc.

252.

placer *to please* (used as impersonal verb and in third pers.)

PRIN. PARTS placer, placiendo, placido, place, **plugo** (*or* plació)
PRES. SUBJ. **plega, plegue,** *or* **plazca** (more common)

253.

poder *to be able (to)*

PRIN. PARTS poder, **pudiendo,** podido, **puedo, pude**
PRES. IND. **puedo, puedes, puede,** podemos, podéis, **pueden**
PRES. SUBJ. **pueda, puedas, pueda,** podamos, podáis, **puedan**
PRETERIT **pude, pudiste, pudo, pudimos, pudisteis, pudieron**
FUT. IND. **podré, podrás,** etc.

254.

poner   *to put, place*

PRIN. PARTS   poner, poniendo, **puesto, pongo, puse**
PRES. IND.   **pongo,** pones, pone, ponemos, ponéis, ponen
PRES. SUBJ.   **ponga, pongas,** etc.
IMPERATIVE   **pon,** poned
PRETERIT   **puse, pusiste, puso, pusimos, pusisteis, pusieron**
FUT. IND.   **pondré, pondrás,** etc.

255.

querer   *to want*

PRIN. PARTS   querer, queriendo, querido, **quiero, quise**
PRES. IND.   **quiero, quieres, quiere,** queremos, queréis, **quieren**
PRES. SUBJ.   **quiera, quieras, quiera,** queramos, queráis, **quieran**
IMPERATIVE   **quiere,** quered
PRETERIT   **quise, quisiste, quiso, quisimos, quisisteis, quisieron**
FUT. IND.   **querré, querrás,** etc.

256.

raer   *to scrape, to become threadbare*

PRIN. PARTS   raer, rayendo, raído, **raigo (rayo),** raí
PRES. IND.   { **raigo,** raes, rae, raemos, raéis, raen
               { **rayo**
PRES. SUBJ.   **raiga, raigas,** etc.; **raya, rayas,** etc.

257.

saber   *to know*

PRIN. PARTS   saber, sabiendo, sabido, **sé, supe**
PRES. IND.   **sé,** sabes, sabe, sabemos, sabéis, saben
PRES. SUBJ.   **sepa, sepas,** etc.
PRETERIT   **supe, supiste, supo, supimos, supisteis, supieron**
FUT. IND.   **sabré, sabrás,** etc.

258.

salir   *to go out*

PRIN. PARTS   salir, saliendo, salido, **salgo,** salí
PRES. IND.   **salgo,** sales, sale, salimos, salís, salen
PRES. SUBJ.   **salga, salgas,** etc.
IMPERATIVE   **sal,** salid
FUT. IND.   **saldré, saldrás,** etc.

259.

ser   *to be*

PRIN. PARTS   ser, siendo, sido, **soy, fui**
PRES. IND.   **soy, eres, es,** somos, sois, son
PRES. SUBJ.   **sea, seas, sea, seamos, seáis, sean**
IMPERATIVE   **sé,** sed
IMPERF. IND.   **era, eras, era, éramos, erais, eran**
PRETERIT   **fui, fuiste, fue, fuimos, fuisteis, fueron**

260.

tener   *to have*

PRIN. PARTS   tener, teniendo, tenido, **tengo, tuve**
PRES. IND.   **tengo,** tienes, tiene, tenemos, tenéis, tienen
PRES. SUBJ.   **tenga, tengas,** etc.
PRETERIT   **tuve, tuviste, tuvo, tuvimos, tuvisteis, tuvieron**
IMPERATIVE   **ten,** tened
FUT. IND.   **tendré, tendrás,** etc.

261.

traer   *to bring*

PRIN. PARTS   traer, **trayendo,** traído, **traigo, traje**
PRES. IND.   **traigo,** traes, trae, traemos, traéis, traen
PRES. SUBJ.   **traiga, traigas,** etc.
PRETERIT   **traje, trajiste, trajo, trajimos, trajisteis, trajeron**
PAST SUBJ.   **trajera,** etc.; **trajese,** etc.

262.

valer   *to be worth*

PRIN. PARTS   valer, valiendo, valido, **valgo,** valí
PRES. IND.   **valgo,** vales, vale, valemos, valéis, valen
PRES. SUBJ.   **valga, valgas,** etc.
IMPERATIVE   **val,** valed
FUT. IND.   **valdré, valdrás,** etc.

263.

venir   *to come*

PRIN. PARTS   venir, **viniendo,** venido, vengo, **vine**
PRES. IND.   **vengo, vienes, viene,** venimos, venís, **vienen**
PRES. SUBJ.   **venga, vengas,** etc.
PRETERIT   **vine, viniste, vino, vinimos, vinisteis, vinieron**
IMPERATIVE   **ven,** venid
FUT. IND.   **vendré, vendrás,** etc.

264.

ver   *to see*

PRIN. PARTS   ver, viendo, **visto, veo,** ví
PRES. IND.   **veo,** ves, ve, vemos, veis, ven
PRES. SUBJ.   **vea, veas,** etc.
IMPER. IND.   **veía, veías, veía, veíamos, veíais, veían**

265.

yacer   *to lie* (down)

PRIN. PARTS   yacer, yaciendo, yacido, **yazco (yazgo,** *or* **yago),** yací
PRES. IND. $\begin{cases} \textbf{yazco} \\ \textbf{yazgo,} \text{ yaces, yace, yacemos, yacéis, yacen} \\ \textbf{yago} \end{cases}$

PRES. SUBJ.   **yazca, yazcas,** etc.; **yazga, yazgas,** etc.; **yaga, yagas,** etc.
IMPERATIVE   **yaz** (*or* yace), yaced

266. IRREGULAR PAST PARTICIPLES

Certain regular verbs have (with their compounds and analogues) irregular past participles.

abrir, abierto	*opened*	**proveer, provisto**	*provided*
cubrir, cubierto	*covered*	**resolver, resuelto**	*resolved*
escribir, escrito	*written*	**romper, roto**	*broken*
freír, frito	*fried*	**ver, visto**	*seen*
imprimir, impreso	*printed*	**volver, vuelto**	*(re)turned*
morir, muerto	*dead*		

NOTE. All verbs ending in **-scribir** have the irregular past participle in **-scrito:**

adscribir, adscrito *ascribed*

circumscribir, circumscrito *circumscribed*

describir, descrito *described*

inscribir, inscrito *inscribed*

prescribir, prescrito *prescribed*

proscribir, proscrito *proscribed*

suscribir, suscrito *subscribed*

REGIMEN OF VERBS

267. COMMON VERBS OF DIFFERING REGIMEN

Following is a list of frequently used verbs in Spanish whose construction differs in some way from that of their English equivalents.

acercarse a	*approach*	**escuchar**	*listen to*
acordarse (ue) de	*remember*	**esperar**	*wait for*
agradecer	*be thankful for*	**fijarse en**	*notice*
aguardar	*wait for*	**gozar de**	*enjoy*
apostar (ue) a	*bet (that)*	**influir en**	*influence*
aprovechar	*take advantage of*	**jugar a**	*play (a game)*
asistir a	*attend*	**mirar**	*look at*
buscar	*look for*	**oponerse a**	*oppose*
cambiar de (tren etc.)	*change*	**pagar a**	*pay (a person)*
carecer de	*lack*	**pagar**	*pay for (a thing)*
conseguir (i)	*succeed in (doing)*	**pedir (i)**	*ask for (a thing)*
cuidar (de)	*care for, take care of*	**renunciar a**	*renounce, give up*
cumplir con	*fulfill*	**reparar en**	*notice, observe*

disfrutar de   *enjoy (a thing)*
entrar en (in America also **entrar a**)   *enter*

resistir a   *refuse*
salir de   *leave*
tirar de   *pull*

268. VERBS GOVERNING DIRECT INFINITIVES

Following is a list of frequently used verbs in Spanish which, being transitive, are followed by the direct infinitive (see Sec. **104.6**).

aconsejar   *advise*
advertir (ie, i)   *warn*
afirmar   *declare, affirm*
ansiar   *be anxious*
asegurar   *assure, declare*
bastar   *be enough*
celebrar   *rejoice, be glad*
confesar   *confess*
convenir   *be suitable* (impersonal)
creer   *believe, think*
deber   *ought, must*
decidir   *decide*
declarar   *declare*
dejar   *let, permit*
descuidar   *neglect*
desear   *desire*
determinar   *determine*
dignarse   *deign*
dudar   *doubt, hesitate*
elegir (i)   *choose*
encargar   *order, entrust*
esperar   *hope*
evitar   *avoid*
figurarse (impersonal)   *it seems*
fingir   *pretend, feign*
gustar   *please, like*
hacer   *make, cause, have*
imaginarse   *imagine*
impedir (i)   *prevent*
importar   *matter*
intentar   *attempt*
jurar   *swear*
lograr   *succeed in, manage*
mandar   *cause, have, order*
merecer   *deserve*
mirar   *watch*

necesitar   *need*
negar   *deny*
ocurrirse (impersonal)   *occur (to one)*
ofrecer   *offer*
oír   *hear*
olvidar   *forget*
ordenar   *order*
parecer   *seem*
pensar (ie)   *intend*
permitir   *permit*
pesar   *grieve, be sorry*
poder (ue)   *can, be able*
preferir (ie, i)   *prefer*
pretender   *claim*
procurar   *try*
prohibir   *forbid*
prometer   *promise*
proponer   *propose*
querer (ie)   *want, wish*
reconocer   *admit, acknowledge*
recordar (ue)   *remember*
rehusar   *refuse*
repugnar   *cause repugnance*
resolver (ue)   *resolve*
rogar (ue)   *beg, ask, request*
saber   *know (how)*
sentir (ie, i)   *be sorry, regret*
servirse (i)   *please*
soler (ue)   *be in the habit of, used to*
sostener   *maintain*
suplicar   *beg*
temer   *fear*
tocar (impersonal)   *be one's turn*
valer más (impersonal)   *be better*
ver   *see*

269. VERBS GOVERNING PREPOSITIONS

Following is a list of frequently used verbs in Spanish which are construed with prepositions.

abandonarse a *give oneself up to*

acabar de *finish, have just;* _____ **con** *finish, exhaust;* _____ **por** *end by*

acertar (ie) a *chance to, manage to; succeed in*

acordarse (ue) de *remember*

acostumbrarse a *be accustomed, get used to*

aguardar a *wait for, until*

alegrarse de *be glad to*

alejarse de *go away from*

amenazar con *threaten to or with*

animar a *encourage to;* _____ **se a** *make up one's mind to*

aprender a *learn to*

apresurarse a *hasten to, hurry to*

apurarse por *worry about*

arrepentirse (ie, i) de *repent of, be sorry for*

arriesgarse a *risk*

asomarse a *appear at, look out of*

asombrarse de *be astonished at*

aspirar a *aspire to*

asustarse de *be frightened at*

atreverse a *dare*

autorizar a or **para** *authorize to*

avenirse a *agree to, consent to*

aventurarse a *venture*

avergonzarse (ue) de *be ashamed*

ayudar a *help to, aid to*

bastar para or **a** *be sufficient to;* _____ **con** *have enough with*

burlarse de *make fun of*

cansarse de *grow tired of*

carecer de *lack*

casarse con *marry*

cesar de *cease to, stop*

comenzar (ie) a *commence to*

complacerse en *take pleasure in*

comprometerse a *obligate oneself*

concluir de *finish,* _____ **por** *end by*

condenar a *condemn to*

confiar en *trust*

conformarse a *conform to*

consagrarse a *devote oneself to*

consentir (ie, i) en *consent to*

consistir en *consist of*
contar (ue) con *count on, rely on*
contentarse con *content oneself*
contribuir a *contribute to*
convenir en *agree to*
convertirse (ie, i) en *become*
convidar a or **para** *invite to*
cuidar de *take care of (to)*
dar a *open on, face;* _____ **con** *come upon;* _____ **en** *persist in*
decidirse a *make up one's mind to,* _____ **por** *decide on*
dedicarse a *devote oneself to*
dejar *let, allow, permit;* _____ **de** *stop,* fail to
desafiar a *dare to, challenge to*
despedirse (i) de *take leave of*
destinar a or **para,** *destine to, assign to*
desvivirse por *do one's utmost to*
determinarse a *make up one's mind*
disculparse de *excuse oneself for*
disfrutar de *enjoy (a thing)*
disponerse a *get ready to*
divertirse (ie, i) en or **con** *amuse oneself by*
dudar de *doubt;* _____ **en** *hesitate*
echarse a *begin to*
empeñarse en *insist on*
empezar (ie) a *begin to*
enamorarse de *to fall in love with*
encargarse de *undertake to, take charge of*
encontrarse (ue) con *find, meet with, come upon*
enseñar a *teach (how) to*
enterarse de *find out*
entrar en *enter;* _____ **a** *enter, enter on*
entretenerse en, con *entertain oneself by or with*
enviar a *send to*
equivaler a *be equivalent to*
esforzarse (ue) a, para, por or **en** *strive to*
esmerarse en *take pains in*
esperar *hope, expect, wait;* _____ **a** *wait for, until*
estar para *be about to;* _____ **por** *be in favor of, be inclined to*
exponerse a *expose oneself to*
extrañarse de *be surprised at (to)*
faltar a *be absent from, fail to (do)*
felicitarse de *congratulate oneself on*
fijarse en *notice*
gozar de *enjoy;* _____ **se en, con** *enjoy*
guardarse de *take care not to*

gustar de   *be fond of*

haber de   *have to, be going to;* ____ **que** (impersonal)   *be necessary*

hacer por   *try to;* **estar hecho a**   *be accustomed to*

hartarse de   *have one's fill of*

huir de   *flee from, avoid*

impacientarse por   *grow impatient for (to)*

incitar a   *incite to*

inclinarse a   *be inclined to*

incomodarse con   *be annoyed at;* ____ **por**   *put oneself out for*

inducir a   *induce to*

insistir en   *insist on*

inspirar a   *inspire to*

instar a or **para**   *urge to*

invitar a or **para**   *invite to*

ir a   *go to;* ____ **se de**   *leave*

jactarse de   *boast of*

limitarse a   *limit oneself to*

llegar a   *come to, go so far as, chance to*

luchar por or **para**   *struggle for (to)*

maravillarse de   *marvel at*

marcharse de   *leave*

meterse a   *take up;* ____ **en**   *become involved in;* ____ **con**   *provoke (a person)*

molestarse en   *take the trouble to*

morirse (ue) por   *be dying for (to)*

negarse (ie) a   *refuse*

obligar a   *oblige to*

obstinarse en   *persist in*

ocuparse de   *pay attention to, mind;* ____ **en**   *busy oneself at*

ofrecerse a   *offer to, promise to*

olvidarse de   *forget to*

oponerse a   *be opposed to, oppose*

optar por   *choose (to)*

parar de   *stop, cease;* ____ **se a**   *stop to;* ____ **se en**   *stop at, bother;* ____
de   *finish*

parecerse a   *resemble*

pasar a   *proceed to, pass on to*

pensar (ie) de   *think of (have an opinion concerning);* ____ **en**   *think of (have in mind)*

persistir en   *persist in*

persuadirse a   *persuade oneself to;* **estar persuadido de**   *be convinced of*

ponerse a   *set oneself to, begin to*

preciarse de   *boast of*

prepararse a or **para**   *prepare oneself to*

prescindir de   *do without, neglect*

prestarse a   *lend oneself to*

principiar a *begin to*

probar (ue) a *try to*

quedar en *agree to;* _____ **por** *remain to be;* _____ **se a** or **para** *remain to*

quejarse de *complain of*

rabiar por *be crazy about (to)*

rebajarse a *stoop to*

recrearse en *amuse oneself by*

reducirse a *bring oneself to*

referirse (ie) a *refer to*

renunciar a *renounce, give up*

resignarse a *resign oneself to*

resistirse a *resist, refuse to*

resolverse (ue) a *resolve to*

retirarse a *retire, withdraw*

reventar por (ie) *be bursting to*

romper a *begin (suddenly) to;* _____**con** *break off relations with*

sentarse (ie) a or **para** *sit down to*

separarse de *leave*

servir (i) de *act as;* _____ **para** *be of use for;* _____ **se de** *use*

soñar (ue) con *dream of*

sorprenderse de *be surprised to*

subir a *go up to, climb, get on*

tardar en *take along to*

terminar por *end by;* _____ **de** *finish*

tornar a *return to; (do) again*

trabajar por or **para** *work to, strive to;* _____ **en** *work at*

tratar de *try to; address as;* _____ **se de** *be a question of*

tropezar (ie) con *come upon*

vacilar en *hesitate to*

valerse de *avail oneself of*

venir a *come to, amount to*

ver de *see to, look to, try to*

volver (ue) a *return to; (do) again*

270. ADJECTIVES AND PARTICIPLES THAT VARY IN MEANING WHEN USED WITH *SER* AND *ESTAR*

Many adjectives and participles can be used with both **ser** and **estar**, with variations in meaning according to the principles laid down in Secs. **17, 20, 149.** In a number of cases these variations in meaning are so considerable as to be rendered by separate English equivalents. Only the masculine forms are given.

	WITH ser	WITH estar
aburrido	*boring*	*bored*
agarrado	*stingy*	*clinging to, fastened to*
alto	*tall, high*	*tall (for one's age), high (location)*
ancho	*broad, wide*	*too broad, wide*
bajo	*low, short*	*too low, short; low (location)*
bueno	*good, kind*	*in good health; tasty*
callado	*silent (taciturn)*	*silent (quiet)*
casado	*(a) married (person)*	*married*
católico	*Catholic*	*(look, feel, taste) sound*
ciego	*blind*	*blinded*
débil	*(a) weak(ling)*	*weak, weakly*
delicado	*delicate*	*in delicate health*
despierto	*wide-awake, clever*	*awake*
distraído	*absent-minded*	*inattentive, confused*
divertido	*amusing*	*amused*
estrecho	*narrow*	*too narrow*
grande	*large, great*	*too large*
imposible	*impossible*	*unendurable*
inquieto	*restless*	*worried*
interesado	*mercenary*	*interested*
joven	*young*	*(look, feel, act) young*
justo	*just, fair*	*exact, fitting*
limpio	*cleanly*	*clean*
listo	*clever, bright*	*ready*
maduro	*mature*	*ripe*
malo	*bad, evil*	*sick, bad condition*
nuevo	*new, another*	*brand-new*
pequeño	*small*	*too small*
rico	*(a) rich person*	*tasty*
sano	*healthful*	*healthy*
verde	*green (color)*	*green (unripe)*
viejo	*old*	*(look, feel, act) old*
vivo	*lively*	*alive*

271. ADJECTIVES THAT VARY IN MEANING ACCORDING TO POSITION

Following is a list of the more frequent adjectives which vary in meaning (or English equivalent) according to their position:

	AFTER NOUN	BEFORE NOUN
alto	*high, tall*	*exalted*
antiguo	*ancient*	*old, former*
bajo	*low, short*	*vile*
cierto	*sure*	*certain (indefinite)*
determinado	*determined*	*certain (indefinite)*
grande	*large*	*great*
malo	*wicked*	*bad*
medio	*average*	*half*
menudo	*small*	*what a! (exclamation)*
mismo	*self*	*very, same*
nuevo	*new*	*another*
pobre	*poor (indigent)*	*poor (pitiable)*
propio	*(one's) own*	*very, same*
único	*unique*	*only, single*
valiente	*brave*	*what a! (exclamation)*
viejo	*aged, worn*	*old*

272. IRREGULAR ABSOLUTE SUPERLATIVES

1. Those having their origin in the irregular Latin superlative are:

   ínfimo *very (most) low*
   máximo *very (most) great*
   óptimo *very (most) excellent*
   pésimo *very (most) bad*

2. Those preserving the Latin root are:

   afabilísimo *very (most) affable*
   amabilísimo *very (most) kind*
   fortísimo *very (most) strong*
   (**Fuertísimo** is also used.)
   novísimo *very (most) new*
   fidelísimo *very (most) faithful*
   nobilísimo *very (most) noble*

3. Those preserving the Latin suffix are:

   acérrimo *very (most) vigorous*
   celebérrimo *very (most) celebrated*
   libérrimo *very (most) free*
   misérrimo *very (most) miserable*
   paupérrimo *very (most) poor*
   (**Pobrísimo** is also used.)

pulquérrimo *very (most) beautiful*
salubérrimo *very (most) healthful*
ubérrimo *very (most) fertile*

273. DEFINITE ARTICLE WITH PLACE NAMES

1. The definite article is used with the names of the following countries, although in some cases it is omitted in local or journalistic usage: **(la) Argentina, el Brasil, el Canadá, el Congo, (la) China, el Ecuador, (los) Estados Unidos, (la) Gran Bretaña, la Guayana, (la) India, el Japón, el Líbano, (el) Paraguay, el Perú, el Senegal, el Transvaal, (el) Uruguay.**

2. With names of many regions and cities, e.g., **la Alcarria** (province of Guadalajara, Spain), **el Callao** (city in Peru), **el Cairo, la Coruña, el Ferrol** (city in Galicia, Spain), **la Florida, La Habana, La Haya** (The Hague), **El Havre** (Le Havre), **la Mancha** (region southeast of Madrid), **La Montaña** (province of Santander, Spain), **La Rioja** (province of Logroño, Spain), **el Rosellón** (the Rousillon), **el Yucatán.**

274. GENDER OF NOUNS

1. Following are some of the more frequent masculine nouns of Greek origin ending in **-a: axioma, clima, cometa, dilema, diploma, drama, enigma, epigrama, fantasma** *(phantom),* **idioma** *(language),* **lema** *(motto),* **mapa, melodrama, panorama, poema, poeta, planeta, problema, programa, síntoma, sistema, telegrama, teorema.**

2. All nouns ending in **-is** are feminine, except **el análisis, el cutis** *(skin of the face),* **el éxtasis, el iris** *(of the eye),* and **el paréntesis.**

275. AUGMENTATIVE SUFFIXES

Augmentative suffixes are **-ón, -azo, -acho, -ote,** and **-arrón,** e.g., **sillón** *armchair,* **manaza** *large hand,* **ricacho** *(small-town) rich person,* **librote** *big book, tome,* **nubarrón** *dark (threatening) cloud.*

276. DIMINUTIVE SUFFIXES

1. The choice of diminutive suffixes depends not only on the meaning of the suffix (Sec. **170**) but also on the structure of the root word. Instead of the usual **-ito, -illo,** and **-uelo,** the following special forms are used:
(*a*) **-cito, -cillo, -zuelo** are applied to words of two or more syllables ending in **-n** or **-r: mujercita** *little woman, darling,* etc., **corazoncito** *sweetheart.*

(*b*) **-ecito, -ecillo, -ezuelo, -achuelo, -ichuelo** are applied
    (1) to monosyllables ending in a consonant, including **y**: e.g., **vocecita** *thin little voice,* **reyezuelo** *petty king;*
    (2) to words of two syllables containing in the first syllable the diphthongs **ei, ie, ue: cuerpecito** *tiny body;*
    (3) to words of two syllables ending in the diphthongs **-ia, -io, -ua:** e.g., **bestiecilla** *little beast;*
    (4) to some words of two syllables ending in **-ío:** e.g., **riachuelo** *small stream;*
    (5) to all words of two syllables ending in **-e:** e.g., **pobrecito** *poor fellow.*
(*c*) **-ececito, -ececillo, -ececzuelo** are applied to monosyllables ending in a vowel: e.g., **piececito** *tiny little foot.*

2. Some of the more frequent exceptions are: **Juanito, Luisito, agüita.**

3. The suffixes **-ico, -cico, -ecico, -ececico, -ín, -ino, -iño** are especially characteristic of regional usage. The inhabitants of Costa Rica, for example, are often known as **ticos** because they are said to use the suffix **-ico** more frequently than other diminutives.

4. The suffixes **-ón** and **-ote** may serve to form diminutives as well as augmentatives: **callejón** *alley,* **ratón** *mouse,* **islote** *islet.*

5. It is possible to combine various diminutive and augmentative suffixes: **chiquitito** *tiny,* **plazoletilla** *small square,* **corpachón** *big body,* **saloncito** *small parlor.*

277. DEPRECIATIVE SUFFIXES

1. Following is a list of depreciative suffixes: **-ete, -ote, -ajo, -ejo, -ijo, -aco, -uco, -acho, -ucho, -uza, -orrio, -orro, -ato, -astro, -alla:** e.g., **pobrete** ←**pobre; feota** ←**feo; libraco** ←**libro; caballejo** ←**caballo; casucha** ←**casa; mujeruca** ←**mujer; poetastro** ←**poeta; villorrio** ←**villa; gentuza** ←**gente.**

2. With depreciatives (and augmentatives) there is often a change in gender: **el familión** ←**familia; la peseta** ←**peso; el tenducho** ←**tienda; la lagartija** ←**lagarto; el caserón** ←**casa; el sillón** ←**la silla.**

278. INTERJECTIONS

Interjections are used much more frequently in Spanish than in English.

1. The more common interjections are:

¡Oh! *(surprise)*	*Oh!*
¡Ah! *(surprise)*	*Ah!*
¡Alto!	*Halt!*
¡Ay! *(lamentation)*	*Oh! Alas! Ouch!*
¡Bah! *(contempt, incredulity)*	*Bah!*
¡Ca! or **¡Qué va!** *(incredulity, denial)*	*Nonsense! No way!*
¡Ea! *(encouragement)*	*Come!*
¡Ea, ea! *(impatience)*	*Come on!*

¡Hola! *(greeting, discovery)*	*Hello!*
¡Huy! *(disgust, admiration)*	*Ouch! Gee!*
¡Ole! or **¡olé!** *(applause)*	*Bravo! Attaboy!*
¡Chitón!	*Hush!*
¡Ya!	*I see!*
¡Zas!	*Crash!*
¡Arre!	*Giddap!*
¡So!	*Whoa!*

2. Imperatives are frequently used as interjections:

¡Anda! or **¡Ande!** *(incredulity, importunity)*	*Go on! Come on!*
¡Basta!	*Enough!*
¡Calla! or **¡Calle!** *(silence, incredulity)*	*Keep quiet! Nonsense!*
¡Diga! or **¡Mande!** *(reply to call)*	*Yes, sir! (what is it?)*
¡Oye! or **¡Oiga!**	*Listen! Look (here)! Say!*
¡Mira! or **¡Mire!**	*Look (here)!*
¡Quita! or **¡Quite!** *(incredulity, annoyance)*	*Oh, no! Stop!*
¡Toma! *(agreement)*	*Of course!*
¡Vamos!	*Come on! Come! Well!*
¡Vaya!	*Well! What a . . . ! Of course!*
¡Viva!	*Long live! Hurrah!*
¡Muera!	*Down with (kill) him!*

3. Nouns and adjectives are frequently used as interjections:

¡Bravo!	*Bravo!*
¡Claro!	*Of course! Sure!*
¡Cuidado!	*Careful! Look (watch) out!*
¡Firme!	*Steady!*
¡Ojo!	*Attention! Careful!*
¡Socorro! ¡Auxilio!	*Help!*

4. Divine names carry no implication of blasphemy when used as interjections:

¡Dios mío!	*Heavens!*
¡Por Dios!	*For Heaven's sake!*
¡Válgame Dios!	*God help me!*
¡Jesús!	*Heavens!*
¡Jesús, María y José! *(after a sneeze)*	
¡Virgen Santísima!	*Goodness gracious!*
Similarly,	
¡Demonio!, ¡Diablo!	*The devil!*

5. **Hombre, mujer, chico, hijo, hija** are frequently used in conversation for emphasis or expostulation. **¡Hombre!** and **¡señor!** are used addressing either men or women.

6. A number of words having the initial syllable **ca-** are used as interjections to express surprise or annoyance: **¡caramba! ¡caray! ¡caracoles! ¡canastos! ¡cáspita!** *Gosh! Gee!*

279. NUMERALS

CARDINALS

0	cero	*30*	treinta
1	un(o), una	*31*	treinta y un(o)
2	dos	*32*	treinta y dos
3	tres	*40*	cuarenta
4	cuatro	*50*	cincuenta
5	cinco	*60*	sesenta
6	seis	*70*	setenta
7	siete	*80*	ochenta
8	ocho	*90*	noventa
9	nueve	*100*	cien(to)
10	diez	*200*	doscientos, -as
11	once	*300*	trescientos, -as
12	doce	*400*	cuatrocientos, -as
13	trece	*500*	quinientos, -as
14	catorce	*600*	seiscientos, -as
15	quince	*700*	setecientos, -as
16	dieciséis	*800*	ochocientos, -as
17	diecisiete	*900*	novecientos, -as
18	dieciocho	*1000*	mil
19	diecinueve	*2000*	dos mil
20	veinte	*1.000.000*	un millón (de)
21	veintiún(o)	*2.000.000*	dos millones (de)
22	veintidós		

ORDINALS

1st	primer(o)
2nd	segundo
3rd	tercer(o) (tercio)
4th	cuarto
5th	quinto
6th	sexto
7th	séptimo
8th	octavo
9th	noveno (nono)
10th	décimo
11th	undécimo

12th	**duodécimo**
13th	**décimo tercio (tercero)**
14th	**décimo cuarto**
15th	**décimo quinto**
16th	**décimo sexto**
17th	**décimo séptimo**
18th	**décimo octavo**
19th	**décimo noveno (nono)**
20th	**vigésimo**
21st	**vigésimo primero (primo)**
22nd	**vigésimo segundo**
23rd	**vigésimo tercero (tercio)**
30th	**trigésimo**
40th	**cuadragésimo**
50th	**quincuagésimo**
60th	**sexagésimo**
70th	**septuagésimo**
80th	**octogésimo**
90th	**nonagésimo**
100th	**centésimo**
101st	**centésimo primero (primo)**
129th	**centésimo vigésimo noveno**
	ducentésimo
300th	**tricentésimo**
400th	**cuadringentésimo**
500th	**quingentésimo**
600th	**sexcentésimo**
700th	**septingentésimo**
800th	**octingentésimo**
900th	**noningentésimo**
1000th	**milésimo**
1.000.000th	**millonésimo**

280. DAYS OF THE WEEK AND MONTHS OF THE YEAR

Days: **lunes, martes, miércoles, jueves, viernes, sábado, domingo.**
Months: **enero, febrero, marzo, abril, mayo, junio, julio, agosto, se(p)tiembre, octubre, noviembre, diciembre.** (The names of the days and months are not capitalized.)

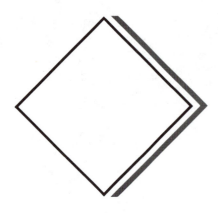

VOCABULARY

SPANISH-ENGLISH

A

a to, at, for (after)
abajo below, downstairs
abarcar take in, comprehend
abogado, -a *m. f.* lawyer
abordar approach; board
abrigo *m.* overcoat; shelter
absolutamente absolutely
absoluto: en ____ absolutely not, not at all
abuelo, -a *m. f.* grandfather, grandmother
abundante abundant
aburrido bored; boring
aburrir bore; ____**se** become bored
abusar de abuse
acabar finish, end; ____ **de** have just; **se acabó** that's all there is to it (Ch. 19)
accidente *m.* accident
aceituna *f.* olive
acera *f.* sidewalk
acercar (se) approach, get closer
acomodador, -a *m. f.* usher
acomodar accommodate, make comfortable
acompañar accompany
acontecimiento *m.* event
acordarse de remember
actitud *f.* attitude

actividad *f.* activity
acto *m.* act
actriz *f.* actress
actuación *f.* role; ____ **del equipo** team play
acudir come (rush) to
acueducto *m.* aqueduct
acuerdo *m.* agreement; **llegar a un** ____ come to an agreement, agree; **de** ____ in accord, agreed, all right
adelante: ¡ ____**!** come in!
además besides, moreover
adiós *m.* goodbye, farewell
adjectivo *m.* adjective
admirable admirable
admiración *f.* admiration
adobe *m.* adobe
adquirir (ie, i) acquire, purchase
aduana *f.* customs
adueñarse (de) take possession of
adusto austere
advertir (ie, i) warn
aeropuerto *m.* airport
afable affable
aficionado *m.* fan; amateur
afirmar affirm
afortunadamente fortunately
afuera outside

agente *m.* agent
agitación *f.* agitation
agosto August
agradable pleasant, agreeable
agradar please
agradecimiento *m.* gratitude
agrandarse become greater
agrupado grouped, huddled
ahí there
ahora now; **por** _____ for the present; _____ **mismo** right away; _____ **que** but, only; now that
ahorrar save
aire *m.* air
aislado isolated, single
álbum *m.* album
alma *f.* soul
alegre joyful, merry
alegría *f.* joy
alegrarse de be glad about
alemán German
alfombra *f.* carpet, rug
alfombrero *m.* carpet maker
Alfonso el Sabio Alfonso X, the Learned (King of Castile and León [1252–1284], founder of Castilian prose literature)
alforjas *f. pl.* saddlebags
algo something; somewhat, rather
alguno any, some; no, none
alistador *m.* recruiter
alistar enlist; recruit
almohada *f.* pillow
almorzar (ue) have lunch
alojarse lodge
alrededor de around
alto high, tall; **lo** _____ the top
altura *f.* height
aluminio *m.* aluminum
alzar raise
alumno, -a *m. f.* student
allá there; **más** _____ beyond, further on, _____ **ellos** so much for them
alquilar rent
amabilidad *f.* kindness
amanecer dawn
amargo bitter
amarillo yellow
ambiente *m.* atmosphere
americana *f.* sport jacket
amigo, -a *m. f.* friend
amistad *f.* friendship
amistoso friendly
ampliación *f.* enlargement
anacronismo *m.* anachronism

anaranjado orange-colored
ancho broad, wide
andanza *f.* wandering
Andalucía *f.* Andalusia (southern part of Spain)
andaluz, -a Andalusian
andante wandering; errant
andar walk, be, go; **¡andando!** let's get going! **¡ande!** come! (coaxing) (Ch. 13)
anglosajón Anglo-Saxon
animación *f.* animation
anochecer become night
ante before (in presence of); _____ **todo** above all
anteojos *m. pl.* eyeglasses
antes before, formerly; **cuanto** _____ as soon as possible
anticipar anticipate
anticuado antiquated
antiguo old, ancient
anunciar advertise
año *m.* year
apagaincendios *m. sing.* fire extinguisher
apagar extinguish; put out, turn off (electrical appliances)
aparato *m.* apparatus, appliance
aparcar park
aparecer appear, look
apariencia *f.* appearance
aparte apart; _____ **de** besides
apasionadamente with great feeling
apenas (si) scarcely
apertura *f.* opening, beginning
apoderarse de seize, take possession of
aposento *m.* room, chamber
apreciación *f.* appreciation
apreciar appreciate
apresurarse hurry
apretón de manos *m.* handshake
apunte *m.* note; **sacar** _____ s take notes
aquí here; **por** _____ (around) here
árabe Arab(ic)
arabesco *m.* arabesque
árbol *m.* tree
arboleda *f.* (grove of) trees
arcada *f.* arcade, archway
archivo *m.* archive
arena *f.* sand
aridez *f.* aridity
aristócrata *m.* aristocrat
arma *f.* weapon
armar arm; (*colloquial*) cause, start
armonía *f.* harmony
armónico harmonious

arquitecto *m.* architect
arquitectónico architectural
arquitectura *f.* architecture
arrabal *m.* suburb; _____**es** outskirts
arrayán *m.* myrtle
arreglar arrange, fix
arrogancia *f.* arrogance
arruga *f.* wrinkle
arte *m.* (*pl. f.*) art; **bellas** _____**s** fine arts
artista *m.* artist
artístico artistic
artículo *m.* article
ascender ascend
asegurar assure
asentado settled
así so; _____ **es que** so that; **una cosa** _____ such a thing
asiento *m.* seat
asilo *m.* asylum
asistir (a) attend
asombrar astonish
aspecto *m.* look, aspect, appearance
aspiración *f.* aspiration
astronauta *m. f.* astronaut
astuto astute
asunto *m.* affair; matter, subject; *pl.* business
asustar frighten; _____**se** become frightened
atacar attack
atardecer become late afternoon
atareado busy
atención *f.* attention
aterrizar land
atleta *m.* athlete
atlético athletic
atmósfera *f.* atmosphere
atractivo attractive
atraer attract
atrás behind
atrasado slow, backward
atravesar (ie) cross
atreverse dare
atribuir attribute
aturdido bewildered, stunned, dizzy
aula *f.* classroom
aún still, yet
aun even
aunque although; even though
autobús *m.* motor-bus
autocar *m.* bus, tourist bus
automóvil *m.* automobile
autopista *f.* turnpike, freeway
autor *m.* author
autorzuelo *m.* wretched author
avenida *f.* avenue

avergonzarse (ue) (de) be ashamed (of)
avión *m.* airplane; _____ **de chorro, de reac-ción** jet plane
avisar to notify, warn, tell, let know
ayer yesterday
ayuda *f.* help
ayudar help
ayuntamiento *m.* city council, town hall
azafata *f.* airline hostess, stewardess
azotea *f.* open housetop
azul blue
azulejo *m.* tile

B

bahía *f.* bay
bailar dance
baile *m.* dance
bajar (carry, come, bring) down; **bajarse** to get off (Ch. 17)
banco *m.* bank
bandera *f.* flag
banquero *m.* banker
barato cheap
barbaridad *f.* (*colloquial*) huge amount; ¡**qué** _____! How awful!
Barcelona *f.* Barcelona (*second largest city in Spain, capital of the Generalitat of Catalonia*)
barco *m.* ship, boat, steamer
barrio *m.* quarter, district, suburb
bastante enough, rather, considerable, considerably
bastar be enough, suffice (Ch. 19)
bastón *m.* cane
bastonazo *m.* blow with a cane
basura *f.* garbage, trash
batalla *f.* battle
baúl *m.* trunk
bebida *f.* drink
belleza *f.* beauty
bello beautiful
biblioteca *f.* library
bibliotecario *m.* librarian
bicicleta *f.* bicycle
bien well, good; **está** _____ all right; **más** _____ rather; _____ . . . _____ either . . . or
billete *m.* ticket; bill (money)
blanco white
blancura *f.* whiteness
bobo *m.* fool, idiot
boca *f.* mouth
bola *f.* ball
bombero *m.* fireman
bombón *m.* chocolate-covered cream, candy

bonito pretty
bordo: a _____ on board
bosque _n._ woods
botella _f._ bottle
botellazo _m._ blow with a bottle
botón _m._ button
botonería _f._ button maker's shop
botones _m. sing._ bellboy
bóveda _f._ vaulted ceiling
bravo fierce, ferocious
brazo: a _____ **partido** hand to hand (with bare fists)
brillante brilliant
brillar shine
bruto brute
bueno good, kind; (_exclamation_) well, all right! **de** _____**as a primeras** point blank
bufón _m._ buffoon
burlón mocking
buscar seek, look for
búsqueda _f._ search

C

¡ca! not at all!
caballo _m._ horse
caber fit, be contained in (Ch. 19)
cabeza _f._ head
cabo: al _____ **(de)** finally, at the end of
cada each
Cádiz Cadiz (_important port on southwest coast of Spain_)
caer fall (Ch. 3)
café _m._ coffee; café; _____ **cortado** espresso coffee with some milk
cafetería _f._ café, restaurant
caída _f._ fall
caja _f._ box; _____ **de ahorros** savings bank
calabazas: dar _____ jilt
calcetín _m._ sock
calentar (ie) heat
cálido warm
califa _m._ Caliph
calor _m._ heat
caluroso warm
callado silent
callarse keep silent
calle _f._ street; _____ **abajo** down the street; _____ **arriba** up the street
callejón _m._, **callejuela** _f._ narrow street, alley
camarero _m._ waiter
camarón _m._ shrimp
cambiante changing
cambiar (de) change

cambio _m._ change; **en** _____ on the other hand
caminar walk
camisa _f._ shirt
campana _f._ bell
campesino _m._ peasant
campo _m._ field; _____ **de cultivo** cultivated fields
canasto _m._ basket
cancelar cancel
canción _f._ song
cansar tire; _____**se** tire, become tired
cantante _m. f._ singer
cantar sing
cante flamenco _m. Andalusian folk songs associated with the gypsies_
cantidad _f._ quantity
canto _m._ rock, boulder
capa y espada "de _____**"** "cloak and sword" (play)
capital _f._ capital
capitán _m._ captain
cara _f._ face
carácter _m._ character
cárcel _f._ jail
cardenal _m._ cardinal
carecer de lack
cargado loaded
carne _f._ meat, flesh
caro expensive
carretera _f._ highway
cartel _m._ poster
cartelera _f._ (bill)board
cartero _m._ mail carrier
Casa de la Moneda _f._ Mint
casa _f._ house, home; firm
casado married
casamiento _m._ marriage
casarse marry
casero domestic, home loving
casi almost
caso _m._ case
castellano Castilian
Castilla _f._ Castile
castillo _m._ castle
castizo traditional, thoroughly Spanish
casualidad _f._ chance
catalán Catalan, Catalonian
catar sample, examine
catavinos _m._ winetaster
catedral _f._ cathedral
causa _f._ cause; **a** _____ **de** because of
celebrarse to be held (concert)
céltico Celtic

cenar dine
censurador censor
central central
centralista centralist
céntrico downtown (*adj.*)
centro *m.* center, downtown
cerca near
cercanía surrounding territory
cercano near
ceremonia *f.* ceremony
ceremoniosamente ceremoniously
cervantino related to Cervantes, the author of the story of "Don Quixote"
cerveza *f.* beer
cicatriz *f.* scar
cielo *m.* sky
ciencia *f.* science; **hombre de ____** scientist
ciento hundred; **por ____** percent
cierto certain; **por ____ que** and by the way, to be sure
cigarrillo *m.* cigarette
cine *m.* movie, cinema
cinematografía *f.* cinematography
círculo *m.* circle
circundado surrounded
ciudad *f.* city
ciudadano *m.* citizen
civil civil
civilización *f.* civilization
claridad *f.* clarity
claro clear; of course; ¡ **____ que sí!** of course!
clasicismo *m.* classicism
clásico classic
clima *m.* climate
coche *m.* car (automobile)
cocinero, -a *m. f.* cook
coger gather, pick (Ch. 2)
colección *f.* collection
colina *f.* hill
Colón *m.* Columbus
color *m.* color
colorido *m.* color(ing)
collar *m.* necklace
comandante *m.* commander; major
comarca *f.* region, area
combatiente *m.* combatant
combinación *f.* combination
comedia *f.* comedy; play; **____ de capa y espada** "cloak and sword" play
comentario *m.* comment
comer eat
cometa *m.* comet

comida *f.* meal, food
como as, since, as if, like
comodidad *f.* comfort
cómodo comfortable
compañero *m.* companion, comrade; **____ de cuarto** roommate
compañía *f.* company
compartimiento *m.* compartment
comparar compare
compartir share
complacer please
completamente completely
completo complete; **por ____** completely
complicado complicated
componer compose
compra *f.* purchase **ir (estar) de ____s** go shopping
comprar buy
comprender understand
comprensión *f.* understanding
comprometerse a to promise to
computadora *f.* computer
comunicar communicate
comunista communist
con with
concebir (i) conceive
concentrar concentrate
concierto *m.* concert
conde *m.* count
condenar condemn
conducta *f.* conduct
conferencia *f.* lecture, talk
confesar (ie) confess
confesor *m.* confessor
confusion *f.* confusion
conjunto *m.* whole; **en ____** all in all, by and large
conocer know, be acquainted with, meet
conquista *f.* conquest
conquistador *m.* conquistador, conqueror
conseguir (i) get, obtain, succeed in
consejero *m.* counselor
consejo *m.* advice; council
conserje *m.* concierge, janitor
considerar consider
consistir en consist of
constar be known; **____ de** consist of (Ch. 16)
construcción *f.* construction
construir build
contador *m.* accountant
contaminación *f.* pollution
contar (ue) tell, relate (Prelim. Les. 2)

contemplar contemplate, gaze
contemporáneo contemporary
contender contend
contendiente contending
contener contain
contentar content
contento happy
contestar answer
continuar continue
continuo continual, continuous
contrario *m.* contrary; opponent; **llevarle la contraria (a uno)** contradict
contratiempo *m.* misfortune, setback, mishap
contraste *m.* contrast
contrato *m.* contract
convencer convince
convenir agree; **lo convenido** the plan (Ch. 11)
conversación *f.* conversation
copa *f.* wineglass
corazón *m.* heart
corbata *f.* necktie
cordialidad *f.* cordiality
Córdoba Cordova
coronel *m.* colonel
correo *m.* mail
correr run
correspondiente respective
corrida (de toros) *f.* bullfight
corriente usual, ordinary, current
cortado espresso coffee with some milk
cortapapel *m.* paper cutter
cortar cut
cortatubos *m. sing.* pipecutter
corte *f.* court, capital
corto short; **quedarse ——** restrain oneself
cosa thing
costa *f.* coast
costar (ue) cost; **—— trabajo** be hard, difficult
costumbre *f.* custom
creer believe, think; **¡ya lo creo!** I should say so! of course!
cresta *f.* crest
criado servant
criollo native American
crisis *f.* crisis
cruz *f.* cross
cruzar cross
cuaderno *m.* notebook
cuadrado square
cuadro *m.* picture, painting
**cual: el —— ** *etc.* which

cualquiera any (at all, whatsoever)
cuando when
cuanto as much as, all that; **en ——** as soon as; **en —— a** as for, as
cuartel *m.* barracks
cuarto *m.* room; fourth, quarter
cuatro four
cubano Cuban
cubierto covered
cubreplatos *m. sing.* dish cover
cuchara *f.* spoon; **meter la ——** butt in
cuenta: darse —— realize
cuentista *m.* story writer
cuento *m.* tale, story; **—— de nunca acabar** endless story
cuero *m.* leather
cuesta *f.* hill; **en ——** steep; **—— arriba** uphill; **—— abajo** downhill
cueva *f.* cave
cuidado care; **tener ——** be careful
culpa *f.* blame
culpar blame
cultura *f.* culture
cultivar cultivate
culto cultured, cultivated
cumpleaños *m. sing.* birthday
cumplir fulfill, execute (Ch. 19)
curiosísimo very curious
curso *m.* course

CH

chaqueta *f.* jacket
charlar chat
chicle *m.* chewing gum
chico small; **-o, -a** *m. f.* boy; girl
chino Chinese
chisme *m.* gossip
chismoso gossipy
chocolate *m.* chocolate
chófer *m.* driver
chorro jet, stream; **avión de ——** jet plane
churro *m.* long thin fritter

D

damasquinado *m.* damascene work (*gold inlaid on black steel*)
daño *m.* harm, damage; **hacer ——** harm
dar give; **me da lo mismo** it makes no difference to me; **——se cuenta (de)** realize (Ch. 6)
datar date

de of, from, with
debajo de beneath, underneath
deber owe, ought, must; *m.* duty
debido fitting, proper
decano *m.* dean
décimo tenth
decir say; **querer** _____ mean (to say); **ni que** _____ **tiene** it goes without saying (Ch. 10)
declaración *f.* declaration
decidir decide; _____**se** decide, make up one's mind
decisión *f.* decision
decorativo decorative
dedicar devote
defecto *m.* defect
defensa *f.* defense
deficiente deficient
definir define
dehesa *f.* pasture land
dejar leave, make; let; _____ **de** stop (Ch. 10)
delante in front of, ahead of
delgado thin
delicado delicate
delicioso delicious
demás: los, las _____ *etc.* the rest
demasiado too (much, many)
democracia *f.* democracy
democrático democratic
dentro: por _____ on the inside; _____ **(de)** within
deporte *m.* sport
depositar deposit
derecha *f.* right wing (politics)
derechista *m.* right-winger
derecho right; *m.* right; law
derroche *m.* lavish expenditure
desagradable unpleasant
desaparecer disappear
desarrollar develop
desarrollo *m.* development
descansar rest
descolgar (ue) take down, unhook
desconocido unknown, strange
descripción *f.* description
descubrimiento *m.* discovery
desde from; _____ **que** since (time)
desear desire, wish, like
desembarcar disembark
desembocar run (empty) into
desesperado desperate
designado chosen
desilusión *f.* disappointment
desmayado faint
desnudo bare, naked

desolación *f.* desolation
desolado desolate
despacho *m.* study, office
despacio slowly
despedirse (i) take leave (of)
despertarse (ie) awaken
despiadado pitiless
despierto awake
desprecio *m.* scorn
destacar stand out
destierro *m.* exile
destinación *f.* destination
desvivirse por outdo oneself in order to
detener(se) stop; arrest
detenidamente carefully
detenido detailed
detrás behind
deuda *f.* debt
devolver (ue) return
diablo *m.* devil; **qué diablos** what the devil
diálogo *m.* dialogue, conversation
diario daily; *m.* diary; daily newspaper
dictador *m.* dictator
dictadorzuelo *m.* petty dictator
diez ten
Diego James
diferenciarse be different
diferente different
diferir (ie) differ
difícil difficult, hard
dificultad *f.* difficulty
dignidad *f.* dignity
dilema *m.* dilemma
dimensión *f.* dimension
dineral *m.* large amount of money
dirigir direct; _____ **la palabra** address
disco *m.* disk, record
discreto discreet
discusión *f.* argument
discutir argue
disponible available
disposición *f.* disposal
dispuesto ready
disputa *f.* argument
distancia *f.* distance
distar be distant
distintivo distinctive
distinto different
diversión *f.* amusement, sport
diversos various
divertido amusing
divertir (ie, i) amuse
divisar see, perceive
doce twelve

docena *f.* dozen
documento *m.* document
dólar *m.* dollar
domador *m.* tamer
domar tame
dominio *m.* dominion
Don Quijote *m.* Don Quixote
donde where
dorado golden
dormir (ue, u) sleep
dos two
dotado gifted
drama *m.* drama
dramaturgo *m.* dramatist
duda doubt
dulce sweet, soft
durante during, for
durar last
duro *m.* five pesetas

E

e and (before words beginning with **i-** or **hi-**)
echar throw, pour; _____ **se (a)** begin to, burst out; **echarse a perder** spoil
edificio *m.* building
educación *f.* good breeding, politeness; education
educador *m.* educator
educar educate; bring up
egoísta *m.* egoist, selfish
ejemplo *m.* example
ejercicio *m.* exercise
electricidad *f.* electricity
electricista *m.* electrician
elegancia *f.* elegance
elegante elegant
elegir (i) choose, pick out, elect
elevado high, elevated
ello it
elogiar praise
embajada *f.* embassy
embajador *m.* ambassador
embalador *m.* packer
embalar crate
embarcar embark
embargo: sin _____ nevertheless
embrujamiento *m.* eeriness, haunting, spell
eminente eminent
emoción *f.* emotion, emotional appeal
emocionante exciting
emocionar move, stir, appeal to
empezar (ie) start, begin
empinado high, lofty

empleado *m.* employee
empobrecer impoverish, become poor
emprendedor enterprising
emprender undertake
en in, on
enamorarse fall in love _____ **de** fall in love with
encantador charming, delightful
encantar delight
encanto *m.* charm
encargar order
encargo *m.* errand, order, commission
encarnar embody
encendedor *m.* cigarette lighter
encender (ie) light
encerrado (en) shut up in
encerrar (ie) shut in
encima in addition; **(por)** _____ **de** above, on top of
encomendar (ie) commend, trust with
encontrar(se) (ue) find, meet
encuentro *m.* meeting
enfadar (se) make (get) angry
enfermarse become ill
enfermedad *f.* illness
enfermo ill
enfrente across the way, opposite
enfriar cool, chill, grow cold
engañador deceiving
engañar deceive
enojado angry
enojarse become angry
enormemente immensely
enriquecer grow rich
enrojecer redden
ensalada *f.* salad
enseñar show; teach
ensueño *m.* reverie
entablar start (a conversation, a relationship)
entendedor *m.* understanding person
entender (ie) understand, make out; _____**se** get along together (Ch. 1)
enterarse (de) find out
entero entire
enterrar (ie) bury
entierro *m.* burial
entonces then, that time
entrar enter; _____**le a uno sueño** (*etc.*) to get (become) sleepy (*etc.*) (Ch. 18)
entre among, between
entregar deliver, hand over
entrenamiento *m.* training
entretener entertain
entristecer sadden, become sad

entusiasmado enthusiastic
enviar send, ship
envolver (ue) involve; wrap
enzarzarse (en) become involved in
época *f.* time, period
equipaje *m.* baggage
equipo *m.* team
errar (ie) err, wander
escala: hacer _____ call at (of a boat or airplane)
escandaloso scandalous
escaso scarce
escena *f.* scene, sight, view; stage
esclarecer brighten, grow light
escribir write
escrito: por _____ in writing
escritor *m.* writer
escuchar listen
esculpir carve
escultórico sculptural
escultura *f.* wood carving, sculpture
esforzarse (ue) strive
esfuerzo *m.* effort
eso that; **por** _____ therefore, that's why; **a**
 _____ **de** about (time); **¡eso es!** that's it
 (right); _____ **sí que no** that's really not it;
 y _____ **que** although, even if
espacio *m.* space
espantar frighten
España *f.* Spain
español Spanish, Spaniard
especial special
especialmente especially
especie *f.* kind
espectáculo *m.* spectacle
espectador *m.* spectator
espejo *m.* mirror
esperar hope; expect; wait (for)
espeso thick
espíritu *m.* spirit
espiritual spiritual
espléndido splendid, magnificent
esplendor *m.* splendor
esquiador *m.* skier
esquiar ski
esquina *f.* (street) corner
estación *f.* station; season
Estados Unidos *m. pl.* United States
estalactita *f.* stalactite
estancia *f.* stay
estar be, stand, lie; look, feel, act (Ch. 13)
estatua *f.* statue
este this
estilo *m.* style; **por el** _____ of the sort, kind

estimar calculate
estimulante stimulating
estirar stretch
esto this; _____ **de** this business of
estrecho narrow
estreno *m.* first performance, premiere
estrepitoso noisy, boisterous
estropear spoil, damage
estudiante *m.* student
estudiar study
estudio *m.* study
eterno eternal, everlasting
Europa *f.* Europe
evocación *f.* evocation
evocar evoke
exagerar exaggerate
excelencia: por _____ par excellence
excelente excellent
excepción *f.* exception
excepcional exceptional
exceptuar except
excesivo excessive
excursión *f.* trip
excusar excuse, avoid
existencia *f.* existence
existente existing
éxito *m.* success
explorador *m.* explorer
explorar explore
explosión *f.* explosion
exportador exporting
exposición *f.* exposition
expresar express
exquisito exquisite
extender (ie) stretch
extenso wide
extrañar surprise
extranjero *m.* foreigner
extraño strange
extraordinario extraordinary
extremo *m.* end

F

fábrica *f.* factory
faceta *f.* facet
fachada *f.* façade
fácil easy
faja *f.* sash; strip (of land, etc.)
falta *f.* lack; **hacer** _____ be necessary
faltar be lacking (Ch. 19)
familia *f.* family
familiar familiar
famoso famous

fantástico   fantastic
faro   *m.* light(house)
fastidiar   annoy, bore
fatigado   tired
favor   *m.* favor; **haga el** _____ **(de)** please
favorecer   favor, flatter
favorito   favorite
felicitar (se)   congratulate
fenicio   Phoenician
fenómeno   *m.* phenomenon
fiesta   *f.* feast, holiday; sport
figura   *f.* figure
figurarse   imagine, think of
fijarse (en)   notice
filigrana   filigree
fin   *m.* end; **al** _____ finally; **en** _____ after all, in short, well
final   *m.* end
firmar   sign
físico   physical
fisonomía   *f.* appearance
flecha   *f.* arrow
flechazo   *m.* arrow shot; (*colloq.*) sudden passion, love at first sight
flor   *f.* flower
fomento   *m.* fomentation, promotion
fondo   *m.* background, rear; **en el** _____ at bottom
fondos   *m. pl.* funds
forastero   *m.* stranger
formar   form
formidable   formidable, "swell," "terrific"
fortaleza   *f.* fortress
fortuna   *f.* fortune
foto   *f.* photograph
fotografía   *f.* photograph
fracasar   fail
fragmento   *m.* fragment
francamente   frankly, really
francés   French, Frenchman
franco   *m.* franc; frank
franqueza   *f.* frankness
frase   *f.* phrase, sentence
frecuencia   *f.* frequency
frecuentemente   frequently
frente   *f.* forehead; front
fruta   *f.* fruit
fuente   *f.* fountain, spring
fuera de   outside of; out of
fuertemente   strongly
fuerza   *f.* strength
fugaz   fleeting
fugitivo   *m.* fugitive
fumador   smoker

fumar   smoke
función (de teatro)   *f.* performance, show
fundar   found
furioso   furious
fusilar   shoot (execute)
fútbol   *m.* soccer

G

gallego   Galician
galleta   *f.* cracker, cookie
gana   *f.* desire; **darle a uno la** _____ **de, tener** _____ **s de** feel like
ganar   earn, win
ganga   *f.* bargain
gasolina   *f.* gasoline
gastar   spend
gato   *m.* cat
general   general; **por lo** _____ in general
generalmente   generally
generalizarse   become general
género   *m.* type, genre
generosidad   *f.* generosity
generoso   generous
geniazo   *m.* strong temper
genio   *m.* temper; character
gente   *f.* people
geográfico   geographical
gerente   *m.* manager
gesto   *m.* gesture
girar   turn; _____ **alrededor de** center on
gitano   *m.* gypsy
gobierno   *m.* government
gobernación   *f.* governing
godo   Goth
gótico   Gothic
grabado   engraved
gracia   *f.* grace; wit; **hacer** _____ amuse, strike as funny; **caerle a uno en** _____ charm someone; **tener** _____ be amusing
gracioso   graceful
gran(de)   great, large, big
granadino   pertaining to Granada, Spain
grandeza   *f.* grandeur, greatness
grandiosamente   grandly
granito   *m.* granite
granizar   hail
grano   *m.* grain; **ir al** _____ come to the point
grato   pleasant
grave   grave, serious
gravedad   *f.* gravity, sternness
gris   gray
gritar   shout
grupo   *m.* group

guante *m.* glove
guapo good-looking
guardajoyas *m.* jewel case
guardapuente *m.* bridge guard
guardia *m.* policeman
guerra *f.* war
guerrero *m.* warrior
guía *f.* guide
gustar like (be pleasing)
guitarra *f.* guitar
gusto *m.* taste; pleasure; **hallarse a** _____ be at ease, enjoy oneself

H

haber have (auxiliary)
hablar talk, speak
hablador talkative
hablante *m.* speaker
hacer do, make; **hace** it is (of weather); **desde hacía tiempo** for some time; _____**se** become (Ch. 12)
hacia toward
hada *f.* fairy
hallar find; _____**se** be
hambre *f.* hunger
hasta until, up to, as far as; _____ **ahora** so far
hay, había *etc.* there is, was; **he de,** *etc.* I am to; **hay que** it is necessary, one (we) must (Ch. 12)
hecho *m.* fact
helado *m.* ice cream
helar (ie) freeze
hermano, -a *m. f.* brother, sister
hermoso beautiful
heroico heroic
hispánico Hispanic
hispanoamericano Hispanic American
historia *f.* history
histórico historic, historical
holgazán lazy
hombre *m.* man; ¡_____! man! Wow!
honor *m.* honor
hora *f.* hour; **tener la** _____ have the time
horario *m.* schedule
hospitalidad *f.* hospitality
hotel *m.* hotel
hoy today
huele it smells
huelga *f.* strike
huerta *f.* truck farm
huérfano *m.* orphan

huir flee
humanidad *f.* humanity
humano human **lo** _____ **y lo divino** everything under the sun
humo *m.* smoke
humor *m.* humor

I

idea *f.* idea
ideal ideal
idiota *m.* idiot
iglesia *f.* church
ignorar be ignorant of, not know
iluminar illuminate
imaginación *f.* imagination, imagining
imaginar (se) imagine
imperial imperial
impermeable *m.* raincoat
imponente imposing
importador importing
importante important
importar matter, be of consequence
imposible impossible
impresión *f.* impression
impresionante impressive
impresionar impress
impulso *m.* driving force
inaccesible inaccessible
inagotable inexhaustible
inatención *f.* inattention
incendio *m.* fire
incidente *m.* incident
inconsciente unconscious
inconveniente *m.* difficulty, disadvantage
increíble incredible
independencia *f.* independence
indescriptible indescribable
indicar indicate
indio Indian
indiscreción *f.* indiscretion
individual individual
individuo *m.* person, fellow
industria *f.* industry
industrial industrial
industrialización *f.* industrialization
industrializar industrialize
infinito infinite
información *f.* information
informe *m.* notice, report
infracción *f.* infraction, violation
ingeniero *m.* engineer
ingenio *m.* wit

inglés English, Englishman
ingreso *m.* receipt; _____**s** income
injusticia *f.* injustice
inmenso immense
inmigración *f.* immigration
innato innate
inolvidable unforgettable
insistir insist
insultante insulting
insultar insult
insuperable insuperable
insurgente insurgent
intelectual intellectual
intención *f.* intention
intentar try, attempt
interés *m.* interest
interesante interesting
interesar interest
interior *m.* interior
interminable endless
internacional international
íntimo intimate; **lo más** _____ the innermost
  (part)
intrigar intrigue
inundar inundate, flood
invitar invite
ir go; _____**se** go, go away, leave; **¡Ah, vamos!**
  Oh, I see! **¡Qué va!** Nonsense! (Ch. 15)
irónico ironic
itinerario *m.* itinerary
izquierda *f.* left wing (politics)
izquierdista *m.* left winger
izquierdo left

J

jabón *m.* soap
jadeante panting
jamás never, ever
jardín *m.* garden
jefe *m.* chief, boss
jersey *m.* sweater
jornalero *m.* day laborer
jota *f. Aragonese folk dance in 3/8 time*
joven young
joya *f.* jewel
judío Jew, Jewish
juez *m.* judge
jugador *m.* player
jugar (ue) play (game) (Ch. 2)
juguetón playful
juicio *m.* judgement
julio *m.* July

junio *m.* June
justo fair, just, proper
juventud *f.* youth
juzgar judge

K

kilo *m.* kilo (*kilogram, 2.2 lbs.*)
kilómetro *m.* kilometer 1000 meters (*approximately five-eighths of a mile*)

L

lado *m.* side
lamentar lament
lápiz *m.* pencil
largo long
lástima: es _____ it is a pity; **dar** _____ be
  pitiful
lata: dar la _____ bore
lavar wash
lección *f.* lesson
lectura *f.* reading
leche *f.* milk
lechería *f.* dairy, creamery
leer read
lejanía *f.* distance
lejano remote
lejos far; **a lo** _____ in the distance
lengua *f.* tongue, language
león *m.* lion
levantarse rise, get up
leyenda *f.* legend
liberal liberal
libertad *f.* liberty
libertar liberate
librería *f.* bookstore
libro *m.* book
liebre *f.* hare
ligereza *f.* agility
ligero light
limitar (se) limit
limpiaparabrisas *m. sing.* windshield wiper
limpiar clean
limpio clean, pure
línea *f.* line; _____ **aérea** airline
Lisboa Lisbon (*capital of Portugal*)
lista *f.* list
listo ready; clever
literario literary
literatura *f.* literature
lo it; _____ **que es** as for
loco mad, wild, crazy

lograr   attain, succeed in
lotería   *f*. lottery
luchar   struggle, fight
luego   then, later; thereupon, therefore; **desde** _____ of course
lugar   *m*. place; **tener** _____ take place
lujoso   luxurious
lunes   *m*. Monday
luz   *f*. light

LL

llamado   so-called
llamar   call, knock
llaneza   *f*. informality
llano   flat
llanura   *f*. plain
llegar   arrive, come to
lleno   full
llevar   take; wear; have; _____ **(se)** take away with; _____**se bien** get along well together (Ch. 17)
lloviznar   drizzle

M

macizo   massive
madre   *f*. mother
Madrid   *m*. Madrid
maduro   ripe, mature
magnífico   magnificent, splendid
mal   badly, not very well
maldecir   curse
maldiciente   slanderous, cursing
maleta   *f*. suitcase
malo   bad; **lo** _____ **es que** the trouble is that
mañana   *f*. morning
mandar   order, have
mandón   bossy
manera   *f*. manner, way, fashion; **de** _____ **que** so that
manía   *f*. mania
manicomio   *m*. insane asylum
manifestación   *f*. manifestation
mano   *f*. hand; _____ **de obra** manual labor
mantener   maintain
mantequilla   *f*. butter
mantilla   *f*. mantilla (*lace shawl worn as head-dress by Spanish women on ceremonial occasions*)
manuscrito   *m*. manuscript
manzana   *f*. block (of houses); apple

mapa   *m*. map
máquina   *f*. machine; _____ **de escribir** typewriter
mar   *m*. and *f*. sea; **la** _____ **de** lots of
maravilla   *f*. marvel; **a las mil** _____s wonderfully
maravilloso   marvelous
marcha: estar en _____ be moving; **ponerse en** _____ start off
marcharse   leave
margen   *m. f*. margin
marido   *m*. husband
más   more
masa   *f*. mass, pile
matador   *m*. bullfighter
matamoscas   *m*. fly swatter
matar   kill
materia   matter; **primera** _____ raw material
material   *m*. material
mayor   larger, largest
mayordomo   *m*. chief steward
mayoría   *f*. majority
me   me
mecánico   *m*. mechanic
medicina   medicine
médico   *m*. physician
medieval   medieval
medio   half; **quitar (algo) de en** _____ get (something) out of the way
medir (i)   measure
meditación   *f*. meditation
mejor   better; **tanto** _____ so much the better
melancólico   melancholy
melodía   *f*. melody
melón   *m*. melon
memoria   *f*. memory
mencionar   mention
menear   shake
menor   smaller, smallest; slightest
menos   less, least; **ni mucho** _____ not in the least, by no means
mente   *f*. mind
mentir (ie, i)   lie
menudo   small
mercader   *m*. trader
merced   *f*. favor, grace
merecer   deserve
mesa   *f*. table
meseta   *f*. table-land, plateau
metálico   metallic
meter   put, place (into); _____**se con** quarrel with; _____**se** enter (Ch. 7)
método   *m*. method

metro *m.* meter (*39.37 in.*)
mi my
mí me
mientras (que) while; _____ **tanto** in the meantime
mil (one) thousand
milagro *m.* miracle, wonder
milla mile
ministro *m.* minister
ministerio *m.* ministry
mío my, of mine
mirador *m. in Cadiz, a turret, in the rest of Spain a glass-enclosed balcony*
mirar look (at)
mismo same, very; self
misterio *m.* mystery
misterioso mysterious
místico mystic
mitad *f.* half
mitin *m.* political rally
modelo *m.* model
modernizado modernized
moderno modern
modo *m.* way, fashion, manner
mole *f.* mass
molestar annoy, disturb, bother
molestia *f.* annoyance, bother
molino *m.* mill; _____ **de viento** windmill
momento *m.* moment
monasterio *m.* monastery
mono cute, nice
monótonamente monotonously
montón *m.* pile
monumental monumental, of (in) monuments
monumento *m.* monument
moro Moorish, Moor
motivo *m.* reason
mozo *m.* youth; servant; _____ **de cuerda** street porter
muchacho *m.* young man, lad
mucho much; long (time)
mueble *m.* piece of furniture
mueblería *f.* furniture store
muerte *f.* death
mujer *f.* woman
mujerzuela *f.* low woman
multar fine
multitud *f.* multitude
mundial world
mundo *m.* world; **todo el** _____ everybody
municipio *m.* municipality
muralla *f.* wall

muro *m.* wall
museo *m.* museum
música *f.* music
músico *m.* musician
muy very

N

nacer be born
nacimiento *m.* birth
nación *f.* nation
nacional national
nadie nobody, no one, anybody, anyone
naipe *m.* playing card
naranja *f.* orange
naranjo *m.* orange tree
natural natural
naturaleza *f.* nature
naturalmente naturally, of course
necesario necessary
necesitar need
negocio business; **hombre de** _____**s** businessman
nevar (ie) snow
ni neither, nor
nieve *f.* snow
ninguno no, none; any
niño boy
no no, not
noble noble
noche *f.* night; **de** _____ at night; **esta** _____ tonight
nombre *m.* name
norte *m.* north
norteamericano (North) American
norteño northern
nosotros we
nota *f.* note; grade; **sacar buenas (malas)** _____**s** get good (bad) grades
notar note
noticia *f.* news
novela *f.* novel
novelista *m.* novelist
noveno ninth
novio -a *m. f.* sweetheart, fiancé(e)
nube *f.* cloud
nublado overcast
nuestro our
Nueva York *f.* New York
nueve nine
nuevo new; **de** _____ again
número *m.* number
nunca never, ever

O

o or
obedecer obey
objetivo *m.* objective
objeto *m.* object
obligar compel
obra *f.* work (of art, etc.); **mano de** _____ manual labor
obrero *m.* worker
observación *f.* remark
obtener obtain
ocasión *f.* occasion, opportunity; **de** _____ second hand
occidental western
océano *m.* ocean
octavo eighth
ocupar occupy
ocurrir (se) occur, think of (Ch. 18)
odiar hate
ofender offend
oficial official, (of) government
ofrecer offer
ojalá I wish, (would) that!
ojo *m.* eye; **costar un** _____ **de la cara** cost a great deal
olivar *m.* olive orchard
olvidar forget
once eleven
opinión *f.* opinion
oportunidad *f.* opportunity
opuesto opposite
ordenador *m.* computer
organización *f.* organization
oriental oriental
original original
orilla *f.* bank (river)
ornamentación *f.* decoration
oro *m.* gold
oscurecer darken, grow dark
oscuro dark
otro other, another; _____**s dos** two more

P

paciencia *f.* patience
pagar pay
país *m.* country, land
paisaje *m.* landscape
paisano *m.* fellow countryman
pajarillo *m.* little bird
pájaro *m.* bird
palabra *f.* word; **de** _____ verbally; **dos** _____**s** a few words

palacio *m.* palace
palmera *f.* palm tree
pan *m.* bread
panadero *m.* baker
panorama *m.* view, panorama
pantalones *m. pl.* trousers
panteón *m.* mausoleum
pañuelo *m.* kerchief; **el mundo es un** _____ the world's a small place
papel *m.* paper
papelero *m.* stationer, papermaker
paquete *m.* package
par *m.* pair, couple
para for, in order to, to; _____ **con** toward, to
parador *m.* wayside inn, hostelry
paraguas *m.* umbrella
parar(se) stop
pardo brownish, grayish
parecer seem, appear, look (like); **¿qué le parece?** what do you think of . . . ?; **¿le parece (bien)?** what do you say?; _____**se** resemble (Ch. 5)
pared *f.* wall
pariente *m.* relative
parque *m.* park
parroquiano *m.* parishioner; customer
parte *f.* part; **a todas** _____**s** everywhere; **(por) ninguna** _____ nowhere
participante participant
participar participate
particular specific
partida *f.* departure
partido *m.* game
pasado mañana day after tomorrow
pasajero *m.* passenger
pasar pass, spend; happen, feel, be; _____**lo bien (mal)** to have a good (bad) time (Ch. 19)
pasear(se) walk, take a walk
paseo *m.* walk; boulevard; **dar un** _____ take a walk
pasillo *m.* corridor
paso *m.* step, pace; **dos** _____**s** short distance
pastel *m.* pastry
pastelería *f.* pastry shop
pastelero *m.* pastry cook
pastilla *f.* tablet; cake
pastor *m.* shepherd
pata *f.* paw, leg; _____ **de palo** wooden leg
patio *m.* patio
patria *f.* native country, birthplace
patrón *m.* master, boss
paz *f.* peace

pedir (i)   ask for, request; ———— **prestado** borrow (Ch. 1)

pegar   strike, to place close; **pegármela** fool me (Ch. 2)

peligro   *m.* danger

pelo   *m.* hair

pelota   *f.* (hand) ball; ———— **vasca** Basque handball (*jai alai*)

pelotazo   *m.* blow with a ball

pena   *f.:* **valer la** ———— be worthwhile

penetrante   penetrating

penetrar   penetrate

península   *f.* peninsula

penosamente   painfully

penoso   painful

pensamiento   *m.* thought

pensar (ie)   think (over)

peñasco   *m.* rock, boulder

pequeño   small

perder (ie)   lose, miss, waste; ———— **de vista** lose sight of (Prelim. Les. 2)

perdonar   pardon

perfeccionarse   improve

perfectamente   perfectly

periferie   *f.* periphery

periodista   *m.* journalist

período   *m.* period

perito   *m.* expert

perla   *f.* pearl

permiso   *m.* permission; **con** ———— excuse me

pero   but

perpetuo   perpetual

perro   *m.* dog

persona   *f.* person, people

personaje   *m.* personage, character

personalmente   personally

perspectiva   *f.* prospect, view

pertenecer   belong

pesado   heavy; boring

pesar   weigh; grieve

pescado   *m.* fish

peseta   *f.* peseta (Spanish monetary unit)

peso   *m.* weight (*monetary unit in some Hispanic countries*)

pestaña   *f.* eyelash

pianista   *m.* pianist

pico   *m.* peak

pictórico   pictoric

pie   *m.* foot; **de** ———— standing

piedra   *f.* stone

pierna   *f.* leg

pieza   *f.* piece

pinar   *m.* pine forest

pintar   paint

pintor   *m.* painter

pintoresco   picturesque

pintorzuelo   *m.* wretched painter

pintura   *f.* paint

pisapapeles   *m. sing.* paperweight

pistola   *f.* pistol

pitillera   *f.* cigarette case

pitillo   *m.* cigarette

placer   *m.* pleasure

plan   *m.* plan

planchar   iron

planear   plan

plantado: dejar———— stand up

plantar   plant

plata   *f.* silver

plátano   *m.* banana

plateresco   plateresque (*style of Spanish architecture in 16th century*)

plato   *m.* plate, dish

plaza   *f.* (town) square; ———— **de toros** bull ring; ———— **Mayor** main square

plazo   *m.* term, time limit; **a** ————**s** on credit, on time

pluma   *f.* pen

población   *f.* population; town

poco   little, few; ———— **a** ———— little by little, gradually; ———— **más o menos** more or less

poder (ue)   be able, can, may; **¿se puede?** may I come in?; **como pude** as best I could; **a más no** ———— to the utmost (Ch. 11)

poesía   *f.* poem, poetry

poético   poetic

política   *f.* politics

político   political

polo   *m.* pole

poner   place, put; ————**se** become, get; put on (Ch. 7)

popular   popular, folk

por   for, by, through, along, about, by way of

porque   because

portarse   behave, do

portero,   *m.* doorkeeper; janitor

posesión   *f.* possession, property

posición   *f.* position

postre   *m.* dessert

potente   powerful

pozo   *m.* well

prado   *m.* meadow

precio   *m.* price

precisamente   precisely, just

precision   *f.* accuracy

preciso: es ———— it is necessary

preferir (ie, i)   prefer

pregunta   *f.* question

preguntar ask (inquire) ——**se** wonder
prejuicio *m.* prejudice, preconceived notion
premio *m.* prize; —— **gordo** first prize
prensa *f.* press
preocuparse worry, bother
preparar prepare
presentar present, introduce
presidente *m.* president
prestar lend
primer ministro *m.* prime minister
primo, -a *m. f.* cousin
princesa *f.* princess
principal principal, main
principio *m.* beginning; **al** —— at first; **en un** —— at first
prisa *f.* hurry; **de** —— quickly
pro: en —— **y en contra** pro and con
probablemente probably
probar (ue) test, try
problema *m.* problem
producir produce
producto *m.* product
profesional professional
profesor *m.* teacher
profundo profound, deep
programa *m.* program
pronto quickly, soon; ¡**hasta muy** —— ! See you soon!
propio own
proponer propose
proporción *f.* proportion
proporcionar give
propósito *m.* purpose; **a** —— apropos, by the way
prosperidad *f.* prosperity
protestante Protestant
proverbial proverbial
provincia *f.* province
provinciano provincial
publicar publish
público *m.* public
pueblecito *m.* little village
pueblo *m.* people, town
puente *m.* bridge
puerta *f.* door, gate
puerto *m.* port
pues well (then); —— **bien** well, then
puesta de sol *f.* sunset
puesto que since, as
pulmón *m.* lung
pulsera *f.* bracelet
punto *m.* point; (vehicle) stand; —— **menos que** practically
puro pure, sheer

Q

que which, who; that; than; **qué** what (a)! what?
¿qué le parece? what do you think?
quedar(se) stay, remain, be, be left; ——**se con** keep (Ch. 14)
quejarse complain
querer (ie) wish, want, be willing
quietud *f.* quietude
quince fifteen
quinientos five hundred
quinto fifth
quitar take away; ——**se** take off (Ch. 5)
quizá(s) perhaps

R

radical radical
radio *m.* radius; *f.* radio
ramplón coarse, vulgar
rapidez *f.* rapidity, speed
rápido speedy
raro rare, strange; —— **as veces** seldom
rascacielos *m. sing.* skyscraper
rastrojo *m.* stubble-field
rato *m.* while; **al poco** —— after a while
razón *f.* reason; **tener** —— be right
reacción *f.* reaction; **avión de** —— jet plane
reaccionario reactionary
real royal; real
realismo *m.* realism
realmente really
rebelde rebel
recado *m.* message; **dejar** —— leave word
receptor *m.* telephone receiver
recibir receive
reclamar claim
recluta *m.* recruit
recoger get
recomendar (ie) recommend
reconcentración *f.* immersion in oneself
recóndito hidden
reconocer recognize, admit
recordar (ue) remember, recall, remind
recorrer cover, visit
recorrido *m.* trip, tour
rector *m.* president (of a university)
recuerdo *m.* memory, remembrance; souvenir
redondo round
reducir reduce, limit
reflejo *m.* reflection
refrescarse freshen up, wash up
regalo *m.* gift

región *f.* region
regresar return
reina *f.* queen
reino *m.* kingdom
relación *f.* relation, account
relacionarse con be connected with
relativamente relatively
reloj *m.* watch, clock
remedio: *m.:* **no tengo más** ———— I can't help it
renacentista Renaissance (*adj.*)
Renacimiento *m.* Renaissance
rendido worn out
rendirse surrender; become exhausted
reparar repair
repeler repel
repente: de ———— suddenly
repertorio *m.* repertory
repetir (i) repeat
representante representative
representar play
reproche *m.* reproach
república *f.* republic
republicano republican
requerir (ie, i) require
residencia *f.* residence
resignarse resign oneself
resolver (ue) resolve
respetar respect
respeto *m.* respect
respirar breathe
resto: el ———— **de** the rest of
resultado *m.* result
resultar result, turn out, happen
resumen *m.* résumé, account
retórica *f.* rhetoric
reunión *f.* gathering, meeting
reunirse (con) meet, gather, join
revés: al ———— contrariwise
revisar check
revista *f.* magazine
revolucionario revolutionary
rey *m.* king
reyezuelo *m.* petty king
rico rich; delicious
rincón *m.* corner
río *m.* river
riqueza *f.* richness, wealth
rival rival
robar rob, steal
roca *f.* rock
rocoso rocky
rodeado surrounded
rodear surround

rodeos: andar con ———— beat about the bush
rodilla *f.* knee
rogar (ue) beg
rojo red
romance *m.* ballad
románico Romanesque
romano Roman
ropa *f.* clothing
ropería *f.* clothing store
rosado rose
rubio blond
ruedo *m.* (bull) ring
ruido *m.* noise
rumbo *m.* course, tack
ruta *f.* route

S

sábana *f.* bedsheet
saber know, be able; **un no sé qué de** an indefinable, certain something (Ch. 3)
sablazo *m.* sabre cut; **dar un** ———— put the bite on (ask for a loan)
saborear sip
sacar take out; ———— **en limpio** deduce (Ch. 8)
sacerdote *m.* priest
saco *m.* bag; (sports) jacket
sala *f.* room
saliente projecting, salient
salir leave, go out, turn out; ————**se con la suya** have one's way (Ch. 18)
saltar jump; ———— **a la vista** be immediately evident or obvious (Prelim. Les. 1)
salud *f.* health
saludar speak, to greet
sanseacabó that's an end to it! Finished!
santo, saint, holy
sección *f.* section
secadora *f.* hairdryer
seco dry
secretario *m.* secretary
secreto *m.* secret
seda *f.* silk
seguida: en ———— immediately, at once
seguir (i) follow, keep on, continue (Ch. 14)
según according to, as
segundo second
seguro sure
selección *f.* selection, choice
sello *m.* stamp
semana *f.* week
sembrado *m.* plowed field
semejante similar

señal *f.* signal, mark
señalar mark
sencillo simple
señor *m.* Mr.; gentleman
sentado seated
sentar (ie) seat (Prelim. Les. 2)
sentir (ie, i) feel, regret, be sorry
septentrional northern
séptimo seventh
sequedad *f.* dryness
ser be; **es que** (but) the fact is that; **sea** for example, that is; **sea como sea** be that as it may (Ch. 13)
sereno serene
serie *f.* series
serio serious; **en ____** seriously
servicio *m.* service
servidumbre *f.* servitude; servants
servir (i) serve, help, be good for (Ch. 1)
severo severe
sevillano from Seville
si if
sí themselves, etc.: **de por ____** of itself
sí yes; **¿ ____ ?** Is that so?
siempre always, ever
sierra mountain range
siesta *f.* siesta, rest after eating
siguiente following
silbar whistle
silla *f.* chair
simpático pleasant, likeable
simpatizar be congenial
sin (que) without
sinagoga *f.* synagogue
sinceridad *f.* sincerity
sino but
síntoma *m.* symptom
siquiera: ni ____ not even
sistema *m.* system
sitio *m.* place
situado situated, located
soberbiamente proudly
sobrar be left over (Ch. 19)
sobre on, upon
sobrino, -a *m. f.* nephew, niece
socialista Socialist
sociedad *f.* society
soler (ue) be accustomed to, usually (do a thing) (Prelim. Les. 2)
solicitud *f.* application, request
solidez *f.* solidity
sólido solid
solitario solitary
sólo only

solo mere, single, only (*adj.*); alone, by oneself
soltero single, unmarried
solución *f.* solution
sombrerería *f.* hat store
sombrero *m.* hat
sonar (ue) sound; **____ a** evoke (by sound)
sonreír (se) (i) smile
sonriente smiling
sonrisa *f.* smile
soportal *m.* arcade, archway
sorprender surprise
sorprendiente surprising
sorpresa *f.* surprise
sospechar suspect
sostener maintain
su its, his, her, their, your
suave soft, gentle
suavidad *f.* softness
subdesarrollado underdeveloped
subir (go, carry, bring) up (Ch. 17)
subrayar underline
suegro, -a *m. f.* father-, mother-in-law
suelo *m.* floor, soil, land
sueño *m.* sleep, dream
suerte de varas *f. the picador's act in a bullfight*
suerte *f.* good luck, fortune
suficiente sufficient
sugerir (ie, i) suggest
sumo: a lo ____ at the most
superficial superficial
superficie *f.* surface
suponer suppose
suprimir suppress
sur *m.* south
surcado lined
suscitar provoke
sustantivo *m.* substantive, noun
sutil subtle
suyo his, her, its, their, your

T

tabaco *m.* tobacco
tacita *f.* (*dim.* **taza**) little cup
tal such (a): **¿qué ____ ?** how (is) . . . ? How are you?
taller *m.* workshop
también also
tan so
tanque *m.* tank
tanto so much, so many
tardar (se) delay, be (take) long (Ch. 15)
tarde late; *f.* afternoon
tarea *f.* task

tarjeta *f.* card
taxi *m.* taxi
taza *f.* cup
teatro *m.* theater, drama
técnica *f.* technique
técnico technical
tecnología *f.* technology
tela *f.* cloth
telefonear telephone
teléfono *m.* telephone
televisión *f.* television
tema *m.* theme
temblar (ie) tremble
temer fear
temor *m.* fear
temporada *f.* period (of time); **pasar una** ___
   spend some time
temprano early
tendido: largo y ___   at full length, in detail
tener have; ___ **que** have to
tenis *m.* tennis
tercero third
terminante final, definitive
terminar (de) finish
término *m.* end
terrateniente *m.* landholder
terraza *f.* sidewalk in front of a café
tertulia *f.* (informal) gathering (*a typical feature of Hispanic social life*)
tesis *f.* thesis
tesoro *m.* treasure
tiempo *m.* time; weather; **más** ___ longer
tienda *f.* store, shop
tierra *f.* land; **en** ___ ashore
timbre *m.* bell
típicamente typically
típico typical, traditional
tipo *m.* type, kind
tirando a almost
tirante tense
tirantez *f.* tension, reserve, aloofness
tirar throw (Prelim. Les. 1)
tocadiscos *m. sing.* phonograph
tocar ring (bell), play (instrument); touch (Ch. 2)
todavía yet, still
todo all
toledano from Toledo
tolerar tolerate
tomar take (Ch. 8)
tono *m.* tone
tonto foolish
topográfico topographic
torero *m.* bullfighter

tormenta *f.* storm
torno: en ___ **(de)** around
toro *m.* bull
toronja *f.* grapefruit
toros *m. pl.* bullfight
torre *f.* tower
tostado sunburned
total total
trabajador *m.* worker
trabajar work
trabajo *m.* work
tradición *f.* tradition
tradicional traditional
traer bring (Ch. 16)
trágico tragic
traición *f.* treason
traje *m.* suit; ___ **de luces** bullfighter's costume (*of silk and gold braid*)
trajín *m.* round (of amusements, occupations, etc.)
tranquilo quiet, calm, tranquil
tránsito *m.* traffic
transportación *f.* transportation
tranvía *m.* trolley, streetcar
tras behind, after
tratar treat; ___ **de** try to; ___**se** to be (a question of) (Ch. 19)
trato *m.* association
travesía *f.* crossing (by sea)
trayecto *m.* journey
tren *m.* train
triángulo *m.* triangle
trigo *m.* wheat
triste sad
tronar (ue) thunder
tropa *f.* troop
tropezar (ie) stumble; ___ **con** meet, run into by chance
trozo *m.* fragment, part
turista *m. and f.* tourist
turístico tourist
tutear use the familiar form of address with someone

U

último last; **por** ___ finally
único only, unique
unido joined
universal universal
universidad *f.* university
uno one, a
unos some

útil useful
utilizar use

V

vacaciones *f.* vacation
vacío empty
vagamente vaguely
valer be worth, avail (Ch. 19)
valiente brave, courageous; ¡ _____ ...! What a ...!
valioso valuable
valle *m.* valley
valor *m.* courage
vanidad *f.* vanity
variedad *f.* variety
varios several
vasco Basque
vaso *m.* glass
vega *f.* plain
vegetal vegetal
veinte twenty
veintitantos some twenty
vendedor *m.* seller
vender sell
venir come; **que viene** next (time)
ventaja *f.* advantage
ventanilla *f.* window (of vehicle)
ver see; ¡**a** _____ ! let's see; _____ **se** be; **está visto** it is clear
verdad *f.* truth; **es** _____ it is true
verdaderamente truly, really
verdadero real, true, genuine
verde green
verificarse take place
verso *m.* verse; line of poetry
vestido *m.* costume, dress
vestir dress

vez *f.* time; **de** _____ **en cuando** from time to time; **una** _____ once; **una** _____ **más** once more
viajar travel
viaje *m.* trip, voyage; _____ **por mar** sea trip
viajero *m.* traveler
vida *f.* life
viejo old
vino *m.* wine
viñedo *m.* vineyard
violinista *m.* violinist
virtud *f.* virtue
visita *f.* visit
visitar visit
vista sight; **a la** _____ in sight
visto bueno (Vo. Bo.) official approval, "O.K."
vitamina *f.* vitamin
vivir live
volar (ue) fly
voluntad *f.* will
volver (ue) return, go (come) back _____ **a** + *inf.* do again (Prelim. Les. 2)
vuelo *m.* flight
vuelta *f.* return; **dar** _____ **s** stroll, walk

Y

y and
ya already, now
yacente lying
yo I

Z

zapato *m.* shoe
zarzuela *f. Spanish light opera*
zona *f.* zone; _____ **azul** zone where parking is by permit only

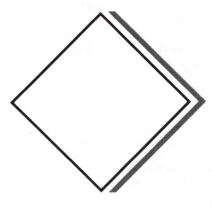

VOCABULARY
ENGLISH-SPANISH

A

ability talento *m.*

able: be ——— **to** poder

about (*concerning*) cerca de, cosa de, unos; **be** ——— **to** estar para

above sobre, por encima de

abroad el extranjero

absent-minded distraído

absent ausente

absurd absurdo

abuse abusar de

academy academia *f.*

accept aceptar

accident accidente *m.*

account: on ——— **of** a causa de, por; **on my** ——— por mí

account cuenta *f.*

accountant contador *m.*

accurately: very ——— con gran precisión

accusation acusación *f.*

accuse acusar

accustomed acostumbrado; **to be** ——— **to** acostumbrarse, tener la costumbre de, soler (ue) que

ache doler (ue)

acquaintance conocido

acquainted: become ——— conocer, llegar a conocer

across al otro lado (de), tras

act acto *m.; v.* obrar, estar

action acción *f.*

actor actor *m.*

actress actriz *f.*

add añadir

addition: in ——— **to** además de

address señas, dirección *f.; v.* dirigir, dirigirse a

admiration admiración *f.*

admire admirar

admit admitir, reconocer

adobe adobe *m.*

advantage ventaja *f.;* **to be to one's** ——— convenirle a uno

adventure aventura *f.*

advertise anunciar

advice consejo *m.* (*usu. pl.*)

advise aconsejar

adviser consejero

affair asunto *m.*

affliction aflicción *f.*

afraid: be ——— **of** tener miedo de, temer (se); **feel** ——— darle miedo a

African africano

after después de, tras
afternoon tarde *f.*
afterwards después, luego
again otra vez, de nuevo; **do** _____ **again** volver (ue) **a** + *inf.*
against contra
age edad, época *f.*; **Golden** _____ Siglo de Oro *m.*
agent agente *m.*
agility agilidad, ligereza *f.*
ago: a year _____ hace un año
agree convenir (en), ponerse (estar) de acuerdo
agreement acuerdo *m.*; **come to an** _____ ponerse de acuerdo
ahead (de) delante
air aire, ambiente *m.*
airsick mareado (en el aire)
album album *m.*
alike parecido; **be** _____ parecerse
alive: be _____ vivir
all todo; _____ **in** _____ en conjunto; **(not) at** _____ nada, en absoluto; de nada
allow dejar, permitir
almost casi, tirando a
alms limosna *f.*
alone solo
along a lo largo de, por
already ya
although aunque; y eso que
always siempre
amateur aficionado
amaze asombrar
Amazon el Amazonas
ambassador embajador *m.*
ambition ambición *f.*
ambitious ambicioso
America América *f.*
American americano; norteamericano
among entre
amount to ascender (ie) a
amusement diversión *f.*
amusing divertido
ancient antiguo
Andalusia Andalucía *f.*
Andalusian andaluz
angry enfadado; **make** _____ enfadar; **get** _____ enfadarse
animal animal *m.*
animated animado
animation animación *f.*
announce anunciar
annoy molestar

answer contestación *f.*; *v.* contestar
anticipate prever
antique shop tienda de antigüedades *f.*
anxious: be _____ desear
any algun(o); cualquiera; (*neg.*) ningun(o)
anyone alguien; (*neg.*) nadie
anything algo, cualquier cosa, (*neg.*) nada
anywhere en (a, por) cualquier (ninguna) parte
apart: far _____ distante
apartment piso *m.*, apartamento *m.*
apiece cada uno
apparently por lo visto, parecer + *inf.*
appeal (to one) emocionar
appear parecer, aparecer
appetite apetito *m.*
apple manzana *f.*
appliance aparato (eléctrico) *m.*
appointment nombramiento
appreciate apreciar
appreciation apreciación *f.*
approach acercarse a
approve aprobar (ue)
approximating tirando a
April abril
apropos (of) a propósito (de)
aqueduct acueducto *m.*
Arab árabe
Arabian Nights Las mil y una noches
Aragon Aragón *m.*
Aragonese aragonés
arcade soportal *m.*
architectural arquitectónico
architecture arquitectura *f.*
argue discutir
argument discusión, disputa
aristocrat aristócrata *m.*
arm brazo *m.*
armchair sillón *m.*, butaca *f.*
around por; alrededor de; a eso de (time)
arrange arreglar
arrest detener
arrival llegada *f.*
arrive llegar
arrogance arrogancia *f.*
art arte *m.* **fine** _____s bellas artes
article artículo *m.*
artificial artificial
artist artista; pintor
artistic artístico
as como; **while** _____ **for** en cuanto a, lo que es, según, conforme, a medida, como; _____ **if** como si, **just** _____ tal y como

ascetic ascético
ashamed: make one feel _____ darle ver-
  güenza a uno
ashore en (a) tierra
ashtray cenicero _m._
Asiatic asiático
aside from aparte de
ask (inquire) preguntar; _____ **a question**
  hacer una pregunta; _____ **for (to)** pedir (i)
  (request) pedir (i)
aspect aspecto _m._
assembly asamblea _f._
association asociación _f._
assure asegurarse
astonish asombrar
astonishing sorprendente
astronaut astronauta _m. f._
asylum asilo _m._
at a, en
athlete atleta _m._
atmosphere ambiente _m._
attend to ocuparse de
attention atención _f.;_ **pay** _____ **to** hacer caso
  de, a (_of persons_)
attitude actitud _f._
attract tirar, atraer
attractive simpático; agradable
aunt tía _f._
austere austero
author autor _m._
authorization autorización _f._
avenue avenida _f._
average _adj._ medio; _n._ media _f._
aviator aviador _m._
avoid evitar
awake despierto
away: be _____ estar ausente, fuera; (_dis-
  tance_), a una distancia de
awfully la mar de

B

back _adj._ atrasado; **be** _____ estar de vuelta
back espalda _f._
background fondo _m._
bad malo; _____ **(ly)** mal
baggage equipaje _m._
Balearic Balear
ballad romancero _m._
bank banco _m.;_ _____ (_river_) orilla _f._
banker banquero _m._
banquet banquete _m._
bare desnudo

bargain ganga _f._
bark ladrar; _n._ **(bark, barking)** ladrar _m._
barren árido, yermo
baseball béisbol _m._
basket cesto, canasto _m._
Basque vasco
bath baño _m.;_ **take a** _____ bañarse
bathe bañar(se)
bay bahía _f._
be ser, estar; haber (_there is_); (_spend time_) llevar
be held (_meeting, concert_) celebrarse
beach playa _f._
bear llevar
beaten vencido
beautiful hermoso
beauty belleza _f._
because porque; _____ **of** por, a causa de;
  just _____ por el solo hecho de
become hacerse; ponerse; llegar, venir, a ser;
  volverse; convertirse (ie, i) en (Ch. 1)
bed cama _f.;_ **go to** _____ acostarse (ue); **stay
  in** _____ guardar cama
bedroom alcoba _f._, dormitorio _m._
beer cerveza _f._
beet remolacha _f._
before antes, ante; _prep._ antes de, ante; **conj.**
  antes (de) que; _____ **me** antes que yo
beg rogar (ue), pedir (i)
beggar mendigo _m._
begin empezar (ie), comenzar (ie)
beginning principio _m._
behind detrás (de); atrás
Belgium Bélgica _f._
believe creer
bell campana, campanilla _f._
bell tower torre _f._, campanario _m._
bellboy botones _m. sing._
belong to ser de, pertenecer a, ser de
below debajo (de), abajo, bajo
belt cinturón _m._
besides además (de)
best mejor; **to do one's** _____ hacer lo posible
  (por)
bet apostar (ue)
better mejor; **had better** mejor sería
between entre
bicycle bicicleta _f._
big grande
bikini bikini _m._
bill cuenta _f.;_ billete _m._ (_banknote_); proyecto
  de ley _m._ (_legislative_)
bind (_books_) encuadernar
birthday cumpleaños _m. sing._

bit trozo, rincón *m.* (*of pieces*); **a** ——— algo, un poco; **not a**——— nada
bite morder (ue)
blame culpa *f.*, **to be to** ——— **for** tener la culpa de; *v.* echar la culpa
blanket manta *f.*, cobertor *m.*
blessed (*iron.*) dichoso
blessing bendición *f.*
blind ciego; *v.* cegar (ie)
block (*city*) manzana *f.*
blockhead majadero *m.*
blond(e) rubio
blood sangre *f.*
blue azul
board: on ——— a bordo (de)
board junta *f.*, consejo *m.*; cartelera *f.* (*theatrical*); ——— **of directors** consejo de administración
boardinghouse pensión, casa de huéspedes *f.*
boat barco *m.*
bonfire hoguera *f.*
book libro *m.*
bookcase estantería *f.*
bookstore librería *f.*
bootblack limpiabotas *m.*
bored aburrido
boredom aburrimiento *m.*
boring aburrido
born: to be ——— nacer
borrow pedir (i) prestado
both los dos, ambos, uno y otro; ——— . . . **and** lo mismo . . . que
bother molestar, molestarse en
bottom: at ——— en el fondo
boulder peñasco *m.*
boulevard paseo *m.*
box caja *f.*
boy chico, muchacho *m.*
bracelet pulsera *f.*
brake: put on the ———**s** frenar
brave valiente
bread pan *m.*
break romper
breakfast desayuno *m.* **have** ——— desayunarse
breathe inspirar
bribe sobornar
bridge puente *m.*
briefcase cartera *f.*
bright brillante, claro
brilliant brillante
bring traer; ——— **along** traerse; ——— **upstairs** subir

broad ancho
bronze bronce *m.*
brother hermano *m.*
brother-in-law cuñado *m.*
brow frente *f.*
brown café, castaño, marrón (pardo)
browned (*by the sun*) tostado
buffoon bufón *m.*
build construir
building edificio *m.*
bulb (*light*) bombilla *f.*
bullfighter torero *m.*
bull toro *m.*
bullet bala *f.*
bullfight corrida (de toros) *f.*
bullring plaza *f.*
burn quemar
burning ardiente
bury enterrar (ie)
bus autobús *m.*
business (*affair*) negocio, asunto *m.*; (*in general*) negocios
businessman comerciante, hombre de negocios *m.*
bustle bullicio *m.*
busy ocupado
buy comprar
but pero, sino, sino que, mas
button botón *m.*

C

Cadiz Cádiz
café café *m.*
Caliph califa *m.*
call llamar; **so-**———**ed** llamado
calm sereno; ——— **down** *v.* calmar (se)
canary canario *m.*; ——— **Islands** Islas Canarias *f.*
candy dulces, bombones *m. pl.*
cane bastón *m.*
cap gorra *f.*
capital (*city*) capital *f.*
capture toma *f.*
car coche *m.*
card (*playing*) carta, *f.*, naipe *m.*
care: ——— **for** cuidar de
careful: be ——— ten cuidado
carefully con cuidado; detenidamente
careless descuidado
carpenter carpintero *m.*
carry llevar; ——— **away (off)** llevarse
cart carreta *f.*

carved esculpido, tallado
case caso *m.*, _____ (*legal*) pleito *m.;* **in** _____ **(that)** en caso de que, como
cash: pay _____ pagar al contado
cashier cajero *m.*
cast moldear
Castile Castilla *f.*
Castilian castellano
cat gato *m.*
Catalan catalán
Catalonia Cataluña *f.*
catch coger, pillar
cathedral catedral *f.*
Catholic católico
cause causa *f.; v.* causar, dar
cave cueva *f.*
celebrated célebre
cement estrechar
cent centavo *m.* (*American*), céntimo *m.* (*Spain*)
center centro *m.*
central central
century siglo *m.*
ceremony ceremonia *f.*
certain cierto; **a** _____ **something** un no sé qué
certainly seguro (que), con toda seguridad, sí que
chair silla *f.*
change cambiar (de), mudar (de)
chapel capilla *f.*
character carácter *m.;* _____ (*in fiction*) personaje *m.*
charge: take _____ **of** encargarse de
Charles Carlos; _____ **V** Carlos Quinto
charity caridad *f.*
charm encanto *m.*
charming encantador
chauffeur chófer *m.*
cheap barato
cheat engañar
check cheque *m.* (*bank*)
cheer up animarse
chemistry química *f.*
chestnut vender castañero, *m.*
chief jefe *m.*
chiefly en su mayoría, principalmente
child niño, -a
choose escoger; elegir (i)
Christian cristiano
church iglesia *f.*
cigar puro *m.*
cigarette pitillo, cigarrillo *m.;* _____ **case** pitillera *f.*

circus circo *m.*
citizen ciudadano *m.*
city ciudad *f.*
City Hall ayuntamiento *m.*
civilization civilización *f.*
class clase *f.*
classic(al) clásico
classmate compañero de curso *m.*
clean limpiar
clear up aclarar
clear claro; **it is** _____ está visto
clearness claridad *f.*
clever listo
cliff peña *f.*, cerro *m.*
climate clima *m.*
climb subir a
close cercano; cerrar (ie); terminar (*letter*)
cloth tela *f.*
clothes ropa *f.*
cloud nube *f.*
cloudy nublado
club club, círculo, casino *m.*
clump masa *f.*
coast costa *f.*
coat-of-arms escudo, blasón *m.*
coat Americana, chaqueta, saco *f.;* **fur** _____ abrigo de piel (es) *m.*
coexistence coexistencia *f.*
coffee café *m.*
cold frío; catarro, resfriado (*ailment*) *m.*
collar cuello, collar *m.*
collect coleccionar, recaudar
collection colección *f.*
college universidad *f.*
collision choque *m.*
colonel coronel *m.*
combination combinación *f.*
come venir; _____ **(along) with** acompañar; _____ **back** volver (ue); _____ **from** nacer de; _____ **in** entrar, pasar, ¡adelante!; _____ **out** salir; _____ **to** volver en sí; _____ **upon** dar, tropezar, encontrarse (ue) con; _____ **up to** acercarse a; **come (now)!** ¡ande! ¡vamos!
comedy comedia *f.*
comfort comodidad *f.*
comfortable cómodo
comical cómico
coming llegada *f.*
commercial comercial
commission encargo *m.*
committee junta, comisión *f.*
commodity subsistencia *f.*

common común
companion compañero *m.*
company compañía *f.*
compartment compartimiento *m.*
compel obligar
complain quejarse de
complete completo
complexion tez *f.*, cutis *m.*
compliment piropo *m.*
compose componer
composer compositor *m.*
computer computadora *f.*, ordenadora *m.*
conceive concebir (i)
concert concierto *m.*
concierge (*Fr.*) conserje *m.*
conclusion conclusión *f.*
concrete *adj.* particular; *n.* concreto, hormigón *m.*
condition estado *m.*, condición *f.*
conduct conducta *f.; v.* conducir
conductor cobrador (*trolley*), revisor *m.*
confine: be ____d to bed guardar cama
confusedly confusamente
confusion confusión *f.*
congenial: be ____ simpatizar
congratulations felicitaciones *f.*, enhorabuena *f.*
connection combinación *f.* (*train*)
conquer vencer
conqueror conquistador *m.*
consent consentir (ie, i) en
consequence: be of ____ importar
consequently por eso, por consiguiente
considerable bastante
constitutional constitucional
consulate consulado *m.*
consult consultar (con)
contain contener
contemporary contemporáneo
content contentar
contented: be ____ contentarse
continent continente *m.*
continual continuo
continue continuar, seguir (i)
contract contrato *m.*
contradict contradecir, llevarle la contraria a uno
contrary contrario; **on the ____** al revés
contrast contraste *m.*
convenience: at your earliest ____ a la mayor prontitud
convenient cómodo
converge converger
convince convencer

cook cocinero
cool fresco
copper cobre *m.*
copy ejemplar *m., v.* copiar
cordial cordial
cordiality cordialidad *f.*
Cordova Córdoba
cork corcho *m.*
corner rincón *m.*, ____ (*street*) esquina *f.*
correct justo, correcto
corridor pasillo *m.*
cosmopolitan cosmopolita
cost costar (ue)
costume traje *m.*
cotton algodón *m.*
cough tos *f.*
cough toser
councilman concejal *m.*
count contar (ue); ____ **on** contar con
Counter Reformation Contrarreforma
counter mostrador *m.*
country house casa de campo *f.*
country (*nation*) país *m.*, (*rural*) campo *m.*
countryman paisano *m.*
couple par *m.*
courage valor *m.*, valentía *f.*
course curso *m.; of* ____ claro (está), desde luego, naturalmente, por supuesto
court patio *m.*, ____ (*royal*) corte *f.;* **tennis ____** campo de tenis *m.*
courteous cortés
cousin primo, -a
cover cubrir; recorrer (*territory*)
coziness intimidad *f.*
crate embalar
crazy loco
creditor acreedor *m.*
critic crítico *m.*
critical crítico
cross cruzar, atravesar
crossing travesía *f.*
crowded atestado
crown coronar
crude sin refinar
crusader cruzado *m.*
cry *n.* quejido, llanto *m.; v.* llorar; ____ **baby** llorón
culture cultura *f.*
cultured culto
cup taza *f.*
curiosity curiosidad *f.*
custom costumbre *f.*
customs: ____ official aduanero *m.*
cut cortar; ____ **it out!** ¡quita!

cute mono
cylinder cilindro *m.*

D

dad papá *m.*
dairy store lechería *f.*
damage daño *m.*, *v.* estropear
damascene damasquinado *m.*
dance baile *m.; v.* bailar
danger peligro *m.*
dare atreverse a
daring atrevido
dark oscuro; (*complexion*) moreno
date fecha *f.; v.* datar
daughter hija *f.*
dawn amanecer
dead muerto
deaf sordo
deal trato *m.;* negocio *m.* **a great (good)** ⸻
  (of) mucho
dean decano *m.*
dear querido
death muerte *f.*
deathbed lecho de muerte *m.*
debt deuda *f.*
deceive engañar
decide decidir
decision decisión *f.*
decorate condecorar
deed hazaña *f.*
deep profundo
defect defecto *m.*
degree grado *m.*
delicious delicioso, rico
delighted encantado
delivery: free ⸻ se sirve a domicilio
denominator denominador *m.*
dentist dentista *m.*
deny negar (ie)
depend depender
derby (*hat*) sombrero hongo *m.*
descendent descendiente *m.*
desert desierto, páramo *m.*
desk escritorio *m.*, mesa *f.*
desolate desolado, desierto
despot déspota *m.*
dessert postre *m.*
destination destinación *f.*
destroy destruir
detail detalle *m.*, **in** ⸻ detalladamente,
  largo y tendido
determine determinar
develop desarrollar; resultar

devil diablo *m.*
devote dedicar
dialogue diálogo *m.*
dictate dictar
dictionary diccionario *m.*
die morir(se) (ue, u)
difference diferencia *f.;* **make a** ⸻ importar; **make no difference** dar lo mismo
different distinto, diferente; **be** ⸻ diferenciarse
difficult difícil
difficulty dificultad *f.;* **get out of the** ⸻
  salir del paso
dignity dignidad *f.*
dim débil
dine cenar, comer
dining room comedor *m.*
dinner comida *f.*, (*evening*) cena *f.*
direct dirigir
director director *m.*
disagreeable desagradable
disappear desaparecer
disappoint desilusioner
disappointment desilusión *f.*
disapproval desaprobación *f.*
disarrange revolver (ue)
discomfort incomodidad *f.*
discuss discutir
discussion discusión *f.*
dismiss despedir (i)
disposal disposición *f.*
dissuade disuadir
distance distancia; lejanía *f.;* **in the** ⸻ a lo
  lejos; **only a short** ⸻ **from** a dos pasos
  de
distant lejano
distinctive distintivo
disturb molestar
divided dividido
dividend dividendo *m.*
dizzy aturdido
do hacer, ⸻ **without** pasarse sin; **have to**
  ⸻ **with** tener que ver con
doctor médico *m.;* (*title*) doctor
document documento *m.*
dog perro, -a *m., f.*
dollar dólar *m.*
domestic doméstico, casero
dominate dominar
Don Quixote Don Quijote
door puerta *f.;* ⸻ **bell** timbre, campanilla
  f.
doorway portal *m.*, portada *f.*
doubt dudar

doubtless sin duda
down: ——— **the street** calle abajo
downstairs abajo; **go** ——— bajar
downtown *adj.* céntrico
dozen docena *f.*
drama drama *m.*
draw sacar, tirar de
drawer cajón *m.*
dreadfully la mar de
dreamer soñador, -a
dress vestido, traje *m.; v.* vestir(se) (i)
dresser cómoda *f.*
drive conducir; **(crazy)** volver (ue) loco
driver (*automobile*) chófer *m.*
drop gota *f.*
drugstore farmacia *f.*
dry seco
dry cleaner's tintorería *f.*
due: be ——— deberse
during durante
dye teñir (i)

E

each cada, todo(s); ——— **other** nos, os, se, el uno al otro
early temprano
earn ganar
earthquake terremoto *m.*
easily fácilmente
eat comer
economic económico
edge extremo *m.*
editor director *m.*
educated culto
eeriness embrujamiento *m.*
eight ocho
eighteen(th) dieciocho
eighth octavo
either o, tampoco
elegance elegancia *f.*
elegant elegante
element elemento *m.*
elevator ascensor *m.*
Elizabeth Isabel
else otro, más; **somebody** ——— otra persona; **nothing** ——— nada más
embarrass confundir
embezzlement malversación (de fondos) *f.*
embody encarnar
embrace abrazo *m.*
emotion(al appeal) emoción *f.*
emperor emperador *m.*

employee empleado *m.*
empty vacío, desocupado
encounter encuentro *m.*
end final *m.;* **at the** ——— **of** al cabo de, a fines de
endless infinito
energetic enérgico
engaged (*busily*) atareado, dedicado a, metido en
engine máquina *f.,* motor *m.*
engineer ingeniero *m.*
English(man) inglés
engraved grabado
engraving grabado *m.*
enjoy oneself divertirse (ie, i), pasarlo bien; estar a (su) gusto, estar a sus anchas
enjoyable agradable
Enlightenment Siglo de las Luces
enough bastante, suficiente; **be** ——— bastar; ——— **of . . . !** ¡basta de!
enter entrar en
enterprise empresa *f.*
enthusiasm entusiasmo *m.* **with** ——— entusiasmado
enthusiastic entusiasmado
enthusiastically con entusiasmo
entire entero, todo el
entirely por completo
envelope sobre *m.*
epic épico
escape escapar(se)
eskimo esquimal .
especially especialmente, sobre todo
essay ensayo *m.*
essentially esencialmente, más que
estate finca *f.*
estimate calcular
Europe Europa *f.*
European europeo
even aún, todavía; hasta; aunque; **not** ——— **if** ni que; ——— **if, though** aunque, y eso que; **not** ——— ni siquiera
evening noche *f.*
ever alguna vez; (*neg.*) nunca, jamás
every todos los, cada; ——— **other** cada dos, un(o) . . . sí, otro no
everybody todo el mundo
everything todo
everywhere en (a, etc.) todas partes
evident evidente; **it is** ———esevidente, se ve, se conoce
evidently por lo visto
evocation evocación *f.*

exactly   precisamente
exaggerate   exagerar
examination   examen *m.* _____ **room** sala de exámenes *f.*
example   ejemplo *m.*
excellent   excelente
except   excepto, menos
exceptional   excepcional
excessive   excesivo
exchange   cambiar
excited   agitado, emocionado
exclude   quitar
excuse   disculpa *f.*
exhaust   acabarse
exist   existir
exotic   exótico
expect   esperar
expense   costa *f.*
expensive   caro
experience   experiencia *f.*
experiment   experimento *m.*
expert   perito *m.*
explain   explicar
explore   explorar
exporter   exportador
exposition   exposición *f.*
express   expresar
express (*train*)   expreso *m.;* rápido *m.*
expression   expresión *f.*
extent: to a lesser _____ en menor grado

F

face   cara *f.; v.* _____ **(on)** dar a
fact   hecho *m.,* **the** _____ **is** (ello) es
factory   fábrica *f.*
fail   faltar; _____ **to** dejar de
fair   (*mediocre*) regular; (*just*) justo
fair   feria *f.*
faith   fe *f.*
fall (*season*)   otoño *m.*
fall   caer; _____ **down** caerse
false   falso
family   familia *f.;* _____ **name** apellido *m.*
famished   muerto de hambre
famous   famoso
fantastic   fantástico
fascinate   fascinar
fashion   moda *f.*
fashionable   de moda
fast   rápido, ligero; *adv.* rápidamente, de prisa
fat   gordo; **get** _____ ponerse gordo, engordar
father   padre *m.*

father-in-law   suegro *m.*
fatigue   cansancio *m.*
favor   favor *m.;* **to be in** _____ **of** estar por (*Spain*), estar a favor de (*America*); *v.* favorecer
fear   miedo *m.; v.* temer
feast (*of wit*)   derroche de ingenio *m.*
February   febrero
feel   sentir (ie, i), estar; _____ **like** tener ganas de; _____ **well** encontrarse bien; _____ **the same way** pasarle a uno lo mismo
feeling   impresión *f.;* **with great** _____ apasionadamente
fellow   individuo, sujeto *m.*
fellow countryman   paisano *m.*
feminist   feminista
fertile   fecundo
feverish   febril
few   unos, unos cuantos, cuatro
fiancée   novia, prometida *f.*
field   campo *m.*
fierce   bravo
fifty   cincuenta
fight   luchar
filigree   filigrana *f.*
fill   llenarse
film   película *f.,* filme *m.*
finally   por fin
finance   costear
find   encontrar (ue), hallar; encontrarse (hallarse) con; _____ **out** enterarse de, saber, averiguar
fine   magnífico, hermoso, bueno
finger   dedo *m.*
finish   terminar, acabar, concluir
fire   fuego; incendio *m.; v.* tirar de
firm   compañía, sociedad, casa, *f.*
firearms   armas de fuego *f.*
firefighter   bombero *m.*
fireplace   chimenea *f.*
first   primero; _____ **of all** primeramente, primero de todos
fish   pescado *m.*
fitting   digno, conveniente
five   cinco
five hundred   quinientos
fix   arreglar, reparar
flag   bandera *f.*
flatter   favorecer
flood   diluvio *m.,* riada *f.*
floor   suelo *m.*
Florida   la Florida
flower vender   florista *f.*

follow seguir (i)
following siguiente
fond: be _____ of ser aficionado a, gustarle a uno
food (*dish of*) plato *m.*
foolishness tontería *f.*
foot pie *m.,* **little _____** piececito *m.*
football fútbol *m.*
for para, por
forbid prohibir
force fuerza *f.*
forever para siempre
foreign(er) extranjero
forget olvidar; **I _____** se me olvida
fork tenedor *m.*
former antiguo; *pron.* aquel
fortress fortaleza *f.*
fortunate afortunado; **be _____** tener suerte
fortunately afortunadamente
fortune fortuna *f.*
founder fundador *m.*
fountain fuente *f.*
fourth cuarto; cuarta parte de *f.*
France Francia *f.*
frank franco
Frank Paco, Pancho (*Sp. Am.*)
frankly francamente
frankness franqueza *f.*
free libre; **set _____** poner en libertad
French francés
frequent frecuente
fresh fresco; **_____ water** agua dulce
freshen up refrescarse
friend amigo, -a; **make _____ s with** conocer, hacerse amigo(s)
friendly amistoso
friendship amistad *f.*
from de, desde; **_____ ... on** a partir de, de ... en adelante
front: in _____ of delante de
fruit fruta *f.;* **_____ orchard** huerto *m.*
fulfill cumplir (con)
full lleno
fundamental fundamental
funny gracioso; **be, strike one as _____** tener, hacer gracia
furious furioso
furniture muebles *m.,* **piece of _____** mueble *m.*
future porvenir *m.*

G

gain ganar
Gallician gallego

game partido *m.;* **_____** (*hunting*) caza *f.*
garage garaje *m.,* cochera *f.*
garden jardín *m.*
gardener jardinero *m.*
gate puerta *f.*
gathering reunión, tertulia *f.*
gem joya *f.*
general general; **become _____** generalizarse; *n.* general; **_____'s wife** generala *f.*
generally generalmente
generous generoso
gentle suave
gentleman señor, caballero *m.*
genuine genuino, auténtico
genuinely genuinamente
George Jorge
German alemán
Germany Alemania *f.*
gesture gesto *m.*
get conseguir, obtener; sacar; recibir; **_____ away** escaparse; **_____ along with (together)** llevarse; **_____ there** llegar a; llegar; **_____ together** reunirse; **_____ up** levantarse; **_____ out** sacar; **_____ on** subir a (*train*)
gift regalo *m.*
gigantic gigantesco
girl muchacha *f.*
give dar; **_____ up** renunciar a; desistir de, abandonar
glad: be _____ alegrarse de; **be very _____ to** tener mucho gusto en
glass vaso *m.*
glasses (*spectacles*) gafas *f.,* anteojos *m. pl.*
glimpse *v.* entrever
glorious glorioso
glory gloria *f.*
glove guante *m.*
go ir, (*become*) volverse; (*turn out*) resultar; **_____ around** dar la vuelta a; **_____ down** bajar; **_____ in for** meterse a; **_____ on** seguir, continuar; **go on!** ¡ande!; **_____ out** salir; **_____ up** subir; **_____ up to** dirigirse a, **_____ with** acompañar
God Dios
goddess diosa *f.*
gold oro *m.*
golden (*colored*) dorado
golf golf *m.*
good bueno
gorge desfiladero *m.*
gossip historias *f.,* chismes *m.; adj.* chismoso
Gothic gótico
government gobierno *m.*
governor gobernador *m.*

grace gracia
graceful gracioso
gradually poco a poco
grandeur grandeza *f.*
grandfather abuelo *m.*
grandmother abuela; **great** ____ bisabuelo (a) *m. f.*
granite granito *m.*
grape uva *f.*
grateful agradecido; **be** ____ agradecer, estar agradecido
grave grave
gray gris **become** ____ ponerse gris
great grande; ____ **many** muchos;
greater: to become ____ agrandarse
greatly mucho, muchísimo (*etc.*)
greatness grandeza *f.*
green verde
greet saludar
greeting saludo *m.*
grief pena *f.*
grilled window reja *f.*
grocery store tienda de ultramarinos (*or* comestibles)
ground suelo *m.*, tierra *f.*
group grupo *m.*
guarantee garantía *f.*
guard guardia, guardian *m.*
guest invitado, -a
guide guía *m.*
gun (shotgun) escopeta *f.*
gypsy gitano, -a

H

habit costumbre *f.*
hair pelo *m.*
half *adj.* medio; *n.* mitad *f.*; ____ **and** ____ a medias
hand mano *f.;* **on the other** ____ a, en cambio; ____ **to** ____ a brazo partido
handkerchief pañuelo *m.*
handle manejar
handsome guapo, hermoso
handwriting letra *f.*
happen pasar, ocurrir, suceder
happiness felicidad *f.*
happy contento, feliz
harbor puerto *m.*
hard: be ____ ser difícil, costar (ue)
hardship fatiga *f.*
hardware store ferretería *f.*
harmonize armonizar
harmony armonía *f.*

harsh severo, adusto
hasten apresurarse a
hat sombrero *m.* **top** ____ sombrero de copa
haughtiness altivez *f.*
Havana La Habana
have tener; contar (ue) con; ____ **to** *m.* tener que
headache dolor de cabeza *m.;* jaqueca *f.*
headstrong terco
health salud *f.*
healthful sano
healthy looking coloradote
hear oír; oír decir; ____ **from** tener noticias de
heart corazón *m.;* **by** ____ de memoria
heat calor *m.*
heated acalorado
heatedly calurosamente
heel: take to one's ____s tomar las de villadiego
Helen Elena
help *n.* ayuda *f.; v.* ayudar; **I cannot** ____ no puedo menos de; **it can't be** ____ed no hay más remedio
Henry Enrique
here aquí; ____ **is** aquí tiene Ud.
heroic heroico
heroism heroísmo *m.*
hidden recóndito
high alto
highway carretera *f.*
hill cuesta (*slope*); colina *f.*
Hispano-Arabic hispanoárabe
hiss silbido *m.*
historic(al) histórico
history historia *f.*
hold tener, encerrar (ie); ____ **back** detener
holiday fiesta *f.*
holy santo
home casa *f.*, hogar *m.*
homebody hombre
honor honor *m.*
hope esperanza *f.; v.* esperar; **lose** ____ perder las esperanzas
horse race carrera de caballos *f.*
horseback: on ____ a caballo
hospital hospital *m.*
hospitality hospitalidad *f.*
hostess azafata *f.* (*air*)
hot caliente; ____ (*weather*) caluroso
hotel hotel
hour hora *f.*
house casa *f.*
housetop azotea *f.*

how? ¿cómo?; ¿qué?; —— **much?** ¿cuánto?
however sin embargo; —— **much** *etc.* por más (muy, mucho) que
huddled agrupado
huge enorme
human humano
humor humor *m.*
(one) hundred cien(to)
hunger hambre *f.*
hungry: be —— tener hambre
hurry darse prisa, apresurarse; **be in a** —— tener (estar de) prisa
hurt hacer daño

I

ice cream helado *m.*
ideal ideal
idiot idiota, bobo *m.*
idleness ocio *m.*
if si; **as** —— como si
ignorance ignorancia *f.*
ill enfermo; —— **ness** enfermedad *f.*
illusion ilusión *f.*
imagine imaginar(se), figurarse
immaterial: be —— no importar; dar lo mismo (igual)
immediately en seguida
immense inmenso
immensely enormemente, muchísimo, la mar (de)
impatience impaciencia *f.*
impatient impaciente
imperial imperial
impertinent impertinente
importance importancia *f.*
importer importador
imposing imponente
impossible imposible
impress impresionar
impression impresión *f.*
impressive impresionante
improve perfeccionarse
incident incidente *m.*
income renta *f.*
inconvenience molestia *f.*
incredible increíble
indefinable: something —— (un) no sé
Indian indio
indicate indicar
indiscreet indiscreto
individual individual
industrial industrial
industrialization industrialización *f.*

industrialize industrializar
influence influencia *f.*
inform avisar, enterar
informal íntimo, de confianza
ingredient ingrediente *m.*
injured herido
injustice injusticia *f.*
inn fonda *f.*
innate innato
innocient inocente
innumerable innumerable
inopportune inoportuno
inside interior *m.;* **on the** —— por dentro
insist insistir en, empeñarse en
insistent insistente
insolent insolente
insolently insolentemente
inspire inspirar
install instalar
instance: for —— por ejemplo
insult insultar, ofender
intellectual intelectual
intelligent inteligente
intend pensar (ie), tener la intención de
intention intención *f.*
interest interés *m., v.* interesar; **be** ——**ed in** interesarse por
interesting interesante
interior interior *m.*
interview entrevista, interviú *f.*
intimate íntimo
intolerant intolerante
introduce presentar
invention invención *f.*
invitation invitación *f.*
invite invitar
involve envolver (ue)
involved: become —— enzarzarse en
Irish irlandés
iron hierro *m.*
ironic(al) irónico
island isla *f.*
isolated aislado
Italian italiano
itinerary itinerario *m.*
its su, sus

J

janitor portero *m.*
Jew(ish) judío
job trabajo *m.*, tarea, colocación (*position*) *f.*
Joe Pepe
John Juan

join reunirse con
joke chiste *m.*, broma *f.*
journalist periodista *m.*
journey viaje *m.*
judge juzgar
judgment juicio *m.*
juicy jugoso
July julio *m.*
jump saltar, dar un salto
June junio
just precisamente, exactamente, sólo; justamente; (*recently*) recién; **have** ____ acabar de

K

keep guardar; tener; (*retain*) quedarse con
kerchief pañuelo *m.*
key llave *f.*
kick dar un puntapié a
kid hablar en broma
kill matar
kilo kilo *m.*
kilometer kilómetro *m.*
kind bueno, bondadoso; grato
kind clase *f.*; género *m.* (genre); **what** ____ **of?** ¿qué clase de . . . ?
kindness amabilidad, bondad *f.*
king rey *m.*
kingdom reino *m.*
kitchen cocina *f.*
knee rodilla *f.*
knife cuchillo *m.*
knight caballero *m.*
knock llamar
know saber, conocer; **let** ____ avisar

L

lack falta *f.*; *v.* carecer de
lady señora *f.*; **young** ____ señorita *f.*
lake lago *m.*
lamb cordero *m.*
lame cojo
land tierra *f.*; *v.* desembarcarse
landlady patrona *f.*
landlord casero *m.*
landscape paisaje *m.*
language idioma *m.*, lengua *f.*
large grande
last último; (*passed*) pasado; *v.* durar; **at** ____ por fin
last final
late tarde; **be** ____ (*train*) llegar con retraso

later on más tarde, después
latest último
Latin latín *m.*
latter: the ____ éste
laugh reír(se) (i)
laughingstock hazmereír *m.*
law derecho *m.*; ley *f.*
lawyer abogado *m.*
lay poner
lead conducir, llevar
leader jefe *m.*
leak salirse
learn aprender, saber, enterarse de
learning ciencia *f.*
least: not in the ____ ni mucho menos
leather cuero *m.*
leave (*behind*) dejar; (*depart from*) irse, marcharse, salir de; (*cease*) pasarse; **take** ____ **of** despedirse (i) de
lecture conferencia *f.*
left: be ____, **have** ____ quedarle a uno
left izquierdo
leg pierna *f.*
legend leyenda *f.*
leisure despreocupación *f.*
lend prestar
lesson lección *f.*
lest no sea que, no vaya a ser que
let dejar; ____ **know** avisar; ____ **on** darse por entendido
letter carta *f.*, letra *f.*
liar embustero *m.*, mentiroso, -a
liberal liberal
liberty libertad *f.*
library biblioteca *f.*
lie yacer
life vida *f.*
light luz *f.*; *v.* encender (ie)
lighter (*cigarette*) encendedor *m.*
likable simpático
like parecido; **anything** ____ **that** una cosa así; ____ **a** parecido a; ____ **that** así; **nothing** ____ **that** nada de eso; **like** *v.* gustar, agradar; **how do you** ____ ? ¿qué le parece?
limit límite
line línea *f.*; renglón *m.*
lion león *m.*
listen escuchar
literary literario
little poco; **a** ____ un poco de
live vivir
living vivo
living room sala *f.*; living (*South Am.*) *m.*

loaded cargado
located situado
location situación *f.*
London Londres *m.*
lonely solitario, solo
long largo; (*time*) mucho tiempo; **(take)** _____ tardar (mucho); **too** _____ demasiado tiempo; **be (take)** _____ tardar; **how** _____? ¿cuánto tiempo?
longer más tiempo; **no** _____ no . . . más, ya no
look mirada *f.; v.* mirar; (*seem*) parecer, estar; _____ **at** mirar; _____ **for** buscar; _____ **here** ¡oiga!; _____ **like** parecer, tener el aspecto de (aire, cara de); _____ **out of** asomarse a, mirar por; _____ **up** ver, mirar _____ **out**!! ¡ojo!
lose perder (ie); _____ **heart** descorazonarse (uno)
lot: a _____ mucho
lots (of) la mar (de)
lottery lotería *f.;* _____ **ticket** billete de lotería *m.*
loud: in a very _____ **voice** en voz muy alta, a gritos; _____**er** más alto
loudspeaker altavoz *m.*, altoparlante *m.*
Louis Luis
love querer, amar
low bajo; **in a** _____ **voice** en voz baja, por lo bajo
lower bajar, (*price*) rebajar
luck suerte *f.*
lunch almuerzo *m.;* **have** _____ almorzar (ue)
lung pulmón *m.*

M

machinery maquinaria *f.*
Madrilian madrileño
magazine revista *f.*
magnificent magnífico
mahogany caoba *f.*
maid criada *f.*, doncella *f.*
mail correo *m.;* _____ *v.* echar (al correo)
main principal; _____ **spring** motiveo *m.*
maintain sostener
majestic majestuoso
majesty majestad *f.*
major comandante *m.*
Majorca Mallorca *f.*
make hacer
manage: _____ **to** llegar, acertar a
manager director *m.*
mansion palacio *m.*

mantilla mantilla *f.*
many muchos (as); **as** _____ **as** tanto como
map mapa *m.*
mark señal *f.;* huella *f.* (*trace*); blanco *m.* (*target*); *v.* señalar
married casado
martial: _____ **law** estado de guerra (*sitio*) *m.*
marvel maravilla *f.*
massive macizo
master amo *m.;* _____ **and mistress** los señores
mate compañero *m.*
matter (*affair*) asunto *m.;* **be the** _____ tener, pasarle a uno; **no** _____ **how** por muy (mucho, más) . . . que
may poder, puede que, probablemente
mayor alcalde *m.*
meal comida *f.* **take one's** _____**s** comer; **very good** _____ muy bien de comer
mean querer decir, significar
means: by no (any) _____ ni mucho menos, eso sí que no
meantime: in the _____ en el entre tanto
measure medida *f.; v.* medir (i)
meat carne *f.*
mechanic mecánico *m.*
medical de medicina
medieval medieval
Mediterranean Mediterráneo
meet encontrar (ue), encontrarse con; conocer (*become acquainted with*); esperar (*go to meet*)
meeting reunión, tertulia *f.*
melancholy melancólico
melon melón
memory memoria *f.;* recuerdo *m.*
mention mencionar; **don't** _____ **it** no hay de qué
mercury azogue *m.*
merit merecer
merry alegre
mess lío *m.*
message recado *m.*
meter metro *m.*
method método *m.*
middle *n.* medio; _____ **Ages** Edad Media *f.*
midst: in the _____ **of** en medio de
mile milla *f.*
military militar
million millón *m.*
millionaire millonario, -a
mind mente; memoria *f.* **to make up one's** _____ decidirse; *v.* tener inconveniente en, importar

mine mina *f.*
ministry ministerio *m.*
Mint Casa de la Moneda *f.*
minute minuto *m.*
misinterpret interpretar mal
misprint errata
miss perder(se) (ie) que; *v.* importar
missionary misionero *m.*
mistake equivocación *f.;* (tener) falta; _____n equivocado
mix mezclar; _____ **in** meterse en; _____ed **with** no exento de
modern moderno
modernity modernidad *f.*
modestly modestamente
moment momento *m.*
monastery monasterio *m.*
money dinero *m.*
monk monje *m.*
monkish monástico
monotonous monótono
month mes *m.*
monument monumento *m.*
moon luna *f.;* _____less sin luna; _____light luz de la luna; **be** _____lit haber luna
Moor(ish) moro, -a
moor páramo *m.*
more más; **the** _____ **the** _____ mientras (cuanto) más . . . más; _____ **and** _____ cada vez más; **all the** _____ **because** tanto más cuanto que
morning mañana *f.*
Moroccan marroquí
mortgage hipotecar
mosque mezquita *f.*
most más; _____ **of** la mayoría, la mayor parte, los más de; **at** _____ a lo sumo, a todo tirar
mother madre *f.*
motion movimiento *m.*
motorcycle motocicleta *f.*
mountain montaña, sierra *f.*
moustache bigote *m.*
mouth boca *f.*
move (*change*) mudarse; _____ **away** alejarse
movie(s) cine *m.;* _____ **actress** actriz de cine *f.*
much mucho; **so** _____ tanto
mud lodo, barro, fango *m.*
multicolored multicolor
murmur murmullo *m.*
museum museo *m.*
music música *f.*
musical musical, músico

must deber (de), tener que, haber de
my mi, mío
myrtle arrayán *m.*
mysterious misterioso
mystery misterio *m.*
mystic místico

N

name nombre *m.;* **family** _____ apellido *m.;* **by the** _____ **of** que se llama
narrow estrecho
nation nación *f.*
national nacional
native *n.* uno del país
natural natural
naturally naturalmente
Navarre Navarra *f.*
near cerca (de)
neat limpio
necessary necesario, **it is** _____ es necesario, es preciso, hay que
necklace collar *m.*
need necesidad *f.,* **there is** _____ **to** *v.* hacerle falta a uno
neglect descuidar
negotiation negociación *f.*
neighborhood vecindad *f.*
neither *conj.* ni; _____ . . . **nor** ni . . . ni; *pron.* ninguno de los dos
nephew sobrino *m.*
nervous nervioso
never nunca, jamás
nevertheless sin embargo
new nuevo; **New Year's** Año Nuevo
New York Nueva York *f.*
news noticia *f.;* algo de nuevo
newspaperman periodista *m.*
newspaper periódico *m.,* **vile low** _____ periodicucho *m.*
next próximo, que viene (*time*); inmediato, de al lado (*place*); *adv.* después
nice simpático
niece sobrina *f.*
night noche *f.;* **at** _____ de noche, por la(s) noche(s); **last** _____ anoche
nineteen(th) diecinueve
no *adj.* ninguno; *adv.* no, nada de; _____body nadie
noise ruido *m.*
noiselessly sin ruido
noisy ruidoso
northern septentrional, del norte
not no

note nota *f.;* apunte *m.*
notebook cuaderno *m.*
nothing nada
notice notar, fijarse en, reparar
nourishing nutritivo
novel novela *f.*
now ahora; _____ **that** ya que
nudge dar un codazo
number número *n.*
numerous numeroso

O

oak grove encinar *m.*
obey obedecer
object objeto *m.*
observation observación *f.*
obstacle obstáculo *m.*
obvious: be _____ saltar a la vista
occasionally a veces, de vez de cuando
occupation profesión *f.*
occupy ocupar
occur ocurrir, pasar; ocurrírsele a uno
oculist oculista *m.*
o'clock: one _____, **two** _____ *etc.* la una, las dos *etc.*
offended ofendido
offer oferta *f.*
office oficina *f.;* dirección *f.* (*hotel*)
officer oficial *m.*
official oficial
often a menudo, con frecuencia
oil aceite *m.*
O.K. visto bueno (Vo. Bo.)
old-fashioned anticuado
old viejo, (*ancient*), (*former*) antiguo; **to be . . . years** _____ tener . . . años
older, oldest mayor
olive aceituna *f.*
once una vez; **at** _____ en seguida; _____ **and again** una y otra vez
only solo (que), solamente, no(nada) . . . más que
open abierto; *v.* abrir; _____ **air** aire libre *m.*
opening night estreno *m.*
opinion opinión *f.* **public** _____ (*gossip*) el qué dirán
opponent contrario *m.*
opportunity ocasión *f.*
oppose oponerse a
opposite opuesto
orange naranja *f.;* _____ **rose** rosado anaranjado; _____ **tree** naranjo *m.*

orchard huerta *f.*
orchestra orquesta *f.*
order orden *f.;* **in** _____ **to** para; **get out of** _____ no funcionar; descomponerse; (*ask for*) pedir (i), mandar
ore mineral *m.*
organization organización *f.*
organize organizar
oriental oriental
original original
orphan huérfano *m.*
otherwise de otra manera (forma)
ought deber
out fuera, a la calle; (*extinguished*) apagado
outdo oneself desvivirse (por)
outside fuera de; afuera
outskirts afueras *f. pl.*, arrabales *m. pl.*
over sobre, encima de; (*approx.*) más de; **be** _____ terminar (se)
overcast nublado; **become** _____ nublarse
overcoat abrigo, gabán *m.*
overseer capataz *m.*
overtake pasar
owe deber
own propio; *v.* tener
owner dueño *m.*
ox buey *m.*

P

package paquete *m.*
packer embalador *m.*
page página *f.*
pain dolor *m.*
painful penoso
painter pintor *m.*
painting cuadro *m.*
pair par *m.*
palace palacio *m.*
pale pálido
palm: a _____**'s length high** de a palmo
palm tree palmera *f.*
panorama panorama *m.*
paper papel *m.;* (*newsp.*) periódico *m.*
paperknife cortapapel(es) *m.*
par excellence por excelencia
parade desfile *m.*
Paraguay el Paraguay
pardon perdonar
parents padres *m.*
part parte *f.;* *v.* despedirse
partner socio *m.*
pass pasar; salir bien en (examinations)
passage pasaje *m.*

passenger   pasajero *m.*
passing   que pasa, *etc.*, pasajero
passport   pasaporte *m.*
past   pasado *m.*
pastry shop   pastelería *f.*
pasture land   dehesa *f.*
path   sendero *m.*, vereda *f.*; **narrow** ____ senderito, veredita
patience   paciencia *f.*
patient   enfermo *m.*
patio   patio *m.*
pay   pagar; hacer (*a visit*); ____ **compliments** echar flores
peak   pico *m.*, cresta *f.*; *v.* colocar, acomodar
peasant   labrador, campesino *m.*
peculiar   peculiar
peculiarly   típicamente
pen   pluma *f.*
pencil   lápiz *m.*
penny   céntimo *m.*
people   gente *f.*; **other** ____**'s** ajeno
percent   por ciento
perched   asentado
perfect   perfecto
perform   (*a play*) representar
performance   función *f.*; **first** ____ estreno *m.*
perfumed   perfumado
perhaps   tal vez, quizá(s)
permanent   permanente
permission   permiso *m.*
persevere   perseverar
person   persona *f.*
personage   personaje *m.*
personally   en persona
perspective   perspectiva *f.*
Peru   el Perú
pervade   penetrar; animar
peseta   peseta *f.*
Philadelphia   Filadelfia
philosophic   filosófico
phonograph   tocadiscos *m.*
piano   piano *m.*
pick up   coger
pickpocket   ratero *m.*, carterista
picture   fotografía *f.*; (*painting*) cuadro *m.*; (*film*) película *f.*; film *m.*; **have a** ____ **of oneself painted or taken** retratarse
picturesque   pintoresco
pier   muelle *m.*
pierce   pasar
pile   montón *m.*
pilgrim   peregrino *m.*
pill   píldora, pastilla *f.*

pine forest   pinar *m.*
pine tree   pino *m.*
pipe   pipa *f.*
pistol   pistola *f.*
pitcher   jarro *m.*
pitiless   despiadado·
pity   lástima, compasión *f.* **it is a** ____ es lástima
place   lugar, sitio *m.; in* ____ **of** en vez (lugar) de; **take** ____ tener lugar; *v.* colocar, acomodar
plain   llanura *f.*
plan   plan *m.* **make** ____**s for** *v.* tener el plan, planear
plastic   plástico
Plate (*river*)   el (río de la) Plata
plateau   meseta *f.*
plateresque   plateresco
play   obra (de teatro) *f.; v.* (*a game*) jugar (ue); ____ **tennis** *etc.* jugar al tenis *etc.*; tocar (*music*)
pleasant   agradable
please   gastar, agradar; hága(me) el favor de, sírvase Ud., por favor
pleasure   gusto *m.*
pocket   bolsillo *m.*
pocketbook   cartera *f.*
poem   poema *m.*; poesia *f.*
poet   poeta *m.*
point; ____ **blank** de buenas a primeras; **that's not the** ____ no se trata de eso
police   policía *f.*
policeman   guardia *m.*
polite   cumplido
politeness   educación *f.*
politics   política *f.*
pollution   contaminación *f.*
pope   papa *m.*
poplar   chopo *m.*
popular   popular
port   puerto *m.*
porter   mozo (*station*); mozo de cuerda
portrait   retrato *m.*
Portuguese   portugués
position   colocación *f.*, puesto *m.*
possess   poseer
possession; take ____ **of** apoderarse
post office   correo(s) *m.*
poster   cartel *m.*
postman   cartero *m.*
postpone   aplazar
pottery   cerámica *f.*
pour   echar
poverty   pobreza *f.*

practically punto menos que

practice practicar, **put in ＿＿** poner en práctica

precede preceder a

precipitous escarpado

precisely precisamente

preconceived (notion) prejuicio *m.*

predicament apuro *m.*

prefer preferir (ie, i)

preferable preferible

preferably preferentemente

preparation preparación *f.*

preparations preparativos *m.*

present (gift) regalo *m.; v.* presentar

present *adj.* presente, (*time*) actual; **up to the ＿＿** hasta ahora; *v.* presentar

preserve conservar

president presidente; rector *m.* (*of a university*)

prestige prestigio *m.*

pretend fingir, echárselas de

pretext pretexto *m.*

pretty bonito

pretty *adv.* bastante

prevent impedir (i)

previously antes, hace (hacía) una semana (*etc.*)

price precio *m.*

priceless sin par

pride orgullo *m.*

primarily ante todo

primitive primitivo

prince príncipe *m.*

principal principal

principle principio *m.*

print grabado *m.*

prisoner prisionero, preso *m.*

private particular, privado

prize premio *n.; ***first ＿＿** (premio) gordo

pro en pro (de)

problem problema *m.*

proclaim pregonar

produce producir, dar

product producto *m.*

program programa *m.*

progress progreso *m.*

prohibit prohibir

project proyecto *m.*

promise prometer

promote ascender (ie)

properly bien; como era debido

property posesiones *f.*

propose proponer

proprietor dueño *m.*

protest protesta *f.*

prove to be resultar

proverb refrán *m.*

provided (that) con tal (de) que, como

province provincia *f.*

provincial de provincia

provision provisión *f.*

prudence prudencia *f.*

public *adj.* público; *n.* público *m.*

publish publicar

Puerto Rican puertorriqueño

pull: ＿＿ out sacar, arrancar (*train*)

pulse pulso *m.*

puncture pinchazo *m.*

purchase compra *f.*

pure puro

purple morado

put poner, meter; **＿＿ in practice** poner en práctica; **＿＿ on** ponerse; **＿＿ out** (*extend*) sacar, (*extinguish*) apagar; **＿＿ up with** aguantar, consentir, pasar

Pyrenees los Pirineos

Q

quarrel reñir (i), meterse con

quarter cuarto *m.;* barrio *m.* (*of town*)

queer raro

quell sofocar

question pregunta *f.*

quickly rápidamente

quiet tranquilo, callado; **be (keep) ＿＿** callarse, estarse quieto; *n.* quietud *f.*

quite muy, todo

Quixote: Don ＿＿ Don Quijote

R

race raza *f.*

radio radio *f.*

rage cólera *f.*

railroad ferrocarril *m.*

rain lluvia *f.;* llover (ue)

raincoat impermeable *m.*

raise levantar

range sierra *f.*

rapidly rápidamente

rare raro; **＿＿ly** pocas (raras) veces

rash: ＿＿ act temeridad *f.*

rate: at any ＿＿ de todos modos, sea como sea

rather más bien; **would ＿＿** preferir (ie, i)

raw materials primeras materias, materias primas

razor (*safety*) maquinilla de afeitar *f.*

reach   llegar a

read   leer; _____**ing** lectura *f.*

ready   listo, dispuesto

real   verdadero; _____**ly** de veras

realism   realismo *m.*

realistic   realista

reality   realidad *f.*

realize   darse cuenta de

rear   (*back*) fondo *m.*

reason   razón *f.*, motivo *m.*

recall   recordar (ue), acordarse (ue) (de)

receive   recibir

recently   recientemente

recognize   reconocer

recommend   recomendar (ie)

record   (*phonograph*) disco *m.*

red   rojo

reddish   rojizo

redhaired   pelirrojo

refer   referirse (ie, i)

refuse   negarse (ie) a, rehusar

regards   recuerdo *m.;* **to be in** _____ **to** tratarse de, ser cuestión de; **with (in)** _____ **to** (con) respeto a, tocante a

region   región *f.*

regret   sentimiento *m.;* sentir (ie, i), lamentar

regularly   con regularidad, generalmente

rehearse   ensayar

rejoice   alegrarse

relative   pariente *m.*

relic   vestigio *m.*

religious   religioso

rely on   contar (ue) con

remain   quedar (se)

remark   observación *f.*

remember   recordar (ue), acordarse de

remembrance   recuerdo *m.*

remind of   recordar (ue)

reminder   recuerdo *m.*, recordativo *m.*

remote   lejano

renaissance   Renacimiento *m., adj.*

renowned   renombrado

rent   *v.* alquilar

repair   reparar

repay   pagar (ie)

repeat   repetir (i)

repel   repugnar, repeler

repertory   repertorio *m.*

reply   contestación *f.; v.* contestar

represent   representar

representative   representativo

reproach   reprochar

request: on _____ a petición

require   requerir (ie, i)

resemblance   parecido *m.*

resemble   parecerse a

reserved   reservado

residence: royal _____ real sitio *m.*

resign   dimitir

resource   recurso *m.* de

respect   respectar

rest: the _____ el resto de, los demás

rest   descanso *n.;* descansar

restaurant   restaurante *m.*

restless   inquieto

result   resultado, producto *m.*

resume   reanudar

retain   conservar

return   vuelta *f.;* _____ **trip** viaje de vuelta; *v.* (*go back*) volver (ue); (*give back*) devolver (ue)

reveal   revelar

rewrite   volver a escribir

rhythm   ritmo *m.*

rice   arroz *m.*

ride horseback   montar a caballo

riding   montado

right   derecho *m.;* **to be** _____ tener razón; _____ **away,** _____ **now** en seguida; ahora mismo; **all** _____ (está) bien, bueno, de acuerdo; **that's** _____ ¡eso es!

ring   (*arena*) ruedo *m.*

riot   motín *m.*

ripe   maduro

rival   rivalizar con

river   río *m.*

road   carretera *f.*, camino *m.*

rob   robar

robber   ladrón *m.*

rock   roca *f.*

role   papel *m.*, actuación *f.*

Roman   romano

Romanesque   románico

romantic   romántico

romanticism   romanticismo *m.*

roof garden   terraza, azotea *f.*

room   cuarto *m.*, habitación, sala *f.*

roommate   compañero de cuarto *m.*

rough   agitado, revuelto (*sea*); tosco (*not smooth*)

round (of activities)   trajín *m.*

row   hilera *f.*

royal   real

rudely   groseramente

rug   alfombra *f.*

ruin   ruina *f.; v.* estropear, echar a perder

ruined   arruinado

run   correr; _____**ning** corriente

rush   lanzarse

S

sad   triste
sadden   entristecer
saddlebags   alforjas *f. pl*
sail   salir; embarcar(se)
sailboat   barco de vela *m.*
Saint Helena   Santa Elena
sake: for its own _____ por sí solo
salary   sueldo *m.*
salesman: traveling _____ viajante *m.*
same   mismo
sample   muestra *f.*
sand   arena *f.*
sandwich   bocadillo, sandwich *m.*
sash   faja *f.*
satisfied   satisfecho
saving   ahorrador
say   decir; **I should** _____ **so (not)** ¡Ya lo creo (que no)!
scandal   escándalo *m.*
scar   cicatriz *f.*
scarcely   apenas (si)
scatter   esparcir
scene   escena *f.*
scenery   decoraciones *f.*
schedule   horario *m.*
scholar   sabio *m.*
science   ciencia *f.*
scientific   científico
scientist   hombre de ciencia *m.*
scold   reñir (i)
scolding: a good, sound _____ un regaño de los buenos
scratch   arañazo *m.*
sea   mar *m. (and f.)*
sea dog   lobo de mar *m.*
search   busca *f.*
seashore   playa *f.*
seasick: get _____ marearse
season (*of year*)   estación *f.;* temporada *f.*
seat   asiento *m.,* localidad (*theater*) *f.,* plaza (*train*) *f.*
seated   sentado
secret   secreto *m.*
secretary   secretario, -a; (*cabinet*) ministro *m.*
section (*of town*)   barrio *m.;* sección *f.*
see   ver, divisar
seek   buscar
seem   parecer
seize   apoderarse de
seldom   raras veces
self   mismo
sell   vender

senator   senador *m.*
send   enviar, mandar; poner, echar (*letter*), *etc.*
sense   sentido *m.*
sentence   frase *f.*
sentimental   sentimental
separate   separar
September   se(p)tiembre
serious   serio
seriously: take _____ tomar en serio
sermon   sermón *m.*
servant   criado, -a
serve   servir (i); _____ **as** servir de
setback   contratiempo *m.*
several   varios, algunos, unos cuantos
severe   severo
sew   coser
shake   menear
share (*of stock*)   acción *f.*
shave   afeitarse
shed   derramar, verter
sheer   puro
shelf   estante *m.*
sherry (wine)   vino de Jerez *m.*
shine   brillar
ship   nave *f.*
shoe store   zapatería *f.*
shoe   zapato *m.*
shoemaker   zapatero *m.* _____**'s wife** zapatera *f.*
shoot   tirar; _____**ing** tiros *m. pl.*
shop   tienda *f.; v.* ir (estar) de compras
shopping: go _____ ir de compras
short cut   atajo *m.*
short   corto; **in** _____ en fin
short story *f.,* cuento *m.*
shortly   en breve; _____ **after** poco (tiempo) después
shoulder   hombro *m.*
shout   grito *m.; v.* gritar
show   función (de teatro) *f.*
show   mostrar (ue); enseñar; conocérsele; _____**up** aparecer
shrewd   astuto
shrine   santuario *m.*
sick   enfermo, malo
sickness   enfermedad *f.*
side   lado *m.*
sidewalk   acera *f.*
sight   vista, escena *f.;* **be in** _____ tener a la vista; _____ **seeing** ver cosas
sign   firmar
silence   silencio *m.*
silent   callado

silk   seda *f.*
silliness   tontería *f.*
silly   tonto; _____ **remark** (*etc.*) tontería *f.*
silver   plata *f.*
similar   parecido
simple   sencillo, simple
simplicity   simplicidad *f.*
simply   a secas; _____ **have to** no tener más remedio que
since (*temporal*)   desde, desde que
sincere   sincero
sincerity   sinceridad *f.*
sing   cantar
singing (*of voice*)   para el canto
single   solo; **not a** _____ ni uno (solo)
sink   (*intrans.*) hundirse
sip   saborear
sir   señor
sit (down)   sentarse (ie)
situation   situación *f.*
skip   saltarse
sky   cielo *m.*
slap   dar (de) bofetadas
sleep   sueño *m.*, *v.* dormir (ue, u); **feel** _____ **y** entrarle sueño a uno; **get to** _____ dormirse
slender   delgado
slight   desairar
slightest   menor
slippery   resbaladizo
slow   lento; **be (run)** _____ atrasar
slowly   despacio, lentamente
small   pequeño, menudo
smell   oler; **it** _____**s** huele (mal)
smile   sonreírse
smoke   fumar; _____**less** sin humo
snow   nieve *f.*
so   tan; (*that way*) así; (*consequently*) así es que; **and** _____ con que; _____? ¿sí?; _____ **that** para que, de manera (modo) que; _____ (*then*) con que
soccer   fútbol *m.*
social   social
socialist   socialista
soil   tierra *f.*
soldier   soldado *m.*
solid   sólido
solitary   solitario
solution   solución *f.*
somebody   alguien
something   algo
somewhere   a (en, por, *etc.*) alguna parte; _____ **around** por ahí
son   hijo *m.* **son-in-law** yerno *m.*
song   canción *f.*

soon   pronto; **as** _____ **as** en cuanto, tan pronto como, así que, lo antes (posible)
sorry: be _____   sentir (ie, i)
sort   clase *f.; of the same* _____ por el estilo
soul   alma *f.*
soundly (*sleep*)   a pierna suelta
south   sur *m.*
southern   meridional
space   espacio *m.*
Spain   España *f.*
Spanish   español
speak   hablar
special   especial *f.*
spectacle   espectáculo *m.*
speech   discurso *m.*
speed   velocidad *f.;* _____**y** rápido
spell   embrujamiento *m.*
spend   gastar (*money, etc.*); (*time*) pasar
spirit   espíritu *m.*
spite: in _____ **of** a pesar de; con
splendid   espléndido
splendor   esplendor *m.*
spoil   echarse a perder, estropear; pasarse (*overcooked, overripe, etc.*)
sport   deporte *m.*
square   *adj.* cuadrado; *n.* plaza; **little** _____ plazuela, plazoleta *f.*
stamp   sello *m.*
stand   estar, estar de pie; (*endure*) aguantar, resistir; _____ **for** pasar; _____ **out** destacarse; _____ **up** ponerse de pie
standard: by American _____**s** según las normas americanas
star   estrella *f.*
start   *n.* principio, primer momento *v.* empezar (ie), comenzar (ie); entablar; echarse a; ponerse a, en movimiento
station   estación *f.*
statue   estatua *f.*
stay   *n.* estancia *f.*, quedarse; parar (*hotel*)
steal   robar
steam   vapor *m.*
steamer   vapor *m.*
steel   acero *m.*
steep   escarpado, empinado
stenographer   mecanógrafa *f.*
steward   camarero *m.* **chief** _____ mayordomo *m.*
still   *adv.* todavía, aún; *v.* **be** _____ seguir (i)
stint oneself   quedarse corto
stocking   media *f.*
stop   *n.* parada *f.; v.* detenerse, parar, suspender; dejar; dejar de, detenerse
store   tienda *f.*

storm tormenta *f.*
story cuento *m.*, historia *f.*
strange raro
stream (*tiny*) arroyuelo *m.*
streetcar tranvía *m.*
street calle *f.*
strength fuerza *f.*
stretch estirar; _____ (**away**) extenderse (*time*)
stride salto *m.*
strike dar, sonar (ue); _____ **one as amusing** hacerle mucha gracia a uno
strike huelga *f.*
strip (*of land*) faja *f.*
stroll vuelta *f.*, paseo *m.; v.* pasear(se)
strong fuerte
stubborn terco
student estudiante *m.*
study estudio, despacho *m.* (*room*); *v.* estudiar
style estilo *m.*
subtle sutil
suburb barrio *m.*, arrabal *m.*
succeed in conseguir (i), lograr
success éxito *m.*
successful: to be _____ tener éxito
such (a) tal; cada; _____ **as** tal como
suddenly de pronto, de repente
suffer sufrir
suggest sugerir (ie, i)
sufficient bastante, suficiente; **to be** _____ bastar
sugar azúcar *m.*
suit convenir (ie)
suit *n.* traje *m.;* **bathing** _____ traje de baño
suitcase maleta *f.*
summer verano *m.*
summon llamar
sun sol *m.;* **everything under the** _____ todo lo humano y lo divino
sunburned tostado
Sunday domingo *m.*
sunny: to be _____ hacer (haber) sol
superficial superficial
supernatural sobrenatural
suppose suponer
suppress (*a newspaper*) suspender
sure seguro
surely (*intens.*) sí que
surprise *n.* sorpresa *f.; v.* sorprender
surround rodear
suspect sospechar
suspend suspender
suspicious suspicaz
sweaty sudoroso
sweet dulce

swiftness ligereza *f.*
swim nadar
swollen hinchado
symbol símbolo *m.*
symbolize simbolizar

T

table mesa *f.*
tack (*direction*) rumbo *m.*
Tagus Tajo *m.*
tail rabo *m.*
tailor sastre *m.*
take tomar, llevar; _____ **away** llevarse; (deprive) quitar; _____ **in** abarcar, comprender; _____ **long** tardar; _____ **off** quitarse; _____ **out** sacar
talk hablar
tall alto
tame manso
tapestry tapiz *m.*
target blanco *m.*
taste gusto *m.; v.* (*be*) estar
taxi *m.;* _____ **driver** chófer del taxi *m.*
tea té *m.*
teach enseñar
teacher profesor *m.*
team equipo *m.;* _____ **play** actuación del equipo
tear lágrima *f.*
tear rasgar
tease tomar (le) el pelo (a uno)
technique técnica *f.*
telegram telegrama *m.*
telephone teléfono *m.; v.* telefonear
tell decir, contar (ue)
temper genio *m.;* **awful** _____ geniazo
temple templo *m.*
tennis tenis *m.*
test prueba *f.*
Texas Tejas
than que, de, del que, *etc.*
thank agradecer, dar las gracias; _____ **you very much** muchas gracias
that *demonstr.* ese, esa, eso; aquel, aquella, aquello
that *conj.* que
theater teatro *m.*
their su, sus, *etc.*
theme tema *m.*
then entonces; luego
there allí
these estos, estas

thin delgado

thing cosa *f.;* **to be a good** _____ **to** convenir (ie)

think creer, pensar (ie); _____ **of** pensar en, pensar de (*opinion*), figurarse

third tercero

thirsty: be _____ tener sed

thirty treinta

this este, esta, esto

thoroughly a fondo

those esos, esas; aquellos, aquellas

though: even _____ aunque, aun cuando

thousand mil

through por, por medio de

thus así

ticket billete *m.,* (*theater*) localidad, entrada *f.*

tide marea *f.*

tie corbata *f.*

tie *v.* atar

tile azulejo *m.*

time tiempo *m.* (*short time*) rato *m.;* (*in succession*) vez *f.;* (*hour*) hora *f.;* **at one and the same** _____ a la vez, al mismo tiempo; **at that** _____ entonces; **what** _____? ¿qué hora?; **have a good** _____ divertirse (ie, i), pasarlo bien; **some** _____ una temporada

timetable guía *f.,* horario, *m.*

tiny chiquitito

tip propina *f.*

tire cansar; **be (get, grow)** _____ed cansarse

tobacco tabaco *m.*

today hoy

together juntos

tomorrow mañana; _____ **morning** mañana por la mañana

tone tono *m.*

tonight esta noche

too (much, many) demasiado

too (also) también

tooth diente *m.,* muela *f.* (*molar*)

top lo alto; **on** _____ **of** encima de; **at the** _____ **of** con toda la fuerza de (*voice*)

topic tema *m.*

torment pena *f.*

tourist turista *m., f.; adj.* de turismo

toward(s) hacia; para con

tower torre *f.*

town hall ayuntamiento *m.*

town pueblo *m.*

tradition tradición *f.*

traffic circulación *f.,* tránsito *m.*

tragedy tragedia *f.*

train tren *m.*

trait rasgo *m.*

tranquility tranquilidad *f.*

transfer trasladar

transform transformar

translate traducir

translation traducción *f.*

travel viaje *m.; v.* viajar

traveler viajero *m.*

traveling salesman viajante *m.*

traveling de viaje

traverse cruzar, atravesar (ie)

treasure tesoro *m.*

Treasury (department) Hacienda *f.*

tree árbol *m.;* _____**less** sin árboles

tremendous tremendo

trick maña *f.;* **dirty** _____ mala jugada *f.*

trip viaje *m.,* excursión *f.*

trolley tranvía *m.*

troops tropas *f.*

trouble: the _____ **is** lo malo es

true verdadero; **be** _____ ser verdad

trunk baúl *m.*

try ensayar; _____ **to** tratar de, procurar

turbulence turbulencia *f.*

turn volver (ue); _____ **out** resultar, salir; (*extinguish*) apagar; _____ **to** convertirse (ie, i) en; **to be one's** _____ tocarle a uno

tuxedo smoking *m.*

twentieth veinte

twenty veinte

twice dos veces

two dos

type tipo *m.*

typewrite escribir a máquina

typewriter máquina de escribir *f.*

typhus tifus *m.*

typical típico

typically Spanish castizo

U

umbrella paraguas *m.*

unawares desprevenido

unbelievable increíble; **it seems** _____ parece mentira

uncle tío *m.*

uncomfortable incómodo

unconsciously sin consciencia

under bajo, debajo de

understand comprender; entender (ie)

understandable: it is _____ se comprende

understanding comprensión *f.*

unemployed: the _____ los sin trabajo, los desempleados

unforgettable inolvidable

unfriendly hostil
unhurt ileso, sin daño
unique único
university universidad *f.; adj.* universitario
unjust injusto
unless a menos que, como no, a no ser que
unpleasant desagadable
unquestionable indudable, innegable
unrealistic poco realista
unsuccessful sin éxito
until hasta que
untrue falso; **be** ―― no ser verdad
unwillingly sin querer
up: ―― **to** hasta; ―― **and down** de arriba para abajo
uphill cuesta arriba
uprising sublevación *f.*
upstairs arriba
Uruguay el Uruguay
use *n.* uso *m.;* ――**less** inútil; *v.* usar, emplear, utilizar, servirse de
usual usual, corriente; **as** ―― como siempre
usually generalmente

V

Valencian valenciano
valuable valioso
varied vario, variado
variety variedad *f.*
various varios, -as
vast vasto, inmenso
veal ternera *f.*
velvet terciopelo *m.*
vender vendedor *m.*
verbally de palabra
very *adj.* mismo; *adv.* muy
vest chaleco *m.*
view vista *f.*, panorama *m.;* **point of** ―― punto de vista *m.*
village aldea *f.*
villager aldeano, -a *m. f.*
vineyard viñedo *m.*
violently violentamente, con violencia
visigothic visigodo
visit visitar
visitor visita *f.*
voice voz *f.;* ――**less** sin voz
volume volumen *m.*, tomo *m.*
voyage viaje *m.*

W

wait (for) esperar
waiter camarero *m.*

wake despertar (ie); ―― **up** despertarse, amanecer
walk *n.* paseo *m.;* **take (go for) a** ―― dar un paseo; *v.* andar, pasear (se); ―― **in** entrar
wall muro *m.;* pared *f.* (*house*)
walled amurallado
wallet cartera *f.*
wanderings andanzas *f. pl.*
want querer
war guerra *f.*
warm **be** ―― tener calor (*persons*); **be** ―― hacer calor (*weather*)
warn advertir (ie, i)
warrior guerrero *m.*
wash up refrescarse
waste perder (ie) (*time*)
watch reloj *m.*
watchman: night ―― sereno *m.*
water el agua *f.;* ――**ing-place** balneario *m.*
way manera *f.*, modo *m.;* **this** ―― (*manner*) así; **this** ―― (*direction*) por aquí, **by** ―― **of** por; **on the** ―― de camino; **on the** ―― **back** de vuelta; **by the** ―― a propósito; **and, by the** ―― por cierto que; **get (have) one's** ―― salirse con la suya
weak débil
wealthy rico, acomodado
wear llevar
weary cansado
weather tiempo *m.*
wedding boda *f.*
week semana *f.*
weekend fin de semana *m.*
weigh pesar
well *adv.* bien; pues; ―― **then** pues entonces; bueno, bien, pues; **as** ―― **as** lo mismo que; igual que
west oeste *m.*
western occidental
what *rel.* lo que; ――? ¿qué? ―― **a ...!** ¡qué ... ! ¡vaya uno! ¡valiente!
wheat trigo *m.*
wheel rueda *f.;* **steering** ―― volante *m.*
when cuando
where? ¿dónde?
wherever donde (quiera)
which *rel.* que, el que, el cual; lo que, lo cual; ¿cuál?
while *conj.* mientras (que)
while *n.* rato *m.;* **a short** ―― (al) poco rato
whirl: my head is in a ―― tengo la cabeza hecha un lío
white blanco
who ¿quién?; que, quien, quién, el que, el cual

whoever   quien (quiera), (todo) el que

whole   entero, todo; **the _____** todo el, entero

wholesale   al por mayor

whose   cuyo

why   por qué; **so that (this) is _____** conque por esto (eso)

wide   ancho

wife   mujer, señora, esposa *f.*

wild   loco

win   ganar

wind   dar cuerda a

winding   tortuoso

window   ventana *f.*, ventanilla

windy: to be _____ hacer (haber) viento

wine   vino *m.*

wish   desear, querer; **I _____ that . . . !** ¡ojalá! (*with subjunctive*)

with   con, de

within   dentro (de)

without   sin, sin que

woman   mujer *f.;* **poor old wrinkled _____** mujeruca *f.*

wonder   milagro *m.; v.* preguntarse

wonderful   maravilloso, a las mil maravillas

wood(s)   bosque *m.*

woolen   de lana *f.*

word   palabra *f.*

work   trabajo *m.*, obra *f.* (*art, literature, etc.*); trabajo (*repairs*), obra *f.; v.* trabajar; funcionar (*of mechanisms*); **be hard _____** costar (ue) trabajo

worker   obrero, trabajador *m.*

world   mundo *m.*

worn out   rendido

worried   preocupado

worry   preocupación *f.; v.* preocuparse

worse   peor; **grow _____** agravarse

worth: be _____ valer; **be _____while** valer la pena

would that!   ¡ojalá!

wound   herida *f.*

wounded   herido

wrinkled   arrugado

write   escribir

write down (*note*)   apuntar

writer   escritor *m.*

writing paper   papel de cartas *m.*

writing desk   escritorio *m.*

written   escrito

wrong: be _____ estar equivocado, equivocarse, no tener razón

Y

year   año *m.;* **last _____** el año pasado

yellow   amarillo

yes   sí

yesterday   ayer

yet   todavía, aún; sin embargo; **as _____** hasta ahora

young   joven, **_____er** menor

your   su, sus, *etc.*

youth   juventud *f.*

Z

zero   cero *m.*

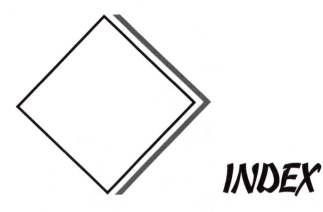

INDEX

References are to page numbers. Section numbers are given in parentheses.